Tamil Language and The Timeless Translations by The Europeans 1543-1887

Pallava rulers at Manchikallu, Mayadivolu and Hirahadagalli were in Prakrit. Thus Prakrit language also had been popular and it had happened much before introduction of Sanskrit. The royal charters issued by the Pallava rulers in Sanskrit were much later in date.[6]

What is the history of translation? In the modern sense March Bloch the historian says that the translation of history is the study of the act of translation in time, which is made up of three levels: the translation agent, the translated works, and the act of translating analyzed and shown diachronically.[7] However it is important to know what was called translating and translation in the ancient past and how it had been handed over down the ages.

Tholkappiyam the Tamil grammar refers to translation with the use of the term '*Athaarpada Yaathal*'. It literally refers the shadow copy made from the original in another language. Tholkaapiyar mentions neatly the two types of texts i.e., from source language and the target language.[8] Further, the translated texts have been referred to be of four kinds such as *thogai nool* (summarization), *viri nool* (elaboration), *Thogai-viri nool* (synthesis of summarization) and *mozhipeyarpu nool* (translation).

Regarding the translation policy to be adopted Tholkappiyar had said that while translating into Tamil those special letters and words of the northern languages should be omitted. He categorically stated that only those suited to Tamil language should be used.[9] We find Sanskrit words like *pangkajam* and *nashtam* have been expressed in Tamil as *pangkayam* and *nattam*. In the *Manimegalai* epic we find Lakshmi the term had been expressed as Lakkumi in Tamil. Hence it is known that translation was very carefully done in Tamil with from word to word.

Sanskrit interaction with Tamil developed during the time of the Pallava ruler Simhavishnu and Nandivaraman II in AD. 730. Sanskrit language came to be patronized by the Pallava rulers and in Tamil country they began to issue royal orders in bilingual. The first portion of the inscription was written in Sanskrit verses as well as in prose and the latter half was written in Tamil. The Pandya rulers and the Cholas also followed the same style and we find numerous bilingual inscriptions in Sanskrit and Tamil. It was at that time Kalidasa the Sanskrit poet came to be introduced to Tamils as we find mention in inscriptions. The *Raguvamsam* of Kalidasa is also mentioned in the Kuram plate of Pallava Parameswaran and also in the

1

Introduction

Evolution of Translation and Translating in Tamil before Print

India the country in the ancient past had people of many dialect and Language speaking groups. In the southern part of the country Tamil was widely spoken on the coast and hinterland. The Romans and the Greeks had established maritime contacts with Tamil coast and these foreign language speaking groups have been mentioned in the *Aganaanuru* and *Pattinapaalai*.[1] The Arabs and the Chinese in the medieval period had also established commercial contacts with Tamil coast. They communicated with each other and had exchanges. However, we have no concrete evidences of development of translation of foreign literary texts to Tamil and vice versa.

The study of the history of translation in India had been though undertaken by scholars the subject of the Tamil language translation had been largely ignored.[2] Tamils came into contacts with people who spoke Pali and Prakrit in the northern India. It happened chiefly because of the rise of the religious contacts of Jainism and Buddhism. The available earliest reference to translation is found in *Manimegalai* an epic in Tamil which contains fourteen lines of text translated from a *pidagam* in Pali language.[3] Myilai Seeni Venkatasamy opines that this translation was done from word for word.[4] *Kundalakesi* another epic in Tamil contains translation from *Therikaathai* in Pali language.[5] Thus contacts of Pali language with Tamil and translation of Buddhist texts had happened at first than any other language of India. It should be mentioned that the early inscriptions of the

LR	Livro Reservado
MPJA	Madurai Province Jesuit Archives, Shenbaganur
NAFR	Nouvelles acquisitions françaises
NAIP	National Archives of India, Pondicherry
NHB	Neue Hallesche Berichte, Neuere Geschichte der Evangelischen
NYPL	New York Public Library
OIOC	Oriental and India Office Collection
SCL	State Central Library, Goa
SII	South Indian Inscriptions
SNLA	Sri Lanka National Archives, Colombo
TNSA	Tamilnadu State Archives, Chennai
UBA	Universiteits Bibliotheek, Amsterdam
UBG	Universitats Bibliotheek Gottingen
UBL	Universiteits Bibliotheek, Leiden
UBU	Universiteits Bibliotheek, Utrecht

Abbreviations

ABSL	The American Bible Society Library, New York
ACL	Academia das Sciencias, Lisboã
AFSt	Archiv der Franckeschen Stiftungen, Halle
AGLTC	Archives of the Gurukul Lutheran Theological College and Research Institute, Chennai
AHU	Arquivo Historico Ultramarino, Lisboã
AMEP	Archives de la Société des missions étrangères de Paris
ARSI	Archivum Romanum Societatis Iesu, Roma
AUTC	Archives of the United Theological College, Bengaluru
BA	Biblioteca da Adjuda, Lisboã
BAMEP	Bibliothèque Asiatique des missions étrangères de Paris
BAV	Biblioteca Apostolica Vaticana, Città del Vaticano
BFBSL	British and Foreign Bible Society's Library, Cambridge
BFSt	Bibliothek der Franckesche Stiftungen, Halle
BL	British Library, London
BNL	Biblioteca Nacional de Lisboã
BNP	Bibliothèque Nationale, Paris
DI	Documenta Indica
EI	Epigraphia Indica
H B	Hallesche Berichte
HKI	Hendrik Kramer Instituut, Oegstgeest
KB	Det Kongelige Bibliotek, Kobenhavn
KBDH	Koninklijke Bibliotheek, Den Haag

List of Illustrations

Contents

Biblioteca Nacional de Lisboã; Biblioteca da Cartuxa, Evora; Biblioteca Apostolica Vaticana, Città del Vaticano; Archivum Romanum Societatis Iesu, Roma; Bibliothèque Nationale, Paris; Archives de la Société des missions étrangères de Paris; Bibliothèque Asiatique des missions étrangères de Paris; Bibliothèque Municipale de Chalon-sur-Saone; Hendrik Kramer Instituut, Oegstgeest; Universitats Bibliotheek Gottingen; Det Kongelige Bibliotek, Kobenhavn; Universiteits Bibliotheek, Leiden; Koninklijke Bibliotheek, Den Haag; Universiteits Bibliotheek, Utrecht; Universiteits Bibliotheek, Amsterdam; Archiv der Franckeschen Stiftungen, Halle; Bibliothek der Franckesche Stiftungen, Halle; Staats-und Universitatsbibliotheek Hamburg Carl von Ossietzy; British and Foreign Bible Society's Library, Cambridge; British Library, London; Bodleian Library, Oxford; British International Bible Society, London; Houghton Library of Harvard University, New York Public Library and the American Bible Society Library, New York for the numerous help and extending great assistance. Further, I also thank the authorities of the Sri Lanka National Archives, Colombo; Archives of the Gurukul Lutheran Theological College and Research Institute, Chennai; Tamilnadu State Archives, Chennai; State Central Library, Goa; Madurai Province Jesuit Archives, Shenbaganur; Archives of the United Theological College, Bengaluru; National Archives of India, Pondicherry and Saraswathi Mahal Library, Thanjavur for permission to consult and use the resources available. Finally my thanks go as well to Shri Abhishek Goel, Kaveri Books for printing the book.

Prof. S. Jeyaseela Stephen

Preface

I developed interest in finding out the literary communication that developed by the foreigners, who came to the Tamil littoral in the age of European commerce and missionary expansion. I could spot jarring omission in the existing historiography of the early modern age, on the remarkable role played by translation from Tamil to other languages and vice versa done by the translators. Hence I commenced my work with special reference to the region of Tamil country, but gradually felt the importance to include the French territory Pondicherry, and also the island of Sri Lanka, chiefly because the Tamil translations occurred had embedded together. The translation works in these territories had involved different styles, scales and needs directed by fundamental divergence in prose. However, Tamil language had stood as the bridging element and culture being the common denominator. Thus the book provides new information on the interesting interconnections and the pivotal role played in communication history and translation studies.

This volume is made possible by an enormous amount of help from many people. I owe a substantial debt to the Fundação Calouste Gulbenkian, Lisboã, for the invaluable help of research grant extended to me in assisting to conduct research in the various archives and libraries in Europe for two years, Instituto de Cultural e Lingua Portuguesa, Ministry of Education, Government of Portugal for awarding a fellowship for one year to do research in the repositories in Portugal. Therefore, I extend my sincere and warm thanks. Many institutions and people shared with me data, information and documents and in this connection I wish to express my gratitude to repositories and authorities of Academia das Sciencias, Lisboã; Arquivo Historico Ultramarino, Lisboã; Biblioteca da Adjuda, Lisboã;

First Published in 2021
ISBN: 978-93-86463-16-6

Cover Illustration: Translation from German to Tamil in 1740 made in palm-leaves (Courtesy: Archiv der Franckeschen Stiftungen, Halle, P/TAM 97)

Published by
Kaveri Books
4832/24, Ansari Road
New Delhi-110002 (India)

Tel: 011-23288140, 4707 2321
E-mail : info@kaveribooks.com
kaveribooks@gmail.com
Website: www.kaveribooks.com

Laser Typesetting by :
Delta Book World, New Delhi - 110 002

PRINTED IN INDIA

Tamil Language and The Timeless Translations by The Europeans 1543-1887

S. Jeyaseela Stephen

Kaveri Books
New Delhi-110 002

Velvikudi grant of the Pandya ruler.[10] The composers of the Sanskrit portion of the inscriptions being students of Sanskrit literature they freely borrowed portions and introduced it. We find even some verses from the *Agni Purana* mentioned in an epigraph praising Udvahanatha at the temple of Tirumananjeri near Mayiladuthurai area.[11]

Ramayanam (the story of Rama) in Sanskrit had been well known to Tamils as mentioned in the sangam literature of Puranaanuru.[12] *Silapathikaaram* the first epic in Tamil also mentions Ramayanam.[13] *Kalithogai* also refers to it.[14] However Ramayanam the epic in Tamil came to be composed by Kambar only in the twelfth century.[15] Sheldon Pollock opines that adaptations from Sanskrit appeared in Tamil opposed to Sanskrit. Hence his view may be called into question for there was no rivalry or monopoly of languages.

Mattavilasaprahasana the farcical play in Sanskrit was composed by Mahendra Varman I the Pallava ruler.[16] The *Bhagavadajjukkam* another play has also been assigned to him.[17] Stories found in Sanskrit had lured the Tamil poets. The story of Sivakan is found in the *uttarapaaham* of *Mahapuranam* in Sanskrit. The same story appears in *Sathya Chintamani* and *Shathira Chudaamani* in Sanskrit. Thiruthakka Devar adapted this story of Sivakan and he composed an epic in Tamil titled *Sivaka Chintamani* in the ninth century.[18] The story of Nazhlan found in one of the branch tales of Mahabharatham was composed by poet Pughalyendi titled *Nazhla Venpa* (the story of Nazhla in venpa metre) in the thirteenth century.[19] Perhaps these stories were not popularly known and imperfectly understood by the people of that period and that had necessitated for adapting into Tamil.

Mahabharatham was translated in Tamil in the seventh century and it is mentioned in the Chinnamanur copper plates.[20] Based on Mahabharatham of Agasthya Bhattar in Sanskrit, Villiputtur Alvar had composed *Villi Bhaaratham* in Tamil during the fourteenth century.[21]

Adaptations and translations from Sanskrit had developed in the post-sangam period and we find *Aasaarakovai* composed by Perivaayin Mulliyar. This is translation of a work in Sanskrit titled *Aaridam*. It contains the moral teachings of Jainism and Buddhism.[22] *Kavyadarsa* the treatise of Dandin on literary science of the late seventh century was adapted in Tamil as *Thandi Alangaram*.[23] This literary art of Dandin was introduced and knowledge was disseminated to the Tamil audience. Adaptation of Mahabharata is also found in *Bharata Venpa* (The Bharta in venpa metre) poetry and it was mixed with prose composed by Perundevanar during the mid-ninth century.[24] Translation from Sanskrit to Tamil had happened and *Rathina Jarakanda Siraavahaasam* dealing with Jainism in Sanskrit was translated in Tamil. It was titled *Arungala Cheppu* in the twelfth century.[25] Translating from Sanskrit to any other language was considered at that time an activity of lower standard. Brahmins only had educational access to Sanskrit. No Brahmin also taught Sanskrit to non-brahmins.

Sanskrit words came to be mixed with Tamil gradually and widely. We find the use of the term '*manipravaala*' referring to the inflected Sanskrit words in Tamil. However Sanskrit terms were not allowed to be used in Tamil poetry. The *Vira Chola Kaarikai* (Treatise for Vira Chola) composed by Buddhamithiran, the lord of Ponparri and probably a vassal of Vira Rajendra Chola (1063-69) speaks of the pure Tamil spoken by the Chola king and it forms the subject matter of the treatise.[26] Kopperunjika (AD. 1231-63) the Kadava chieftain had abiding interest and deep love for Tamil language and he is called *Penu senthamizh vaazhlappirantha kadava* (The Kadava born to foster and protect pure Tamil).[27] *Nannul*, the new Tamil grammar composed by Bhavanandhi in the early thirteenth century notes that Sanskrit influence of words and usage had never been allowed in Tamil language. *Mahapurana Sanghiragam* in Sanskrit dealing with Jainism got translated in Tamil in the fifteenth century and it was called *Sripuranam*.[28] Since texts in Sanskrit have been adapted and translated into Tamil, can we call the language relations as domination or subordination? Certainly it is not the case. It is chiefly a matter of reputation for the writer when there are more readers if the text gets translated. While getting translated from Sanskrit to Tamil could be like in modern days an Indian language translation into English.

The history of translation in Tamil country can be broadly divided into two main areas: the history of oral translation (or interpreting), and written translation history. We can also divide the history of translation in Tamil country into centuries. This division does not mean that writing the history of translation has been chronological, or that its evolution and way of thinking has developed in a linear fashion, as many of the events in one period are repeated in another, in addition to the various perspectives which have been reinvented from earlier times. In the history of Tamil translation the historical sense is very much needed and we have observed that the focus is often on history of translation into Tamil and from it into other languages, besides in terms of tradition.

In the existing literature, most of the writers have mentioned the translation of Ramayanam Uththara Kaandam from Sanskrit by Sittrambala Desikar and Thirukural translated from Tamil to English by F.W. Ellis and getting printed at Fort St. George College press in 1815 and 1816 respectively. They have marked the beginning of translation under the rule of the English East India Company and tried to link up with the help of scholars of the College of Fort St. George where many men were engaged in promoting translation. Further, the development of translation found in Tamil journals and periodicals in the nineteenth century had also been noted.[29] However, the earlier phase with the advent of the Portuguese and translation in Tamil had not been covered therefore this book aims to fill the gap. The Portuguese were the first to arrive on the Tamil coast in the sixteenth century followed by the Dutch, Danes, German missionaries and French in the early modern age. They came into contacts with Tamils and did their best to learn the language and do translation. We shall therefore examine what they have done and how they carried out the work of translation and how translations made rapid progress.

The introduction chapter situates the scenario of translation and translating in Tamil country since the pre-Christian era. Chapter two opens up the life cycle of books, which is very important from the point of view of both book history and translation studies. It examines the importing of books from Portugal to India and making translations from Latin, Portuguese, Italian and English into Tamil by the Catholic missionaries developed between 1543 and 1865. The Franciscan missionaries first arrived at Cochin on 26 November 1500. Books were sent from Portugal to India regularly from 1509 to 1541 for the purpose of education and evangelization. The Jesuits arrived in 1542 and the supply of books continued from Portugal to India. It was at that time books of fiction and tales of chivalry were banned from reading during the voyages from Portugal to India. The missionaries in Tamil country after the conversion of the Hindus in 1536 desired to translate and Francis Xavier did translation of the prayers and sermon from Portuguese into Tamil during 1543 and 1546. Translating ‘Cartilha’ the prayer book was done in Portugal from Portuguese into Tamil and it was printed in Lisbon in 1554.

Translating the book of Catholic doctrine from Portuguese and Latin into Tamil developed and we find Anrique Anriquez the Jesuit translating the book of Catholic doctrine from Portuguese into Tamil between 1557 and 1577. He printed this book *Thambiran Vanakkam* at Quilon in 1578. Anriquez also did translation of the book of Marcos Jorges on Catholic doctrine from Portuguese into Tamil between 1568 and 1578. The book was printed under the title *Krisiththiyani Vanakkam* at Cochin in 1579. Anriquez also translated the book on the lives of saints from Portuguese and Latin into Tamil and the book was printed in Goa in 1586. He also translated the book on the life of Christ in 1598-9 from Portuguese into Tamil under the title *Sesunaathar Sarithiram*. Missionaries like Roberto Nobili followed the translation trend set up by Anriquez and the Christian doctrine of Marpur de Lavradio was translated from Portuguese into Tamil under the title *Chinna Kurippidam* in 1612. Translating the book of Antonio Fernandes on the life of the Blessed Virgin Mary from Portuguese into Tamil was undertaken by Jean-Venant Bouchet in 1715 and it was titled *Devamaathaavin Sarithiram*. As the Jesuit printing press ceased to function around 1680s after the advent of the Dutch, the translated books could not be printed. However, translated books in Tamil appeared in print only in 1840s when the Catholic missionaries had set up a printing press in Pondicherry. In the mean while we find translation of books from English to Tamil had been undertaken in Sri Lanka and the books got printed in Colombo at the Catholic press. *Sathiya Vetha Bhodhaga Surukkam* printed in Colombo got reprinted in Pondicherry in 1846 to meet the requirements of the laity. Translating Alphonse Maria de Ligouri's book on the passion and death of Jesus Christ into Tamil titled *Aathuma Nesam* was done by Fr. C. Gnaanapragasa Nathar a native priest of Kumbakonam who worked in Pondicherry mission. It was printed by Louis Savinien Dupuis the Pro-vicar Apostolic in Pondicherry in 1860. Again translation of Thomas Kempi's Imitation of Christ was executed by C. Gnaanapragasa Nathar and the book was printed in Pondicherry in 1863. Biblical translations by C. Gnaanapragaasa Nathar titled *Sathiya Vetha Sarithira Surukkam* had been executed and the book was printed by L.S. Dupuis in Pondicherry in 1865. Thus the chapter lays emphasis on the beginnings of translation and the difficulties encountered in printing and the progress made by the Catholic missionaries.

Chapter three highlights the shipping of books from the Netherlands,

Denmark, Germany and England to India and Sri Lanka and making translation of Protestant religious texts from Dutch, German and English into Tamil by the missionaries that developed between 1661 and 1825. The prayers and catechism in the beginning came to be translated from Dutch into Tamil by the *predikants* of the Reformed Church. The book of Jacobus Borstius on the doctrine of faith of the Reformed Church was translated by Abraham Bronsveld from Dutch into Tamil and it was printed in Colombo in 1754. The liturgy of the Reformed Church was translated from Dutch into Tamil by Philippus de Melho and it got printed in Colombo in 1760.

In Tamil country translating the pastoral letters began from German to Tamil by Bartholomäus Ziegenbalg in Tranquebar during 1708-12. He also translated the books of Lutheran doctrine and liturgy from German to Tamil. The book of Johann Anastasius Freylinghausen titled *Grundlegung der Theologie* was translated from German to Tamil and it was printed at Tranquebar under the title *Vetha Sasthiram* in 1717. Johann Wilke's *Communions Buch* on the Lutheran liturgy was translated from German to Tamil by Peter Malayappan the catechist in Tranquebar in 1721-2. The Portuguese book on the passion of Jesus Christ was translated into Tamil by Benjamin Schultze in 1723-40. The book of Wolfgang Seber titled *Biblisches Lust-Gärtlein* was translated from German to Tamil by Benjamin Schultze under the title *Vetha Thottam* in 1739-40. Thomas Kempi's Imitation of Christ was translated from German to Tamil by Benjamin Schultze in 1740-1. Johann Arndt's *Paradies-Gärtlein* was translated from German to Tamil jointly by Benjamin Schultze and Rayanayakkan in 1747 and the book was printed at Halle in Germany in 1749-50 under the title *Gnaana Mandira Selva Pungaavanam*. Johann Arndt's another book *Fünff Geistreiche Bücher vom wahren Christenthum* was translated from German to Tamil during 1736-49 by Benjamin Schultze and it was printed at Halle in Germany in 1751 under the title *Gnaana Kannaadi*. Translation of hymns from German to Tamil was undertaken by the Lutheran missionaries and printing was done at Tranquebar during 1713 and 1756. Translation of hymns continued from German to Tamil and books were also printed in Madras during 1774 and 1825.

Chapter four examines the translations from English to Tamil by the Protestant missionaries and the Tamils during 1714 and 1857. Religious controversy that broke out strongly in Tamil country between the Roman

Catholics and the Protestant missionaries had necessitated polemical writings. The booklets published in England came to be translated. We find '*Pappu margaththukku ethiriyaana tharkka chuvadi*' being circulated. Prayers of the Anglican Church got translated from English to Tamil by Benjamin Schultze in 1726. Further the translation of John Bunyan's Pilgrims' Progress from English to Tamil was done and it was printed at the Vepery press in Madras in 1793. Daniel Pillai the catechist in Tranquebar made translation of books on Protestantism into Tamil and they got printed at Vepery in Madras. Translations from English to Tamil had continued by the missionaries between 1814 and 1857. The role of the Tamils in doing translations from Sanskrit, Marathi, Bengali and Telugu into Tamil had been situated during 1826 and 1851. Thus the gamut of translation of Protestant books into Tamil language and the energy spent by the missionaries had been thoroughly examined in this chapter. Further how the translation society in Madras helped in preparing and printing Tamil books during 1847 and 1857 had been discussed.

Chapter five investigates into the inter-lingual and inter-cultural phenomena, documenting the material and social aspects of translation through history. It explores the growth and development of translation of Tamil texts into Portuguese, Latin, Danish, English, German and French languages during 1661 and 1887. Roberto Nobili's *Gnaanopadesam* composed in Tamil came to be translated into Portuguese by Balthasar da Costa in 1661 and it got printed and dedicated to the king of Portugal. Beschi wrote *Paramaartha guru kathaigal* in Tamil and this short story was translated into Latin in 1744. Following this, several other short stories in Tamil attracted the Europeans for translation and we find *Theruntha Vaasagam*, *Arichandran Kathai* and *Pancha Thanthira Kathai* translated from Tamil to Danish and *Kavilai Vaasagam* translated from Tamil to English. The early modern translating and printing activities had been closely inter-related, and both translation and print were also found essential for the dissemination of knowledge. The furthering of communication between peoples, and the spread of social, cultural and religious contacts had happened on a large scale from Tamil country to continental Europe. Ziegenbalg the missionary in Tranquebar had envisaged a plan to translate *Anda Kooru Thaththuvam* and *Thirikaala Chakkaram* from Tamil to German but he could not do so for it was difficult to find equivalent philosophical terms. However, he was very successful in his translation of

Neethi Venpaa, *Ulaga Neethi* and *Konrai Vendhan* into German in 1708. Thirukural which was the most popular text among the Tamils had attracted several Europeans and as a result we notice translation of *Thirukural* into Latin by Beschi (1724-25), into German by Johann Z. Kiernander (1742), into English by Nathaniel Edward Kindersley (1794) and to German by August Friedrich Caemmerer (1799-1803). This was the only text which got translated into so many languages at that time. Christoph Samuel John translated *Aathichoodi* and *Moothurai* into German between 1791 and 1796. Mariadass Pillai in Pondicherry translated *Bhaagavatha Puranam* and *Vaana Sasthiram* from Tamil to French during 1769-89. We find numerous translation of letters from Tamil to Danish and German (1712-30) and plenty of commercial and legal records translated from Tamil to French (1718-38) for it was the need of the hour by the East India trading companies and missionaries. Popular Tamil medical texts known for the best cure of diseases like *Agasthiyar Irandaayiram* got translated into German by Johann Ernst Grundler in 1712. The text *Agasthiyar Vaidhiyam* was translated into Danish by Theodor Ludvig Friedrich Folly in 1798. Korakkar Siddhar's *Kalpasthanam* was translated into English by Benjamin Heyne in 1800. Translations from Tamil to English by the Protestant missionaries and the natives in Madras had developed between 1798 and 1863. The chapter finally makes an overall assessment on the various textual translations undertaken by the Europeans from Tamil manuscripts.

Chapter six locates the Bible translation of the Roman Catholic missionaries from Latin into Tamil that commenced in 1554 till printing the first Catholic New Testament in Pondicherry in 1857. The early translation of the biblical passages is gleaned from Latin to Tamil by Anrique Anriquez (1554-86). The Jesuits of the Madurai mission had ardently continued their work in this direction and we find the growing translation of passages of the Bible from Latin to Tamil (1625-1760). Jácome Gonçalves in Sri Lanka wrote his chronicle of the history of the Old Testament and the New Testament in Tamil (1725), and he prepared a dictionary of biblical words in Tamil (1731), besides offering *Suvisesha Viruththi Urai*, a book of Gospel reading for Sundays and feast days (1732). Finally the New Testament translation was successfully done by Fr Louis Marie Mousset and Fr Arul a native priest in Pondicherry mission (1844-56). Fr Louis Savinien Dupuis the Pro-vicar Apostolic took great efforts in printing the first Catholic Tamil Bible at the mission press in Pondicherry in 1857. The translation of the various individuals had been presented and analyzed with reference to the policy of the Popes in the Vatican and the practices that developed in the Roman Catholic Church.

Chapter seven examines the Bible translation of the Protestant missionaries from Hebrew, Greek, Portuguese, German and English into Tamil. It begins with the role of Bartholomäus Ziegenbalg and his Tamil translation of the New Testament (1710-3), printing the New Testament in Tamil in two parts by Ziegenbalg and Johann Ernst Grundler in 1714-15, reprint of the New Testament translation of Ziegenbalg in 1722, translation of the Old Testament by Ziegenbalg in 1711 and printing the first part in 1723, translating the Book of Psalms by Benjamin Schultze and its printing in 1724, translating the Old Testament from Hebrew into Tamil by Benjamin Schultze in 1723 and printing the second part of the Old Testament in 1726, printing the third part of the Old Testament in 1727, translating and printing the Book of Apocrypha in Tamil by Ziegenbalg and Benjamin Schultze in 1728, reprinting the Book of Psalms in Tamil (1747) and the reading habit of the Tamils and the printing impact. The study continues further by examining the scathing attacks and criticism of the Catholic missionaries on the Tamil Bible translation of the Tranquebar missionaries (1728-41), planning and revising the Tamil translations of the Gospel by the missionaries of Tranquebar (1737-9), Bible translation from Portuguese to Tamil by the Dutch, Bible translation from Greek to Tamil by Adolphus Cramer in Colombo (1732-48), Bible translation from Koine Greek to Tamil by Philippus de Melho in Colombo and Jaffna (1759), translating the Old Testament from Hebrew to Tamil by the Dutch in 1790, translating the Bible from Hebrew to Tamil by Johann Philipp Fabricius and its printing in Madras and Tranquebar (1772-96), printing Tamil New Testament at Serampore in Bengal in 1813, translating the New Testament from Greek to Tamil by Karl Theophilus Ewald Rhenius and its printing in Madras in 1827, 1833, and printing in Jaffna in 1843 and in Madras in 1844, and translating the Bible from English to Tamil by Peter Percival and Arumuga Naavalar and printing done in Jaffna in 1850. The chapter traces how some translators have prepared dictionaries for Bible and it examines the dictionary of Biblical Tamil words by Benjamin Schultze (1728) and by Philippus De Melho (1790).

Chapter eight situates the complete Tamil translations of the Bible and the prose texts with special reference to the growth and development of prose and its style through analytical and comparative method. It locates the translation of the Lord's Prayer into Tamil from the Gospel of St. Mathew (1554-1739), the Sermon on the Mount of Jesus and its translation into Tamil from the Gospel (1578-1857), translation of the Genealogy of Jesus Christ from the Gospel printed by Ziegenbalg in Tranquebar and its comparison with the Dutch printed version in Colombo (1715-1741), psalms translated and printed by Benjamin Schultze in Tranquebar and its comparison with the printed version of Johann Philipp Fabricius in Madras (1724-1772). Finally the translation by Ziegebalg in Tranquebar (1715), Fabricius in Madras (1772), Karl Theophilus Ewald Rhenius (1827) in Madras and Fr Mousset in Pondicherry (1857) had been examined towards the prose development and contribution.

Chapter nine deals with conclusion and the findings of the study have been reported. There is the select bibliography given at the end. The book thus outlines the importance of Tamil translations and how Tamil language reached across the globe through the efforts of the Europeans besides the life-cycle of translations as material and cultural products in early modern Tamil world. The work had also been planned to provide the scholars of Tamil translation in the period with a critically adequate tool for the investigation of this under-researched area. It thus opens up new lines of discussion and research particularly many avenues that had remained virgin to be explored like the relationship between the printed and manuscript translations in an age when the development of print was closely interlinked with a still flourishing manuscript Tamil culture. The book throws light not only on translation scholars, but also the crucial role played by translation and translators in the period of the advent of Tamil print. As the book contains refreshingly new material I am sure that it would be most welcomed by the readers.

NOTES

1. *Aganaanuru*, eds., N.M. Venkatasamy Nattar and R. Venkatachalam Pillai, 3rd edn., South India Saiva Siddhanta Pathippu Kazhagam, Madras,1957, song no. 67, 127 and, 211. U.V. Swaminatha Ayyar, Pattinapaalai in *Pathupaatu*, Madras, 1974, song no. 211.
2. Tariq Khan, ed., *History of Translation in India*, Mysuru, 2017. This work omits the study of Tamil.

3. *Manimegalai*, ed., N.M. Venkatasamy Nattar, South India Saiva Siddhanta Pathippu Kazhagam, Tirunelveli, 1992, see Samayak kanakkar tham thiram ketta Kaathai.
4. N. Murugesa Pandiyan, *Mozhipeyarppiyal*, Chennai, 2016, p. 155.
5. Ibid., p. 156.
6. Marc Bloch, *Apologia da História*, Rio de Janeiro, Jorge Zahar, 1997.
7. Chitra Madhavan, *History and Culture of Tamil Nadu as Gleaned from the Sanskrit Inscriptions, vol. I, Up to C. AD. 1310*, New Delhi, 2005, p. 3.
8. *Tholkaappiyam*, South India Saiva Siddhanta Pathippu Kazhagam, Tirunelveli, 1982, see, Porul Athikaaram, Marabiyal, Noorpa, 643. The text runs thus: 'thoguththal viriththal thogaiviri mozhipeyarthu Atharpada yaththalodu anaimarabinavae'. G. J. V. Prasad, 'Caste in and Recasting Language: Tamil in Translation' in *Decentering Translation Studies: India & Beyond*, eds. Judy Wakabayschi and Rita Kothari, Amsterdam, 2009, pp. 17-28, see, p.19.
9. Tholkaappiyam, 1597. The text runs thus: 'vadasor kilavi vadavezththori yezhuthodu punarntha solaagume'.
10. C. Sivaramamurti, *Epigraphical Echoes of Kalidasa*, Madras, 1944, p. 29.
11. S. Gurumurthy, *Education in South India*, Madras, 1975, p. 157.
12. *Puranaanuru*, ed., U.V. Swaminatha Ayyar, Madras, 1971, song no. 378.
13. *Silapathikaaram*, ed., N.M. Venkatasamy Nattar, South India Saiva Siddhanta Pathippu Kazhagam, Tirunelveli, 1992, see Purancheri Iruththa Kaathai, 65.
14. *Kalithogai*, ed., M. Kasi Visvanatha Chettiar, Third edition, Madras, 1947, 101.
15. Sheldon Pollock, *The Language of the Gods in the World of Men: Sanskrit, Culture and Power in Pre-modern India*, Berkeley, 2006, p. 384.
16. *South Indian Inscriptions*, (Publications of the Archaeological Survey of India) vols., I to XXVI, New Delhi, 1890-1990 (hereafter *SII*), vol. IV, no. 8, p. 6.
17. C. Minakshi, *Administration and Social Life under the Pallavas*, Madras, 1975, p. 336.
18. N. Murugesa Pandiyan, Mozhipeyarppiyal, p. 155.
19. Ibid., p. 157.
20. SII, vol. III, pp. 451-63. The Chinnamanur copper plate text runs: Maa bhaaratham Thamizhpaduththum Madhuraapurich Changam Vaiththum.
21. N. Murugesa Pandyan, Mozhipeyarppiyal, p. 157.
22. Ibid., p. 154.

23. Sheldon Pollock, The Language of the Gods, p. 163.
24. Ibid., p. 384.
25. N. Murugesa Pandiyan, Mozhipeyarppiyal, p. 156.
26. Sheldon Pollock, The Language of the Gods, p. 398.
27. *Epigraphia Indica* (hereafter EI), volumes, Calcutta/Delhi, 1892, vol. XXIII, no. 27, lines 3-7 p. 180.
28. N. Murugesa Pandiyan, Mozhipeyarppiyal, p. 156.
29. Thomas R. Trautmann, *The Madras School of Orientalism: Producing Knowledge in Colonial South India*, New Delhi, 2009; T.V. Venkateswaran, 'Representation of Natural World in the Popular Science Texts during the Nineteenth Century Tamilnadu', *Indian Journal of History of Science*, vol. 39.3, 2004, pp. 279-305; T.V. Venkateswaran, 'Science and Colonialism: Content and Character of Natural Sciences in the Vernacular School Education in the Madras Presidency, 1820-1900', *Science and Education*, vol. 16, 2007, pp.87-114; Pa. Manimaaran, *Thamizh Nazhlithalgalil Mozhipeyarppu Kalai*, Thanjavur, 1999; S. Jeyaseela Stephen. *A Meeting of the Minds: European and Tamil Encounters in Modern Sciences, 1507-1857*, Delhi, 2016, pp.787-825; S. Jeyaseela Stephen, *Missioner Tamil Written and Printed in Pondicherry: Literature and Louis Savinien Dupuis, 1841-73*, Pondicherry, 2017, pp. 174-177; Stuart H. Blackburn, *Print, Folklore and Nationalism in Colonial South India*, New Delhi, 2003.

2

Importing Books from Portugal to India:

Making Translations from Latin, Portuguese, Italian and English into Tamil by the Catholic Missionaries, 1543-1865

The fleet of Vasco da Gama consisting of four ships left Lisbon on 9 July 1497 reached Kappad near Calicut on Sunday, 20 May 1498. Thereafter ships annually began to sail and reached India. The king of Portugal appointed viceroys and developed diplomatic relations with the native rulers. Affonso Albuquerque the second Portuguese viceroy of India (1509-1515) visualized a society which should be dependent and loyal to the Portuguese, and he felt that it was the need of the hour. Hence he wished to Latinise or lusitanise them in more ways than one. He planned to provide education that consisted of not only in making of the Catholic Christian tenets known through religious books and canonical tracts, but also wished to impart teaching of the Portuguese language.[1] Books printed in Portugal and other parts of Europe were brought to India. People who sailed in ships from Portugal to India brought the printed books for reading during the long voyage.

The Arrival of the Franciscan Missionaries: Shipping Books from Portugal to India for the Purpose of Evangelization and Education, 1509-1541

Affonso de Albuquerque passed an order to send the young native men to attend the school which he started in the Portuguese settlement of Cochin in order to learn to read and write.[2] He also requested the king of Portugal to send necessary books to Cochin in the ships that sailed from Portugal. In 1512, Albuquerque acknowledged the receipt of primers for the use of children at the school in Cochin that functioned under a *mestre* (master/teacher) who taught the Portuguese language. It has been reported that the school had catered to the needs of the *panikkar* children.[3] The same school later came to be administered by the Franciscan missionaries of the Convent of Santo Antonio in Cochin under the guidance of Frei Antonio de Loureiro. Catechism books sent from Portugal were received in 1517 and the strength of the children in the school had by then increased to 150 students. Frei Antonio was held responsible for running the school and imparting education and he continued to receive parcels consisting of catechism books printed in Portugal for use in Cochin.[4]

Lopo Soares de Albergaria the next Portuguese Governor of India in 1518 also made efforts to imparting education and he had requested the king of Portugal to supply 300 books to the Franciscan missionaries in Cochin.[5] His request was heeded to and 100 copies of book titled 'An account of the destruction of Jerusalem' and 'The story of the most noble Vespasian, emperor of Rome' (Estoria *de muy nobre Vespesiano emperador de Roma*) by Valentim Fernandes printed in Lisbon in 1496 had reached.[6] The list of other books include Augustine Jacopo Filippo Foresti da Bergamo's '*Supplementum chronicarum*', a voluminous treatise on oriental wonders, first published in Venice in 1483 and also got reprinted several times, the monumental four volumes of Portuguese version of *Vita Christi*' by Rudolf of Saxony.[7] Further we find three copies of '*Summa Theologica*' of St. Thomas Aquinas the Spanish edition and four copies of '*Bosco Deleytoso*' printed in Lisbon by Hermão de Campos in 1515.[8] It is known that 100 copies of catechisms covered in parchment, 12 copies of small catechisms, 20 copies of '*flos sanctorum*' (Lives of saints), 30 copies of '*Livro e legenda que fala de todo los feytos e payxooes dos santos marties*' (Book and legend on the accomplishments and passions of the holy martyrs) printed in 1513 in Lisbon by Buonhomini de Cremona had also found way.[9] All these books safely reached through the ships were kept at the Franciscan monastery in Cochin.

The Portuguese learning primer book was in high demand and so it had continued to be supplied through the ships. In 1521 it is reported that 200 spelling primers had arrived for learning Portuguese language.[10] Dom Duarte de Menezes the Portuguese Governor of India thereafter entrusted fifty copies of the primers to the Portuguese factor in Goa for use. He also at that time gave five copies of lives of saints and one copy of the four

Gospels of the New Testament for use in Goa.[11] The scarcity of books in fact led to a complaint lodged by Sebastião Pires, the vicar-general in Cochin to the king of Portugal.[12]

The teaching of Latin represented the knowledge of Christian religious rites brought to India by the missionaries. Prayer books circulated were bilingual (in Latin and Portuguese). The church in Cannanore in 1538 received four large books for religious offices of high quality binding from the king of Portugal.[13]

Three distinct groups of people in society in India had been identified at that time as needing Catholic religious instruction. The lack of knowledge in matters related to the Christian faith both amongst the growing number of *mestiço* children as well as the neo-converts was cause for much concern. Another group of people to whom religious instruction had to be imparted were the Christians of St. Thomas in Malabar as the Portuguese called. There is evidence of a college established in 1540 by Frei Vicente de Lagos, a Franciscan at Cranganore that offered elementary education and studies in Latin and theology. It catered to the training of the Saththanars of the Malabar Christians.[14] It was amongst these groups that the Portuguese had sought alliances and hoped to build their future plan and activities. A few years later Frei Vicente de Lagos submitted a request to Dom João III the king of Portugal for the supply of books to the college and he attached a long list including small breviaries, psalters, books of daily prayers, a large missal for the church, six copies of small missals and grammar books needed.[15] There were continuous requests for many books by the Franciscan missionaries of Cochin, Cannanore, Quilon and Ceylon too.[16]

The Arrival of the Jesuits and the Supply of Books from Portugal to India, 1542-1555

The Jesuit missionaries arrived in Goa in 1542. Martim Affonso de Sousa the Portuguese governor of India (1542-45) at that time came to India and he brought the book '*De vitis pontificum historia*' composed by the Italian humanist Bartolomeo Sacchi (under the name of Platina) which was printed in 1518 in Venice and he used it for reading.[17] Captain Baltasar Jorge de Valdez who sailed from Lisbon in 1543 brought '*Vita Christi*', '*Flos Sanctroum*', and '*Cronica do condoestrabre de Portugal Nuno Alvarez Pereyra* (Chronicle of the Constable of Portugal Nuno Alvares Pereira) printed in Lisbon in 1526 by Simão Galharde.[18] He also brought books that include 'An account of the destruction of Rhodes' by Giacome Fontana, 'The story of El Cid', 'The Grammar' by Erasmus and the book of Guglielmus Lilius, '*De octo orationis partium constructione libellous*' printed in Paris in 1534 and texts by Seneca, Valerius Maximus and Petrarch.[19]

Since books were to be carried in ships to India in large numbers, Dom Joao III the king of Portugal had advised Pero Fernandes Sardinha the master of the ship who sailed to India from Portugal in 1545 to allot separate space for keeping them.[20] Miguel Vaz the vicar-general had sent a request to the king of Portugal in 1545 for supply of grammar books and Portuguese language teaching books for use. These books were also supplied.[21]

After three years of arrival of the Jesuits (i.e., in 1545) the college of St. Paul in Goa which was founded by the Franciscans of the province of mercy was handed over to the Society of Jesus. The Colegio de Santa Fe (College of the Holy faith) as commonly came to be called was transformed into a centre for advanced studies.[22] Nicola Lancilloto the Jesuit in Goa sent a request to the king of Portugal in 1545 for the supply of books to the Jesuit College. He mentioned that the Jesuits used books and they had only 40 books including short Latin compendiums with texts by Virgil and Terence all of them were very old and dissolute.[23] Hence he requested the king of Portugal to make a donation of new and good books. He also asked for subsidy for the purchase of books, paper and quills needed for the Jesuits.[24] This matter was considered very favourably by the king and we find Nicola Lancilloto in 1546 listing the new supply and arrival of books in Goa for teaching. It included Terence's comedies, Virgil's Eclogues, Ovid's Metamorphoses, Cato's Libri minors, St, Jerome's Opera and the treatise by Erasmus '*De duplici copia verborum ac rerum*'.[25]

Within ten years (in 1555) the Jesuit library in Goa had grown and it had many books. Marco Maarulic's '*Livro Insigne*' (A book of eminent people) a famous compilation of biographies of saints, the Latin edition, '*Opusculum*' of St Thomas Aquinas printed in Coimbra in 1545 by João da Barrieria and João Alvares, the works of Plato, Aristotle's Ethics, Ptolemy's Geography, the Portuguese translation which was appended to Pedro Nunes's '*Tratado da Sphera*' (Treaty of sphere) printed in 1537 in Lisbon by Germão Galharde, '*Vita Christi*' by Ludolfo de Saxonia, book of Thomas

Kempis '*Contemptus mundi*' first printed in Lisbon in 1542 by Germão Galharde, '*Historia de la Iglesia*' (The history of the Church) printed in Lisbon in 1541 by Luis Rodrigues, St. Augustine's Confession, Henricus de Herpf's '*Espelho de Perfeycam*' (The mirror of perfection) printed in Coimbra in 1553 at the Santa Cruz monastery, St Bonaventura's '*Livro chamado stimulo de amor a divino*' (Stimulus of divine Love) printed in Lisbon in 1550 by Germão Galharde had been in the library.[26] Thus the list prepared shows chiefly books including bibles, breviaries and concordances.

Banning the Books of Fiction and Tales of Chivalry from Reading during the Voyages from Portugal to India, 1544-1578

People brought the printed books which they wished to enjoy reading during the voyages in the ships sailing from Portugal to India. The Jesuits began to control and they wanted to ban reading fiction and tales of chivalry. We find growing number of censorship found mention in the Jesuit records.[27] The Jesuits banned books on the tales of chivalry that included Giovanni Boccaccino's '*Libro llamado Fiametta*', printed in Lisbon by Luis Rodrigues in 1541, '*Las obras de Boscan y lacunas de Garcilasso de la vega*' (The works of Boscan and Garcilasso da la vega) printed in Lisbon in 1543 by Luis Rodrigues, and '*Cronocia del valiente y esforcada principe dom Florando d'Ingla Terra*' (The tales of the valiant and dedicated prince Florent of England) printed in Lisbon in 1545 by Germão Galharde.[28] In 1547 the Jesuits banned the books of fiction to be read by people in the ships. The missionaries stated that these were solely for entertainment purpose which would make the faithful astray from the path of rectitude advocated by the Catholic Church.

However, people continued to bring books what they wished for reading in the ships. A priest in 1560 complained about many profane books found aboard and he exhorted his fellow passengers to throw away such books overboard because they were prejudicial to them. He went as far as tearing away certain books that were really bad which were found in the hands of the children.[29] In 1562 another priest had bitten the arm of a young man so that he would let go of a bad book he was reading. After throwing the book overboard the missionary gave the youth three good books in return so that the young man was made happy.[30] To keep people away from the less orthodox books throughout the voyage, some priests did public readings from books on ecclesiastical history and other spiritual books.[31] A Jesuit letter written in 1564 mentions that many books banned for reading were brought by people for reading in the ship during the voyages. These forbidden books were seized and thrown overboard.[32] In 1566 a Jesuit who sailed to India recommended to his superior that all missionaries who travelled to India should take with them a large number of religious books, so that they could exchange them on board if caught the pernicious books read by passengers.[33]

Translation of Prayers and Sermon from Portuguese to Tamil by Francis Xavier, 1543-1546

After the conversion of the Hindu Paravas to Christianity in 1536 by the Franciscans in Tamil country, the missionaries evinced keen interest to teach the Catholic tenets and developed interest in translating prayers. Further they also thought of doing translation of many Catholic doctrinal works into Tamil. The prayers available in Latin and Portuguese were planned to be done in Tamil to disseminate the Christian knowledge among the Tamil converts. They decided to undertake simple projects of translation rather than massive works of Catholic religious literature. There was an urgent and immediate need to provide the Christian tenets to the Tamil reading audience.

Francis Xavier the Jesuit missionary (1506-52) arrived in Goa in 1542 and he had an important luggage which consisted of books given to him by Dom João III, the king of Portugal.[34] On his arrival at Tuticorin in Tamil Country in 1543 he continued to write on the most essential parts of the small catechism in Portuguese. He got them translated by employing three local seminarians who had knowledge of Portuguese and Tamil.[35] It has been reported that on his way from Goa to the pearl fishery coast, Xavier was also accompanied by these three Tamils, of whom, Gaspar and Emmanuel were the deacons who spoke both Portuguese and their own language very well. The translation of Xavier's small catechism in Tamil was the work of these two young seminarians.

Sermons were lectures, centred on religious theme. Xavier had composed in Portuguese a sermon and he delivered on what it meant to be a Christian, what heaven and hell are, and who goes to the one and who goes to the other. He got this also translated into Tamil. It is an early attempt on making available the Christian literature to the new converts.[36] In course of time, Xavier's small catechism grew into big catechism with the addition of the declaration of the articles of faith. Xavier mentioned it in his letter that he sought out individuals who understood both Portuguese and Tamil. He got the prayers translated from Latin into Tamil. After having translated in Tamil, he himself had at first learnt by-heart. He later went through the villages teaching the prayers in Tamil by assembling the people with the help of a bell in his hand.[37]

In 1546 when Xavier was in Melaka he composed a reading on the explanation of the articles of faith which he got it translated into Tamil by Fr Francis Coelho a fellow Jesuit who had skill in the language.[38] It has been reported by Anrique Anriquez (1520-1600) that he was busy in correcting the Tamil prayers which Xavier's collaborators had made which contained a number of mistakes.[39] The Tamil version did not see the light of printing. The Portuguese version of the catechism text was copied and sent to all Jesuit missionaries as a manual for teaching Christian doctrine. In 1556, with the introduction of the printing press in Goa, Xavier's catechism in Portuguese was printed.[40]

Writing Tamil in Roman Script: Translating the Prayer Book from Portuguese to Tamil and Printing in Lisbon in 1553-54

The first prayer book in Tamil was successfully prepared for use in 1553-4. It is titled Cartilha in Portuguese, otherwise called the primer that contained abridged versions of the Christian doctrines. The work also contained the common prayers like *Pater Noster*, *Ave Maria*, *Credo*, besides *Salve Regina* and the Ten Commandments of the Old Testament. The book was written in the colloquial Tamil language. This elementary work was the first one prepared by the Portuguese missionaries including for the study of Tamil alphabets. The prologue was written by three Luso-Tamils then living in Lisbon and their names are also mentioned (Vicente de Nazareth, Jorge Carvalho and Thome da Cruz). These three men were responsible for the entire work and the printing work of the book was supervised by Fr João Villa de Conde. The book printed is still preserved and a copy of it is kept in the Biblioteca da Cartuxa, Evora.[41] Copies of the cartilha prayer book in Tamil printed in Lisbon had reached Tamil coast.

The missionaries had sent a delegation of the three young Tamil converts to Lisbon and the first objective was to publicise the spiritual inroads that the Franciscans had made in Tamil country in order to gain the renewed material support from the king of Portugal and to raise a new missionary zeal amongst young Europeans. The second objective was to provide the Tamil envoys to have the first hand opportunity to see Portugal and thereby on return to India they were able to confirm the things of the missionaries.

Translating the Book of Catholic Doctrine from Portuguese and Latin into Tamil

Doctrina Christiana composed in Goa in Portuguese in May 1542 by Francis Xavier was printed in Goa in 1557. This short Catechism follows the official structure of catechesis in four parts (the Sign of the Cross, the Creed, the Prayers of Our Father, Hail Mary, Hail Holy Queen and the Decalogue) but it lacks the explanation of the Seven Holy Sacraments. Other catechetical statements added are the Five commandments of the Church, the Confiteor, Mortal sins, Mortal virtues, Theological virtues, Cardinal virtues, Corporal works of mercy, Spiritual works, Bodily senses, Three powers of the soul, Three enemies of the soul, prayer to the holy host, Prayer to the chalice, and invocations.[42] In 1566, following the Decrees of the Council of Trent, the first catechism was published with the imprimatur of the Roman Catholic Church. The original Latin version of the *Catechismus ex decreto Concilii Tridentini ad parochos*, thus came to be generally known as *Catechismus Romanus*. It formalized the four-fold canon of catechism (1. the articles of the Creed, 2. the Sacraments, 3. the Decalogue and the laws of God i.e. Ten Commandments, 4. the prayers).[43]

Anrique Anriquez and His Translation of the Book of Catholic Doctrine from Portuguese to Tamil, 1557-1577: Printing the Book titled Thambiran Vanakkam at Quilon in 1578

An initiative was made by Anrique Anriquez for better education and instruction of the Tamil Christians who were converted and it was the translation of a book printed in Portuguese. It has been mentioned that Anriquez had begun to translate the prayers found in the book titled ‘Doctrina Christam’ with the assistance of Fr Manuel de São Pedro. This work in Tamil was called *Thambiran Vanakkam* (Adoration to God) and in Portuguese it was titled *Doctrina Christam en lingua Malauar Tamul*.[44]

2.1: The title page of Thambiran Vanakkam printed at Kollam in 1578 (Courtesy: Houghton Library, Harvard University, Cambridge, Massachusetts, USA)

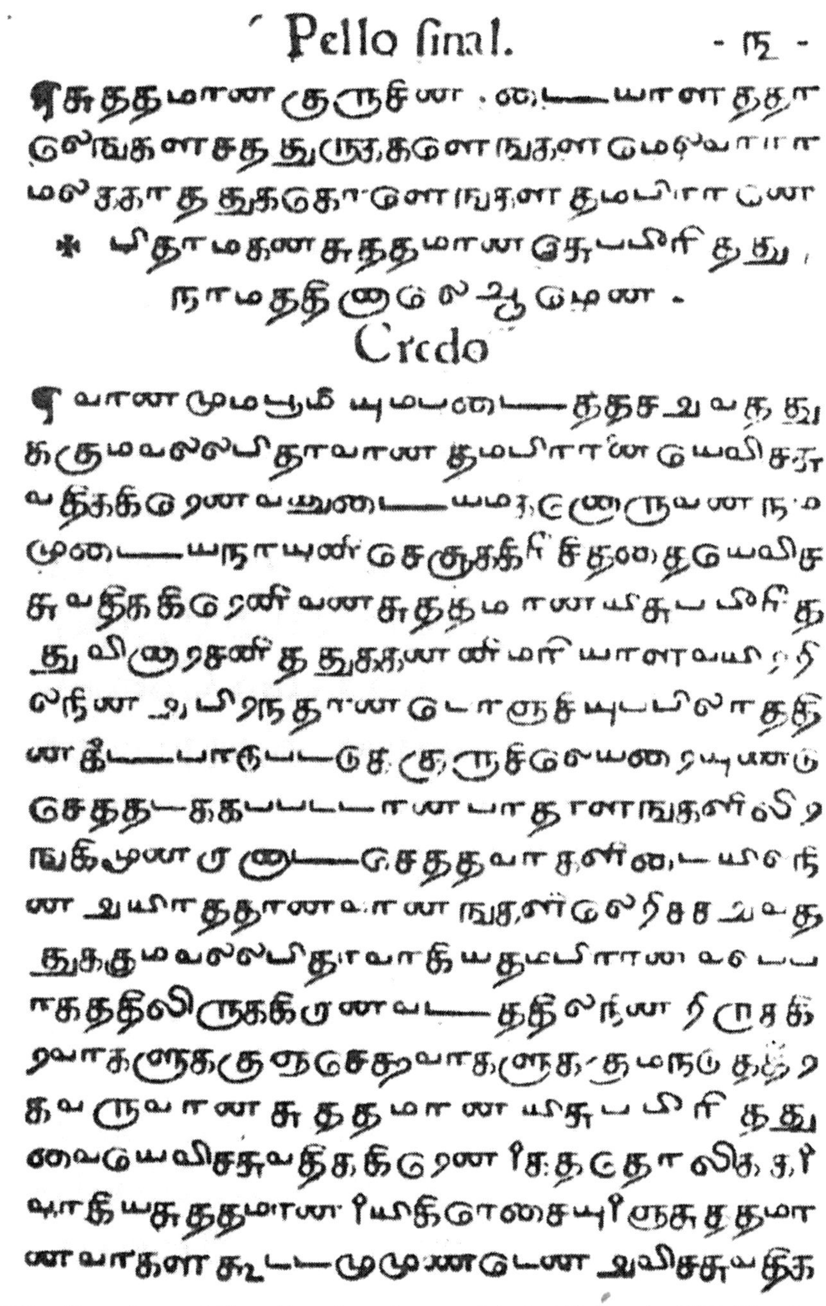

2.2: Page three of Thambiran Vanakkam printed at Kollam in 1578 (Courtesy: Houghton Library, Harvard University, Cambridge, Massachusetts, USA)

This book was also based on Francis Xavier's earlier *Doctrina Christam* in Portuguese that had already been printed in Goa in 1556. To assist those who know Portuguese, Anriquez and Manoel de São Pedro, the authors had given the titles of the sections in Portuguese as follows:

Pello sinal	– The sign of the cross
Credo	– The apostle's creed
Os mandamentos	– The ten commandments of God
Os mandamentos de igreija	– The precepts of the Church
Padre nosso	– Our Father, The Lord's Prayer
Ave maria	– Hail Mary
Salve regina	– Hail holy queen
A confissao	– Act of contrition
Os artigos de fe	– Articles of faith
Os sacramentos da igreija	– The sacraments of the church
Os pecados capitais	– Capital sins or vice
As obras de misericordia	– Works of mercy, both the corporal and the spiritual
Os cinco sentidos	– Five senses
As vitrudes theologais	– Theological virtues
As virtudes cardeais	– Cardinal virtues
Os imigos de alma	– Enemies of the souls
As cousas derradeiras	– Final ends
As oyto beauenturancas	– The eight beatitudes

According to Jesuit records, Anriquez began to translate this *Doctrina Christam* into Tamil on 20 February 1557. Fr Manoel de São Pedro who was then in Sri Lanka had come to Punnaikayal in 1562 to assist him after five years in completing this work. The work was stated to be in progress again after five years when Fr João Villa de Conde paid a visit to Punnaikayal during October 1567. He expressed his admiration at the monumental work that was then in progress for around ten years in total. Anriquez continued to make corrections in the Tamil prayers with the help of natives even as late as in 1569. This catechism book which was planned much earlier actually was ready only in the year 1570. It took another eight years to reach the final shape. This book was titled finally *Thambiran Vanakkam* which contains the collection of prayers. The printed book has no preface. The second page mentions that this small catechism was printed on 20 October 1578, in the Collegio do Saluador in Coulam. Hence the view of some writers that *Thambiran Vanakkam* was a translated version of the Bible may therefore be called into question.[45] The co-author of the catechism is also mentioned as Padre Manoel de São Pedro. Thus many persons had helped in translation at different levels in the beginning.[46]

Anrique Anriquez and his Translation of the Book of Marcos Jorges on Catholic Doctrine from Portuguese to Tamil, 1568-1578: Printing the Book titled Krisiththiyani Vanakkam at Cochin in 1579

Dialogues (conversation style sheet) had been a popular format, used to illustrate and explain aspects of Catholic religion in Europe. This was felt well suited for disseminating the Christian revelation. Marcos Jorge (1524-1571) based on this model had composed a book titled '*Doctrina Christam, Ordenando a maneira de dialogo, para ensiar os minios*, and it was dealing with Catholic doctrine which was printed in Lisbon in 1561.[47]

Anrique Anriquez aimed to translate this book from Portuguese into Tamil titled *Krisiththiyaani Vanakkam* (Adoration to Christianity). He had the translation into Tamil during 1577-79. There were twelve chapters in the Portuguese book and Anriquez translated all of them. The book was printed on Saturday, 14 November 1579 at Cochin as found in the second leaf of the book. It ends with the words of the Holy Scripture 'There is no salvation except through this name (Jesus)'. This monumental work is also a collection of prayers and doctrinal explanations in Tamil to help the Christians to grasp the tenets of the Catholic faith. Anriquez wrote an introduction in the work both in Tamil and in Portuguese. It appears in the printed book on the front page and at its back, which also says that Fr Anriquez the Jesuit translated into Tamil the Christian Doctrine which was originally written in Portuguese by Marcos Jorge.

The twelve chapters in this book Krisiththiyaani Vanakkam are as follows:

Chapter 1 : What is Christianity? – It has been explained

Chapter 2-6 : Sign of the cross, Pater Noster, Ave Maria, Salve Regina & Credo

Chapter 7 : Articles of faith

Chapter 8-9 : Ten Commandments of our Lord, The precepts of the Church

Chapter 10-11 : Capital sins & Sacraments

Chapter 12 : Acts of mercy, virtues, eight beatitudes (Sermon on the Mount)

Finally the book ends with the confession prayer.

The details of the chapters are also given in Portuguese titles as follows:

I - que quer dizer chirstao pello sinal

II - do sinal do Christao que he a sancta cruz

III - do padre nosso

IV - da Ave Maria

V - da salve regina

VI - do credo

VII - dos artigos da fe

VIII - dos mandamentos da ley de deos

IX - dos mandamentos sa sancta madre igreija

X - do sete peccados, que comummete se cha mao mortais

XI - dos sete sacramentos da sancta madre igreija

XII - das obras de misericordia

Teaching penny catechism had by that time had been felt necessary by the Portuguese missionaries and so *Krisiththiyaani vanakkam* contained instructions and prayers. It is mentioned that the place where the prayers are taught to the children, the catechist should teach the children at first to make the sign of the cross and he should also do it. After making the sign of the cross, one child had to be asked to go up on a raised platform and he or she should ask the questions and the interesting conversation had been furnished in Tamil. The dialogical text is between a teacher (*vaathiyar*) and a disciple (*seeshan*), and it was read—except that men "practiced" (recited) it on Sunday and Friday after the Mass and the women on Tuesday. The author mentions that as the wax melted by nature and whatever is imprinted is fixed very well, so also the case when these religious instructions were given to the children when they are young, it bears good fruit.

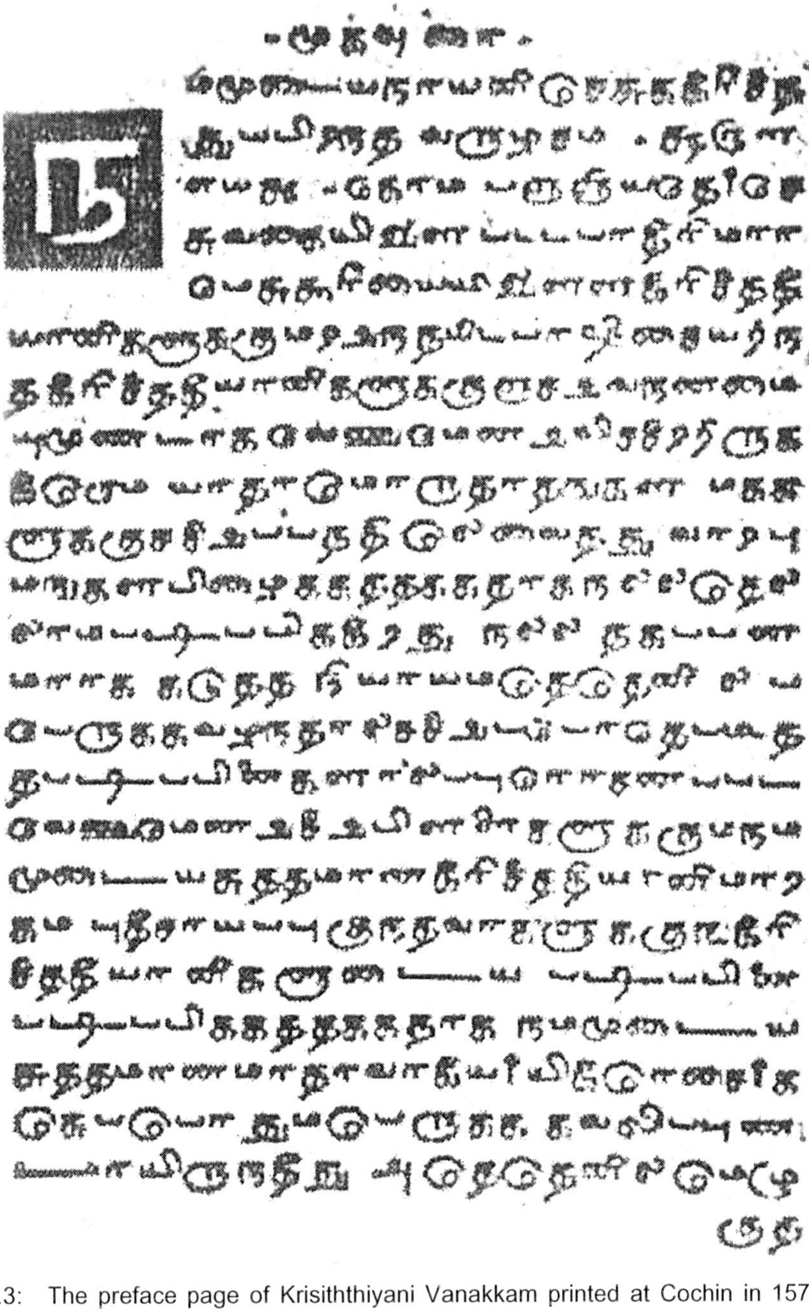

2.3: The preface page of Krisiththiyani Vanakkam printed at Cochin in 1579 (Courtesy: Bodleian Library, Oxford)

Nuno Rodrigues the Jesuit in Cochin mentioned in his annual letter written dated 30 December 1582 that the Tamil Christians continued with the recitation practice of the prayers and it was done for the pious men on Sunday afternoon and Fridays at night, for the women it was done on Tuesday after the Mass, with the catechism of *Thambiran Vankkam* for the girls and boys with more zeal with the catechism by Father Marcos Jorge with questions, which was translated into Tamil and this had produced much fruit, and many persons knew parts of it by-heart.[48]

With the arrival of Alessandro Valignano in 1575, Anriquez's energies were directed towards translations and publications of Christian literature in Tamil. *Thambiran vanakkam* and *Kirisiththiyani vanakkam* had remained nevertheless, tied to the Portuguese and Latin originals. Printing *Krisiththiyani vanakkam* in Cochin was entirely managed by Pero Luis the Tamil Brahmin, the only Indian Jesuit who was then admitted into the Society of Jesus.

Translating the Book of Confession Manual of 1556 from Portuguese to Tamil by Anrique Anriquez during 1578-79 and Printing it in Cochin in 1580

The decrees of the Council of Trent restored the annual obligation of confession first laid down in AD.1215 at the fourth Lateran Council with the canon *Omnes Utrisque Sexus*. The correct administration of the reformed sacrament of penitence made it necessary to train confessors and instruct penitents. Hence the confession manual came to be prepared through which the priests were required to be able to examine and evaluate sins and the penitents were made to know with a view to recognize and confess their sins. Confession manual in Portuguese language was prepared based on Juan de Polanco's *Breve directorium ad confessarii ac confitentis munus recte obeundum*, printed in Latin in Rome in 1554. It was translated from Latin into Portuguese by Alvaro de Torres and got printed in Portugal in 1556.[49] It was widely used in Portugal and copies of the same book had been brought through ships that sailed to India for use. We find in this confession manual the penitent is told that the sacrament of confession was introduced by Jesus Christ to cure the diseases of the soul just the same way as the doctors cure physical ills. Jesus Christ appointed the priests to be doctors of the souls and to forgive sins. Just like a person that goes to the doctor wishing to be cured and tells him all his sickness without hiding anything, so also he who goes to the confession tells all his sins to the priests without hiding anything. Even though the priest is human nothing should be hidden from him with shame or fear because at that time of hearing the confession he is in the place of God, and all the sins told to him he cannot tell to any living being.

Girolamo da Palmero the Dominican theologian renowned for his piety and doctrine and a staunch defender of the Franciscan spirit and assiduous lover of poverty composed in Italian a confessionario and it was printed in 1557 in Venice.[50] It became so popular that it also got reprinted with added information and observations of great importance in Brescia by Tommaso Bozzola in 1561 and reprinted in Naples in 1564.[51] It was further reprinted in Brescia in 1567.[52] This printed confession manual of Girolamo da Palmero was also brought in ships and reached Goa for use by the missionaries.

The Catholic missionaries on the Tamil coast introduced among the new converts the practice of making confessions. The Tamil Christians were told at least once a year, during the Holy Week or Christmas to make confessions. It is reported by Anrique Anriquez the Jesuit in 1558 that he desired to write a *conficioneyro* in Tamil to help the Christians.[53] After ten years (in 1568) it is reported by him that the manual could not be prepared for he lacked adequate knowledge of Tamil Language. Native Christians at Virapandyanpattinam made confessions to Anriquez and he was hearing. It is also said that people have not made their confession for long in the absence of the missionaries.[54] Hence Pero Luís, the Tamil brahmin who was admitted to the society of Jesus was allowed to hear confessions in 1569 to meet out the requirements of the faithful.[55]

It has been mentioned in the letter of Fr Luís Frois in 1578 that Fr Francisco Rodrigues the Jesuit had felt the need to have more copies of the printed book confessionario which was in high demand for use in India. Fr António de Quadros the superior felt the need for confession manual and so he had ordered in 1578 the manual for confession in Portuguese to be printed in Goa. The missionaries planned to print and circulate it during the Lent. A devotee had come forward to supply the paper free of cost for printing and so it was printed for the love of God to be placed into the hands of Christians of Goa in 1578. When printed copies of the same were sent to the Portuguese settlements on the Tamil Coast for distribution, the

Jesuits in Punnaikayal wished to translate it at the earliest into Tamil.[56] Anriquez undertook the translation of the manual of confessionario for he felt it as an immediate requirement for pastoral work.[57] He successfully did the work and translated the confessionario from Portuguese into Tamil. Thus the manual of confession in Tamil came to be published at the Collegio da Madre de Deus in Cochin on the 31st of the month of May (*vaikasi*) in 1580.[58] The manual for confession has no Tamil title page but we find it in Portuguese.

In this manual of confession an instruction is given to the readers and it encourages the penitents to read with pious concentration. The text runs thus: 'When you read this book, don't read them carelessly; you must read them deeply with attention and with the thought that your soul would benefit from it. This book printed is devotional in nature and it saves souls. If you read them, it will help you with good thoughts and good desires and would bring light/enlightenment and knowledge'.[59]

Anriquez mentions that we need to confess frequently since we commit sins. The confession making with simplicity and truth would help the Christians to lead a good life. One must admit that he is a sinner before God and he is not eligible to receive any good from him when he sets a bad life. One should confess his sins to a *padre* (priest) with fear and devotion and should not hide the sins that he had committed knowingly. He should reveal the sins without any shy and he should tell it to the *padre* who is the representative of God. The almighty listens and grants pardon through the priest. The individual should make a resolution that he will not repeatedly commit these sins. For a true Christian it is necessary to make confession at least once a year. As Lord Jesus Christ is present in the Holy Eucharist and in order to receive him, confession is essential.

The manual in Tamil teaches the penitent how to prepare him or herself for confession. The preparation was twofold—internal and external. One had to learn the art of introspection and then the right words to express oneself during the confession, and what was to be said during confession. Various chapters in the book describe the process. Chapter four of the confession manual particularly teaches how the sinner should approach the confessor/the *padre*. As the one who confesses is an offender, and as he had offended his *raasa* (king), he would expiate his sins. Hence the sinner should kneel down on the floor on both knees with great humility. Having said the proper prayer which is made for that, he must make the sign of the cross. As soon as he made the sign of the cross, he must say the salutation to the priest that 'I am a great sinner'.[60] The section that follows about introductory instructions indicate that both the penitent and confessor need this manual for confession. The penitent for being new to the new doctrine and in need of knowing when he failed and the priest confessor who has difficulties with language and needs to understand what the penitent wants to say, even when he responds with just yes or no to the questionnaire.

When we compare the Portuguese confession manual printed with the Tamil confession manual translated by Anriquez we find that it does not tally in many respects. We notice mainly the questions to be asked a sinner under the Ten Commandments. Anriquez has added many new things situating it to the local Tamil scenario. It records types of sins committed against the first commandment containing several new things. It mentions the Hindu (the pagan) practices and superstitious beliefs which are treated as mortal sins according to Catholic doctrine. The confessor here commands the sinner to remember well and recite the superstitious and idolatrous acts committed in words, thoughts, and desires which include celebrating demons and goddesses, selling palm-leaf books which contain the religion of those who have not embraced the Christian religion, believing in and using *viththai* (magic) and black magic (*sasthiram*), consulting astrologers and wizards using love potions, finding thefts by magic, believing in bird omens and gecko omens and the *paktchi dhosham* (disease caused in children by the birds flying over them), using magical plates, observing auspicious time and using various roots and herbs, keeping iron objects and bracelets to ward off demons, and doing magical prayers against the sharks.[61] Thus the types of sins listed had been very long which are not found in the Portuguese confession manual. The Catholic priest demands the details of the sins committed to say without fail, instead of the sinner confessing on his own. We find some type of nonsense had crept in Tamil translation though the confession manual was prepared by Anriquez desires to know the way of life of the new Tamil converts. It is found to be a mere foul play or trick adopted to know the heathen (Hindu) behaviour which the missionary wanted to keep off from Hinduism.

The confession manual continues to contain the list of sins committed against the second, third, fourth and the fifth Commandments. It refers to elicit information in the case of the sixth commandment, the transgression against another person. The confession table had become the site of pleasure of hearing about the sexual matters and we find the bachelor priest in the name of God or his representative sitting and raising questions about the sins of sex. Though it is really ridiculous, a spiritual tone had been added by the Catholic Church in the confession manual. It mentions the fear of the Lord and it depicts God as a judge and as a witness who will demand an accounting for all the sins people have committed, without missing anything. People would fear that they would be weeping forever, later suffering in Hell, having lost the heavenly seat.[62] Love, on the other hand, has been shown that Lord's creation, and the Christians who love and serve the Lord would receive unlimited happiness, which would be no less than the happiness of the saints.[63]

We find mention of the seventh commandment i.e., Thou shall not steal. A question is found 'Have you stolen items from the church?'.[64] There is a question with regard to the ninth commandment and we find 'Have you, a married woman, taken from or given to anyone without the agreement of your husband?'.[65] There are questions raised with reference to the tenth commandment and we find 'have you paid off the loan?' 'Have you refused any time to give the salary or wages due to the labourers/porters or those who do menial jobs/slaves'.[66] 'Have you taken the wealth of some one? Do you think that you want to give out of your portion, if you have taken excess? Thus questions have been included for sins committed against all the commandments.

Anriquez has not only translated the manual from Portuguese but aimed to adapt the practices of Tamils with confessionary zeal. It is more structured and bureaucratized in approach in dealing with sin and introspection. An examination of the printed text shows that words from languages such as colloquial Tamil, Sanskrit, besides Latin and Portuguese had been profusely used. The Tamil vocabulary provided in the confession manual includes many words and Christian concepts which are untranslatable from Portuguese such as attrition, contrition, and penitence. Hence he had merely transliterated phonetically into Tamil and they are found in brackets with a diamond-shaped sign to mark their presence in the printed page. Ines Zupanvo had looked into this confession manual as a Jesuit dialogical and catechetical text. She laid emphasis on how the manual had captured and condensed Tamil voices and arguments in a network of Jesuit normative vocabulary and offered a language of self-knowledge expressed in affective vocabulary. However it looks different and the manual is not strictly composed following the model of—the dialogue played out with a series of questions and responses between Master (*guru*) and Disciple (*shishya*). Zupanov is of the view that this confession manual should not be considered only a strategy for missionary manipulation but also an important tool for the social self-empowerment of the new convert.[67] Anriquez had accomplished through this manual in Tamil, by tackling the emotional process of confession and penance, injecting key elements of the spiritual exercises into a hypothetical dialogue between a confessor and a penitent. The manual had merely functioned as conscience-fashioning manual teaching converts to think, feel, talk, and act in a Christian way. In doing so, Tamil penitents had acted out a ritual of some familiarity and approachability which inherently carried Christian and not the Jesuit principles.

It was through confessions and preaching that the missionaries sought to combat the vices and other customs that they saw as contrary to the teachings of the church. Hearing confessions of the natives was considered an important pastoral activity of the missionaries. Confession manual which was already prepared in Europe and available in Portuguese and Italian had followed no uniform style but also differed through some sort of translation had been carried out with additions and deletions. Hence Anriquez had put the same model almost in a new pattern suitable for the use of Tamil converts though the sins and the sinners in the entire universe were almost the same. Direct contact with God was frowned upon by the spirit of Counter Reformation which prized mediation. The sacrament of penance was belittled by the reformed church. The translation of the confession manual in Tamil was made to serve the native Catholic penitents a guide to make accurate examination of conscience and an effective confession of their sins.

Translating the Book on the Lives of Saints from Portuguese and Latin into Tamil by Anrique Anriquez in 1580 and Printing the Book in Goa in 1586

The book titled '*Ho flos sanctorum em linguajem portuguesa*' (Admonitions of the saints in Portuguese language) was an extensive compilation of edifying biographies of saints, and it was printed in Lisbon in 1513 by Hermão de Campos and Roberto Rabello.[68] *Flos Sanctorum* was a compendium of the acts of the saints. It is a set of edifying tales of devotion and martyrdom compiled and adapted from religious works. In 1521, Dom Duarte de Menezes the Portuguese Governor of India entrusted five copies of the lives of saints to the Portuguese factor in Goa for the use of the people.[69] Baltasar Jorge Valdés (d.1546), a Portuguese noble who travelled to India in 1540 had carried twelve books and one of them was the lives of saints.[70] In 1554 Melchior Nunes Barreto (1520–71) the Jesuit had brought a copy of the lives of saints and it was used in the college in Goa.[71] Thus the book had been a very popular one both used in Europe and in India.

Flos Sanctorum for the second time appeared in print in Portuguese in 1567. It was titled '*Historia das vidas e feitos heroicos e obras insignes dos sanctos*' printed in 1567 at Braga by Antonio de Mariz.[72] A mere four years after the Council of Trent's closing and even before the reformed breviary (1568), the new legendary work of Flos Sanctorum was ordered to be prepared by Friar Bartolomeu dos Mártires, the Archbishop of Braga, Primate of Hispania and a participant of Trent, to the Dominican Friar Diogo do Rosário (who spent most of his life as the prior of the Dominican convent in Guimarães, 50 kilometres north-east of Porto). This was done exclusively with the explicit goal of replacing the earlier histories of the lives of saints that had been printed in Portuguese in 1513 which contained some very uncertain and apocryphal matters.[73] Lives of Saints edition printed in 1567 were brought by the Portuguese missionaries to India for use. *Flos Sanctorum* had been revised again and it was printed at Coimbra in 1577. Portuguese missionaries had also brought this book to India for use.

The Jesuits desired the Tamil Catholic converts to lead an exemplary life according to the Christian tenets. Hence they decided to translate the book of the lives of saints to edify the people. Anriquez undertook this great task and he mentions three different sources which he had used for translation. According to him he used the book of Frei Diogo do Rosário (History of the lives, heroic exploits and signal works of the saints with many sermons and spiritual instructions to be used for many feasts of the year' printed in Braga in 1567). It must be stated that Rosário's *Flos Sanctorum* was no pocket book. It had approximately 1,000 folio-sized pages (305 by 483 mm), and it was a large book. Anriquez also had access to the next edition of Coimbra in 1577 and he used for his translation.

It had been reported by Anriquez that he used the book 'Sanctorum *Priscorum Patrum Vitae*' (Lives of the saints and ancient fathers), four volumes printed in 1551-54 in Venice by Luigi Lippomano (the Apostolic Nuncio in Portugal, 1542-1546, who later became the Bishop of Modena, Verona and Bergamo. Anriquez had stated that he did not use all the 163 saints and their lives found in this work, but he made a selection of saints particularly chose the lives of 49 saints for translation in Tamil.[74]

Anriquez also had mentioned that he used Joachim Périon's *Derebusgestis vitis que Apostolorum liber* (Book on the deeds and lives of the apostles, published by Charles Perrier, printed in Paris in 1551 for his translation. However Anriquez did not refer to the specific parts contained in this which he used for translation of the lives of saints in Tamil.[75] The translation began in 1580 took six years for completion. The translated text was examined by Dom Matheus de Medina the Bishop of Cochin and by the lords of inquisitors. It was approved and permission was granted for printing by the Bishop of Cochin and the councillors. The book was printed in Goa in 1586.

The Tamil translation contains seventy-three topic entries on saints, matter from the New Testament, giving accounts of the life of Christ, the Virgin Mary and the apostles.

Saint	***Type of feast/ saint***
Advent	Christ Feast
Andrew (1st century)	Apostle
Augustine (354–430)	Bishop
Adrian	Identity unclear
Alexis (4th–5th century)	Confessor
The Holy Guardian Angels	Observance
Agatha (3rd century)	Martyr
Ascension of Jesus	Christ Feast
Blaise	Bishop and Martyr
Benedict of Nursia (c.480–c.547)	Patriarch of Monks
Bernard of Clairvaux (1090–1153)	Abbott/Theologian
Christine	Martyr
Cecilia	Martyr
Circumcision of Jesus	Christ Feast

All Souls	Observance
Our Lady of Sorrows	Marian Feast
Eustace (d.118)	Martyr
Eugenia	Virgin and Martyr
Epiphany	Christ Feast
Incarnation of Jesus	Christ Feast
Felicity and the Seven Sons	Martyr
Final Judgment	–
Ignatius of Antioch (c.35–c.108)	Bishop and Martyr
Martin	Identity unclear
Mary of Egypt (5th century)	Penitent
Margaret	Identity unclear
Christmas	Christ Feast
Birth of Mary	Marian Feast
Our Lady of the Snows	Marian Feast
Paulinus of Nola (353–431)	Bishop
Purification of Our Lady	Marian Feast
Passion of the Christ	Christ Feast
Lent	Observance
Resurrection of Christ	Christ Feast
Pentecost	Christ Feast
Sophia and her daughters	Identity unclear
Martyr Seven Sleepers	Identity unclear
Holy Trinity	Observance
Thaïs	Penitent
Vincent (d.304)	Martyr
Nicholas (270–343)	Bishop
Lucy (283–304)	Virgin and Martyr
Thomas (1st century)	Apostle
Stephen (1st century)	Martyr
John the Apostle (1st century)	Apostle
Sylvester (d.335)	Pope

Circumcision of Jesus	Christ Feast
Epiphany	Christ Feast
Sebastian (d.288)	Martyr
Apollonia (d.249)	Virgin and Martyr
Matthias (1st century)	Apostle
Philip (1st century)	Apostle
James the Lesser (1st century)	Apostle
Invention of the Holy Cross	–
Corpus Christi	Feast
Anthony of Padua (1195–1231)	Franciscan
John the Baptist (1st century)	–
Peter (1st century)	Apostle
Paul (1st century)	–
Mary Magdalene (1st century)	Follower of Jesus
James the Greater (1st century)	Apostle
Christopher (3rd century)	Martyr
Dominic (1170–1221)	Founder and Confessor
Lawrence (c.225–258)	Martyr
Assumption of Mary	Marian Feast
Bartholomew (1st century)	Apostle
Matthew (1st century)	Apostle
Michael the Archangel	Archangel
Jerome/Geronymo (c.347–420)	Confessor and Doctor
Francis of Assisi (1181/2–1226)	Founder
Simon and Jude (1st century)	Apostle
All Saints	–
Catherine of Alexandria (c.287–c.305)	Virgin and Martyr

Source: BAV, Vaticani Indiani 24, Flos Sanctorum; Anrique Anriquez, Flos Sanctorum enra Adiyaar Varalaaru, Thuthukudi, Thamizh Ilakkiya Kazhlagam, 1967.

The lives of saints translation done by Anriquez was not verbatim for he had assembled facts contained in all the three sources. It appears practical

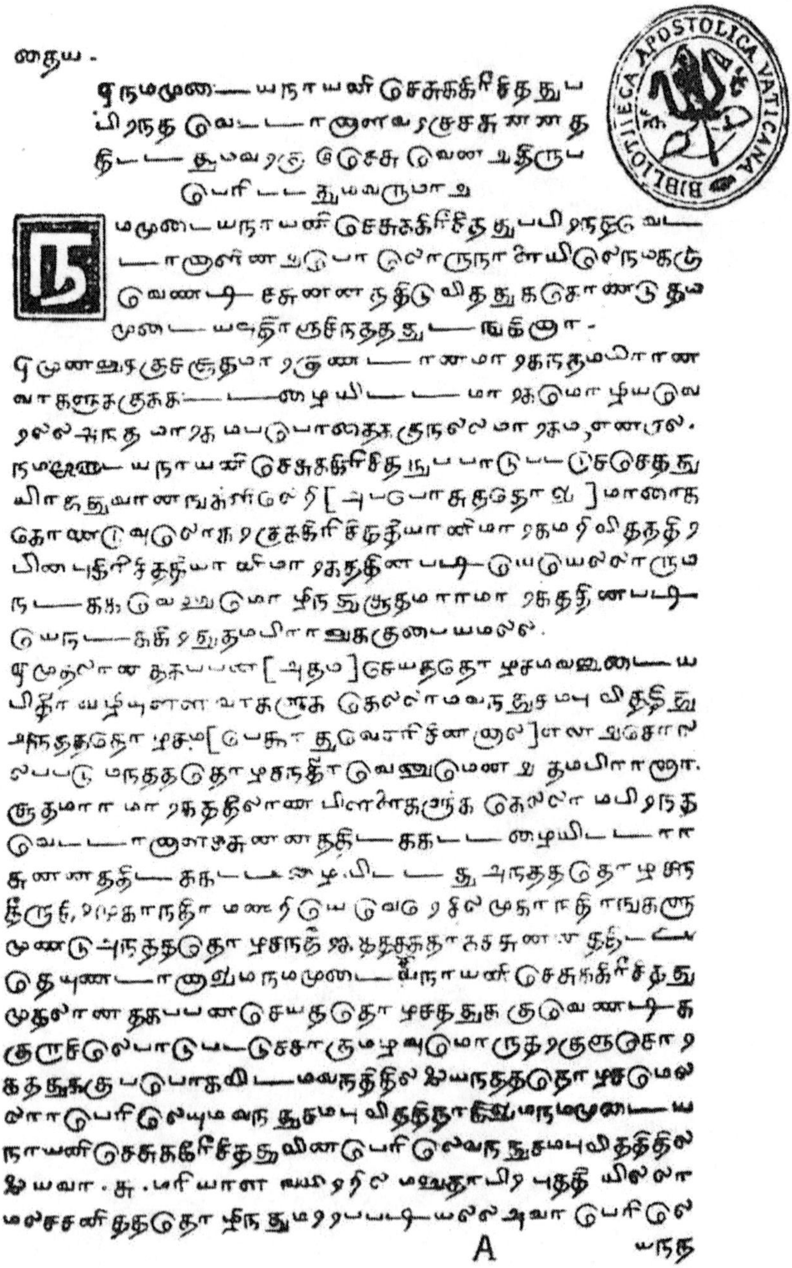

2.4: A page from Flos Sanctorum printed in Goa in 1586 (Courtesy: Biblioteca Apostolica Vaticana, Città del Vaticano)

because Anriquez had also used some contents from the New Testament of the Bible, but he made no claim to be a translation of the Bible, since it was prohibited. Anriquez had made a selection of popular saints like Antony of Padua, (miracle-maker and helps to find lost things) Cecilia (patron of singers), Lucia (helper of cure for eye-ache), Sebastian (plague disease) besides the martyrs from the early church. He had also included the founders of the religious orders, such as the Franciscans, Dominicans, and Benedictines. The noted theologians like Augustine, Jerome, and Bernard of Clairvaux did not escape his attention.

Anriquez in the beginning of the book had written that Jesus was born as a man and at the time of his birth there were no Muslims except Jews and Tamils. As soon as he was born, an angel appeared and made known the news of his birth to the Jewish shepherds. After he was born a star had appeared to the three Tamil kings.[76] This Anriquez had inserted to give a local setting while introducing this book to Tamil readers. In fact the idea is not at all found in original three books which he had used for translation.

Anriquez had carefully arranged the feasts of the saints according to the Church calendar from the month of January to December. The related portion from the book was read out to the public on the days of the feast of the saints by the catechist.

Flos Sanctorum translation is important because this devotional literature refers to works that concentrates on individuals for spiritual edification. This is completely different from other translations of catechisms, dialogues and sermons which assigned priority to Catholic doctrine and theology. Anriquez gave names like St. Lucy as 'su. Uluciyaal'; St. Matthew as 'su. Mattecu' because these names were untranslatable. The proper names in print appear between diamond-shaped marks. The book also contains the untranslatable words from Portuguese and Latin. In the translation process, the ideas or words from European languages were not translated exactly into another, since the cultures were very different, but a degree of meaning of the Christian message had been attempted by Anriquez is praiseworthy for it helped to reach the Tamils in their mother-tongue.

Translating the Book on the Life of Christ from Portuguese to Tamil titled Sesunaathar Sarithiram by Anrique Anriquez, 1598-99

The Life of Christ (*Vita Christi*) by Ludolph of Saxony (1300-78) was an important work and it was among Ignatius of Loyola's cherished readings.[77] It contains an embryonic theology of both the missionaries and the imaginative meditation that later characterized the Society of Jesus. The printed book Life of Christ in Lisbon was of the size of missal and it contained all events till the ascension of Jesus well illuminated. Gil Eanes Pererira had brought a copy of the book from Portugal to India and he used it in Bengal.[78]

Portuguese missionaries thought the book was essential to preaching Christ in the native language. Gaspar de Leão who was appointed the archbishop of Evora in 1540 later became in 1560 the first archbishop of Goa. He desired to write a book on Christian life and composed '*Compendio spiritual da vida christaa*' (Spiritual compendium of Christian life) and it was published by João de Quinquencio and João de Endem in Goa in 1561. This book was a manual of doctrine and prayer but contained a history of the life of Jesus.[79]

Anrique Anriquez desired to write in Tamil on the life of Christ based on the printed books in Portuguese in Lisbon and Goa. He therefore used large extracts contained in the books. He included themes such as the mystery of redemption, annunciation, before nativity, nativity, after nativity, Visit of the Magi, presentation, fled to Egypt, Return to Judea, Jesus among Doctors, in Nazareth, baptism, fast, apostles, teaching, miracles, Jewish enmity, tricks, agony, arrest, before Caiaphas, humiliations, Before Pontius Pilate, Herod, scourging, crowning, condemnation, way of the cross, death, after death, after burial, resurrection and ascension into heaven. He completed the translation in 1598 and titled the book *Sesunathar Sarithiram*.[80] It has been mentioned in the Jesuit annual letter of the year AD.1600.[81] Further, the Jesuit annual letter of 1612 also remarked that the book on life of Christ had been translated into Tamil some years ago from the printed book of Life of Christ.[82] Hence the view of Rajamanickam that *Sesunathar Sarithiram* was the work of Roberto Nobili is called into question.[83]

Translating the Christian Doctrine of Marpur de Lavradio by Roberto Nobili from Portuguese to Tamil titled Chinna Kurippidam, 1612

The essential educational tool for the conversion of the natives in India used had been initially the book of Dom Diego de Vilhegas, the Bishop of

Cute, titled '*Catechism pequeno*' (small catechism) printed in Lisbon in 1504 by Valentim Fernandes and João Pedro Buonhomini de Cremona.[84] Doctrina Christiana in question-answer format of Cardinal Roberto Bellarmine (1542-1621) was first translated into Portuguese by Marpur de Lavradio. It was decided by the Jesuits to translate this catechism into Tamil. Further *Catechismus Catholicus* by Girolamo da Palmero the Dominican theologian was printed in Venice by Giordano Ziletti e Soci in 1571. Another catechism printed in Latin in Venice in 1583 was also found useful for translation. The work was entrusted to Roberto Nobili stationed at Madurai. A copy of the same after translation was promised to be sent to Europe vide the Jesuit letter written from Madurai dated 13 November 1610.[85] It is gleaned that translation had taken two years to complete and this is mentioned in the Jesuit annual letter of 1612.[86] It was called *Chinna kurippidam* (Penny Catechism) in Tamil.

Balthasar da Costa (1610-73) the fellow Jesuit refers to *Chinna Kurippidam* (*Catechismi examen*) by Roberto Nobili which consists of seven small chapters. The first chapter treats of the Triune god, the second of creation and fall, the third of redemption, the fourth of the church, the fifth of the last things, the sixth of precepts and sin and the seventh treats of the sacraments in general and baptism, confession and eucharist in particular. The Jesuit annual letter of 1656 mentions this translation work by Nobili which the children learnt with great enthusiasm before receiving the first holy communion.[87] The youngsters again had to use and have a faithful rendering which was necessary before marriage. The prayers in the *Chinna kurippidam* were directed by the missionaries to be learnt by-heart. Catechists were also instructed by the Jesuits to use before baptism and conversion to Christianity.

Translating the book of Alphonso Mendez on the Life of the Blessed Virgin Mary from Portuguese to Tamil by Jean-Venant Bouchet titled Devamaathaavin Sarithiram, 1715

Jean-Venant Bouchet (1655-1732) the Jesuit who was at Ariyankuppam near Pondicherry had made a mention of his work in Tamil on the Blessed Virgin Mary vide his letter dated 21 September 1714 to Fr Jean-Baptiste Du Halde (1674-1743) in Europe.[88] He had great devotion to Mary and translated the printed book in Portuguese titled 'Life of the Blessed Virgin

Mary, the Mother of God Our Lady' by Patriarch Alphonso Mendez and published from the Jesuit college press in 1652 in Goa.[89] The book in Tamil translated was titled *Devamaathaavin sarithiram* (Life of Mother of God). It contains the details of her birth, dedication in the temple, marriage, annunciation visitation, Joseph's anxiety, nativity of Jesus, presentation- fleeing to Egypt, Jesus lost and found in the temple in Nazareth, public life of our Jesus Christ, his passion and resurrection, The primitive church, Mary's appearance, her death, soul in heaven, burial, her bodily appearance, her help, St. Bernard's prayer, her miracles, refuge of the sinners and conclusion. Hence the view of Rajamanickam that *Devamaathaavin Sarithiram* was the work of Roberto Nobili is called into question.[90]

Translating the Biography of St. Ignatius of Loyola from Italian into Tamil by Angelo de Franceschei in 1740

The biography of Ignatius of Loyola the founder of the Society of Jesus appeared and the books were printed in Italian in Venice in 1585 and 1586.[91] Devotion to Ignatius of Loyola in Tamil country had been recorded in the Jesuit annual letter written from Kollai dated 8 May 1677 and in the next Jesuit annual letter of 1678.[92] Angelo de Franceschei the Jesuit who worked in the Carnatic Mission translated the biography of Ignatius of Loyola from Italian into Tamil in 1740.[93] However the translation did not see the light of printing as the Jesuit press had ceased functioning by this time. The book was printed by L.S. Dupuis in Pondicherry in 1869.[94] The translated Tamil text of Ignaciyar Sarithiram has been wrongly attributed by S. Rajamanickam as the work of Roberto Nobili.[95]

Translation of Catholic Tenets from English to Tamil in Sri Lanka and Printing in Colombo and Reprinting the Book Sathiya Vetha Bhodhaga Surukkam in Pondicherry in 1846

Fr. L.S. Dupuis the manager of the mission press in Pondicherry had printed the book *Sathiya Vetha Bhodhaga Surukkam* in 1846. The title page of the book runs thus:

> Sathiya vetha bhodhaga surukkam: Iguthu christhu vetha visuvasikalukku piraiyosanamaaga vetha virpannargalal inglishu bahsagyri pirayogikka patta vannath thamzhilil mozhipeyarthu ilangapuriil maha maatchimai poruthiya don Caetano anthoni

2.5: The title page of Sathya Vethabhodhaga Surukkam printed in Pondicherry, 1846 (Courtesy: Bibliothèque Asiatique des missions étrangères de Paris)

> mettrani aandavargal anumathiyil kolumbil vyagula maria naayaggiyin dharma sampradhya achchu kudaththil achchil pathikka patta pragaarame, romapurin ninru vantha utharaththin padiye 1846 varusham puthuvaiyir sanmavirakkini maatha koilai serntha achchu kudathir pathikka pattathu.

It is gleaned that Sathi*ya Vetha Bhodaga Surukkam* was translated from English into Tamil for the use of the Christians and it was printed by the permission of Dom Caetano Joseph the Bishop of Sri Lanka and it was printed at vyagula mariya nayagi press at Colombo. An order was issued from Rome and so it was reprinted in Pondicherry in 1846.[96]

Translating Alphonse Maria de Ligouri's Book from Latin to Tamil titled Aathuma Nesam by Charles Michele Bertoldi and Printing in Pondicherry in 1860

C. Gnaanapragaasa Nathar Swami (Charles Michele Bertoldi, 1662-1740) the Jesuit worked in the Madurai mission. He undertook the translation of St. Ligouri's meditations and prayers on the passion and the death of Jesus Christ and it was called *Aathuma Nesam* in Tamil. The translation was widely used by the missionaries and circulated among the native Catholics for long. It did not see the light of printing. Louis Savinien Dupuis the MEP missionary and the manager of the mission press at Pondicherry had decided to print it for the use of Tamil Catholics. The book got printed on receipt of an order from the Superiors in Rome and permission was granted by the Bishop in Pondicherry in 1860.[97] In this printed book we find the dedication to St. Ligouri by the translator (pp. 1-2) followed by the prayer to Jesus and Mary. The preface of Ligouri is also found translated in Tamil. The biography of Alphonse Maria de Ligouri (1696-1787) is given where it is stated that St. Ligouri was born on 26 September 1696 and Francisco Heronimus had made a prophecy that Ligouri would become a bishop and he would not die before the age of 90. There are 16 chapters translated and given in the book. We find chapter 6 dealing with commencement of Jesus at Mount of Olive sweating of blood and chapter 13 concludes with end of the passion and death of Jesus. The last utterances of the sacred words of Jesus had been given. It ends with the prayer of Bonaventure. The total printed pages are 308 in the book.

சேசுமரியாயி சூசை துணை.

மிகவும்பெயர்பெற்ற வேதசாஸ்திரியும்
மேற்றிராணியாருமாகிய
அர்ச். லிகோரியார்
அருளிச்செய்த
ஆத்தும நேசம்,
அல்லது
நமதாண்டவராகிய சேசுகிறிஸ்துநாதருடைய
திருப்பாடுகளின்பேரில்
பத்தியுள்ள தியானம்.

இஃது
ஞானப்பிரகாசநாதனென்னும்
குருசுவாமியாரவர்களால்
மொழிபெயர்க்கப்பட்டு
அதிசிரேஷ்டருடைய அநுமதியுடன்
உரோமாபுரியினின்று வந்த
உத்தாரத்தின்படியே

௲௮௱௬௰-ஆம்
புதுவை-சன்மவிராக்கினி மாதாக்கோயிலைச்
சேர்ந்த அச்சுக்கூடத்திற் பதிப்பிக்கப்பட்டது.

2.6: The title page of Aathuma Nesam printed in Pondicherry, 1860 (Courtesy: Madurai Province Jesuit Archives, Shenbaganur)

Translation of Thomas Kempi's Imitation of Christ from Latin to Tamil by Charles Michele Bertoldi and Printing in Pondicherry in 1863

Charles Michele Bertoldi translated the book of Imitation of Christ by Thomas Kempis (1380-1471) from Latin to Tamil. L.S. Dupuis, the MEP missionary and Pro-vicar Apostolic in Pondicherry felt the importance of the Tamil translation for the use of the Catholics. Therefore he took steps and got printed the book in 1863. The title page of the book mentions that *De Imitatione Christi, Kristhunaathar Anusaaram*, whose author was Thomas A Kempis and the translator was C. Gnaanapragaasa Nathar and permission was granted by Bishop Isidore Joseph Godelle in Pondicherry for printing.[98] The book contains four sections. The first section has 25 chapters dealing with the theme of the useful admonitions to spiritual life (pp.1-80). The second section has 12 chapters and deals with the admonitions concerning interior things (pp.81-125). The third section has 59 chapters and it deals with special features of the interior consolation (pp.126-173). The fourth chapter has 18 chapters and it deals with the Blessed Sacrament (pp.174-374). The prayers are given at the end. The book contains 390 printed pages.

Biblical Writings Translated by Charles Michele Bertoldi and Printing the book Sathiya Vetha Sarithira Surukkam in Pondicherry in 1865

L.S. Dupuis had also printed the book titled *Sathiya Vetha Sarithira Surukkam* translated by Charles Michele Bertoldi. The title page of the printed book mentions that C. Gnaanapragaasa Nathar had translated the book and Bishop Isidore Godelle had granted permission for printing.[99] The author of the book and the language in which it was composed and available being used for translation had not been stated anywhere in the printed book. There are two sections while the first is called *Vari Vetham* that deals with the Old Testament beginning with the creation of the world, Adam and Eve and the text goes on and ends at page 170. The second section is titled *Arul Vetham* and it deals with the New Testament, commencing from the birth of Jesus to his ascension to heaven and the text ends at p. 338. The contents had been given at the end (pp.339-44). The book contains 344 printed pages.

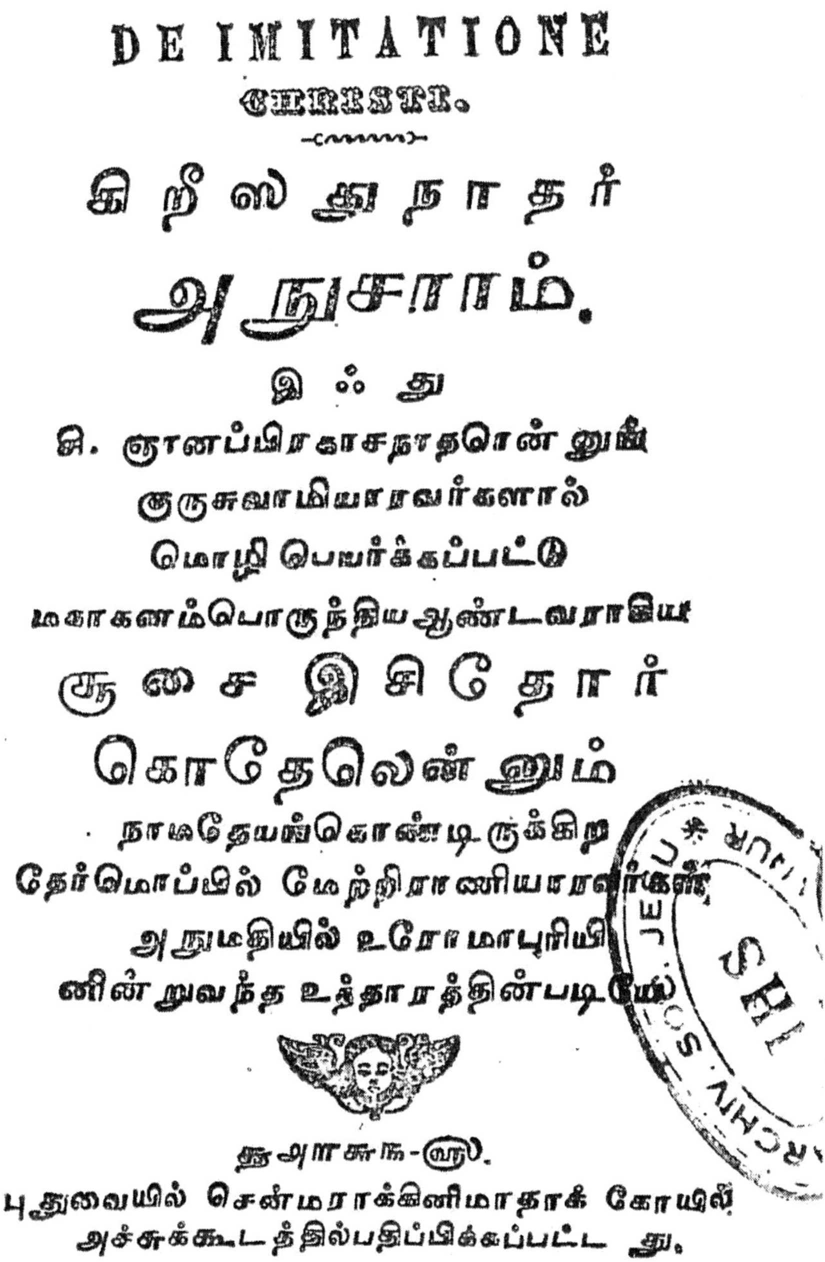

DE IMITATIONE
CHRISTI.

கிறீஸ்துநாதர்
அநுசாரம்.
இஃது
சி. ஞானப்பிரகாசநாதனென்னுங்
குருசுவாமியாரவர்களால்
மொழிபெயர்க்கப்பட்டு
மகாகனம்பொருந்திய ஆண்டவராகிய
ஞொசெ இசிதோர்
கொதேலென்னும்
நாமதேயங்கொண்டிருக்கிற
தேர்மொப்பில் மேற்றிராணியாரவர்களின்
அநுமதியில் உரோமாபுரியி
னின்றுவந்த உத்தாரத்தின்படியே

௲௮௱௬௩-ஹூ.
புதுவையில் சென்மராக்கினிமாதாக் கோயில்
அச்சுக்கூடத்தில்பதிப்பிக்கப்பட்டது.

2.7: The title page of Kristhunaathar Anusaaram printed in Pondicherry, 1863 (Courtesy: Madurai Province Jesuit Archives, Shenbaganur)

சேசுமரியாயி சூசை துணை.

சத்தியவேத சரித்திரச் சுருக்கம்.

இஃது

ஞ. ஞானப்பிரகாசநாதரென்னுங்
குருசுவாமியாரவர்களால்
மொழிபெயர்க்கப்பட்டுப்
புதுவையிலெழுந்தருளியிருக்கும்
மகாகனம்பொருந்திய ஆண்டவராகிய
சூசையிசிதோர்
கொதேலென்னு
நாமதேயங்கொண்டிருக்கிற
தேர்மொப்பில்
மேத்திராணியாரவர்களநுமதியில்
உரோமாபுரியினின்றுவந்தஉத்தாரத்தின்படியே

௲௮௱௬௰௫
புதுவையிற்சன்மனிராக்கினிமாதாக்கோவிலைச்சேர்ந்த
அச்சுக்கூடத்திற்பதிப்பிக்கப்பட்டது.

2.8: The title page of Sathya Vetha Sarithira Surukkam printed in Pondicherry, 1865 (Courtesy: Madurai Province Jesuit Archives, Shenbaganur)

To conclude it may be said that the Catholic missionaries had translated books from Latin and Portuguese into Tamil and got most of them printed at the Jesuit printing press in Quilon, Cochin and Goa. These missionaries had made the body of Tamil literature attain a new identity particularly Catholic Christian in the larger gamut of the existing old religious literatures of South India. They saw an undercurrent in the various religious literatures of the Jains, Buddhists, Hindus and Muslims after translation chiefly remaining in manuscripts without reaching a larger audience through print. It must be stated that Anrique Anriquez stands a unique figure while translating prose works from Latin and Portuguese into Tamil. He had coined several new terms mixed with Portuguese words. The main concern of the Catholic missionaries in the sixteenth century was the religious instruction in Tamil associated with the need to latinise the converts. Therefore there was the growing involvement and sense of teaching the Christian tenets of Catholicism to Tamils in their local tongue. The practical support had come from the king of Portugal. The missionary translators played an important role within the Tamil social and intellectual mediating networks. Printing had contributed to shaping reading habits and literary tastes by facilitating the circulation of books. The relationship between the Jesuit translator, the Jesuit printer, and Catholic Church the institution of religious power is nowhere better illustrated than encouraging translation and granting permission for publishing besides extending financial patronage. Thus the activities of the translator and the printer of Tamil translations had become inseparable. In fact the Jesuits had the exclusive privilege to print the translated Tamil books of devotional literature. Later the MEP missionaries had printed the translated books with the permission of the Sacred Congregation for the Propagation of Faith in Rome and from the local Bishop in Pondicherry at the Mission press since 1846.

NOTES

1. Fernão Lopes da Castanheda, Manuel Lopes de Almeida, ed., *Historia do descobrimentos e conquista da India pelos portugueses*, 2 vols, Porto, 1979, vol. I, p. 689.
2. António da Silva Rego, ed., *Documentação para a historia das missões do Padroado Portugues do oriente*, 12 vols., Lisboã, 1947-1958, vol. I, document 143, pp. 336-338.
3. António da Silva Rego, *Historia das Missões do Padroado Portugues do Oriente*, Lisboã, MCMXLIX, p. 134.

4. António da Silva Rego, *Documentação para a historia*, vol. 1, p. 338.
5. Ibid., vol. I,.pp. 336-39.
6. João Jose Alves Dias, ed., *No Quinto Centenario da Vita Christi, Os Primeiros Impressores Alemaes em Portugal*, Lisboã, 1995, p. 32.
7. Ibid., pp. 45-47.
8. Maria Alzira Proença Simoes, *Catalogo dos impressos de tipografia do seculo XVI: A Coleção da Biblioteca Nacional*, Lisboã, 1990, p. 68.
9. António Joaquim Anselmo, *Bibliografia das obras impressas em Portugal no seculo XVI*, Lisboa, 1926, p. 146.
10. António da Silva Rego, Documentação para a historia, vol. 1, pp. 419-421.
11. Ibid.
12. Ibid., vol. I. p. 437.
13. Ibid., vol. I, p. 411.
14. Ibid., vol. II, p. 328.
15. Ibid., vol. IV, p. 206.
16. Luis de Matos, ed. *Imagens do oriente no seculo XVI: Codice Casanatense*, Lisboã, 1889, rpt., Casa da Moeda, 1985, pp. 33-34.
17. Garcia da Orta, *Coloquios dos simples, e drogas he cousas medicinais da India*, Lisboã, 1963, col. 2, fl. 7v.
18. Maria Alzira Proença Simoes, Catalogo dos impressos, p. 116.
19. Jose Vitorino de Pina Martins, *Au Portugal dans lle Sillage d'Erasme*, Paris, 1977, pp. 93-94.
20. Armando Cortesão and Luis de Albuquerque, ed., *Obras Completas de Dom João de Castro*, 4 vols., Coimbra, 1968-1981, vol. III, p. 53.
21. Jose Wicki and J. Gomes, *Documenta Indica* (hereafter DI), 19 vols., Roma, 1944-88, vol. I, p. 88.
22. Georg Schurhammer, *Francisco Javier: Su vida y Su Tiempo*, 4 vols., Pamplona, 1992, vol. III, pp. 317-336.
23. D.I., vol. I, p. 35.
24. Ibid., p. 36.
25. Ibid., vol. I, p. 136.
26. António Joaquim Anselmo, Bibliografia das obras, pp. 66, 175,179; Maria Alzira Proença Simoes, Catalogo dos impressos, pp. 127, 149.
27. Gaspar de Leão and Eugenio Asensio, ed., *Desengano de Perdidos*, Coimbra, 1958, pp. xxxviii-lx.
28. António Joaquim Anselmo, Bibliografia das obras, pp. 181, 299, 302.

29. D.I., vol. IV, p. 614.
30. D.I., vol. V, p. 531.
31. D.I., vol. VI, p. 295.
32. Ibid., p. 308.
33. D.I., vol. VI, p. 772.
34. António da Silva Rego, Documentação para a historia, vol. III, pp. 24-25.
35. Georg Schurhammer, *St. Francis Xavier: His Life, His Times*, 2 vols., Rome, 1977, vol. II, pp. 308-09.
36. Ibid., p. 310.
37. M. Joseph Costelloe, trs., *The Letters and Instructions of Francis Xavier*, Anand, 1993, pp. 64, 92.
38. Georg Schurhammer, *Epistolae S. Francisci Xaverii alia que eius Scripta*, Roma, 1944, vol. I, pp. 427, 429.
39. D.I., vol. I, pp. 491-2, 581; vol. II, p. 302.
40. Georg Schurhammer and E. A. Voretzsch, *Ceylon zurr Zeit des Konigs Buvaneka Bahu und Franz Xaviers, 1539-1552*, 2 vols., Leipzig, 1928.
41. Biblioteca da Cartuxa, Evora, E.2098; Jean Filliozat, *Un Catechisme Tamoul du XVIe Siecle en Lettres Latines*, Pondicherry, 1967; Xavier S. Thaninayagam, 'The First Printed Books in Tamil', *Tamil Culture*, vol. VII, no.3, July, 1958, pp. 288-308.
42. M. Joseph Costelloe, The Letters and Instructions of Francis Xavier, pp. 41–5.
43. *Catechismus ex Decreto Concilii Tridentini ad Parochos*, Roma, MDLXVI.
44. Houghton Library, Harvard University. USA, Thambiran Vanakkam, AD 1578; Anrique Anriquez, ed., Thamizh Naadaan, *Thamizh Mozhhiyin Muthal Achchu Puththagam*, Salem, 1995, pp. 1-12.
45. C.T. Indra and R. Rajagopalan, eds., *Culture, Language, Identity: English-Tamil in Colonial India, 1750-1900*, Abingdon, 2018, p.6.
46. Georg Schurhammer and G. W. Cottrell, 'The First Printing in Indic Characters', in *Orientalia*, Roma/Lisboã, 1963, p. 321.
47. Marcos Jorge, *Doctrina Christam, Ordenando a maneira de dialogo, para ensiar os minios*, Lisboã, 1561. Bodleian Library, Oxford, Vet. Or. f. Tam.1. *Kirisiththiyaanai Van akkam*, Cochin, 1579. Anrique Anriquez, Krisiththiyaani Vanakkam, AD 1579, ed., S. Rajamanickam, *Vanakkam*, Thamizh Ilakkiya Kazhagam, Tuticorin, 1963.
48. D.I, vol. XII, p. 718.

49. Juan de Polanco, *Breve directorium ad confessarii ac confitentis munus recte obeundum*, Roma, apud Antonium Bladum, 1554; See, Alvaro de Torres, *Directório de confessores e penitentes*, Lisboã, João Blavio, 1556.
50. Rosa Marisa Barraccini, 'An unknown bestseller: The Confessionario of Girolamo da Palemero' in Flavia Bruni & Andrew Pettegree, eds., *Lost Books: Reconstructing the Print World of Pre-industrial Europe*, Leiden, 2016, pp. 291-309, see p. 295.
51. *Confessionario Raccolto da Dottori Catolici, Per lo Revr. Maestro Girolamo Panormitano del Ordine de Predicatori, con Privilegio*, in Napoli, Appresso Gio Mario Scotta, 1564.
52. Biblioteca Vallicelliana, Roma, Girolamo da Palmero, *Confessionario Raccolta da i dottori Catolici Nuouamente ampliato di alcutli avisi & osservationi d'importanza Per F. Andrea Alchero de Materno*, Brescia, 1567.
53. D.I., vol. IV, p. 159.
54. D.I., vol. VIII, p.175, vol. VII, p. 562.
55. Archivum Romanum Societatis Iesu (hereafter ARSI), Roma, MSS Goa, vol. VIII, fls. 694r-98v, see the letter of Diogo do Soveral to the members of São Roque in Lisbon written from Punnaikayal dated 18 December 1569.
56. D.I., vol. III, p. 711.
57. Anrique Anriquez, Flos Sanctorum, ed., S. Rajamanickam, *Adiyar Varalaru*, Tamil Ilakkiya Kazhagam, Tuticorin, 1967, pp. 559, 648.
58. Bodleian Library, Oxford, Vet. Or. F. Tamil.1, *Kompeciyonaryu*, 1580, fl. 2b.
59. G.W. Shaw 'A Lost Work of Henrique Henriques: The Tamil Confessionary of 1580', *The Bodleian Library Record*, No. 11, 1982, pp. 26-34; *Kompeciyonaryu*, 1580, fl. 75a.
60. *Kompeciyonaryu*, fl. 10b.
61. Ibid., fls.10a-18a.
62. Ibid., fl. 84a.
63. Ibid., fl. 90b.
64. Ibid., fl. 40a.
65. Ibid., fl. 41b.
66. Ibid., fl. 40b.
67. Ines G. •upanov, 'I Am a Great Sinner: Jesuit Missionary Dialogues in Southern India, (Sixteenth Century)', *Journal of the Economic and Social History of the Orient*, vol. 55, 2012, pp. 415-446.
68. Biblioteca Nacional de Lisboã (hereafter BNL), RES. 157A, *Ho flos*

sanctorum em lingoajem portugues, Lisboã, Hermão de Campos e Roberto Rabello, 15 Março 1513; Fr. Gauberto de Vagad O. Cist, *O Flos Sanctorum em Linguagem Português*, 1513.

69. António da Silva Rego, Documentação para a historia, vol. I, pp. 419-421.

70. Marcel Bataillon, *Erasmo y España: Studios sobre la historia spiritual del siglo XVI*, 2nd edn, trans. Antonio a la Torre, Mexico, Fondo de Cultura Económica, 1966, p. 807.

71. D.I., vol. III, p. 202.

72. António Joaquim Anselmo, Bibliografia das obras, pp.119-120.

73. Diogo do Rosário, *Historia das vidas & feitos heroicos & obras insignes dos sanctos, que nesta segunda parte se contem: com muitos sermões & praticas spirituaes que servem a muitas festas do anno. Reuistas & cotejadas cõ os seus originaes autenticos: de mãdado do muy Illustre & Reuerendiss. senhor dõ frey Bartholomeu dos Martyres Arcebispo & senhor de Braga, Primas das Hespanhas, & c.*, Braga, António de Mariz, 1567, see, Proemio.

74. Biblioteca Apostolica Vaticana (hereafter BAV), Città del Vaticano, VAT Baago 3, Flos Sanctorum; Det Kongelige Bibliotek (hereafter KB), Kobenhavn, Orientalske Afdeling, 1531, Flos Sanctorum.

75. Ibid. see also, Antonio Franco, *Synopsis Annualium Soceitatis Jesu in Lusitana ab annis 1540 usque ad annum 1725*, Haeredum, MDLCCXXVI, see Index materiam dequibus tracarunt Lusitane Provinciae scriptores ab initio Societatis ad annum 1724, p. 517.

76. BAV, VAT Baago 3; S. Rajamanickam, *Flos Sanctorum enra Adiyaar Varalaaru*, Thuthukudi, Thamizh Ilakkiya Kazhlagam, 1967, p. 7.

77. *Vita Christi domini saluatoris nostri a r.p. Ludolpho Saxone Cartusiano ante CCL annos ex sacris evangelijs, veterumque patrum sententijs contexta, atque ita disposita, nihil ut eorum, quae tum ad historiae, tum ad homiliarum totius anni rationem spectant, deesse quidquam possit. Opus ut vere pium, ac eruditum, ita singulis christianae pietatis alumnis plurimum & solatij, & utilitatis allaturum. A Io. Dadraeo, Parisiensis scholae doctore theologo, multis notationibus illustratum, postrema hac Venetaeditione innumeris mendis purgatum, pulcherrimisque figuris exornatum. Indices accessere necessarii,* Venetiis : apud Guerraeos fratres, & Franciscum Zilettum, 1581.

78. D.I., vol. XI, p. 424.

79. New York Public Library (hereafter NYPL), New York, *COMPENDIO SPIRITVAL DA VIDA CHRISTAA, tirade de muitos autores pello primeiro ARCEBISPO de Goa, ó per elle pregado no primeiro anno a seus fregueses, pera Gloria ó horra de IESV CHRISTO nosso SALVADOR, ó edificacam de*

suas. Na seguinte folha se decrara o conteudo neste Tratado. Impresso em Goa: por Ioão Quinquencio, ó Ioao de Endem, ó por madao do Senhor Arcebispo, 1561. Acabouse este presente liuro a honra ó louuor de Deos todo poderoso, ó da sacratissima Virgem Maria, aos 2. De Iulho, 1561 Annos. Gaspar de Leão had sent a copy of Compendio spiritual da vida Christaa in November 1561 is mentioned in a Jesuit letter. See, D.I., vol. V, p. 231.

80. S. Rajamanickam, ed., *Sesunathar Sarithiram*, Tuticorin, 1964.
81. Antonio Franco, Synopsis Annualium Soceitatis Jesu, p. 516.
82. ARSI, Roma, MSS Goa, vol. 51, fls. 187-192.
83. A. Sauliere, *His Star in the East* (Revised and reedited by S. Rajamanickam), Anand, 1995, p. 480.
84. Maria Alzira Proença Simoes, Catalogo dos impressos, p. 241.
85. *Catechismus ex decreto Concilii Tridentini ad parochos. Pii V pont. max. iussu editus*, Venetiis : apud Fabium, August, Zoppinos, fratres, 1583. ARSI, Mss Goa, vol. 51, fls.170-5.
86. Ibid., fls.187-192.
87. Ibid., Mss Goa, vol. 53, fls.239-58.
88. Bibliothèque Nationale, Paris (hereafter BNP), Rue Richelieu, MSS Nouvelles Acquisitions Françaises (hereafter NAFR), no. 1168, fl.78, see the letter of Jean-Venant Bouchet to Du Halde dated 21 September 1714.
89. Biblioteca Publica, Oporto, Portugal, see, *VIDA DA SANTISSIMA VIRGEM MARIA MAY DE DEOS, Senhora Nossa, Composto pello Padre Antonio Fernandes da Companhia de Iesvs Portuguez natural de Lixboa, Em Goa co licenca dos Inquisidores & Ordinario*, Impresso no Collegio de Sam Paulo da Companhia de Iesv, anno, de 1652, pp.1-183. This book is a Portuguese translation by Patriarch Alphonso Mendez of a book written by Antonio Fernandez in the Armaranic language.
90. S. Rajamanickam, ed., *Archsishta Devamatha Sarithiram*, Tuticorin, 1964. See, A. Sauliere, His Star in the East, pp. 479-80.
91. Giovanni Pietro Maffei, *De vita et moribus Ignatii Loiolae, qui Societatem Iesu fundauit*, libri III, Venetiis, apud Iolitos, 1585; Pedro de Ribadeneyra, *Vita del p. Ignatio Loiola fondatore della Religione della Compagnia di Giesù*, In Venetia, appresso i Gioliti, 1586.
92. S. Jeyaseela Stephen, *Letters of the Portuguese Jesuits from Tamil Countryside, 1666-1688*, Pondicherry, 2001, pp. 85-86, 146.
93. D. Ferroli, *The Jesuits in Mysore*, Calicut, 1955, p.186.
94. Bibliothèque Asiatique Missions Etrangères de Paris (hereafter BAMEP), *Archiasishta Ignaasiyaar Sarithiram*, Pondicherry, 1869.

95. S. Rajamanickam, *The First Oriental Scholar*, Palayamkottai, 1972, p. 112.
96. BAMEP, TA 193, *Sathiya Vethabhodhaga Surukkam*, Pondicherry, 1846.
97. Madurai Province Jesuit Archives (hereafter MPJA), Shenbaganur, No. 221/58, *Aathuma Nesam*, Pondicherry, 1860.
98. British Library, London, 14170.a.20, *De Imitatione Christi, Kristhunathar Anusaaram*, Translated from Latin by S. Gnaanapargaasa Nathar, Pondicherry, 1863; See also, MPJA, 221/191, Accession number 141000, *Kristhunaathar Anusaaram*, Pondicherry, 1863.
99. MPJA, 221/209, Accession number 006366, *Sathiya Vetha Sarithira Surukkam*, Pondicherry, 1865.

3

Shipping Books from the Netherlands, Denmark, Germany and England to India and Sri Lanka:

Making Translations from Dutch, German and Portuguese into Tamil by the Protestant Missionaries, 1661-1825

The Protestants in Europe had a separate identity and their approach was also different in the matter of policy of conversions from that of the Catholics. On the doctrinal side, there was strong opposition between the Protestants and Catholics. Among the Protestants also there were denomination such as the Dutch Reformed Church and the German and Danish Lutherans. The missionaries brought printed books of Protestantism from Europe to Tamil coast and Sri Lanka and they also began to translate the Christian prayers for worship.

The Prayers and Catechism Translated from Dutch to Tamil by the Predikants of the Reformed Church, 1661-1739

Philippus Baldaeus (1632-1671), the Dutch *predikant* who worked at Nagapattinam in 1660 and at Tuticorin in 1661 translated the Lord's Prayer. It was circulated in handscriften (handwritten form). The Dutch East India Company (VOC) at that time had established its governance in Sri Lanka but the trading settlements on the Tamil coast were placed under its control. The activities of the missionaries on the Tamil coast were directed mainly from Sri Lanka to Tamil ports like Pulicat, Sadurangapattinam, Nagapattinam and Tuticorin.

The Lord's Prayer translated in Tamil by the Dutch appeared in print in four folios, printed on one side. This is the first document to be printed at the VOC press in Colombo in 1739. Copies of Lord's Prayer were sent for circulation to Tamil coast. It had the Dutch title '*Het Gebed Onses heeren in de Tamilsche Tale met de tweed sort der Malabaarsche*'. We find next the letters in s'Compagnies Drukkery tot Colombo, gedrukt den 28 April 1739.[1] A copy of this Lord's Prayer printed in Tamil in 1739 is preserved at the Royal Library in The Hague, The Netherlands.[2]

The Dutch Reformed Church desired to have a catechism in Tamil prepared. Hence steps were taken for translation and we find a catechism and prayer book printed in 1739. It is titled in Dutch '*Mallebaars Catechismus, en Gebede-boek Gedrukt tot Colombo ten dientse der Scholen Anno 1739*'. It has 88 pages. The book has the title, table of contents, Tamil title with the VOC crest, the table of contents in Tamil and the Tamil text. This catechism and prayer book was meant for use in the schools. Hence 2100 copies were printed and a statement is also found in Dutch Governor Imhoff's Memoir, prepared for his successor in 1740.[3]

Translating the Book of Jacobus Borstius on Doctrine of Faith of the Reformed Church by Abraham Bronsveld from Dutch to Tamil and Printing in Colombo, 1754

The Dutch missionaries used Jacobus Borstius's work on the Synopsis of the Christian faith in Dutch. They desired its translation into Tamil for use by the converts. Hence Abraham Bronsveld who had a good command of Tamil began to do the translation and completed the job. This book titled '*Kristhavargaludaya vetha padippinaiyin surukkamaana thogai*' was printed in 1754. Its Dutch title is *Kort Begryp Der Christelyke Religie, Voor Die zig willen begaven tot des Heeren heilig Avondmaal; ten dientse der kerken en Schoolen, In de Tamulsche Spraak overgezet, En, op Goedkeuring Van de Hooge Overheid deezes Eilands, In t' Licht gegeven, Door Sigisbertus Abrahamsz Bronsveld Bedienaar des H. Evangeliums in Christi gemeinte Te Colombo*'. Then we find in the book mention 'Gedrukt te Colombo, in s' Comps: gewoone Drukkery: Door Johann Bernhardt Arnhardt. 1754'. It has 40 pages with Dutch title, Johan VI.53 (a four-line quotation followed by the imprimatur, Tamil title, the Tamil text of Johan VI.53. Voorreeden, dated 16 September 1754, Colombo, and the Tamil preface.[4]

Translating the Liturgy of the Reformed Church from Dutch to Tamil by Philippus de Melho and Printing in Colombo, 1760

The Dutch missionaries desired to have the liturgy of the Reformed Church which was available in Dutch to be translated. Philippus de Melho the native began the work and he completed the translation into Tamil. It was tilted '*Thiruththapattta thiruchabaigazhin vazhipaatu allatha murai noolhal*' (The Liturgy of the Dutch Reformed Church) and it got printed in 1760. The title in Dutch is *Liturgie der Gereformeerde kerken, ofte De Fornulieren by Dezelve in den uiterlyken dienst gebruykelyke: I in't doen van de gemeene gebeden; II. In de bedieninge der H.Sacramenten; III. Ind'inzegeninge des Houwelyks; en Iv.int' vertroosten der zicken. uit de hollandsche in de tamulsche taale overgezet ten dientse van de Christelyke Tamulsche gemeenten, door Philippus de Melho, Bedienaar des Godlyken words, in de Gemeente Jesu Christi te Jaffanapatnam, En naar kerk order behoorlyk overzien*. Then we find mention of Gedrukt te Colombo, in's comps: gewoone drukkery, door Pieter Bruwaart, Anno 1760. The book has 120 pages with Dutch title, Tamil title, text in Tamil and table of contents. We find at folio h2a, a large tail-piece of a flower pot.[5]

It may be mentioned here that the Dutch East India Company which had set up a printing press in Sri Lanka had been fully and thoroughly utilized for printing the Tamil translation of prayers, catechism, doctrine of faith and liturgy of the Dutch Reformed Church between 1739 and 1760. The Dutch had totally abandoned the practice of keeping the sacred literature stored in palm-leaf and instead used the paper and its printing though it was a costly affair at that time.

Translating the Pastoral Letters from German to Tamil by Bartholomäus Ziegenbalg in Tranquebar, 1708-12

The arrival of the Protestant missionaries at Tranquebar (Tharangambadi) on the Tamil coast on 9 July 1706 under the patronage extended by King Friedrich IV of Denmark inaugurated a new era in the spread and expansion of Christianity. These missionaries brought into their work the pietistic inspiration and practices they had received at Halle. Pietism gave to Lutheranism a personal and affective devotion which demanded a true conversion of heart and mind. Regular prayer meetings centred on Bible were held and works of charity were insisted upon. These missionaries learnt Tamil and they desired to introduce the Protestant message to the Tamils and convert the people.

Letter writing in Tamil is known through the literary of works of *Silapthikaaram* and *Perungkathi* in the ancient period. Letters are called *madal* or *nirupam* in Tamil had continued to be in practice during the early modern period. We find Protestant missionaries of the Danish-Halle Mission in Europe were writing letters to their pastors in Tranquebar from time to time which came by ships. August Hermann Francke wrote a letter on 8 September 1708 and Bartholomäus Ziegenbalg (1683-1719) at that time desired to have a translation in Tamil for it was edifying to be presented to the new converts. It was translated verbatim including the last line with date. It was titled '*Ayiroppa yengira seermaiyaiirukkira alley yengira pattanathil irunthu tharanganpadiiley navamaay naatapatta thiruchabaikku yezhuthi anupiina nirupam*' (The letter which was written and sent from the city named Halle in the country of Europe to the newly created holy church in Tranquebar). According to the translation the letter begins with the blessing in Tamil '*Cholamadlathiley navamayy naatapatta yesukristhuvinudaya thiruchabaikku devaparsaadamum, kirubahiyum undaagakadvathu*' (Divine mercy and grace to the newly. erected church of Jesus Christ in Coromandel through God the father and Christ). The translation was immediately prepared in a palm-leaf as per the Tamil tradition for circulation among the Tamil converts. Another copy of the same was prepared and it was sent to Halle for information.[6]

Johann Lysius the pastor in Berlin wrote a letter to the missionaries of Tranquebar on 15 September 1708. Ziegenbalg again translated it verbatim. It was in Tamil titled '*Ayiroppa seermaiyin naduvileyirukkira beralin yengira pattanathil irunthu tharanganpadi pattanathiley iruukikra thiruchabaikku yezhuthi annupina nirupam*' (The letter which was written and sent from the city named Berlin in the country of Europe to the newly erected church in Tranquebar). A scribe was appointed and asked the translation to be made in a palm-leaf manuscript for circulation among the Tamils. Another copy of the same palm-leaf manuscript also got ready and it was sent to Halle. Ziegenbalg in his letter dated 14 February 1708 from Tranquebar to Kamenz his friend in Germany mentioned that he had written 14 small books during the last two years.[7]

Joachim Lange, the Rector and pastor in Berlin wrote a letter to the missionaries of Tranquebar in 1709. Ziegenbalg again translated it verbatim and it was in Tamil titled '*Ayiroppa engira seermaiiley beralin yengira pattanathil irunthu tharanganpadi pattanathiley iruukikra thiruchabaikku yezhuthi annupina nirupamaavathu*' (The letter which was written and sent from the city named Berlin in the country of Europe to the holy church in the city of Tranquebar). A palm-leaf manuscript was prepared for local circulation and another copy prepared was sent to Halle in the ship that sailed for Copenhagen.[8]

Ziegenbalg had developed and nurtured the culture of translating the pastoral letters in Tamil which the missionaries received. He found it as a means to propagate ideas of Christianity and got them circulated among the natives with Protestant ideas. We find many such letters composed by him in Tamil and circulated widely in Tranquebar area. One such is '*Parraparavasthuvaahiya sarvesuran cholamandalathiley vaasamaayirukkira thamzihlar yelaarukkum yezhuthi annupina nirupam*' (The letter written and sent by the Supreme god Paraaparavasthu to all the Tamils living in the region of Cholamandalam) dated 1709. In this he outlined the great significance of embracing Christianity. Many copies of the palm-leaf manuscript were made and sent to various persons in Europe and the same is available and well preserved even now in Halle, Stuttgart and London.[9] Thus there are many letters available in Tamil in palm-leaf. In 1712 Ziegenbalg brought out a translation of Professor Francke's five questions on the order of grace.

Translating the Books of Lutheran Doctrine and Liturgy from German to Tamil by Ziegenbalg

Ziegenbalg desired to have many more writings in Tamil based on Lutheran doctrine and liturgy. He wished to have in Tamil, the 'small catechism' (Enchirihion) of Martin Luther (1483–1546).[10] A palm-leaf manuscript in Tamil titled '*Sathya vethathiley adanki irukkira gnaana upadesangal yellathaiyum surukkamaaga vezhipaduthugirathakka sasthiram*' (A short treatise on the most important teachings contained in the true veda, i.e., the Bible) was prepared in 1709.[11] It is gleaned that as late 1844 the protestants missionaries in Tamil country had printed the same which was so popular and got circulated this tract in Tamil (under the title *Sathya vetham*) at the American Mission Press in Madras.

Ziegenbalg was keen to introduce the Protestant message of Christianity as inspired very much from the interpretation made by Philip Jakob Spener (1635–1705). Therefore he translated the book '*Einfache Erklaerung der Christlichen Lehre*' printed in 1677 from German to Tamil. It was titled in Tamil '*Martin Luther enbavarin gnaanaopadesak kuripidathai visthaarikkum vinaa vidaigal*' and it was completed by him in 1711. This Protestant catechism was very different that of the Catholics and also his own catechism prepared earlier. Luther's catechism was translated by Ziegenbalg with word for word explanations and it was published from Tranquebar in 1713.[12]

Johann Ernst Grundler in his letter from Tranquebar to Francke in Halle dated 27 February 1719 mentioned that five books had been translated from German to Tamil and they were busily engaged in verifying and checking the translations. Ziegenbalg in his writings used the everyday spoken Tamil of Tranquebar, and not the Tamil poetry of the elite, though the Tamil tradition and custom did not approve of the colloquial spoken Tamil for writing. He had twelve copyists to transcribe his translations, tracts and letters on palm-leaf. Most of the writings were distributed among the interested Muslims and Hindus too who could read. Hundreds of palm-leaf manuscripts were thus prepared and circulated, including matters related to explaining why conversion to Christianity is necessary.[13]

Martin Luther's Catechism translated in Tamil and printed earlier was desired to be reprinted as the second impression at Tranquebar in 1730. The book has 24 pages and we find a title page in Tamil and a title page in Portuguese. The Tamil title was '*Mandira Chuvadi: Ithile vethapramaanitinapadiye padikavendiya anju mandirangalaiyum athukaanna viyachiyangalum anthantha vezhaigaliley sevikkapadathakka sepangalum adangi irukkuthu, rendaam visai, kristhu pirantha 1730 varushaththiley tharanganpaadi achchiley pathipikkapattathu*'.[14]

Protestant missionaries in Tranquebar translated the catechism of August Hermann Francke from German into Tamil and the book was called *Krisiththamaana upadesathin muthal paadam* got printed at the Tranquebar press in 1734. The book contains 22 questions and answers and it follows significant teachings contained from the Holy Bible.[15]

Johann Philipp Fabricius (1711–1791) the Protestant missionary who lived in Madras and served there under the English East India Company opposed the Anglican catechism, when his colleague Johann Ernst Geister introduced it in 1737 to the congregation in Cuddalore. This was something new for the congregation in Madras for it had been established as a Lutheran one. This catechism was too lengthy for the children and catechumens had to learn by-heart. It was found extremely difficult also to understand it plainly. Fabricius therefore felt that it would be creating a confusing among the Tamil Christians. He felt that the converts would have an exposure to learn the Ten Commandments in a different order and also there was a need to change the article of the Lutheran church.[16] As a result, the Anglican catechism was dropped, shortly after its introduction, but without its coming to the notice of the officials in England. Thus we find also various catechisms of the Protestants were in circulation.

August Hermann Francke's Rudiments of Christian Doctrine was translated by the Tranquebar missionaries from German to Tamil and the book was printed in 1734. It has a title page in Latin and in Tamil. The Tamil tile page is '*Krisithamaana upadesathin muthal paadam.*[17]

Translating the Book of Johann Anastasius Freylinghausen titled Grundlegung der Theologie from German to Tamil and Printing the Book titled Vetha Saasthiram in 1717

Johann Anastasius Freylinghausen (1670-1739) had published his book *Grundlegung Der Theologie* in 1703 and it helped the cause of a church union between the Reformed and Lutheran confessions, even if that was not his intention. In the section of the book dealing with the Lord's Supper, Freylinghausen refrained from emphasizing the differences between the two confessions understanding of the sacrament. This down-playing of theological incongruities helped pave the way for the eventual union. Johann Anastasius Freylinghausen's works on Protestant theology and catechism appeared in print in Germany in 1703 and 1705 were brought by Ziegenbalg to Tranquebar. He planned to translate Freylinghausen's '*Grundlegung der Theologie: Darinn die Glaubens-Lehren aus Göttlichem Wort deutlich fürgetragen, Und zum Thäthigen Christenthumb wie auch Evangelischen Trost angewendet werden. Zum Gebrauch des PAEDAGOGII REGII daselbst*', published in Halle in 1703 from German to Tamil. He did the translation at first in a summary form titled in Tamil '*Sarvesvaranukku adutha upadesathathai bhodishivikkira vetha sasthirathinudaya muthalam*

JOH. ANASTASII Freylinghausens/
Past. Adj. zu Glaucha an Halle/
Grundlegung
Der
Theologie/
Darinn die
Glaubens-Lehren
aus Göttlichem Wort deutlich fürgetragen/
Und zum
Thätigen Christenthumb/
wie auch
Evangelischen Trost
angewendet werden.
Zum Gebrauch des PÆDAGOGII REGII daselbst.

HALLE/
In Verlegung des Wäysen-Hauses / MDCCIII.
Mit Königl. Preuß. und Churf. Brandenb. Freyheit.

3.1: Vetha Sasthiram translated and printed in Tranquebar in 1717 from Johann Anastasius Freylinghausen's Grundlegung der Theologie (Courtesy: Bibliothek der Franckesche Stiftungen, Halle) *vaguppaavathu*' (The first part of the systematic theology which teaches the doctrine of God). Later Ziegenbalg decided to translate the entire book and so Johann Ernst Grundler joined hands with him and they did the work and completed it in 1709 and it was printed in Tamil titled *Vetha Sasthiram* (Theological treatise).[18] After many years it was again rewritten in a dialogue form and Ziegenbalg got it printed in three parts from the printing press in Tranquebar in 1717. The Tamil title of the book is '*Vetha Sasthiram: Ithiley karaierugiradhukku ariya vendina gnaana upadesamagira sarvesvaranukku adutha upadesathamum, manushanukkadutha upadesamum, sathiya vethathiley adangi irukkira piradhana upadesangalyellaam thezhiva vezhipadutha pattirukkuthu*' (A systematic theology that clearly explains all the important teachings of the Bible on God and humankind that are necessary for salvation').[19]

The second part of Johann Anastasius Freylinghausen's translation in Tamil *Vetha Sasthiram* was titled '*Manushanukkadutha upadesaththai pothivaikira vethasasthirathin udaya rendaam vaguppu*' (The second part of the theological treatise dealing with the doctrines on human beings) and the work is dated 1709 and it is now available in a paper manuscript. The translation was carried out by Ziegenbalg with the assistance of Grundler.[20] The third part of the translation in Tamil was completed and this third part of *Vetha Sasthiram* was also printed at Tranquebar.[21]

Translating Johann Wilke's Communions Buch from German to Tamil by Catechist Malayappan in Tranquebar, 1721-22

Interestingly we find the significant help extended by the Tamil catechists in the translation of Protestant Church liturgy. Johann Wilke's book '*Communions Buch*' in German was translated to Tamil by catechist Malayappan in 1721 with the title '*Archishista narkarunaikku paathiramullavanaaga seravenumennu irukkiravan athukku thaaney entha piragaaramaaga aayatham panna venumennu pothichivikkira posthagam*' (A book which shows how a person who wants to worthily participate in the Lord's supper ought to prepare himself).[22] The printing of this book began at Tranquebar on 14 June 1721 and completed on 13 February 1722.[23] It may be mentioned that Peter Malayappan went to Europe along with Ziegenbalg and visited Denmark, Germany and England between October 1714 and September 1716. He knew German as he had delivered a speech in German before the King of Denmark and his court officers as early as on 26 July 1715. Benjamin Schultze wrote in his report and mentioned that a communion book had been already translated in Tamil on 7 October 1723.[24] Peter Malayappan took the assistance of Benjamin Schultze in the course of translation.

Translating the Book on the Passion of Our Lord Jesus Christ from Portuguese to Tamil by Benjamin Schultze, 1723-40

Benjamin Schultze noticed in Tranquebar a book on the passion of Jesus Christ and it was the work of Johaan Ernst Grundler in Portuguese in narrative form. He mentioned this book vide his letter to Francke on 13 August 1723.[25] Polycarp Jorden in his letter from Tranquebar to Francke in Halle dated 4 October 1713 mentioned that Grundler learnt Portuguese for two years and he had translated books and got printed in Tranquebar. Schultze thought that it may be useful to natives and so he desired the translation of the same book into Tamil and he also mentioned it vide his letter 28 August 1713.[26]

Schultze began the translation and he completed. It was titled '*Meyyana sarvesuranum meyyana manushanum onnaairukkira yesu kristhu naatharaanavar intha bhoologathiley sagala manusargalay paavathinudaya adumaithanuthuleyum yenyennaikkum nirkira naragathinudaya aakkineyulum ninru meezlkkathakathaaga thammudaya sarirathileyum thammudya aathumathulayeum yethinai ninaivugalaiyum vethanaigaleyum kadaisiliey maranaththaium sollappadaatha porumaiyodu paadupattuirunthathu surukkamaaga vezhipaduthugira sarithira posthagam*' (The history book which describes how the lord Jesus Christ, who is the true god and true man in one person bore with indescribable patience, much pain and torment in his body and in his soul and finally died, so that the people of the whole world might be saved from the slavery of sin and from eternal hell). The book was printed in Tranquebar in 1723.[27] The same book was again reprinted as a second edition with the title '*Manushavathaaram pannina devasuthanaagira yesu kiristhu swami manusha jathiyai retchikka paadupattu marithathanri uyirthu paralogathuku ezhuntharliya sarithiram: Irandaam pathithal*' from Tranquebar in 1740.[28]

Translating Differença da Christandade the Booklet from Portuguese to Tamil and Printing in Tranquebar, 1731

A booklet '*Differença da Christandade*' was composed by João Ferreira de Almeida in Portuguese and got printed at first in Jakarta in 1668 and it got reprinted at the printing press in Tranquebar in 1728.[29] This work got translated into Tamil with the help of Peter Malayappan, the catechist and Tamil school-master in Tranquebar and the reason for such a production was owing to the dispute with the Roman Catholic missionaries which started in 1726 intensively. The Tamil translation titled '*Kristha Maargathinudaya Vettrumai*' appeared in print at Tranquebar in 1731 and got widely circulated.[30] Though both the Catholics and Protestants were preaching the same Gospel of Jesus Christ they considered each other as enemy. Each of them felt in their work as hindrance to the progress of the respective churches while working among the natives in Tamil country making their occupation useless. They accused each other as evil spirits opposing all that had been done in the extension of Christ's kingdom. Therefore they wrote to the Tamils in polemical style explaining do not let this discourage them, to remain faithful to the respective church so as to be pleasing to the Lord Jesus Christ.

Translating the Book of Wolfgang Seber titled Biblisches Lust-Gärtlein from German to Tamil by Benjamin Schultze titled Vetha Thottam, 1739-40

Benjamin Schultze also wanted to translate Wolfgang Seber's book *Biblisches Lust-Gärtlein* published from Leipzig in 1688. Therefore he began the work in 1739 and the portions that dealt with the Christian doctrine of god the trinity, creation of the world angels, death and human beings were translated into Tamil in summary form and he called book in Tamil *Vetha Thottam: Muthalaam Vaguppu* (The book of Biblical garden: part one).[31] He continued to translate Wolfgang Seber's book and completed the translation of the portions from chapter eleven to thirteen in summary form which dealt with on sin, free will, pre-destination, penitence and ordination to pastoral office (useful particularly to the Tamil catechists) and he called book in Tamil *Vetha Thottam: Rendaam Vaguppu* (The book of Biblical garden: part two).[32]

Schultze further continued to translate Wolfgang Seber's book and he completed the translation of the portions from chapter fourteen in summary form that dealt with the Christian church, freedom, the sacrament of baptism, Lord's supper, pain and prayer and he called in Tamil '*Vetha Thottam: Munaam Vaguppu*' (The book of Biblical garden: part three). He completed the translation work in 1740. The palm-leaf manuscript prepared was sent to Halle via Copenhagen besides other copies prepared were meant for circulation among the natives.[33] He continued to do the rest of the book of translation and successfully completed the portions that dealt with worldly authority, marriage, death, the end of the world, the resurrection of the dead, the last judgment, hell and eternal life. He called the book in Tamil, *Vetha Thottam: Naalaam Vaguppu* (The book of Biblical garden: part four).[34] The four parts of the Vetha Thottam did not see the light of printing and it was circulated only in palm-leaf among the Protestant Tamil Christians.

Translating the Book of Thomas Kempi's Imitation of Christ from German to Tamil by Benjamin Schultze, 1740-41

Imitation of Christ composed by Thomas A. Kempis (1380-1471) was popular and famous widely used in Europe among the Christians. Schultze desired that this work should be made available in Tamil. He used Thomas von Kempen's book, *Vonder Nachfolgung Christi*, published from Cologne in 1699 for translation. He started the translation work on 14 (Purattasi month) September 1740 Wednesday. He completed the translation work on 22 April 1741.[35] The work was titled in Tamil '*Nammudaya kartharaagiya yesu kiristhu naatharai yeppadi pinsella venum engirathin periley thome they kempishenravar yezhuthi vaitha gnaana posthagam*'.[36] It was widely circulated only in palm-leaf and did not see the light of printing till 1764. Missionary reports from Tranquebar mention that this book had the title in German '*De Imitatione Christi, Buchelin vom heiligen abendmahl in Tamulschen*' printed in 1765.[37]

Translating Johann Arndt's Paradies-Gärtlein from German to Tamil by Benjamin Schultze and Rayanayakkan in 1747 and Printing the book titled Gnaana Mandira Selva Pungaavanam in Halle in 1749-50

Benjamin Schultze also planned to translate Johann Arndt's *Paradies-Gärtlein, Voller Christlichen Tugenden, Wie solche Durch geistreiche*

ஞானசங்கீதங்களுடைய
பொஸ்தகம்.

முதலாஞ் சங்கீதம்.

உ. சங்கீதம்.

3.2: The first page of the Book of Psalms in Tamil reprinted in Tranquebar in 1747 (Courtesy: Bibliotheca Nacional de Lisboã, Portugal)

Gebete in die Seele zu pflantzen; Worzu ietzo kommen, 1. Dreyzehn Wunder-Geschichte, welche sich mit diesem Büchlein, und dieses Mannes andern Schriften begeben. 2. Bernhardi völlig verteutschtes Jubel- und Jesus- Lied und 3. Ein dreyfaches Register, so den Nutz und Gebrauch dieses Gebet-Büchleins weiset, Magdeburg, Druckts Christian Leberecht Faber published in 1727. He made a reference to the translation of this work done by Rayanayakkan the Tamil catechist stationed in Thanjavur. The work was completed perhaps also through the assistance of Schultze by 1747.[38] The translated matter was sent to Europe and the first part of the book was printed in 1749 at Halle in Germany.[39] It had the Tamil title, '*Gnaana Mandira Selva Pungaavanam: Athinudaya muthalam vaguppiley paththu karpanaigaludaya varisayin padiey kristhavargalukkotha punniyangaliley vathikka thakkathaaga seyya veyndina 48 sevangal adangi irukkuthu*' (The rich flower garden of spiritual prayers: Its first part contains 48 prayers ordered according to the ten commandments which would help further the increase of Christian qualities). The book also had a title in Latin '*Libellus Precum Religiosissimarum, Dictus Hortulus Paradisiacus, et eius quidem Pars Prima, Ex Germanico in Tamulicum convertit Beniamin Schulzius, Missionarius Evangelicus, Halae Magdeburgicae, 1749*'.

The second part of the book was printed in 1749 at Halle in Germany with the Tamil title, '*Gnaana Mandira Selva Pungaavanam: Athinudaya rendaam vaguppiley thiruthivamaagira yega sarvesuranaagira pithaa suthan parisuthammana arubiyaaanavar aruliseytha nanmaigalukkaagavum, ubagarangalukkagavum seyya vendia 29 thothirangal adangi irukkuthu*' (The rich flower garden of spiritual prayers: Its second part contains 29 thanksgiving prayers for the benefits and help wrought by the Triune god, father, son and the holy spirit).[40]

The third part of the book was printed in 1749 at Halle in Germany with the Tamil title, '*Gnaana Mandira Selva Pungaavanam: Athinudaya munaam vaguppiley ubathdiriyathai anupavikkira kaalathiley aarudhal peratthakkathaga seyya vendina 31 sepangal adanagi irukkuthu*' (The rich flower garden of spiritual prayers: Its third part contains 31 prayers to be said in the period of suffering and to get consolation).[41] The fourth part of the work has no individual title but it is brought out along with part three. This fourth part contained 12 prayers used from the 26th Sunday after Trinity and contained order of the readings for prayers and prayers for each day in the year and on festival days (*Gnaana Mandira Selva Pungaavanam: Athinudaya naalam vaguppiley sarvesuranyudaya thirunaamathukku sangaiundagavum, thuthiundaagavum seyya vendina gnaana santhosham uzhla 12 isthothirangal adangi irukkuthu*'. It dealt with liturgy and religious worship and it was printed in Halle in 1750.[42]

Translating the Book of Johann Arndt's Fünff Geistreiche Bücher vom Wahren Christenthum from German to Tamil during 1736-49 by Benjamin Schultze and Printing the Book titled Gnaana Kannaadi in Halle in 1751

Benjamin Schultze felt the importance to translate Johann Arndt's *Fünff Geistreiche Bücher vom wahren Christenthum*, published from Leipzig in 1696.[43] He began the translation of this work that dealt with aspects of true Christianity on 1 June 1736.[44] He translated 42 chapters into Tamil and called it as part one of the work and these portions described how the old man Adam should accept Jesus Christ and be transformed into his image. The book was printed at Halle in 1751. There is a Latin title followed by the Tamil title of the book which runs: '*Unmaiulla Kirisithiyaniyudaya Magimaiyai Thezhlivaaga Kaanpikkira Gnaana Kannaadi: Athinuadaya muthalaam posthangathilay adangiirukkira 42 athigaarangal, kristhu piranthu 1751 varushamaagirapoothu saasoniley irukkum aalley pattanathiley ithu achiley pathikapattathu*' (The spiritual mirror which clearly shows the glory of True Christianity: Part One containing 42 chapters).[45]

He began to continue the translation and completed the next portion successfully on 27 December 1736. The translated 58 chapters he called it part two of the work and these portions described how love, humility, suffering, hope and prayer are important in Christian life. The book was printed at Halle in 1751. The Tamil title of the book is '*Unmaiulla Krisithiyaniyudaya Magimaiyai Thezhlivaaga Kaanpikkira Gnaana Kannaadi: Athinuadaya Rendaam Postham: Ithiley adangiirukkira 58 athigaarangal, kiristhu piranthu 1751 varushamaagirapoothu saasoniley irukkum aalley pattanathiley ithu achiley pathikapattathu*' (The spiritual mirror which clearly shows the glory of True Christianity: Part Two containing 58 chapters).[46] It has 48 pages. Graham Shaw wrongly attributes that this book was printed at Tranquebar in 1750. In fact the book was printed at Halle in Germany in 1751.[47]

3.3: Gnaana Kannadi translated and printed in Halle in Germany in 1751 from Johann Arndt's Funff Geistreichte Bucher vom wahren Christenthum (Courtesy: Bibliothek der Franckesche Stiftungen, Halle)

Schultze continued the third part of the translation and he began the work on 2 January 1737 and completed it successfully on 27 December 1737.[48] The translated 23 chapters he called it part three of the work. The book was printed in Halle in 1751. The Tamil title of the book is '*Unmaiulla Kirisitiiyaniyudaya Magimaiyai Thelivaaga Kaanpikkira Gnaana Kannaadi: Athinuadaya munraam posthangathilay adangiirukkira 23 athigaarangal. kiristhu piranthu 1751 varushamaagirapoothu saasoniley irukkum aalley pattanathiley ithu achiley pathikapattathu*' (The spiritual mirror which clearly shows the glory of True Christianity: Part Three containing 23 chapters).[49]

Schultze began the final part of the translation work on 4 March 1738 and completed it successfully on 1 October 1738.[50] He translated into Tamil the fourth portion that dealt with creation and it contained forty six chapters in total. He called it as the part four of the work. The book was printed in Halle in 1751. The Tamil title of the book is '*Unmaiulla Kirisithiyaniyudaya Magimaiyai Thezhlivaaga Kaanpikkira Gnaana Kannaadi: Athinuadaya naalam posthangathin muthalam vagupille aaru athigaarangalum rendaam vagupilley 40 athigaarangalum adangiirukkuthu*' (The spiritual mirror which clearly shows the glory of True Christianity: Its fourth book contains six chapters in its first part and 40 chapters in its second part).[51]

Translation of Hymns from German to Tamil by the Lutheran Missionaries and Printing at Tranquebar, 1713-56

Ziegenbalg with the assistance of Grundler aimed to translate songs in Tamil and we find 48 hymns successfully done from German to Tamil in 1713 and they were set to Tamil music. These hymns for translation were taken from the song book of Johann Anastasius Freylinghausen in German.[52] In 1715 we find songs were printed in the hymn book containing 48 songs that are sung by the Christians belonging to the newly erected Church of Jerusalem in Tranquebar and this was the first Tamil hymnal printed.

When Ziegenbalg was in Europe Grundler began to revise the hymnal and he carried out the work since 22 November 1714. After that the corrected matter for printing was ready and it was finally given to the press for printing. The hymnal had 48 songs and it was printed at Tranquebar on 24 January 1715.[53] The Tamil title of the book was *Pirathani Posthagam* and it was in octavo size and the print order was 300 copies.[54]

Grundler had mentioned that the *Hymnologia Sagrada* awaited publication in 1713 with 100 songs translated from German into Tamil and we find that a hymn book printed at Tranquebar only in 1719.[55] The translated hymns of 48 from German to Tamil for worship were again reprinted in 1721. This was the next hymn book (second edition) published. This hymn book had 48 songs in Tamil meter and also according to the Tamil music scale.[56]

According to evidences, Schultze had successfully translated various songs numbering 112 hymns from German to Tamil and the book '*Gnanap-paatukalin posthaham*' got printed in Tranquebar in 1723.[57] This was the third edition of hymns that appeared with 160 songs compiled by him.[58] It contained such well known German hymns such as '*Wach auf mein hertz und singe*', '*Christus der ist mein heben*' and '*Dancksei gott in der Hohe*'.[59] Schultze's *Hymnologia Tamulica* containing 112 hymns was again printed in 1725.

Christian Friedrich Pressier and Christoph Theodosius Walther the two missionaries also translated hymns from German to Tamil and it was printed in 1747. The Latin title is '*Hymnologia Tamulica*'. This book contained 307 songs. This is the fifth edition of hymns appeared in 1756. The Tamil title is *Puthithaay thamizha paduthapatta gnaana paatukkal adangiirukkira posthagam*. The Latin and the Tamil titles have been partly printed in red.[60]

Translation of Hymns from German to Tamil and Books Printed in Madras, 1774-1825

Johann Philipp Fabricius the Protestant missionary in Madras translated hymns from German to Tamil. The new hymnal of book *Gnaana Paattukkal* with 336 hymns was first printed at Vepery press, Madras in 1774.[61] Its second edition enlarged one with a new appendix of 12 hymns appeared in print in1797 from the same Vepery press.[62] The third edition appeared in 1820. Fabricius had continued to add many more songs and the books had appeared in print from Madras. The hymns translated from German to Tamil by Fabricius the fourth edition got printed in the Vepery press in 1825.[63] The pages and the sections are found as per the Tamil numbering system. Every section starts with the German title for example the first section reads '*Seht da ist euer Gort*' (See there is your God).[64]

To conclude it may be said that the Dutch missionaries had translated a few selected books chiefly dealing with prayers, catechism, doctrine and liturgy of the Dutch reformed Church into Tamil and got them printed in Colombo. However, the Lutheran missionaries in Tranquebar undertook large scale translation of pastoral letters, prayers, catechism, Lutheran doctrine, liturgy and the prominent protestant writings available in German to Tamil. We also find natives like Peter Malayappan and Rayanayakkan translating works from German to Tamil and they contributed to the growth of Protestant Christian literature. Tamil Christians used these books translated and printed in Tranquebar in their daily spiritual life. Some of the books of big volumes after translation in Tamil got printed in Halle in Germany. The main reason may be that sufficient quantity of paper was available in Europe for printing. However printed Tamil books travelled in ships from Copenhagen to Tranquebar and these were circulated amongst the natives for worship and prayer.

NOTES

1. Koninklijke Bibliotheek, Den Haag (hereafter KBDH), The Netherlands, Handscriften, Oude Drukken, 82 H 9, see plate no. XIV.
2. Archiv der Franckesche Stiftungen (hereafter AFSt), Halle, M2 B6:54a; KBDH, Handscriften, Oude Drukken, 82 H9, Tamil translation of the Lord's Prayer printed at Colombo, 1739.
3. Hendrik Koaemer Institut, Oegstgeest (hereafter HKI), K-116; Universiteits Bibliotheek, Leiden (hereafter UBL), 1497 C 43; S. Anthonisz-Pieters trs., *Memoir of Gustaaf Willem Baron van Imhoff to His Successor Willem Maurits Bruynink, 1740*, Colombo, 1911. The Dutch text runs 'op deese 2000 gedrukt den January Ao: 1768'.
4. *Kristhavargaludaya Veda Padippinaiyin Surukkamaana Thogai*, Colombo, 1754, pp. xii+ 22, in HKI, K-134; KBDH, 1117 D 59; UBL 877 G6 and 1144 B 45; British Library, London (hereafter BL), no. 14170. b.15.
5. *Thiruthapattta Thiruchabaigazhin Vazhipaatu Allatha Murai Noolhal*, Colombo, 1760, (Translated by Philippus de Melho) pp.115+ii, in KBDH, 1117E 51; UBL, 877 G 7; BL, no. 1410.a.25
6. AFSt, MSS P:TAM, 37 I, fls.196v-200v.
7. AFSt, Letter of Ziegenbalg dated 14 February 1708 to Kamenz in Germany; AFSt, P:TAM, 37 J, 200v-202r.
8. AFSt, P:TAM, 37 K, 202r-207r.
9. AFSt, MI B59:22; AFSt, P:TAM 37, fls.207-220r; BL, Oriental

MS:13864.106C; Wurttembergischen Landesbibliothek, Stuttgart, Cod. Or. fl.38.

10. Hans-Werner Gensichen, 'Abominable Heathenism': A Rediscovered Tract by Bartholomäus Ziegenbalg', *Indian Church History Review*, vol.1, no.1, 1967, pp. 29-40, p. 33.
11. AFSt, P:TAM 37, 194-196r.
12. Bibliothek der Franckesche Stiftungen, Halle (hereafter BFSt), 190 F 21, *A Expliçāo da Doutrina Christaa Segundo a Ordem do Catecismo do B. Luthero, em Perguntas e Repostas Proposta, e Com Necessarias Testemunhos da Escritura Sagrada Provada: Traduziada em Lingoa Portugueza Pelos Minsitros da Palavra de Deus e Missionarios del Rey de Dennemark, Tranquebar Em India Oriental na Costa de Coromandel*, na Estampa dos dittos Missionarios, no Anno de 1713; BL, no. 14170.a.33.5; no. 14170.a.25, *Martin Luther Enbavarin Gnaanopadesa Kuripidathai Vistharikkum Vina Vidaigal* (A Catechism of Protestant doctrine based upon P.J. Spener's "Einfache Erklarung det Christlichen Lehre" embodifying and amplifying Luther's Kleiner Catechismus, Translated into Tamil by Bartholomäus Ziegenbalg, Revised by A. Blomstrand), third edition, Tranquebar, 1872, p.160.
13. AFSt, Letter of Johann Ernst Grundler from Tranquebar to Francke in Halle dated 27 February 1719; Hans-Werner Gensichen, Abominable Heathenism, p. 30.
14. KB, 3-471; KB, HJ 376. The Portuguese title page is '*A verdadeira religiao em hum compendio summariamente comprehendida e com testemunhos da escritura sagrada provada, Segundo impressao, Trangambar, na officina real Missao de dinamarca, anno de 1730*'.
15. BFSt, 54 H 30, *Doctrinae Christiane Rudimenta Olim ab Autore Beato A.H. Franckio Theologo Halensi Germania Edita: Nunc in Lingual Tamulicam Translata: Accessit Brevis Notitia de S. Scriptura Religione*, Trangambariae, Typis Missionis Danicae, MDCCXXXIV.
16. Arno Lehmann, *It Began at Tranquebar* (Translated by M.J. Lutz), Madras, 1956, p. 80.
17. BFSt, 54H30. The Latin title page is *Doctrinae Christiane Rudimenta olim an autore Beato A.H. Franckio Theologo Halensi Germanica Edita: nunc in Linguam Tamulicam translata; Accessit brevis notitia de S. Scriptura & religione*, Trangambariae, Typis Missionis Danicae, MDCCXXXIV.
18. AFSt, P:TAM 36, *Vetha Sasthiram*; See also P:TAM 37, fls.91-151r; BL, no. 3559.c.13, J.A. Freylinghausen, *Theologia Thetica...in Lingua Tamulica Scripta a...B. Ziegenbalg et J.E. Grundler*, reprint, 1856.

19. KB, 3-470; KB, HJ 485; BFSt, 54 G1. The book is titled in Latin *Theologia Thetica: In qua Omnia Dogmata ad Salutem Cognoscendi Necessaria Perspicua Methodo Tractantur ac Dictis Classicis Probantur, ad Propagationem Evangelii Christi intergentes Orientales in Lingua Damulica Scripta a Bartholomaeo Ziegenbalgio & Johanne Ernesto Grundlero*, Tranquebariae 1717. The translation in Tamil is based on the two works of Johann Anastasius Freylinghausen, *Grundlegung der Theologie: Darin die Glaubens-Lehren aus Göttlichem Wort deutlich fürgetragen und zum thäthigen Christenthum wie auch Evangelischen Trost angewendet werden zum Gebrauch des Paedagogii*, Halle, Verlegt im Wäysenhause, 1703 and J.A., Freylinghausen, *Compendium oder kurtzer Begriff der gantzen christlichen Lehre in XXXIV Articuln/ nebst einer Summarischen Vorstellung der Göttlichen Ordnung des Heyls in Frage und Antwort einfältig und Schrifftmäßig entworffen*, Halle, Verlegt im Wäysenhause, 1705.
20. AFSt, P: TAM 85.
21. BFSt, 54 G1, pp. 173-735.
22. AFSt, P:TAM 81, fls.1-242
23. KB, HJ, 484, *Archayasista Narkarunaikku Paathiram Ullavanaka: Solidissima Instituto Sanctae Coenae: Inqua Ostenditu qua Praeparatione Ante: Qua Exteriorum Interiorum que Morum Observationae irca: et qua Novitiate Vitae post Usum Sanctae Coenae Digne Sacramentum Celebraturus se Probare Debeat in Gratiam Christianae Gentis Damulorum Exhibita a Missionaria Danica Benjamin Schultze*, Trangambariae, Typis ac Sumptibus Missionis Danicae, MDCCXXII.
24. *Der Königl. Dänischen Missionarien aus Ost-Indien eingesandter ausführlichen Berichten, Von dem Werck ihrs Ams unter den Heyden, angerichteten Schulen und Gemeinen, ereigneten Hindernissen und schweren Umstanden; Beschaffenheit des Malabarischen Heydenthums, gepflogenen brieflicher Correspondentz und mundlchen Unterredungen mit selbigen heyden*, Teil 1–9, (Continuationen 1–108) Waiserihaus, Halle, 1710–1772 (hereafter HB), vol. II, continuation 19, p. 346; AFSt, D16a, Diary of Benjamin Schultze, 14 July 1720.
25. HB, Vol. II, continuation 19, p. 342. Benjamin Schultze, born at Sonnenburg in Brandenburg 1689, studied at Halle, had embarked at Deal in a ship on 20 March 1719, and he landed at Madras 25 July 1719. He was ordained at Tranquebar in 1720 and began the Madras Mission in 1728. He sailed to Europe in 1743, and died at Halle on 25 November 1760.
26. AFSt, Letter of Polycarp Jorden from Tranquebar to Francke in Halle dated 4 October 1713; see also, HB Vol. III, continuation 33, p. 928.

27. BFSt, 63F 28; BL, Or.90.a.67; BL, no. 14170.a.24; The book is titled in Latin *Historia Passionis, Jesu Christi Fili Dei et Mariae Virginis Damulice, ex Quatuor Evangelistis Conscripta a Benjamin Schultze Mission Danico*, Tranquebariae, Offic. Missionis Danicae, MDCCXXIII. The book has 77 pages.
28. BFSt, 63F 33, The book is titled in Latin *Historia Passionis, Mortis, Resurrectionis et Ascenscionis Jesu Christi Fili Dei et Mariae Virginis, Tamulice, ex quatour Evangelistis Conscripta. Editio Secunda, Penitus Recognita Er Ad Textum Graecum Conformata*, Trangambariae, Missionis Danicae, Anno 1740.
29. KB, HJ 486; KB, 3-469; *Differenca da Christandade: Em que Claramente de Manifesta a Grande Desconformidade Traduzida da Castelhano em Portuguez Pelo P. Joãm Ferreira A. d'Almeida, Ministro Pregador do S. Evangelho na India Oriental: Conforme a Impressão de Batavia de 1668*, Segunda Impressão, Trangambar, na Officina da Real Missão de Dinamarca, 1728. The booklet has 32 pages.
30. HB, vol. II, continuation 22, pp. 862-3.
31. AFST, P:TAM 71 fls.1- 214.
32. Ibid., P:TAM 72 fls.1-175.
33. Ibid., P:TAM 73 fls.1-200; P:TAM 62; P:TAM 74; P:TAM 75.
34. Ibid., P:TAM 76; P:TAM 77.
35. *Notices of Madras and Cuddalore in the Last Century from the Journals and Letters of the Earlier Missionaries of the Society for the Propagation of Christian Knowledge*, London, 1858, p.183.
36. AFSt, P:TAM 88.
37. HB, continuation 99, p. 305; continuation 101, p.501; continuation 103, p. 713.
38. AFSt, M2 B72:13; BL, no. 14170.bbb.7; *Gnaana Mandira Selva Pungaavanam*, 4 pts, Halle, 1749-1750. Part I and II have distinct title pages and pagination. See, Notices of Madras and Cuddalore, p. 194; Heike Liebau, 'German Missionaries as Research Workers in India: Their Diaries as Historical Sources (Benjamin Schultze, 1689-1760, Exception or Norm?)', *Studies in History*, new series, vol. 11, no. 1, 1995, pp.101-18.
39. BFSt, C:5B.
40. Ibid.
41. Ibid.
42. The book was printed in 1750. Part III and IV have a common title page and a continuous pagination.
43. HB IV, continuation 42, p. 834.

44. The Latin title of the book is *Joannis Arndtii...de Vero Christianismo Liber Primus...Ex Germanico in Tamulicum Convertit Benjamin Schulzius*, Halle, 1751, BL, no.G.19737. The book has v+399 pages. There is a book with the title *Gnaana Kannadi*, and it is the third edition printed at Pondicherry in 1906. See, MPJA, It has 136 pages.
45. BFSt, C: 70; AFSt, 32 M 12.
46. HB IV, continuation 48, p. 1632.
47. BFSt, C: 70; AFSt, 32 M 12.
48. BFSt, C:38:97; C:38:98; C:38:99; Graham Shaw, *The South Asia and Burma Retrospective Bibliography, Stage1: 1556-1800*, London, 1987, p. 98.
49. HB IV, continuation 48, p. 1633.
50. BFSt, C: 70; AFSt, 32:M 12.
51. HB IV, continuation 48, pp. 1635, 1649.
52. BFSt, C:70; AFSt, 32:M 12.
53. Rosenkilde Volmer, Printing in Tranquebar, 1712-1845, *The Library Series 5*, vol. 4, 1949, pp. 179-95, see p. 185.
54. AFSt, P:TAM 92, *Tharanganbaadiiley navamayamaakkapatta Thiruchabaiyaagira Yerusalem engira kovilukku ulpatta kristhavargal paadugira naarpaththettu piratiniaigaludaiya posthagam, Tharangambadi*, 1714; Daniel Jeyaraj, ed., *Olai Chuvadigalil Thodakakaala Thamizh Kristhava Iraineri Paadalgal, 1714: Mulamum Vizhakkamum*, Chennai, 2014; Rosenkilde Volmer, Printing in Tranquebar, op. cit., p. 186.
55. HB, vol. II, continuation 13, p. 35; J.E. Gründler, *Piratthanai Posthagam*, Gesang-Buch Den 24 Jan 1715, in HB, vol. III, continuation 33, pp. 929, 933.
56. KB, Kobenhavn, Hjelmst, 1314, *Hymnologia Sagrada: Isto he, Espirituaes Cantigas Para Excitação da Christaa Devoção, E para Edificação em Fe e Piedade, Com Real Licenca, Tranquebar, Em India Oriental na Costa de Coromandel,* em a Estampa da Real Missão de Dennemark; no Anno 1719.
57. Arno Lehmann, Es begann in Tranquebar, pp. 26, 61.
58. BL, London, 14170b.17; see also, Or.90.8.61; *Gnaana Paatugalin Posthagam: Hymnologia Damulica, Sive ex Germanico in Damulorum Idioma, Observatis usque et Melodiis et Rhythmis Odarum, Translatorum Centum et Sexaginta Hymnorum Spiritualium Fasciculus, in Gratiam Juventutis Damulicae Aeque ac Ecclesiae Hujus Gentis, Christo Nomen Dantis, Exhibita a Benjamin Schultze*, Tranquebariae, MDCCXXIII. The book has xii+200 pages.
59. BFSt, 54 G5, *Gnaana Paatugalin Posthagam: Hymnologia Damulica, Sive*

ex Germanico in Damulorum Idioma, Observatis usque et Melodiis et Rhythmis Odarum, Translatorum Centum et Sexaginta Hymnorum Spiritualium Fasciculus, Tranquebariae in Littore Coromandelino, Typis & Sumptibus, Missionis Danicae Edito Tertia. The book has viii+ 200 pages.

60. Ibid.

61. KB, 4-425, KB, 1-189; KB, HJ 490; BL, London, no. 14170.b.39; BL, Or.90a.60(2), *Puthithaay Thamizha Paduthapatta Gnaana Paatukkal,* Tharanganpadi, 1756. This fifth edition is without Latin title, containing 295 hymns and an appendix of 13 songs. The book has x+315 pages.

62. Georg Christian Knapp., et.al., *Neuere Geschichte der evangelischen Missions-Anstalten zu Bekehrung der Heiden in Ostindien aus den eigenhändigen Aufsätzen und Briefen der Missionarien erausgegeben*, Teil 1–8, (Stück 1–95) Waisenhaus, Halle, 1770-8/ 1795-1848 (hereafter NHB), 11, p. 1474; NHB, 13, p. 48.

63. NHB, 52, pp.379, 382.

64. Archives of the Gurukul Lutheran Theological College and Research Institute, Chennai (hereafter AGLTC), Microfilm accession no. 578, Roll no. 53, Johann Philipp Fabricius, *Hymn Book* (Tamil & English), Fourth edition, Vepery, Madras, 1825.

4

Translations from English, Sanskrit, Marathi, Bengali and Telugu into Tamil by the Protestant Missionaries and the Tamils, 1714-1857

Translations undertaken by the Europeans had an impact on Tamils who were also interested to undertake the work. Many natives who had fluency and command over the language began to translate and the books came to appear in print from time to time. Hence this chapter explores the translations from English, Sanskrit, Marathi, Bengali and Telugu into Tamil by the Tamils and also by the Protestant Missionaries in Tamil Country.

Translations from English to Tamil, 1714-1800

Religious controversy broke out strongly in Tamil country between the Roman Catholic missionaries and the Protestant missionaries. The main reason was that the Protestants had converted the Roman Catholic converts once again to Protestantism. This had in a large measure irritated the Jesuits for they did not obstruct the Hindus being converted by the Protestant missionaries. In Europe too there was intense rivalry and between the Roman Catholic missionaries and Protestants. Polemical essays came to be composed and they got circulated. The Protestant missionaries in Tamil country translated the English booklet 'A Short Refutation of the Principal Errors of the Church of Rome' which was printed in London in 1714. It was titled in Tamil '*Pappu margaththukku ethiriyaana tharkka chuvadi*' and the translation was circulated widely among the public.[1]

The Lutheran missionaries of Tranquebar came to act as chaplains of the English company servants in Madras. Benjamin Schultze who came from Tranquebar to Madras on 1 September 1726 was very much supported by the Society for the Propagation of Christian Knowledge (SPCK) founded earlier in 1699 in London. It has been reported that Christianity had spread well and there were 442 Lutheran Christians in Madras area by 1731.[2] Schultze wanted the protestant doctrine in Tamil to reach out to the natives. Hence he began to do some translation of Christian doctrinal works from English to Tamil. He translated the English liturgy of the prayer book into Tamil. He used the 'Book of Common Prayer Book and Administration of the Sacraments according to the Use of the Church of England' together with the psalms of David from English and he translated it from English to Tamil in 1726. It was titled '*Varushathiley ovvoru naazhl kaalame seygira sepathinudaya ozhungaavathu*' (The order of prayers that are to be said every day morning). The same was made in a palm-leaf manuscript for circulation among the converts and another copy was prepared and it was sent to Halle.[3]

The translation of John Bunyan's Pilgrims' Progress from English to Tamil was done and it was printed at the Vepery press in Madras in 1793. This bilingual text represents a major development. We find poetry in between the Tamil prose text. The translation achieved a story telling technique unprecedented in Tamil.[4]

Daniel Pillai the Catechist in Tranquebar and His Translation of Books on Protestantism into Tamil and Printing at Vepery in Madras

Daniel Pillai (1740-1802) was born in Tranquebar and he studied in Tamil missionary school. He was of *vellala* caste and knew German and Danish very well.[5] Hermann Jacob Forck the Danish Governor appointed him as the second interpreter in the Danish East India Company's service in the beginning. Later under Hermann Abbestee the Danish Governor (served for two terms, 1761-75 and 1779-88) he became the first interpreter of the Royal Danish Government. According to records Daniel Pillai worked in the native court of Justice in Tranquebar.[6] Christoph Samuel John (1747-1813) the missionary in Tranquebar had written the biography of Daniel Pillai.[7] He realized the talent of Daniel Pillai and he engaged him to be a part of the mission work.[8] As he became the Protestant catechist of Tranquebar Daniel Pillai translated two books from German to Tamil titled *Onru Kuraiyathu* (One Thing Needful) and '*Gnaana Padalam*' (The Chapter on Wisdom). Daniel Pillai had been identified as the translator to the Danish government who devoted one hour a day for 40 years to

THE

PILGRIM'S PROGRESS

FROM

THIS WORLD

TO

THAT WHICH IS TO COME:

Delivered under the SIMILITUDE of a

DREAM

Wherein is discovered

I. The Manner of his SETTING OUT,

II. His dangerous JOURNEY; and

III. His safe Arrival at the DESIRED COUNTRY

Written by JOHN BUNYAN.

I have used Similitudes, Hosea xii. 10. 1793

Printed in the Office of the Mission at Vepery near Madras. MDCCXCIII

4.1: The translation of John Bunyan's Pilgrims' Progress from English to Tamil printed at the Vepery press in Madras in 1793 (Courtesy: British Library, London)

translating several Christian books.[9] Those published include '*Paraaparan udaiya pillaigalin aabharana petti*' (The Golden treasury of the sons of God) by Carl Heinrich von Bogatzky printed in Vepery in 1800 and it contained hymns and prayers for every day in a year.[10]

Translations from English to Tamil by the Missionaries and Natives, 1814-1857

Philip of Birmingham's book Renunciation of evil ways was translated by Joseph Knight from English to Tamil. The same book saw the third edition printed in Jaffna in 1814. The book had 16 pages.[11] Liturgies of the Church of England was translated from English to Tamil by Christian David and the book was printed in Madras in 1818.[12] Again the book of common prayers with the occasional services and Psalter was translated from English to Tamil by Johann Peter Rottler and the book was printed at the Government press in Madras in 1819.[13] The same book got reprinted under the title Pothuvaana Sepanagal in Madras in 1828.[14] Puthuvai Gnaanapragasa Mudaliar translated the sketch of ancient history from English to Tamil and it was printed in Madras in 1828 which had 39 pages.[15] He also translated the summary of the history of Hindoosthan from the Mahomedan invasion from English to Tamil and it was printed at the press in Vepery in 1830. This book had 89 pages.[16] Jonathan Edmonson's five sermons on the nativity, the crucifixion, the resurrection, the ascension of Jesus and the decent of the Holy Spirit was translated to Tamil. The book was printed in Madras in 1831 and it had 63 pages.[17]

Needhi Neri Vizhlakkam of Kumaragurupara Thambiran was translated to English by H. Stokes and it was printed in Madras in 1830. The first 24 chapters of the Kural, with the commentary of Parimelazhagar, and of Ramanuja Kavirayar had been translated to English by W.H. Drew, and it was printed in Madras in 1840. *Grammatica Tamuliensis*, an English translation of Nannul with references was done by W. Joyes and S. Samuel Pillai of Thanjavur and the book was printed in Madras in 1858. All the three books were taken to Leipzig by Karl Graul the German missionary.[18] Further a book was translated from English to Tamil titled *Gnaana Desaanthiri* and it got printed in Madras in 1841.[19]

The English East India Company in Madras took efforts to translate the official records from English to Tamil. We find the Regulations and Acts translated for the internal government of the Madras territories from

January 1802 to June 1844 and the two volumes were printed in Madras in 1845-46. Again the Regulations and Acts were translated from English to Tamil by S. Ranga Nayakalu Chettiar and the two volumes were printed in Madras in 1844-45. The circular orders of the court of *Sudt Udalut* were translated to Tamil by S.R. Chettiar and the book was printed in Madras in 1845. Further the circular orders of the court of *Foujdary Udalut* had also been translated to Tamil by S.R. Chettiar and the book was printed in Madras in 1845.

Persian Stories were translated into English by Henry George Keene and the same had been translated into Tamil by C. Jesudasen Pillai. The book was printed in Madras in 1840 and it had 104 pages.[20] Sarah's 'The Walk of Purity' was translated by L. Spaulding and the book saw the second edition of printing in Jaffna in 1842. The book had 12 pages.[21] Christian Gottolob Barth's a brief history of the church of Christ was translated from German and the same book appeared in English was also translated to Tamil by J.A. Regel. The book got printed in Madras in 1845 and it had 656 pages.[22] Thomas Hopkins Gallaudet's the book of natural theology was translated from English to Tamil and it was printed in Madras in 1846 which had 267 pages.[23] Prayers translated from English to Tamil by J.P. Rottler appeared in print in Madras in 1846. The book had 216 pages.[24] Pleasing tales had been translated from English to Tamil and it got printed in Madras in 1847. The book had 42 pages.[25] Philip Doddridge's 'The Rise and Progress of Religion in the Soul' was translated and abridged (in English and Tamil) under the title *Meygnanodhaya Viruththi* and it was printed in Jaffna in 1848. It had 339 pages.[26] Aesop's fables were translated by A. Thiruvengada Pillai from English to Tamil and it was revised by Kuvamaa nagaram (C.) Rajah Soobboroya Moodeliar and the book got printed in Madras in 1853.[27] Hannah More's 'Parley the porter' was translated to Tamil and the same was printed in Jaffna in 1856. The book had 36 pages.[28] Favell Lee Mortimer's 'The Peep of Day' was translated from English to Tamil by John Christian Arulappan. We find the third edition of the book that appeared in print in Madras in 1852. It had 228 pages.[29] The book of Calvin Cutter on anatomy, physiology and hygiene in English was translated into Tamil by S.F. Green. The book also saw the second edition and it was printed in Madras in 1857 which had 204 pages.[30] With the assistance of Paaripakkam Muniyappa Mudaliar, an English Grammar in Tamil got printed in Madras in 1862. It was compiled by Rev. John Perkins Ashton. The book had 108 pages.[31]

The Role of the Tamils in Translations from Sanskrit, Marathi, Bengali and Telugu into Tamil, 1826-1851

A law book was translated from Sanskrit to Tamil titled Dharuma Nool by Kandasami Pulavar of the College of Fort St George and it was printed in Madras in 1826. The printed book has dots for some words over the consonants and also there are no dots over consonants for many words.[32] *Tharka Sangiragam* (Treatise of logic) was translated from Sanskrit by Ramakrishna Sastriar. *Sita Vijayam* was translated from Sanskrit by Sundra Asariyar. *Nalachakravarthy Kathai* (story of the Emperor named Nala), from the Sanskrit prose was translated and edited by Subbraya Upadhiyar into Tamil. *Nyana Vasishtam* was translated from Sanskrit into Tamil by Muni Alavandhar and the book was printed in Madras in 1850. Karl Graul the German missionary had taken all these books to Leipzig in Germany.[33] Thiruvilaiyaadar Puranam narrating 64 sacred sports in 3363 quatrains and 72 chapters had been translated from Sanskrit to Tamil. It was edited on the basis of the work executed by Saravana Perumal Iyer and Nagur Thyagaraja Mudaliar. The book was printed at Chintadripettai near Madras in 1850. It had 456 pages.[34]

Thandavaraya Mudaliar translated Panchathanthira Kathai from Marathi to Tamil. The book was printed in Madras in 1826 and it had 100 pages.[35] Henry Martyn Scudder translated Rama Vasu's work from Bengali to Tamil. The book was printed in Madras in 1851. It contained a series of Christian lyrics with prose commentaries directed against Hindu religious systems. The book printed had additions made by Scudder and had 124 pages.[36]

Some books were translated from Telugu to Tamil. *Saguna Nool* of Somasundaram a Telugu school teacher was translated by Sittambala Mudaliyar and it was printed in Madras in 1807. *Malika Sangalitam* (Medical handbook) from Telugu was translated to English but the work had Tamil names of medicine. It was printed in Madras in 1835. *Atmabodha Prakasikei* of Sankaracharya commented in Telugu by Krishna Sastri was done in Tamil by Ramanuja Kavirayar in 1840.[37] Karl Graul the Protestant missionary had taken all these books to Germany in 1853.[38]

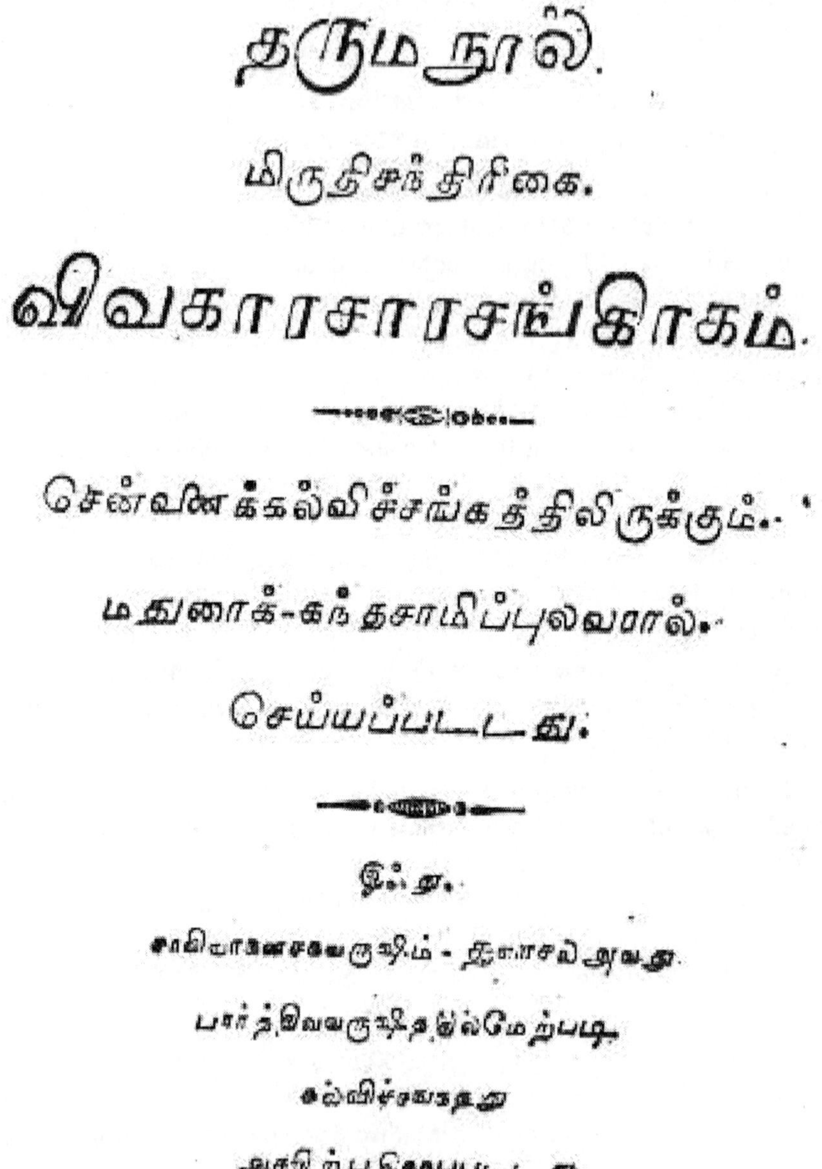

தருமநூல்.

மிருதிசந்திரிகை.

விவகாரசாரசங்கிரகம்.

சென்னைக்கல்விச்சங்கத்திலிருக்கும்.

மதுரைக்-கந்தசாமிப்புலவரால்.

செய்யப்பட்டது.

பார்த்திவவருஷத்தில்மேற்படி

கல்விச்சங்கத்தது

அச்சிற்பதிக்கப்பட்டது.

4.2: The law book translated from Sanskrit to Tamil titled Dharuma Nool by Kandasami Pulavar, printed in Madras in 1826 (Courtesy: British Library, London)

ஞானதேசாந்திரி

தன்பாவங்களினிவாரணம்பண்ணும் வகையையும்

மோட்சகதியையுந்தேடிக்கண்டறிந்து

பாக்கியனுனைதச்சொல்லிய

சரித்திரம்.

இது

இங்கிலீஷ்பாஷையிலிருந்து

தமிழ்ப்பாஷையிலே திருப்பப்பட்டது.

MADRAS:

PRINTED AT THE AMERICAN MISSION PRESS, FOR THE
MADRAS TRACT AND BOOK

1841.

4.3: Translation of the book from English to Tamil titled Gnaana Desaanthiri printed in Madras in 1841 (Courtesy: British Library, London)

The Translation Society in Madras: Preparing and Printing Tamil Books, 1847-57

While the Madras School Book Society could not completely meet the educational demands for modern textbooks due to the inconsistent and wavering policies of the government, a translation society called *Madras Upayukta Grandha Karna Sabha* (the Society for the Production of Useful Books) was established in 1847 at the initiative of the past pupils of Madras University.[39] Several elementary works were brought out by this society in Tamil, which was provided with a grant of 500 rupees in 1854.[40] The formation of the native society should be seen in the context of the institution of the Council for Education set up in 1845 in place of the University Board. The University Board had a large number of natives, whereas the Council for Education consisted of Europeans sympathetic to Christian causes. The society brought out books in Tamil such as (1) Primer, (2) Arithmetic, (3) Geography, (4) History of the Discovery of America, (5) History of Rome, (6) History of England, (7) History of India, and (8) Brief exposition of Kindred science.[41] The South India Christian School Book Society was established in 1854 for the purpose of furnishing the mission schools with suitable books both in English and Tamil.[42] In 1858 this Society was merged with the Christian Vernacular Education Society. Though the main objectives of this society were the training of school-masters, the inspection and improvement of indigenous schools and the circulation of Christian literature, it also published books dealing with science. Ilamayil Kalvi (Conversation on The Heavenly Bodies for Native Children) composed by Rev. W.T. Sattiananadan was published by the society in 1857.[43]

To conclude it may be said that translations from English to Tamil in a large scale had been undertaken mainly by the missionaries and the works were chiefly dealing with Protestant Christian literature. Textbooks for the use of children in the schools were done satisfactorily to some extent. However, translation of texts from Indian languages like Sanskrit, Marathi and Telugu into Tamil were very few and only certain important literary pieces got selected by the natives.

NOTES

1. S. Jeyaseela Stephen, *Missioner Tamil Written and Printed in Pondicherry: Literature and Louis Savinien Dupuis, 1841-1873*, Pondicherry, 2017, p. 72.

2. H. Grafe, 'Benjamin Schultze and the Beginnings of the First Indian Protestant Church in Madras', *Indian Church History Review*, vol. III, 1969, pp. 35-41.
3. AFSt, P:TAM 69, fls.1-165; P:TAM 99; BFSt, 63 F 28, *Ingilis Missionar Kovil Posthagam.*
4. British Library, London, No.14170.cc.1. John Bunyan, *The Pilgrims' Progress from This World to That Which is to Come: Delivered under the Similitude of a Dream (Oru Paradesi Intha Logathaivittu Marumaikku Nadantherinathu Sorpanamenru Uvamaiyiley Kaanpikkapattirukkuthu* , Vepery, MDCCXCIII.
5. AFSt, M1 K5:16
6. HB, continuation 102, p. 672.
7. AFSt, M1 K5:16
8. Ibid.
9. Dennis D. Hudson, *Protestant Origins in India: Tamil Evangelical Christians, 1706-1836*, Surrey, 2000, p. 160.
10. BL, London, no. 14170.c.26, *Paramandalangali Thangal Pokkisham Undenirukkira Paraaparanudaya Pillaigalin Aabarana Petti*, Translated into Tamil by Daniel Pillai, Vepery, 1800. The book has 732 pages.
11. BL, 14170b.1.(31), *Dhunneri Vilakku,* Translated by J. Knight, third edition, Jaffna, 1814.
12. BL, 14170b.51, *The Tamul translation of the book of common prayer*, Madras, 1818.
13. BL, 14170.cc.4, *The book of common prayers with the occasional services & Psalter translated into Tamil by J.P. Rottler*, Government press, Madras, 1819.
14. BL, 3406.df.20, *Pothuvaana Seppangal*, SPCK Press, Madras 1828.
15. BL, 14170.k.11, *Aathikaala Sarithira Sangiraham by P. Gnanapragasa Moodaliar*, Madras, 1828.
16. BL, 14170.k.12, *Industhaani Sarithira Sangiraham by P. Gnanapragasa Moodeliar*, Vepery, 1830.
17. BL, T.2124 (6), Jonathan Edmonson, Five sermons on the nativity, the crucifixion, the resurrection, the ascension of Jesus and the decent of the Holy Spirit, translated into Tamil Madras, 1831.
18. Karl Graul, 'Notizen, Correspondenzen und Vermischtes. Die Tamulische Bibliothek der Evan. Luth. Missionsanstalt zu Leipzig', *Zeitschrift der Deutschen Morgenländischen Gesellschaft*, vol. VII, Leipzig, 1853, pp. 558-568.

19. *Gnaana Desaanthari: Than Paavangalai Nivaaranam Pannum Vagaiyum Motch Gathiyayum Thedik Kandarindhu Paakiyanaarathai Solliya Sarithiram. Ithu Ingilisu Bhashayilirundhu Thamizh Bhashaiyile Thiruppiyathu,* Madras, Printed at the American Mission Press for the Madras Tract and Book Society, 1841.
20. BL, 14172.e.2, *Pershiyan Kathaigal*, Madras, 1840.
21. BL, 14170.b.1 (24), *Thuyya Nadai*, Jaffna 1842.
22. BL, 14170.a.4, *Kristhu Sabhaiyain Sarithira Surukkam*, Madras, 1845.
23. BL, 14170.b.35, *Thaththuva Vetham*, Madras, 1846.
24. BL, 1107.f.24, *Pothuvaana Sepa Puththagam*, SPCK, Madras, 1846.
25. BL, 14171.aa.14 (1), *Inimayaana Kathaigal: Pleasing tales or stories designed to improve the understanding and direct the conduct of young person with a Tamil translation*, Madras 1847.
26. BL, 14170b.36, *Meygnnaodhaya Viruththi*, Jaffna, 1848.
27. BL, 14170.k.32, Rajah Sooboroya Moodeliar, *Kattu Kathaigal*, Madras, 1853.
28. BL, 14170.a. 33 (3), *Kaavalappan Kathai*, Jaffna, 1856, No.1, New Series of the Jaffna Religious Tract Society.
29. BL, 14170.b.32, John C. Aroolappan, *Satta Thittam*, Madras, 1852.
30. BL, 14172.h.55, S.F. Green, *Angaathi Paatha Sugarana Vaatha Udarpaalana Nool*, second edition, Madras, 1857.
31. BL, 14172.h.45, *Inglishu Ilakkanam*, Madras, 1862.
32. BL, 14170.g.15, *Dharuma Nool: Mirudhisandrikai, Vivaahara Sangiragam Chennai Kalvi Sangathin Madurai Kandasami Pulavaraal Seyyapattathu Iguthu Salivaahana Saka Varusham 1748vathu Parthiva Varushathil Merpadi Kalvi Sangaththu Acchir Pathikkapattathu: An Abridgment in the Tamil Language of the Smriti Chandrica, a Treatise on the Municipal Law of the Hindus by Madura Condaswami Pulavar of the College of Fort St. George,* Madras, printed at the College Press, AD.1826.
33. Karl Graul, 'Notizen, Correspondenzen, pp. 558-568.
34. BL, 14170.ee.1, *Thiruvilaiyaadar Puranam*, Chintadripettai, 1850.
35. BL, 14171.c.4, *Iguthu Thandavaraya Mudaliyaaraal Mozhipeyartha Panchathanthira Kathai*, Madras, 1826.
36. BL, 14170.a.28, *Nisthaara Rathnaakaram*, Madras, 1857.
37. BL, 14048.c.44, *Athma Bhoga Paritchai*, Madras, 1840.
38. Karl Graul, 'Notizen, Correspondenzen, pp. 558-568.
39. *Report on the Administration of the Department of Public Instruction for the Year 1858–1859*, Madras, 1859, pp. 3–4.

40. *Report on the Administration of the Department of Public Instruction for the Year 1855–1856*, Madras, 1857, pp. 54–5.
41. Ibid., see the letter from the Director of Public Instruction to the Chief Secretary dated 26 January 1856.
42. *Report on the Administration of the Department of Public Instruction for the Year 1858–1859*, Madras, 1859, pp. 3–4.
43. Henry Morris, *The Life of John Murdoch*, Christian Literature Society, Madras, 1906, pp. 73, 76–7.

5

Translation from Tamil to Portuguese, Latin, Danish, English, German and French, 1661-1887

Missionaries from Europe who came to work in Tamil country learnt Tamil. Many of them were very serious in mastering the literary Tamil while some of them were contented with spoken Tamil as they preferred to preach the Gospel moving from place to place. A few who were highly talented among them took up voluntarily the job of composing Christian literary works, besides translation. We find even mention in the records where missionaries were asked and directed to compose literary texts.

The experience of Gonçalo Fernandez (1560-1621) the Jesuit in Madurai from 1595 to 1617 is worth mentioning. He said that he found difficulty in writing Tamil because his style was not polished. Therefore he apologized for the many obscure things found in his translation. This happened because of his unwillingness to change the words of Portuguese origin which he felt would kill the meaning in Tamil. Fernandez also particularly pointed out the fact that translating the Hindu Tamil text was extremely difficult and that both the literal translation and over-reading of the same could be dangerous.[1]

The Jesuits had obtained training in literature and philosophy and were committed to defend the orthodoxy in Catholic doctrine. Roberto Nobili said that the preacher must be a man of irreproachable life and bearer of a doctrine which, by its very soundness, would be a refutation of error.[2] He began his instruction from Christian philosophy, from the true nature of god and his attributes and said that some arguments were difficult to understand and were also unfamiliar to many in Tamil country. Hence he had to write them time and again in different ways so that the Christian doctrine might be understood easily by Tamils.[3] *Gnaanopadesam* (Spiritual

Instruction) the work he wrote in Tamil in five parts, was his masterpiece.[4] We find volume one, (part 1 and 2) printed at the Jesuit press at Ambalakaadu near Cochin in 1677, volume two (part 3) printed in 1678 and volume 3 (part 4) printed in 1678.[5] It has 88 separate sections explicating the mysteries of the Christian truths. Nobili wrote in Tamil prose. These were not translations from any other work. Nobili had referred to Aathuma Nirnayam the work he composed in 1623 in part one of the Gnaanaopadesam. He also referred to *Nithiya Jeevana Sallapam* composed by him in 1625 and *Dushana Dhikkaram* composed by him in 1641-42 in part two and three of the Gnaanopadesam. He cited all his three works in part of four of the Gnaanopadesam. Hence it may be concluded that Nobili began writing around 1624 and completed it after 1643. After translating the short prayers and liturgical formulae, Nobili realized the necessity of writing a magnum opus on Christian theology. He knew that translation of the missionaries earlier had met with great difficulty because they had to coin new words equivalent from Latin, Greek and Portuguese.

Translating Roberto Nobili's Gnaanopadesam from Tamil to Portuguese by Balthasar da Costa, 1661

Balthasar da Costa (1610-1673) the Jesuit decided to translate the *Gnaanopadesam* in Tamil to Portuguese. He completed the work in 1661. It is mentioned that this work translated into Portuguese was dedicated to Dom Affonso VI (1656-1667) the King of Portugal. The Portuguese title of the work runs thus: *Catecismo em que se explição todas as verdades catholicas necessaraias para a salvação e o exem ordem confutao se tambem clariosmamente todas as seitas gentilicos do oriente composta em lingoa Tamul pello venerabel P. Roberto Nobili do Comphania di Jesu fundadaor da missão de Madure, Traduziodo em lingoa Portugueza pello Padre mesma missão em obsequio dos missionaries da India oriental – Dedicado ao muy alto & muy Poderosos Senhor D. Affonso VI, Rey de Portugal etc Ano de 1661* (*Gnaanopadesam* in which are explained with perfect method all the Catholic truths necessary for salvation; in which are also most clearly refuted all the heathen sects of the East: A work truly suited to convert the heathens composed in Tamil by the venerable Fr. Roberto Nobili of the Society of Jesus, founder of the Madurai Mission, Translated into Portuguese, by Fr. Balthazar da Costa of the same Society and Mission for the use of missionaries in India, dedicated to the Most

High and Most Puissant Lord Dom Affonso VI, King of Portugal etc, 1661).[6] Balthasar da Costa mentioned that to dedicate to his Majesty, this work was no free action, but due obligation, because in it is contained the holiest law of God and the order with which it should be preached among the gentiles of the East. He referred to the famed vision of Dom Affonso Henriques, where Christ chose him not only as King of Portugal but also as defender and preacher of his holy law by means of his vassals. Accordingly the present Portuguese king had inherited the scepter and the good distribution of the divine law which was contained in this book. This dedication was dated from Madurai, on 12 February 1661.[7]

The introduction of this work is not fitting to Nobili's catechism. Balthasar da Costa talks about Madurai mission as a part of the Portuguese empire and he states that the King of Portugal must financially support the missionaries with the same good-will he supports the army, because the Portuguese empire was a neo-Israel, the establishment of God's rule all over the world and to all nations, under the Portuguese flag and by natural and divine right. This divine right he speaks about was allegedly given after a vision the first Portuguese king is said to have had, in which he received the cross as the symbol of the kingdom, for that under and after this cross the King should rule. Balthasar da Costa further compares the Portuguese army with Joshua and the Portuguese missionaries under Padroado with Moses. Then he recalls the period about the fight between the Israelites and Amalec as a symbol of the Portuguese fight against the Dutch, stating also that the Portuguese would not win this battle if the king of Portugal did not pay more attention to the conversion of souls. According to him, to support the missionary work was equivalent to the supporting of Moses arms by his servants. And only when Moses had his arms straight to the air, Joshua won. Whenever his arms had been laid down, Joshua started to lose and he referred to (Exodus 17, 8-16) here to the biblical period. Balthasar da Costa in his view concluded and mentioned to the King of Portugal, almost giving a recipe. We are this God's army and people. God gave you the right to rule all over the world and to work in the defeat of Protestant Dutch heresy, a Luciferian enterprise. To win this battle, is simple, support the missionaries and you will win.

Balthasar da Costa in his introduction continued to write that Roberto Nobili did preach Christ crucified, but with due order and caution, so as not to give that which was holy to dogs or pearls to swine. In this he was following, without the slightest deviation, the example and teaching of the Apostles and of Christ himself, the model of all preachers. Christ accommodated himself to the capacity of his hearers so much so that he never preached to them but in parables.[8]

The translation of Balthasar da Costa in one volume is not only as a treatise of Catholic dogma but a creation of a new genre by Nobili. Hence he had translated it from Tamil to Portuguese. Balthasar da Costa who knew Tamil very well successfully translated it from Tamil so that it might be further translated into many languages.

To the reader Balthasar da Costa addressed a vigorous defense of Nobili's method, before explaining the purpose of his translation using a mercantile metaphor. He said that by knowing the difficulty that missionaries had in learning the language such that many were struck mute like merchants who left the shore to search for necessities each day with too large a coin. Costa explained the work would allow missionaries to be merchants who not only had the large coin of wisdom, but also the little one of words with which they could communicate. The preface bespoke of Costa's ardent commitment to Tamil language. The work was an act of translation an attempt to bring Madurai into conversation with Portugal.

He stated that in this catechism three categories of truths were treated by Nobili. Under the first part come those truths which are within the orbit of human reason, such as the existence of god and his six attributes. The first part has 8 chapters and they deal with the nature of catechism (chapter 1); god and his attributes (chapters from 2 to 7); while the world is for man, man is for god, whom he must adore (chapter 8).[9]

The second part comprises those mysteries which through not exceeding the nature of the intellect are still beyond its power as they depend on the free will of god. Created intellect cannot know them without divine revelation, though it can understand them when once they are revealed. Such mysteries are the creation of angels and of men, their nature, fall and the consequences which result from that. These are treated in the second part and the chapters 1 to 2 on angels, 3 on demons, chapter 4 on Adam and Eve, 5-7 on marriage, chapter 8 on paradise, chapters 9 to 12 on sin and its consequences, chapter 13 and 14 on false religion, 15 and 16 on religious life, 17 and 18 on the gravity of sin and it remedy, chapter 19 and 20 on Mary.[10]

The third part comprises those mysteries which are beyond the orbit of human intellect. Even after god had revealed them man could not fully grasp them. Though they are beyond human understanding, they are in agreement with reason. Such mysteries are the holy trinity, incarnation, redemption, sacraments etc., these are treated in the third part. It mainly deals with the New Testament with chapters 1-2 on Holy Trinity, 3-4 incarnation, 5-6 visitation and the precursor, chapters 7-9 nativity, shepherds and the magi, chapter 10 on presentation, 11 innocents, 12 at Egypt, Nazareth and in the temple, 13 on baptism, 14 on genealogy, chapter 15 tempted in the desert, 16 Baptist's martyrdom, chapter 17 on public life-apostles, chapter 18 Lazarus raised, chapters 19-20 last supper, chapters 21-25; passion, chapter 26 on Christ's suffering and salvation, 27-28 resurrection, chapters 29-33 on church established, chapters 34-36 on Mary, 37-39 end of the world and chapters 40-41 on judgment, heaven and hell.[11]

The fourth part explains the following prayers: the sign of the cross, Pater Noster, Ave, Credo and Decalogue.[12]

The fifth part gives the notes of the divine religion. Such notes are thirteen in number that include 1. Forbids sin and provides remedies, 2-3 contains mysteries but they are rational, 4-5 has no contradictions but has prophecies, 6 wonderful propagation 7-8 on miracles, 9 conversion of sinners, 10 martyrdom, 11 and 12 on true humility and holiness 13, persecuted by the devil and Nobili's profession of faith.[13]

Balthasar da Costa who translated all the five parts of the catechism mentioned that Nobili knew quite well that the only books in this Tamil country are books of difficult verse absolutely useless to the preachers, determined to put at their disposal his own extensive knowledge of the language, acquired during forty years of labour, and that was the reason he taught his people, and this was the book still taught by Jesuit missionaries who had succeeded him in Tamil country. Costa said that if the tree was known by its fruit, then this catechism will reveal to all with what clearness and method its author preached Christ crucified. But since Tamil was not understood by all, he had undertaken the task of translating it into Portuguese. It seemed to him that he should be doing thereby some service to all the missionaries of the East, as this book would be a help to them if each one translated it into the language of the particular region where he resided.[14]

Antão Proença (1625-1666) the fellow Jesuit of Nobili and Balthasar da Costa considered that this work of catechism the best ever composed in the church of god considering the order and arrangement of the matter, which are excellent to persuade and convince the understanding, or the energy and force of the arguments used to prove the mysteries of Catholic Christianity, and it would be clearly seen that Nobili was specially enlightened by god to write this work.[15]

Translating Short Stories: Paramaartha Guruvin Kathaigal Composed by Beschi and its Translation from Tamil to Latin, 1744

Beschi laid the foundation for the development of short stories in Tamil prose, because earlier the Tamils had even their stories composed in poetry. His classic example was Paramaartha Guruvin Kathaigal. He first wrote in Tamil prose in 1744 and then translated it into Latin.[16] The title given is first found in Latin and then in Tamil. So as to the stories he gave in Latin at first and then in Tamil. It is titled *FABULA De Ethnicorum Magistro Paramartaguru Dicto A.P. Josepho Constantio Beschi Societatis Jesu Tamulica Lingua scripta et ab Ipso Auctore in Latinam versa.*[17] The preface is written in Latin and here he noted that he prepared and created this book for the use of those Europeans who were employed under the services of the East India Companies in order to assist them in learning Tamil. He stated that those stories which are comic and laughable heard in the surroundings had been written in this book without spoiling the Tamil language tradition. Europeans who would learn Tamil newly would be very much enthused and interested to read the comic stories than the ordinary fables. Hence in his opinion stories become stories and at the same time it would help easily to learn the Tamil language grammar. This would, he said, at one and the same time assist in learning and enjoying could also be done. Further, the stories were given in Latin to help the Europeans who would benefit to learn Tamil. The doubts that arise in the Tamil portion could be solved by reading the corresponding Latin text. Hence Beschi said that he had composed it in both the languages. Thus the purpose of writing Paramaartha Guruvin Kathaigal had been thus neatly spelt out.[18]

There are eight stories. 1. Transitus Fluvii (Crossing the river) 2. Emptio Ovi Equini (Purchase of horse egg) 3. Actum Conducto Bove Iter (Journey undertaken after hiring the ox) 4. Piscatura Equi (Throwing a fish hook to catch a horse) 5. Iter in Equo (Journey to a village on a horseback) 6. Prophetia

Brachmanis (The Brahman's prophecy) 7. Lapsus Magistri ex Equo (Falling off the horse and 8. Magistri Sepultua (The interment of the guru).[19]

The prose text in Tamil contains usages such as nerthi kadan, nilzhalakkum, adaisi ninran, sannay, asaikini and these are used mostly in the southern Tamil country. Many colloquial words such as nammathu, kadikuthu are also found. However, through Paramaartha Guru Kathaigal Tamil prose particularly literary fiction was newly introduced. This was as a forerunner to the novels of the late nineteenth century that emerged and got experimented. This prose development had major impact on modern Tamil literary culture.

T. P. Meenakshi Sundaram called Beschi as the father of short stories.[20] Kailasapathy mentioned that Beschi was the forerunner of the modern comic writers and said that Beschi had made us laugh in Tamil prose through Paramaartha Guruvin Kathaigal.[21] It may be mentioned that following Beschi many more short stories such as Aviveka purana guru kathai and Madhana kaamarasan kathai had come to be published later.

Translating Theruntha Vaasagam, Arichandran Kathai and Panchathanthira Kathai from Tamil to Danish and Kavilai Vaasagam into English

Gnaana Pragasa Pandaaram composed the work called Theruntha Vaasgam in poetry. It was the story of a king by name Serkanse who at all times acted strictly within the rules of justice. Once his own son committed a petty crime and the father had him executed. This theme with its story and history had interested the Danes in Tranquebar. Hence it was translated into Danish.[22]

Arichandran Kathai was popular among the Tamils and so it attracted the Danes in Tranquebar. King Arichandran was said to have reigned 2000 years at the beginning of the world. It is said of him that he never told a lie. At one time a prophet named Viswamithiran came to him attended by a dancing girl. He was much pleased with her dancing, and promised to give the prophet whatever he asked. The prophet asked as much money as would suffice to make a great offering, but refused to receive it till his return, when the principal and the interest became equal to the value of the whole kingdom, and as the king would not tell a lie he gave of the whole kingdom, himself, his wife, and his children, all of whom became slaves to this intriguer. After a sufficient trial of his patience the god came and took him and his family to heaven. Arichandran Kathai was translated into Danish by the missionaries.[23]

Yet another work called Panchathanthira Kathai was found very interesting by the Danes. It is a series of conversations between different animals and birds, with the shrewdness of some, the dullness of others, and the consequences, prosperous or adverse, that attended certain courses of conduct. As this was very similar to its style and design to Aesop's fables the missionaries in Tranquebar had translated Panchathanthira Kathai from Tamil to Danish.[24]

Kavilai Vaasagam another work was noticed by the missionaries in Madras with interesting events narrated. It contains a fable of a cow which had been seized by a tiger in the jungle. The cow in a pathetic manner craves permission to go to her house where her young calf would be expecting her with great anxiety, at the same time assuring that she would return again. The tiger grants the request, and the cow goes to see her calf and recommending it to the care and protection of the other cows, retires into the forest. The tiger amazed and astonished at her fidelity did not make her his prey; instantly appears the god Iswaran, who transforms both the cow and the tiger and removes them to a higher state of bliss. This Tamil work also got translated into English.[25] Thus several Tamil stories which were highly popular got translated into Danish and English which was a new development in the early modern age. These Tamil short stories had only paved way for the development of Tamil novel literature as they were very closely associated with. Hence the view of some scholars that novels were imported from the west and introduced in Tamil may be called into question. Novel writers of the nineteenth century in Tamil have pointed out that they wrote novels to remedy the absence of Tamil prose with imagination and for recreational purpose.

The Early Plans of Ziegenbalg to Translate Anda Kooru Thaththuvam and Thirikaala Chakkaram from Tamil to German

Bartholomäus Ziegenbalg collected Tamil manuscripts, studied them carefully and later thought of translating some of them from Tamil to German. He said that originally he planned to translate *Anda Kooru Thaththuvam* into German but he was unable to understand all the philosophical terms in Tamil properly. Further he had no philosopher at hand whom he could consult in Tranquebar. Therefore, rather than to write something incorrect, he had postponed this idea until, at a later date, he could obtain the necessary assistance. According to him Anda Kooru Thaththuvam the philosophical work on the elements-the five senses and connected subjects was very little known and it could not be understood by the *pandaarams*, brahmins and poets.

Similarly Ziegenbalg also had in his mind an idea to translate *Thirikaala Chakkaram* a mathematical description of the seven worlds below and the seven above; also of seven oceans together with the paradise called Thabayam the seat of Iswaran. Ziegenbalg though kept his mind open to do this translation but later gave it up because he found difficulty in tracing numerous matching words and terms from Tamil to German.[26]

Ziegenbalg's Successful Translation of Neethi Venpaa (30 August 1708), Ulaga Neethi (3 September 1708) and Konrai Vendhan (4 September 1708) into German

Bartholomäus Ziegenbalg had decided to translate Neethi Venpaa (Nidi Wunpa) into German and he completed the translation successfully. The preface of his work is dated 30 August 1708: The German version runs thus: Neethi Venpaa or the Tamil moral teachings consists of 96 small worldly rules which were composed more than 700 years ago, in Tamil verses which are all translated word by word by Bartholomäus Ziegenbalg.[27]

In the preface to Neethi Venpaa he stated that most Christians in Europe suppose the Tamils to be a very barbarous people, but this arises from the Europeans who have been amongst them not understanding their language, so that they have not been able to read their books, but have drawn their conclusions from outward appearances. He said that he must acknowledge that when he first came amongst them he could not imagine that their language had proper rules, or that their life had the laws of civil order, and took up all sorts of false ideas on their actions as if they had neither a civil nor a moral law,—but as soon as he had gained a little acquaintance with their language and could talk to them on various subjects, he began to have a much better opinion of them and when at last he was able to read their own books he found that the Tamils discussed the same philosophical subjects as the savants of Europe, and that they had a regular written law, wherein all theological subjects were treated and demonstrated. This surprised him extremely, and he was delighted to be thoroughly instructed in their heathenism from their own writings.[28] The preface is followed by text of Neethi Venpaa.[29]

Ziegenbalg very accurately translated the verse by verse into German together with its commentary. According to him, this work on the ethics and morality of the Tamils is the expression of the honest respect of a man confronting the inhabitants of his chosen homeland objectively and without bias. The opening words of his foreword to Neethi Venpaa mentions that when he saw not unfitting equations and life rules were therein continued, he considered it indicated to translate this from Tamil to German, not that the Christians do not have sufficient rules of morality in the holy scriptures for them to learn them from mere heathens, but merely and solely to see what extent a heathen, devoid of the scriptures, and only by virtue of natural enlightenment, could attain cognition of the law of morality, and how those Tamil Hindus equal those former Latin and Greek heathens in this detail, might read the *bibliotheca malabaricum*, composed by him and sent to Europe.

In the preface to Neethi Venpaa he categorically stated that he had accurately rendered the meanings of the Tamil sayings with their commentaries. He placed his own additions in parenthesis so that all readers could easily identify what the original Tamil text means and what he himself had said. Thus he was very careful not to alter and add anything to the original.[30]

It has been reported that whenever Ziegenbalg visited a school and asked the Tamil text Ulaga Neethi (literally Worldly Justice) to some youngsters what certain things meant, they were always unable to give him a satisfactory answer. He said that the same happens in the case of other books dealing with ethics, they are learnt by-heart but without proper understanding; just as the Christians often learn the catechism by-heart without understanding it.[31]

Ziegenbalg decided to translate Ulaga Neethi into German the work by poet Ulaga Naathan. He successfully translated it to find out what kind of morality existed amongst the Hindus.[32] The title page in German runs thus: *Ulaga Nidi oder Weltliche Gerechtigkeit, bestehende in fünff und sechzig lebensreguln, der sich langen jahren von einem heydnischen poeten, der sich Ulaga Naden genennet hat, in Malabarischen versen aufgescheieben worden, nunmehro in die hochteutsche sprache versetzt von Bartholomaeo Ziegenbalg, seiner Königlichen Majestät zu DEnnemarch und Norwegen etc. verordneten Missionario unter den heyden in Ostijndien auf der küste Cormandel zu Tranquebar*. The title is followed by a preface dated 3 September 1708.[33] Then the text of Ulaga Neethi had been furnished.[34]

Ziegenbalg translated Konrai Vendhan into German (*Kondrei Wendhen*) composed by Avvaiyar. He said that he had translated it into German as an offering to those who are anxious to know the moral principles of the Hindus.[35] The title page in German runs thus: *Kondei Wenden oder Malabarische Moralia so da nach aussage der Malabarischen Poeten vor 750 jahren von der göttin der weisheit Auwiar genant, aufgeschrieben seijn, besthende in neuntzig versen oder sittenlehren aus der Malabarischen sprache im hochteutsche versetzt von Bartholomäus Ziegenbalg, seiner königchen Majestaet zu Dennemarck und Norwegen etc. Verordnetem Missionario in Ostijndien unter den Malabarishcen Heijden, Geschrieben in Ostijndien auf der Küst Coromandel zu Tranquebar*. Ziegenbalg had also given a preface to Konrai Vendhan.[36]

It may be mentioned that the three Tamil literary works that were popular booklets of epigrams were translated into German in 1708. These had maxims written in a single line. Hence Ziegenbalg must have thought it proper to undertake this exercise as a beginning of improving his skill in Tamil language. He was also very confident to do this work and sent it to Hermann August Francke (1663-1727) who considered that these Tamil works were heathen nonsense and he had shelved them underneath the heap of material that he had at the orphanage in Halle.

Ziegenbalg was the earliest missionary who made sincere efforts to collect a selection of ethical maxims written by the old poetess Avvaiyaar and he translated them. Since hardly any moral value of Tamil knowledge was then known to the European audience, his work seemed to be of great service to the gentle readers in Europe who desired to have a taste of it.

Translating Agasthiyar Irandaayiram into German by Johann Ernst Grundler in 1712

Johann Ernst Grundler (1677-1720) who reached Tranquebar in 1708 developed an interest in studying palm-leaf manuscripts on the subject of medicine. He moved from Tranquebar to Poraiyar, a nearby village on 20

February 1710 where he spent two years in studying medical manuscripts.[37] In order to learn about Tamil culture more intimately he started eating and dressing like Tamils. He was mainly interested to learn about disease, diagnosis and dosages as found in Tamil medical texts. He noted carefully how the Tamil physicians diagnosed the diseases by pulse, phlegm, urine, tongue, and eye tests and how they prescribed proper medicine by identifying certain special characteristics of the diseases and related them to three separate groups of people—men, women and children. He desired to disseminate the rich medical knowledge, so he translated the palm-leaf medical text '*Agasthiyar Irandaayiram*' from Tamil into German. He stated his intention as a translator was to be of service to European men. He completed the treatise, referred to here as 'The Tamil Physician', in 1712. The text was sent by Grundler to Halle in Germany via Copenhagen by a ship that left Tranquebar in 1712. This manuscript entitled '*Der malabarische medicus, welcher kurzen Berricht gibet, theils was diese Heyden in der medicin vor Principia haben; theils auf was Art und mit welchen Malabaren Zusammen getragen u.ubersetzet von Johann Ernst Grundler*' is preserved in the *Archiv der Franckesche Stiftungen* in Halle.[38] Grundler mentioned in this work that he had compiled and translated the details from the Tamil manuscript into German. He also furnished details related to the circumstances under which medicines were given to cure diseases by the natives. In his preface he gave a short medical account obtained from a brahmin explaining how studies in medicine were conducted and taught to pupils in Tamil schools.[39]

The manuscript 'The Tamil Physician' has two parts. The first contains ten themes:

(1) Arrival of the Doctor and the arrangements to be made to attend the sick.

(2) On pulse and its types.

(3) How to recognize the main disease?

(4) The diseases that emerge from the *tridosha siddhantam*, i.e *vaatham*, *pitham* and *kapam*.

(5) The origin of those diseases.

(6) The diet which have to be observed in these diseases.

(7) Fever.

(8) On unconsciousness/fainting (anaesthesia).

(9) On the symptoms that indicate a patient will live or die.

(10) The manners of these diseases which occur among the Hindus.[40]

The second part of the manuscript contains twelve themes:

(1) How to purify/pulverize some plants which have to be made into medicine?

(2) By which medicines fever can be cured?

(3) Medicines by which fainting can be cured.

(4) Medicines by which different poisonous diseases and ulcers can be cured.

(5) Head diseases.

(6) Eye diseases.

(7) Diseases of the ears, nose and mouth.

(8) On the diseases of the chest and stomach.

(9) On diarrhoea.

(10) On venereal and several other urinary diseases.

(11) On female diseases.

(12) On child diseases. Finally, we find notes to part one and two appended, along with a dictionary of medical terminology.[41]

Grundler elaborated different kinds of medicines used by Tamils for the cure of various diseases. The prescription details contain the ingredients used to make medicines such as sesame (*Sesamum orientale*), *vashambu* (*Acorus calamus*), *erukkai* (*Calotropis gigantea*), *nochi* (*Vitex negundo*), *agaththi* (*Sesbania grandiflora*), *kaatunelli* (*Phyllanthus emblica*), *inji* (*Zingiber officinale*), *murungai* (*Moringa pterygosperma*), *saaranay* (*Trianthema portulacastrum*) and salts like *induppu* and *madaleippu*. The old usages of weights and measures were also given in the text.

On analysis and scrutiny of this Grundler text, it is noticed that he followed exactly the pattern and details of the Tamil manuscript '*Agasthiyar Irandaayiram*'.[42] The Tamil work conforms fully with part one of Grundler's account dealing with the doctor and disease and part two on medicine for various diseases. Grundler's work was used by those Germans who had evinced interest in the siddha medical system. Doctors in Copenhagen read, used and also taught the Tamil medical system. Thus siddha medical knowledge was communicated to a wider audience and information was passed on by Grundler from time to time.

Translation of Thirukural into Latin by Beschi (1724-5), into German by Johann Z. Kiernander (1742), into English by Nathaniel Edward Kindersley (1794) into German by August Friedrich Caemmerer (1799-1803) into English by Francis Whyte Ellis (1816) into German by Karl Graul (1865)

Thirukural attracted the attention of Beschi for it had moral teachings with each couplet had seven words, four in the first line and three in the second. Beschi translated 108 chapters of Thirukural into Latin and he completed the work in 1724-25. He often quotes Thirukural in all his works including Thembaavani completed in 1726. Copies of this manuscript *Moralia Tiruvalluver, RRP C.J. Beschius, Societatis Iesu* had been sent to France during the eighteenth century.[43] V.M. Gnanapragasam who had published it had omitted the explanation of the meanings of five chapters like kadvul vaazththu, vaan sirappu, neeththaar perumai, aran valiyuruththal and uzh. But he gave the Latin translation and its Tamil corresponding kurals. We can be however satisfied that at least five chapters of his Latin translations have been given in Tamil.[44] Those who do not know Latin could not enjoy understanding the nuances of Beschi's own ideas expressed by him in his Latin translation of Kural.

Beschi at first gives the Tamil text of every Kural. Then he gives its transliteration which was followed by the translation and commentary. After that follows an almost word by word translation, in which some grammatical and linguistic peculiarities are given. The first kural reads:

> Kadavul Vaazhlthu, Dei Laus.
>
> Agara mudala elutt ellam aadhi bhagavan mudhatte yulagu (Tamil version in Tamil characters)
>
> Litterae Omnes caput habent; litteram A. Mundus caput habet Deum.
>
> Agaram, littera A/mudala, mudattu, isem, ac mudelai yueittadu, principium habent et habet/ adi pagaven, dues/ulagu, mundus.

It is to be noted that Beschi often gave his own meanings and explanations such as kural no. 37. The translation agrees with the traditional meaning in most of the couplets. For a good many of the couplets, Beschi

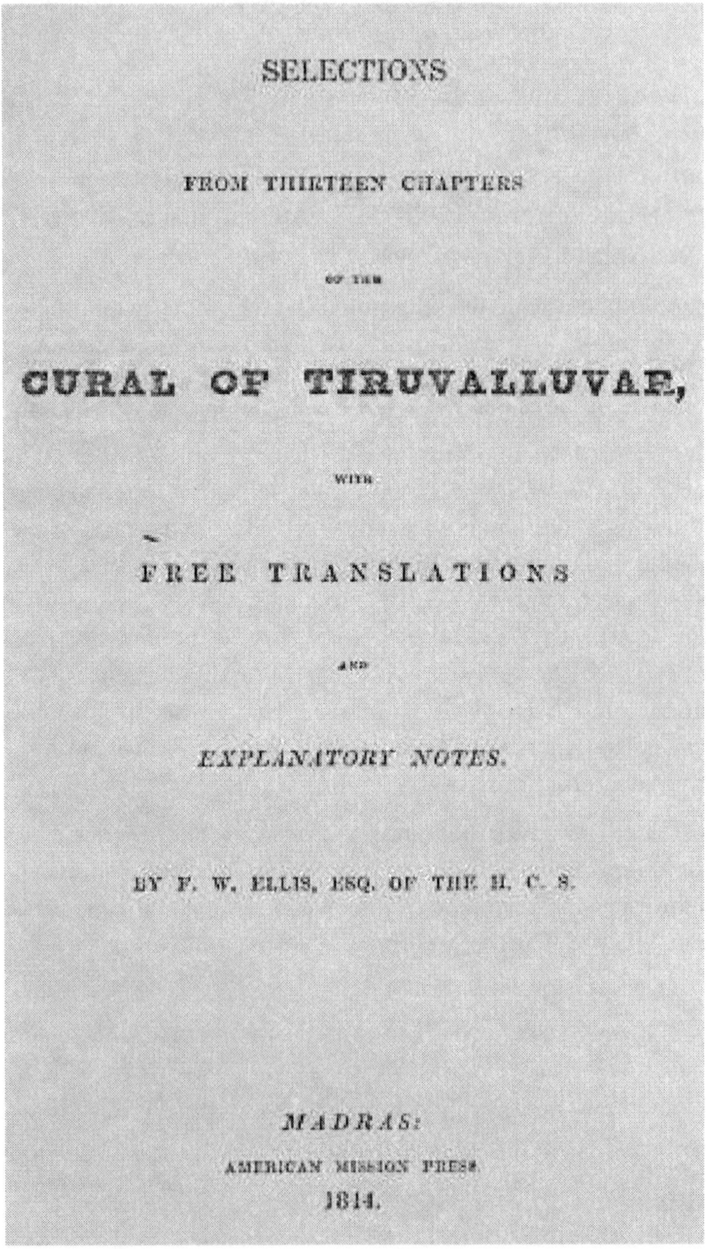

SELECTIONS

FROM THIRTEEN CHAPTERS

OF THE

CURAL OF TIRUVALLUVAR,

WITH

FREE TRANSLATIONS

AND

EXPLANATORY NOTES.

BY F. W. ELLIS, ESQ. OF THE H. C. S.

MADRAS:

AMERICAN MISSION PRESS.

1814.

5.1: Thirukural translated by F.W. Ellis printed in Madras in 1814 (Courtesy: British Library, London) gives a long explanation along with the translation to make the meaning clear as found in the kural.[45] It is also well known that he gave explanations for the western readers and audience. After kural 621 Beschi quotes Seneca: *Adversa adversis adversa now sunt sed aversis* and also explaining the meaning.

K. Meenakshisundaram in his study opines that Beschi has interpreted the verses ingeniously except where they are opposed to Christian beliefs. He also stated that Beschi's reading destroys the metre and he gave an example.[46] G.U. Pope felt that Beschi's translation was erroneous in kural numbers 913 and 919.[47] What-ever may be the criticisms, it may be said that Beschi did translation in his own way being Latin known very well. Moved by a deep love for Kural Beschi translated only aram (virtue) and porul (wealth) and he omitted inpam (love) the third theme of kural into Latin, because he was a Roman Catholic priest for he did not wish to do it.[48] In his Thembaavani he used kurals from kaamathupaal and we find kural number 1091, 1100, 1101, 1121, 1161 and 1285 (twice, 29.51; 30.78). Again he also used kurals from Kaamathu paal in his work *Thonnul Vizhlakkam* vide suththiram no 18, and we find kural numbers 1115, 1200 and 1263.

Through Thirukural translation Beschi had brought the significance of the literary work to the notice of the European literati. This paved way for translation into other European languages such as German and English languages. The Europeans were attracted towards Thirukural which was the holy book and by that incomparable ethical love rendered it into various European languages.

Johann Z. Kiernander, born at Linkoping in Sweden on 1 December 1710, studied at Uppsala and Halle, was ordained at Wernigerode in 1739, embarked at Gravesend on 1 April 1740 and landed at Cuddalore 28 August 1740. He laboured there till 1758 and went to Bengal, where he carried on his missionary work. Johann Kiernander in his letters from Cuddalore to Herrn Berein in Germany dated 21 January and 1 February 1742 mentioned his translation of Thirukural. He quoted the first kural that "As the alphabet 'A' is the first letter so is the praise of the wise god is the best in the world'. However, he gave the commentary of the kural and not exactly the poetic version of Valluvar. The Tamil text runs: Yezhuthugalukkellaam Agara Yezuthu Muthalaay Irukkumaapoley, Ulagathukkellaam Saruva Gnaana Swami Thothiram Muthal Yenravaaru. The German translation runs: *Gleichwie in allen Alphabeten der Buchstab A der erste ist, also ist auch das Lab des allweisen gottles in der gantzen welt das vornehmste.*[49]

Nathaniel Edward Kindersley (1763-1831) was doing banking business in Madras. Later he entered into the services of the English East India Company and became the collector of North Arcot in 1790 and served in it till 1792.[50] During this period he developed abiding interest on Hindu texts and had translated Thirukural into English in 1794.[51]

Missionaries of Tranquebar were highly impressed by Thirukural. They began to quote Thirukural often in their missionary reports in German. We find kural no. 260 from the chapter *Pullal maruththal* (abstaining from meat eating) and the text 'Kollaan pullaalai maruththaanai kaikoopi yella vuirium thozhum' being quoted.[52] In an another report of the missionary we find kural no. 4 and 7 from kadvaul vaazththu chapter one on Praising God 'Venduthal vendaamai ilannadi senthaarku yandum idumbai ila' and 'Thankuvamai illathaan thazhlsenthaarkallal manka kavalai mattral aridhu' published.[53] Stories of Thiruvalluvar holding in great reverence were found also in the missionary reports sent in German.[54]

However Thirukural again came to be translated into German during the end of the eighteenth century. August Friedrich Caemmerer born at Wusterhausen in Brandenburg on 22 June 1767, studied at Halle, was ordained at Copenhagen 1789, suffered shipwreck at the Cape, and arrived in Sri Lanka and then reached Tranquebar 1791. He worked as a missionary for many years and died on 22 October 1837. Caemmerer learnt Tamil and was very much impressed by the work of Thiruvalluvar. He began to translate Thirukural into German published it titled '*Des Tiruvalluvar Gedichte und Denkspruche*' (Poems and maxims of Tiruvalluvar) in Nurnberg in 1803.[55] This enabled the German reader to get an idea in his own language about Thirukural. Francis White Ellis translated Arathuppal of Thirukural into English and the book was printed in Madras in 1816.[56] *Thirukural* again attracted the attention of Karl Graul the German missionary and so he did the translation, but the book was posthumously published by William Germaan in 1865.[57]

Translating Aathichoodi and Moothurai by Christoph Samuel John into German, 1791-96

Christoph Samuel John (1747-1813) the missionary in Tranquebar thought of translating Aathichoodi, the Tamil literary text of Avvaiyar and in 1791 we find a selection of the ethical maxims written from Aathichoodi and Moothurai translated by him.[58] In the introduction C.S. John says 'as the Tamils value these books highly, and since hardly any of their moral knowledge is known to us, it seems to me of service to present to the gentle reader a taste of it. One can see these how remote their insights are and that, at least they do not altogether lack good moral foundations.[59]

It may be mentioned here that Moothurai was felt as an important Tamil literary work by Ziegenbalg himself. He said that one could truly say that he had found a much higher level of morality in their books such as Moothurai and in their speech than was common among the Greek and Romans. Therefore, if one Hindu leads a pious and virtuous life amongst them, they are in full agreement with Christians and they love those who have devoted themselves to virtue; but if one tells them about Jesus Christ, the importance of baptism, and other things necessary for the attainment of bliss, then they will not argue but at the same time they will refuse to accept one's word, saying that a man who leads a good life will reach a good place after his death, one who leads an evil life will find himself in an evil place of residence whether he was a Hindu, a Turk, a Jew, or a Christian. It is extremely difficult to contradict their faulty way of reasoning and show them the necessity of having faith in Christ. On the other hand, if one tells them about the absurdities which surround their own gods and asks how they can possibly believe in them then they just laugh, indicating by their behaviour that they themselves have but little faith in them. Often they will put such sentiments into words, mostly when there is a large crowd present to listen. One almost meets amongst those heathens a situation similar to the one the New Testament relates about Jesus, whenever he preached to a large crowd he almost caused a friction because there were always some who accepted the truth of his words and others who blasphemed him. In the same way whenever, in all modesty, if one talks to those Hindus about the truth of Christianity and the absurdities of their own gods, two groups will form themselves, some will listen with reservations whereas others will accept everything with great humility and never grow tired of asking further questions. But just as the Bible tells us that even amongst those who believed Jesus' words only a few agreed to be baptized, though this was the aim of his sermons, in the same way there are many Tamils who have a high opinion about our Christian religion but only a few will agree to be baptized.[60] Christoph Samuel John was much attracted towards Moothurai and so he translated it.[61] It may be said that after Ziegebalg translations of Tamil literary works, C. S. John had made important contribution in translation from Tamil to German. We find examples in these works such as 1) Please do well 2) Mother and father are the first god head whom one acknowledges 3) When someone gives you charity, don't consider him to be obliged to do this always. 4) Use it to your own best, as the coconut tree uses the water with which it is wetted: to its own growth and to bear fruit after. Poet Muthu Thaandavar's work Pottiamalei was translated by C.S. John from Tamil to German and it got published in German periodicals.[62]

Translation of Tamil Texts into German, 1791-1865

Avvaiyar's *Kalvi Ozhukkam* available in palm-leaf was translated from Tamil to German by Johann Christian Christoph Rudiger and it was printed in Halle in 1791. The book had 28 pages.[63] *Athma Bhodhaga Paritchai* composed by Ramanuja Kavirayar and the commentary made by Krisha Sastri had attracted the Germans. Hence the extracts of the text and the commentary had been translated into German. The book got printed in 1854.[64] Johann Georg Theodor Graesse translated *Paramaartha Guru Kathai* and the book got printed in Dresden in 1856. It had 81pages.[65]

Karl Graul was director of the Leipzig Mission Society. He visited Madras, Tranquebar, Sirkazhli, Cuddalore, Thanjavur, Tiruchirapalli and Sri Lanka. He wrote a voluminous work titled Bibliotheca Tamulica. The first volume contains the German translation of the Vedantha teachings called *Kaivalya Navaneetham* of Thandavamoorthy Swamigal and *Pancadasa Prakarana* of Vidhyanarayana Swamigal. The second volume contains the English translation of Kaivalya Navaneetham with a short Tamil grammar. A collection of Tamil poems including Thirukural had been translated were found in the book that got printed in Erlangen in 1865. It had 227 pages.[66]

Translating Letters from Tamil to Danish and German, 1712-30

Ziegenbalg wrote a letter addressed to the Hindus in Tamil titled 'Tharangambadiyile irukkura Gurumaargal Intha Desaththaaraay irukkira Thamizhar yellarukkum yezhuthina nirupam' in 1712. It was printed in Tamil at Tranquebar press on 17 December 1717 and it got widely distributed. This letter in Tamil was translated into Danish by Rasmus Hansen Attrup, the secretary to the Tranquebar Commandant's Privy

Council and the same was printed in 1719.[67] Further the same Tamil letter was again translated into German in 1730.[68]

Translation of Commercial and Legal Records from Tamil to French, 1718-38

Business records from Tamil to French got translated by the French East India Company in Pondicherry during the eighteenth century. It has been noticed that sale of shops in the bazaar and plot of lands in Pondicherry were carried out extensively through documents prepared in Tamil. We find three big shops and newly built small shops in the bazaar by Velayudhan had been sold to the Jesuits in Pondicherry for a sum of fifteen *pagodas* in 1718.[69] Further sale of a plot of land in the weavers' street in 1726 was done by Arockianatha mudaliar to Kalpaga pillai.[70] Again we find a sale agreement for a plot of land in the brahmin street was executed by Subba Ayyar to Sitarama Ayyar for a sum of 36 *pagodas*.[71] All these Tamil records were translated into French for the purpose of administrative convenience and we find them in the collection of *Acte Tabelliones* preserved at the National Archives of India, Pondicherry.

Numerous commercial transactions of the natives were carried out through signed agreements and bonds both in palm-leaf and paper were executed in Tamil. These were translated into French for administrative purposes. We find some interesting evidences of translations from Tamil into French such as a bond in Tamil executed in 1732 by Mangaan to Muthaiya pillai, a palm-leaf bond in Tamil executed in 1734 by Arulappan to Muthu, a bond in 1732 executed by Sankaradasu to Chinna Thambi chetti for a sum of 119 *pagodas*, a bond executed in 1736 by Poonjolai to Ravanappa chettiar for a sum of seven *pagodas*, a bond in Tamil executed in 1740 by Thandavaraya pillai to Savarimuthu for a sum of ten *pagodas*, a bond executed in 1741 by Muthu Chittambala chettiar to Poomalanda Muthambala chettiar for a sum of 12276 ¾ *pagodas*, a bond executed in 1742 by Savariappan to Kulandaiyappa mudali for a sum of 32 *pagodas*, a bond executed in 1742 by Solaiyappa Annamalai to Ananda Ranga pillai for a sum of 100 *pagodas*, a bond executed in 1742 by Mannapan and Saravanan to Mariyappa mudaliar for a sum of 124 *pagodas*, a palm-leaf agreement of 1744 in Tamil by Kumarappa pillai to Vasudeva pandara Iyer for a sum of 100 *pagodas* with interest at one per cent payable per month, a palm-leaf bond executed in the Tamil year sadharana (1731) by Thillaiyam

Bala mudaliar to Thimmaji for a sum of 200 *pagodas*, and an agreement in Tamil in 1743 executed by Paapu Reddiar and his son to Kalyana Thandava pillai for a sum of 303299 *pagodas* and 320 *panams*.[72] Thus money transactions ranged from petty sums to large amounts got translated from Tamil to French by the company administration in Pondicherry.

Mortgage bonds prepared and used in Tamil were translated into French. We find translation of a mortgage bond in Tamil executed by Vasudava ayyan to Kumarappan for a sum of 24 *pagodas* in 1736, a mortgage bond of 1742 in Tamil mentioning the details of land and house in the chetti street, executed by Anda chetti to Nagpur Appachi Rama for a sum of 18 *pagodas*, and an agreement of 1742 in Tamil executed by Kottai Subayyan to Kumara pillai for the mortgage of land and garden at Ozhugarai for 170 *pagodas*.[73]

Tribunal de Chaudrie though accepted the legal documents prepared in Tamil but the translation of the same from Tamil to French were prepared to suit the administrative needs. We find translation of a sale agreement of a plot of land for a sum of ten *pagodas* by Neelakara Ramabadran to Vadakattu Velayutha chetti done under the orders of *Tribunal de Chaudrie*, and a partition deed of Thirukami chetti and his brother in 1738 done in Tamil and French at the instance of *Tribunal de Chaudrie* and a sale deed of a plot of land with hay stack at the Sozhiyar street by Gangadharan to Annapayar mestri for a sum of 33 *pagodas*.[74]

Many untranslatable words such as *contrat*, (contract) *billet* (receipt) etc., in French got transcribed into words in Tamil in the course of translation. Writers then could not find equivalent words and new words could not be coined for documentary use. Thus the administrative needs of the French in Pondicherry had necessitated development of translation culture. Over a long period of time business/commercial Tamil spoken in Pondicherry had many words borrowed from French and came to be used widely in a corrupted form both in spoken and written Tamil.

Translating Bhaagavatha Puranam and Vaana Sasthiram from Tamil to French by Mariadass Pillai in Pondicherry, 1769-89

Missionaries produced works which were Christian in nature and other spiritual texts for the use of converts in the course of evangelization. However, progress of knowledge through translation of native writings and literary works into French is found. Bhaagavatha Puranam was one of the eighteen puranams was first written in Sanskrit. Later it was translated into Tamil and available to Hindus in Pondicherry. Mariadass Pillai (1723-1790) a native of Pondicherry made a translation into French based on the Tamil manuscript.[75] It is interesting to note why and how Mariadass Pillai translated Bhaagavatha Puranam. Foucher d'Obsonville an officer of French East India Company who came to Pondicherry in 1752 and lived here till his return to France in 1769 was interested to get Bhaagavatha Puranam being translated into French. So he requested Mariadass to do the work and agreed to pay twenty five rupees per month for the translation work. Mariadass therefore began doing the work. After departure of Foucher to France in 1769 the salary to Mariadass was arranged to be paid through his attorney residing in Lyon. In a letter dated 5 October 1772 by Coeurdoux to Anquetil du Perron it had been reported that Mariadss Pillai was well educated and an officer of the French East India Company had employed him for long and painful translation work of the Bhaagavatham, not to speak of considerable expenditure that had been incurred. Coeurdoux added that a layman living in the family was not in a position to complete the work of translation very fast since he was otherwise engaged.[76] Mariadass successfully completed the work of translation into French by the end of the year 1772 and the manuscript reached the Royal Library of the King of France in 1773. Thereafter it was made known in France in the same year through a publication. It stated that Bhaagavatha Puranam was translated to French by Mariadass Pillai an Indian interpreter of the French Company in Pondicherry. The work had been divided into twelve parts which dealt with the creation, the conservation and the destruction of the universe, the divinity the perfect life, the metamorphosis of Vishnu and the origin of the subaltern god. Mariadass Pillai had dedicated his translation to M. Bertin, the Minister and Secretary of State who had zeal for the progress of knowledge.[77] Foucher finally edited and published Bhaagavatha Puranam in 1788 without acknowledgement and mentioning the name of Mariadass Pillai.[78]

Mariadass Pillai was engaged in the translation work of Vaana Sasthiram from Tamil to French. He completed this work on astronomy and the same was sent to France in 1787. Finally it got printed in Paris in 1790.[79] In the first chapter of treatise, we find the notion of the world, *nakshatrams* in Tamil and Sanskrit, mentioning twenty seven stars, twelve signs of the zodiac (*rasi*), twelve lunar months in detail from April to March.[80] In the second chapter we notice recording sixty years, fifteen *thithis*, days and the week in Tamil.[81] In the third chapter explanation of the sun, the moon and the planets. In the fourth chapter we find the details of the moon and Mariadass gave the calculations in *naligai* and *vinadi* for each month.[82] Then he proceeded to mention Mars, Mercury, Jupiter, Venus and Saturn. He then provided the calculations of the longitude of Mars and other planets from 10 April 1786, the *Prabhava* year, and ended by furnishing the details till 14 April 1786.[83] Mariadass gave details of the lunar eclipse of 30 June 1787, and this was followed by details of the next solar eclipse.[84] Mariadass's treatise proves that brahmins were not the only repositories of cultural and intellectual knowledge of Tamil country. The French found other caste men of literate interlocutors and they chose to use their services.

Translation of Tamil Texts into French, 1826-1887

Jean Antoine Dubois (1765-1848) the MEP missionary translated the *Panchathantra Kathai* into French. He also translated the *Paramartha Guru Kathai* into French. The books were printed in Paris in 1826.[85] *Pancha Thantra Kathai* got reprinted in Paris in 1872.[86] Paramartha Guru Kathai also got reprinted in Paris in 1897.[87] Arputham the son of Saveriyakutti Udaiyar in Pondicherry translated the easy lessons and the method of learning Tamil into French and the bilingual book with Tamil text got printed in Pondicherry in 1850 and it had 147 pages. It was based chiefly on the book composed by T. Robertson.[88] Fragments of Thirukural in French translation was done by Edouard Simon Ariel (1818-1854) the French navy officer and it appeared in *Journal Asiatique* published from Paris in 1848 and 1852.[89] Guerrier de Dumast translated Tirukural and it also got printed from Paris in 1854 and 1857.[90] Madurai Kandasamy Pulavar composed *vyavahara–sara-Sanghra* and the book was printed at Madras in 1826 which attracted François Eugene Sice who translated it into French. The book was printed in Pondicherry in 1857 which had 251 pages.[91] Philippe van der Haeghen translated the popular Tamil maxims into French and the bilingual book was printed in Paris in 1858.[92] Louis Jacollist (1837-1890) translated the four parts of the Tamil drama composed by Parasuraman on the *devadasis* and the book was printed from Paris in 1868.[93] *Saakuntala Vilaasam* composed by Ramachandra Kavirayar was translated into French by Gerard Deveze and it appeared in the Journal of Linguistics and Comparative Philology from Paris in 1886-87.[94] Julien Vinson (1842-1926) translated a fragment of the Tamil epic *Seevaka Chintamani* poetry into French and it also appeared in a journal in 1883.[95]

Translating Agasthiyar Vaidhiyam into Danish by Theodor Ludvig Friedrich Folly in 1798

Theodor Ludvig Friedrich Folly was born in 1740 in Itzehoe, a town in the Duchy of Holstein in the northern part of present day Germany. In 1769 he was employed as second surgeon on one of the ships of the Danish Asiatic Company. He also worked in the dispensary of the Royal Frederick's Hospital in Copenhagen. He was employed later as second surgeon in the ships of the Danish Asiatic Company from 1770 to 1775 and he sailed thrice in the voyages conducted from Copenhagen to Tranquebar. In 1777, he was appointed as second surgeon in the military hospital of Tranquebar and he left Copenhagen in 1778 and arrived at Tranquebar in 1779. He worked along with Gottlieb Friedrich Böttger the head surgeon from 1779 to 1786. Folly became the head surgeon in-charge of the military hospital in 1786 and later died in Tranquebar on 30 July 1803.[96]

Theodor Ludvig Friedrich Folly was interested to know the details of siddha medicine and he studied the medical manuscripts through a local assistant. He developed a particular passion to study the medical texts of Agasthiyar. He composed a series of essays in Danish during 1795 and 1801 and these were not printed.[97]

There exists a manuscript now preserved at the rare manuscripts section in Det Kongelige Bibliotek, Kobenhavn.[98] There is also another manuscript at Kirurgisk Akademi, Kobenhavn.[99] Both are entitled in Danish '*Anmærkning Om Mallebar Lægernes Kundskab i Chirurgien, 1798*'. We find here that Folly had translated the process of mercury sublimation from the Agasthiyar's manuscript. He stated the purpose and reason for undertaking his painstaking work of translation; that it would help Danish and German doctors. It is stated that –

> one palam (Tamil ounce of which thirteen makes up one English pound) or the weight of twenty pagodas of singaaram (alum) and two palams or the weight of twenty pagodas of rasam (mercury) must be taken and rubbed together for four saamam (twelve hours) with the juice of pasu manjal (Curcuma domestica), thulasi leaves (Ocimum sanctum), alangi root (Alangium salvifolium) and lemon

> fruit. Then this mass should be poured into a kasi kuppi (glass flask of Benares) and it should be wrapped up with old rags on which the kaliman (literally clay in Tamil but referring here a sort of lime prepared out of small ground gravel stones mixed with jaggery, egg white, sour milk, oil and butter) was to be mixed and rubbed. A stone or a piece of an old clay pot had to be put over the mouth of the flask, and to be wrapped with the rags. The flask should be placed in the sun to dry. Afterwards, a fireplace in the ground was to be dug. A saddi (clay pot) had to be placed over it. Then sand should be put underneath into the fireplace to a height of two fingers width. The flask should be then placed into it, so that it stood upright. Then the flask had to be burnt with a deepam (lamp) at first for four saamams (twelve hours), again with a kamalam (metal plate which was used as an oil lamp with ten wicks) for four saamams and then again with fire wood for four sammams, in total fire should last for one and a half days. Afterwards it should be allowed to cool. Then the flask should be broken, and then rasakarpuram (the mercury) would be found.

According to Folly this mercury was very an excellent drug and used for the treatment of syphilis in siddha medicine. He had also finally stated that what he had translated from the Tamil siddha medical manuscript about the preparation of mercury by the Tamils might not be acceptable to the learned in Europe.

Folly attempted in October 1799 to collect medical manuscripts of Agasthiyar, Bogar, Karuvurar, Konganavar, Sattainathar, Theraiyar, Tirumular, Punnaikisar, and Pulasthiyar, the nine great siddhars. He said that these manuscripts contained the description on the preparation of medicine, the simples and composita. He stated that he was not successful in collecting the manuscripts because they were not then available with physicians whom he had contacted.

Translating Korakkar Siddhar's Kalpasthanam into English by Benjamin Heyne, 1800

Benjamin Heyne was born at Dobra in Germany in 1769. He reached Tranquebar in 1792 as a surgeon to the Moravian Mission and later appointed as a botanist at Samalkota in 1794, became an assistant surgeon in Madras in 1799. He went on leave to Europe from 1812 to 1815. Heyne returned to Madras and continued his medical practice there. He died at Madras in 1819.[100]

Heyne was entrusted with the responsibility of suggesting and prescribing the bazaar medicines that were needed for the supply of army of the English company.[101] This gave Heyne occasion to study siddha medicine in detail. The English Company at Madras welcomed surgeons and physicians to conduct studies and medical investigations and it responded very positively and helped the doctors in their venture. The suggestions given to the company by the European doctors were felt very important for the progress of medical science. Heyne who learnt Tamil was interested in the local vegetation. He engaged seriously in the study of 'Kalpasthanam' a medical text on native drugs.[102] He planned to translate it into English. This medical work by Korakkar Siddhar dealt with general rules of pharmacy. Heyne mentioned that he could not understand the meaning of the author of the manuscript of Kalpasthanam. Further he found the local plant names very difficult to trace.

Heyne in his translation said that the first section of the work discussed vegetable medicines. The second section related to mineral remedies and was less abstrusely written. The third section was wanting in the copy of the manuscript and so Benjamin Heyne did not have an opportunity of perusing it.[103]

Part one of the Kalpasthanam manuscript dealt with climate, weather and nature of different soils, the proper method collecting medicines as prescribed in the *sastras* and the manner of making nectar like medicines of the same. It gave a list of plants most in use as medicines. The parts of the plants listed included tuberous and bulbous roots, bark of large trees, trees possessing a peculiar smell, leaves, flowers, fruits, seeds, acrid and stringent vegetables, milk plants, gums, and resins, also contained types of medicine like decoction, pills, powders, and oils.[104]

Part two was the treatise on medicine, consisting of nine chapters. Chapter one gave advice to physicians. Chapter two dealt with the pulse. Chapter three contained the diagnosis of the three principal disorders. Chapter four mentioned the principal diseases which arose from *vaatham*, *piththam* and *kapam*. Chapter five dealt with the causes of diseases. Chapter seven mentioned the diet. Chapter eight dealt with fevers. Chapter nine gave an account of fever with epilepsy. Chapter ten dealt with prognosis and mentioned the medicine *paspam* of tutanag (zinc), *senduram* of irumbu (iron) and *paspam* of thamira (copper).[105]

Kalpasthanam manuscript dealt in particular with the medicinal value of *Korakkar muli* (opium, *Cannabis sativa*). The text was also concerned with the medicines for fevers, and a few other disorders besides preparation of medicines including *vatacilerpane kunam* (the nature of rattling caused by phlegm), *puta centura navakutori marunthu* (the preparation of medicines by mixing the nine ores through a kind of heating process with metallic oxide), *vaciyam* (subjugating potions), *perumpattukku marunthu* (medicine for menstrual problems), *navamulattirkup parpamum neyyum* (powder and ghee for nine types of piles), the reason for *kirani* (chronic dysentery), its nature and *suranam* (powder), *kunma kutori senduram* (remedies prepared through processing nine ores which help avert indigestion), the ways to prepare medicine from salt, the medicinal value of salt, *cippiyantan sangu parpam* (the powdered medicine made out of chunk lime of the shell), the emission of the acid water from the body, *irata parpatukku amuthamaka suranam* (the method of preparing medicinal powder out of mercury), *tamira parpam* (calcinated white powder of copper), *makaraca pupati senduram* (decoction to cure asthma) and *makatica uppa cayanir* (medicine for the segregation of acids in the cardinal points).

Heyne opined that the native customs were less cultural advanced than the British and considered most Tamil medical practitioners to be quacks. However, he said that medical knowledge of the Tamils was not altogether false. He reported that the medical works of Tamil Hindus were neither to be regarded as miraculous productions of wisdom, nor as repositories of nonsense. Their practical principles on which their medical practice was founded were similar to those of the Europeans. He stated that the theories of the Hindus could be reconciled easily with those of the Europeans, adding that allowances should be made for the ignorance of the Hindus on anatomy. Thus siddha medical knowledge written in English came to be circulated in London.

Translations from Tamil to English by the Protestant Missionaries in Madras, 1798-1844

Benjamin Guy Babington translated Shen-Tamil grammar written in Latin by Beschi into English and returned to England. Vidwan Swaminatha Pillai of Pondicherry prepared the manuscript of Shen-Tamil for publication in 1798.[106] The translation of 'Historia Eclessiastica' in Tamil entitled Thiruchabhaiyin Saithira Posthagam was printed at the press in Tranquebar in 1799.[107] E. Hools, a Wesleyan missionary translated *Vethiyar Ozhukkam* from Tamil to English and he printed it in Madras in 1844. He also translated *Vetha Vizhlakkam* into English.[108] Hools made translation of Beschi's poems and he also published them.[109] Thonnul Vizhlakkam composed by Beschi was printed by a native Christian at Pondicherry.[110]

Rev. Karl Gottlieb Ewald Rhenius came to Madras and he moved to Palayamkottai and preached the gospel and worked in 1820.[111] He felt the need to teach the seminarians and so translated into Tamil the history and geography of the various countries written by European authors.[112] On 23 September 1834 Rhenius completed his work on the English and Tamil Grammar.[113] In 1836, he published the book Grammar of Tamil Language a volume of 300 pages.[114]

Translations from Tamil to English by the Natives and Missionaries in Madras, 1811-1863

Thiruverkadu Subburaya Mudaliar's *Thamizh Vizhlakkam* was translated into English and the book was printed in Madras in 1811. It had 97 pages. This book saw the second edition and it got printed in Madras in 1817.[115] Benjamin Guy Babington translated the *Paramartha Guru Kathai* from Tamil to English and the book got printed in London in 1822.[116] Hudleston Stokes translated 120 stanzas of *Neethineri Vizhlakkam* of Kumara Gurupara Thambiran into English and the book was printed in Madras in 1830 which had 112 pages.[117] *Vethaala Kathai* was translated by B.G. Babington into English and the book got printed in 1831.[118] J. Walker made selections from *Neethineri Vizhlakkam* for translation into English and a book titled *Neethimozhi Thirattu* in bilingual appeared in print in 1841. It had 39 pages.[119] An English version of *Nannul* containing only one chapter and six parts had appeared in print in Madras between 1848 and 1850. The translation was done from Tamil to English by W. Joyes and S. Samuel Pillay and it was revised and corrected by Rev. T. Brotherton.[120]

Henry R. Hoisington translated *Sothi Sasthiram* into English which was translated from Sanskrit into Tamil by Ullamudaiyan. This book titled Oriental Astronomer got printed from Jaffna in 1848. It was bilingual and had two parts respectively with 77 pages and 145 pages.[121] Henry R. Hoisington also translated Tiruvennainallur Meykanda Devar's *Sivagnaana Bhodam* the philosophy of Saiva-siddhantham into English and it appeared in print in Boston in the American Journal of the Oriental Society in 1854.[122] He also translated Seshadri Sivanaar's *Thaththuva Kattalai* into English and it appeared in print in the same Journal in 1854.[123] Umapathi Sivachariyar's *Sivaprakasam* was also translated into English by him and it also appeared in the same journal in 1854.[124] Vira Sami Pillai's Hindu Dharma Sasthiram was translated from Tamil to English by Thomas Lumisden Strange and the book got printed in Madras in 1857. It had 99 pages.[125]

Thomas Foulkes was an outstanding figure for he translated Seshadri Sivanar's *Naanaseevavaatha Kattalai* into English and this book on the elements of Vedantic philosophy got printed in Madras in 1860 and it had 33 pages.[126] Thiruthuraiyur Santhalinga Swami's *Avirotavuntiyar* was translated by Foulkes and the book appeared in print in Madras in 1860 and it had 20 pages.[127] Thattuvaraya Swami's *Sasivarna Bhodam* was also translated by Foulkes into English and the book got printed in Madras in 1862 which had 19 pages.[128] K. Sabapathi Mudaliar's *Saiva Samaya Vizhlakka Vinaa Vidai* was translated into English by Foulkes and the book got printed in Madras in 1863.[129] It had 82 pages. *Sivapragasa Kattalai* was translated by Foulkes and the book was printed in Madras in 1863.[130] Muthu Kumaraswami Mudaliar had translated Ranga Pillai's *Arichandra Vilasam* into English and the book got printed in London in 1863. It had 262 pages.[131]

An Assessment on the Translations Undertaken by the Europeans from Tamil Manuscripts

Manuscripts in Tamil were found in poetry and many of them were in short verses and some were long. The siddha medical texts were composed in *andaadhi yaapu* (anaphora) style. The exact year, month and date when such works were composed or completed by the poets remain unknown. It is not very difficult to find out the probable period based on the language style by examining the texts. Copyists were employed always to make new palm-leaf manuscripts based on the available old manuscripts. The new ones were meant for circulation since printing was unknown to Tamils. The copyists had very neatly furnished their name, year, month, date and day of completion of the work besides sometimes with other related details such as name of the place and the person who possessed the manuscript.

The medical manuscripts in Tamil often contained Sanskrit words that were then in usage. Several colloquial terms such as *arachu* (grind), *kulundu* (cool), *vedichu* (burst) and *vevikka* (boil) were commonly used. Literary forms of expression such as *thaamarai vazhaiyam* (*thandu* or stem), *thengin ennai* (coconut oil) have also been been found in the medical manuscripts. Herbal names in the manuscripts were changed with letters in the beginning such as *kuronidha suram* (*suronidha suram*), *kodisa paalai* (*kudasap paalai*), *singani naadi* (*sangani naad*) and *permati* (*peramutti*). Similarly we also find changes in the alphabets in the middle of words such as *koovazhai* (*koovizhai*) and *maathazhlam* (*maathuzhlam*). We find alphabets too changed at the end like *karikonnai* (*karikonrai*), *thripala* (*tripalai*), *ponnaangkaani* (*ponnaangkanni*) and *milakuraiyan* (*milakaranai*). Sometimes one word itself had changed as another word in the manuscripts like such as *kodi sappani* (*kudasapaalai*), *thiga merukkam* (*thigal erukkam*) and *mudakkotkai* (*mudakottraan*). It is difficult to say with precision whether these were deliberate strategies aimed at rendering the contents secret or to make only accessible to those aware of the code language. Under these circumstances, the Europeans found it extremely difficult to read since they had not acquired such mastery and the necessary linguistic skill to understand the contents of the siddha medical manuscripts; small wonder given the poetic form of most texts. They had employed *dubashis* (linguists) with whose help and assistance it was possible to comprehend the contents and compose prose versions of the texts in French, Danish, German and English. They thereby rendered a very valuable service to the society.

In order to enable the European reader to form some judgment of the merits of the siddha medicine, the missionaries and company surgeons ventured upon translations. In fact they desired a compilation of everything that the Tamils have written on siddha medical science. The Europeans therefore attempted at first a literal translation of siddha works but after many trials they were obliged to give up the task since it was beyond their capacity and power. The next alternative plan made by them was to make extracts but the style of the Tamil authors had rendered it very difficult. What they then wished to present to the reader was a kind of medium between the two plans. In some places they adhered to the Tamil authors of the siddha manuscript very closely, while in some others they had abridged, and had omitted many quotations which appeared to them quite useless to the European reader. The missionaries and company surgeons considered it impossible to make an exact and faithful translation of the siddha works into the European languages like the French, Danish, German and English on account of the complete difference in the genius of writing in the two languages. They found siddha medical manuscripts, as a result of their poetical style abounding in similes, metaphors and all kinds of figures. The Tamil medical texts were of course replete with allusions unintelligible to the Europeans.

It may be said that in Europe, 'The Salerno Regimen of Health' written in the eleventh century and published in 1480 was widely used as the medical text at that time. It also dealt with only the diet and not on medical care and cure. In the Tamil coast there were innumerable number of ayurvedic and siddha medical texts and so the Europeans collected plenty of information on cure of disease and medicine. They converted the same into a body of knowledge generally called the Indian system without neatly making difference between ayurvedic and siddha. In order to make the validity of knowledge fool-proof the Europeans also began to check them through conduct of experiments. Each of them made a selection and study of particular medical text as interested in Tamil medicine.

European doctors on the Tamil coast were at a loss to understand and treat the various diseases in the beginning that were peculiar to local climatic and weather conditions. They made some experiments with herbs but could not obtain the desired results. They also made comparison of diseases in Europe and mixed up things. They finally felt the need to study the Tamil medical treatises so that they could know the secrets of local medicine. On realization of the rich contents in the medical texts they devoted themselves and plunged seriously into the study of Tamil language without which they could do nothing. Thereafter they consulted, tried to purchase a copy of the medical texts. Some Europeans had obtained command over Tamil language while some others took the assistance of *dubashis* who explained the details found mention in the medical texts. The moment when they learnt the secrets and the salient features of the various types of medicine they wrote in their own mother-tongues and communicated the details to Europe. At times they purchased manuscripts and sent them for preservation in the repositories in Europe with a view to store the knowledge for posterity.

Thus the medical knowledge and ideas of Tamils were transferred to the West.

To conclude it may be said, what was available in Tamil language and literature came to be told in several European languages and at that time the translators tried to preserve the juice of the meaning between the two languages. The transfer and communication of ideas between Tamil language and European languages posed and encountered difficulties. Tamil translation of Thirukural, Neethi Venpaa, Ulaga Neethi, Kondari Vendhan, Aathichudi and Moothurai had begun by the Europeans situating the high level of Tamil ethics towards fellow human beings and other creatures. Europeans after acquiring skill in root language and also having the expertise in knowing the tradition of the Tamil language spoken by the people had examined the text at four stages such as word, meaning, idea and expression. Hence we find word to word translations had begun by Ziegenbalg and Beschi in addition to use of foreign words in Tamil, coining new words equivalent and synonyms. No European had come forward to translate the Hindu epics in Tamil for they were Hindu texts and they never attracted them for doing the translation. Beschi only used some selected songs from Silapathikaaram, Bhaaratam, Kambaramayanam and in his own work Thembaavani cited them as examples and he gave the meanings in Latin translation. Babington also made the same translation into English and published. Missionaries were clear in their thinking while making translation. They knew for whom they are addressing and what was the need or purpose for which it is written. They followed three points such as understanding for all and direct, clarity, brevity and short. They began to follow the Tamil tradition.

Religious text like Gnaanopadesam in Tamil came to be translated into Portuguese is important to note. It may be mentioned that we find this first translated text from Tamil to Portuguese by Balthsar da Costa had the links between the translator and the patron, the King of Portugal for whom it was dedicated. Short stories like Paramaartha guru kathai from to Tamil to Latin, Theruntha vaasagam, Arichandran kathai and Panchathanthira kathai from Tamil to Danish and Kavilai vaasagam into English is astonishing to find the enthusiasm shown by the Europeans for circulating Tamil literature across the globe. Moral teachings of Neethi venpaa, Ulaga neethi and Konrai vendhan translated into German by Ziegenbalg, translation of Aathichoodi and Moothurai by Christoph Samuel John into

German, 1791-96 again proves the rich contents of Tamil poetry. Translation of Thirukural into Latin by Beschi (1724-5), into German by Johann Z. Kiernander (1742), into English by Nathaniel Edward Kindersley (1794) and to German by August Friedrich Caemmerer (1799-1803) had been an outstanding exercise in this connection and noted for its significance. Translating medical texts like Agasthiyar Irandaayiram into German by Johann Ernst Grundler in 1712, Agasthiyar Vaidhiyam into Danish by Theodor Ludvig Friedrich Folly in 1798 and Korakkar Siddhar's Kalpasthanam into English by Benjamin Heyne in 1800 are examples of availability of excellent Siddha medical texts. Translation of Vaana sasthiram from Tamil to French by Mariadass Pillai in Pondicherry shows passing on the Tamil astronomical knowledge to Europe. Thus translation growth and development from Tamil encompassed all types of literature. The translation of stories like Paramaartha Guruvin Kathaigal, Arichandran Kathai, Panchathanthira Kathai, Theruntha Vaasagam, and Kavilai Vaasagam besides classics like Thirukural, Aathichoodi, Moothurai, Neethi Venpaa, Ulaga Neethi and Konrai Vendhan became integral to European literature and as timeless masterpieces.

NOTES

1. Jose Wicki, ed., *Tratado do P.e Gonçalo Fernandes Trancoso sobre o Hinduismo, Madure, 1616*, Lisboa, 1973, p. 219.
2. S. Rajamanickam, ed., *Robert de Nobili on Adaptation*, Palayamkottai, 1971, p. 9.
3. S. Rajamanickam, ed., *Punar Janma Atchepam*, Tuticorin, 1963.
4. Bibliothèque Nationale, Paris (hereafter BNP), Rue Richelieu, MSS Indien, Roberto Nobili, Gnaanopadesam, (Catechismus Romanus, 1720), no. 459, fls.1-366; British Library (hereafter BL), London, no. 14170.bb.9, Yagappa Pillai, ed., *Gnaanopadesam*, Second edition, St. Joseph's Printing Press, Madras, 1891; S. Rajamanickam, ed., *Gnaanopadesam*, Tuticorin, vols. I-II, 1966, vol. III, 1968.
5. State Central Library (hereafter SCL), Goa, Gnaanaupadesam: *Thathuvapothaga Swamigal Udayathu, Muthal Kaandam*. Ambalakaadu, 1677. The Portuguese title is *Catechismo Madurense: Escripta em Tamul pelo Padre Robert Nobili S.J. em 1674 e divido em duas partes, Impressoe em Ambalacatta no officina de Ignacio Archamanio em 1677. Gnaanaupadesam: Rendaam Kaandam*, Ambalakaadu, 1677. The Portuguese title is Catechismo Madurensa em lingoa Tamulica, por Pe.

Roberto Nobili da Companhia de Jesus, e 2a parte. The permission and recommendation letter of the Jesuit priest from Travancore was dated in September 1674 and it was printed in Latin in the book. The names of the priests who signed are padre Johannes Philippus Grandi and padre Dominicus de Azevedo, the Jesuit Provincial of the Malabar mission. The members of the Censor Board i.e., the Tribunal de Inquisition of 1675, 1676, 1677 in Goa included the signatories padre Simon Martims of the Jesuit college of Sam Paullo in Goa and Franciscus Delicatus de Mattos of the Tribunal of the holy office in Goa. The two volumes contain xiv+51+200 pages.

6. Academia das Ciencias, Lisboã (hereafter ACL), Serie Vermelha 698, Balthasar da Costa, *Catecismo em que se Explição Todas as Verdades Catholicas Necessaraias para a Salvação com Excellentissima Ordem*, 1661; SCL, Goa, MS no. 6, Pe. Roberto Nobili, *Catecismo em que se explicaõ todas as verdades catholicas em tamul por ... & traduzido pelo Pe. Balthazar da Costa*, 1661.
7. S. Jeyaseela Stephen, *Portuguese in the Tamil Coast: Historical Explorations in Commerce and Culture, 1507-1749*, Pondicherry, 1998, p. 351; See on Baltazar da Costa, Ananya Chakravarti, *The Empire of Apostles: Religion, Accommodation and the Imagination in Modern Brazil and India*, New Delhi, 2018.
8. S. Rajamanickam, Gnaanopadesam, vol. I, pp. 14-5.
9. Madurai Province Jesuit Archives, (hereafter MPJA), Shenbaganur, Archive object 47, Shelve "Nobiliana", Typescripts, Roberto Nobili, *Catecismo em que se explição todas as verdades catholicas necessarias pera a salvação com excelentíssima ordem.*
10. Rajamanickam is incorrect in saying that Nobili's Gnaanopadesa Kandam appeared in print in 1665. S. Rajamanickam, *The First Oriental Scholar*, Palayamkottai, 1972, p. 229.
11. BNP, MSS Indien, no. 460, fls.1-362, Roberto Nobili, *Catechismus Romanus, Tertia Pars*; SCL, Goa, *Gnaanaupadesam: Thathuvapothaga Swamigal Udayathu, Munram Kaandam*, Ambalakkadu, 1678. The Portuguese title is *Catechismus P. Roberti Nobili, Tamulico idiomate scriptus ... Pars Tertia*, Ambalacatta: no officinal de Ignacio Archamonio, 1678. The book contains 336 pages.
12. Bibliothèque Municipale de Chalon-sur-Saone, France, *Gnaanopadesam: Thathuvapothaga Swamigal Udayathu, Naankaam Kaandam*. The Portuguese title is R.P. Roberti Nobili Romani Societate Iesv, *Catechism Romani Qvarta Pars, Ambalacatta, no officinal de Ignacio Arcchamonio*, 1678.
13. A. Sauliere, *His Star in the East* (Revised and reedited by S. Rajamanickam), Anand, 1995, p. 482.

14. Ibid., p. 483.
15. Ibid., p. 482.
16. Benjamin Guy Babington, *The Adventures of the Gooroopararmartan: A Tale in the Tamil Language, Accompanied by a Translation & Vocabulary Together with an Analysis of the First Story*, London, MDCCCXXII. In this edition dots are used over consonants. However, some mistakes are there without making difference between the nedil and kuril (long and short) letters. We find long 'pae' instead of short 'pea' 'paeyarai' on line 6, the last line of the page.
17. Bibliothèque Asiatique Missions Etrangères de Paris (hereafter BAMEP), TAM5, *Aathichuvadi*, Mission Press, Pondicherry, 1844, see, Viramaamunivar Thanthapadi Aaraynthu Suththa Pirathiyakkapatta Paramaratha Guruvin Kathai, pp. 45-84; Archives de la Societe des Missions Etrangères de Paris (hereafter AMEP), Paris, 0627.6, Aathichuvadi, Pondicherry, 1844; *Veeramamunivar Thamzhililum Lathinilum Thanthapadi Aaranynthu Sutha Prathiyakkapatta Paramaarthaguruvin Kathai*, Puducherii, E Typographio Missionariorum Apostolicorum Congregationis Missionum as Exteros, 1845. The book has 41 pages and the book was reprinted in 1851 and 1865. C.J. Beschi, *Paramaartha Guruvin Kathai*, Third edition, Pondicherry, 1904.
18. Ibid., The preface in Latin runs: EXCERPTA E PRAEFATIONE REVERENDI PATRIS J.C. BESCHI; Cum amanuensium ignorantia partim, partim desidia, factum sit ut e pluribus vulgaris Tamulicae linguae libris, ne paginam quidem as orthographiae erroribus immunem reperire possimus, quod sane tyronibus negotium ac damnum parit, non abs re censui typis mandare familaris Tamulici sermonis veluti exemplar. Quo tyrones st dictionum usus et syntaxoes leges sub oculis habere, et minibus tractare possent, et in quo servarentur omnia quae in vulgaris orthographiae legibus vigent. Placuit ad hoc eligere fabulam satisfacetam et in his regionibus celebrem, ut utile dulci commiscendo, fastido satis ac taedio plenum hujus linguae stadium levare, ac hilari illitum fuco concinnare possem, quo animos alliceret simul et oblectaret. Ad faciliorem tyronum usum omnia latine reddidi; sed quantum licuit Tamulicis verbis consonantiam assequi conatus sum.
19. Ibid., pp.1-41.
20. T.P. Meenakshi Sundaram, *History of Tamil Literature*, Madras, 1965, p.175; Aaa. Sivasubramanian, *Sirukathaiku Vitthitavar*, Tuticorin, 1982, p. 12.
21. K. Kailasapathy, *Thamizh Naaval Ilakkiyam*, Madras, 1968, pp.63-4.
22. Det Kongelige Bibliotek (hereafter KB), Kobenhavn, *Collectanea Europaeorum de Lingis et Litteris Indicis*, MSS no. 31; *Codices Orientales*

Biblithecae Regiae Havniensis Jussu et Auspiciis, Regis Daniae Augustissims Christiani Octavi Enumerati et Descripti, Pars Prior Codices Indicos Continens Havnicae, Exofficina Fratrum Berlin, 1846, p. 96.

23. Ibid., MSS no. 33.

24. Ibid., MSS no. 34.

25. Ibid., MSS no. 35.

26. Albertine Gaur, 'Bartholomäus Ziegenbalg's Verzeichnis der Malabarischen Bucher', *Journal of the Royal Asiatic Society of Great Britain and Ireland*, no. 3-4, October, 1967, pp. 63-95, See pp. 84, 88.

27. Bibliothek der Franckesche Stiftungen (hereafter BFSt), Halle, *Kleinere Schriften*, A12; Willem Caland, ed., *Bartholomäus Ziegenbalg's Kleinere Schriften*, Amsterdam, 1930, pp. 1-87. The title runs thus: Nidi Wunpa oder Malabarische Sitten-Lehre, bestehende in sechs und neuenzig Gleichnissen und Lebens Reguln, so da vor mehr als ssieben hundert Jahren von einem Ostijndischen heuyden in Malabarische versen geschrieben aber nunmehro von Wort zu Wort in die hochteutsche Sprache versetzt worden von BARTHOLOMAEUS ZIEGENBALG, seiner königchen Majestaet zu Dennemarck und Norwegen etc. Verordnetem Missionario in Ostijndien unter den Malabarishcen Heijden, Geschrieben in Ostijndien auf der Küst Coromandel zu Tranquebar 1708, den 5 Sept.

28. Ibid., pp. 12-26.

29. Ibid., pp. 26-50, See the text of Neethi venpaa, pp. 54-68.

30. Wilhelm Caland, ed., *Ziegenbalgs Malabarisches Heidenthum: Herausgegeben und mit Indices versehen von W(illem) Caland*, Amsterdam, 1926, p. 25.

31. Albertine Gaur, Bartholomäus Ziegenbalg's Verzeichnis der Malabarischen Bucher, op. cit., pp. 84-5.

32. Archiv der Franckesche Stiftungen (hereafter AFSt), Halle, M 2 B7:8.

33. KB, Oriental Department, Cod Tamul 5, Ulaha Nidi oder Weltliche Gerechtigkeit; AFSt, M 2 B 7:8; The preface runs thus: Dieses gegenwärtige kleine buchlein ist von einem Malabarischen Poeten, der sich Ulaganaden gennent hat, in einer sehr leichten versarth geschrieben worden. Nach aussage der Malabaren sol les über tausend jahr alt seyn. Es faszet in sich sehr feine Moralia und zeigt, welcher gestalt diese heyden auf ein sehr tugendsams leben tringen: jedoch sind alle die darinnen befindlich reguln um bloz aus der matur genommend und gehen lange noch nicht auf ein solch einerlich Christliches leben und heiligen wandel, als sonderlich im Neuen Testemente. Damit aber die Christen wiszen möchten, wie weit gleichwohldie heyden vermöge des natürlichen liehes in denen tugenden gekommen sind, so hab

ich diese Büchlein aus den Malabarischen versen in das teutsche versetzen wollen, in hoffnung dasz es dem geneigten leser nicht miszfallen ware. Ich bin mir aber nichts anders bewust, als dasz ich alle Malabarische worte gantz accuraat in meine muttersprache versetzet habe, ohne dasz ich fast bey einder jedweder regul eine kurtze erklärung gschrieben, so als wie selbige mir von demjenigen Malabarischen poeten ist gesaget worden, den ich dazumal bey mir hatte. Er wird dieses büchlein in den Malabarischen schulen von der jugend auswendig gelernet, aber doch so, dasz es oftmahls nicht einmahl von denen schulmeistern recht verstanden wird, geschwiege denn von den schülern. Dahero, wenn ich dann und wann in ihre schule gekommen und sie aus diesen und anderen büchlein examinieret habe, so haben sie mir das allergeringste nicht antworten können, sagende, dasz es ihnen nicht erkläret würde. Nebst diesen sind annoch sehr viele moralische bücher unter diesen heyden zu finden, davon ich einige gelesen, einige aber noch nicht überkommen habe. Wil der genügte leser hiervon etwas mehres wiszen, so kan ihm meine anjetzo überschickte Bibliotheca Malabarica nebst zwey andern moralischen buchlein, hierzu einige anleitung geben. Wird indeszen der geneigte leser fleiszig vor mich bitten, dasz ich länger in gesundheit mein ambt unter diesen heyden führen kan, so dörffte vielleicht annoch dieses und jenes aus tagelicht kommen, was bishero von diesen heyden aus ihren eigenen büchern noch nicht hat können berichtet warden. Hiermit ergebe ich dem geliebten leser göttlicher gnade und verbleibe allen liebhabern der tugenden zu gebet und liebe verbundener BARTHOLOMAEUS ZIEGENBALG diener des wortes Gottes unter den heyden. Geschrieben in Ostijndien auf der küst Coromandel zu Tranquebar 1708 den 3 Sept.

34. Wilhelm Caland, ed., Bartholomäus Ziegenbalg's Kleinere Schriften, pp. 73-87.

35. AFSt, M1 C29b:106.

36. Willem Caland, ed., Bartholomäus Ziegenbalg's Kleinere Schriften, op. cit., p. 53. The preface to Konrai Vendham runs thus: Ich erinnere mch annoch dasz ich in meiner jugend die heydnischen bücher auf schulen mit sehr groszen verdusz gelesen habe, stets umgehende mit der heiligen schrifft, als darinnen ich auch weit gröszere und höhere weisheit angetrtoffen, als ich in allen heidnischen schrifften, habe auch aus selbigen weit gröszere gelegenheit gehabt die wahre ethica und phisica zu lernen als etwan aus des Senecae oder Aristotelis praecepten hat geschehen können. Daher scheinet es fast wider meinen vorigen eifer zu seyn, dasz ich nunmehro selbsten einige heydnische bücher aus tagelicht bringe, die doch noch niemahls unter den Christen bekant gewesen sind, aber nachdem man biszhero gemenet als wären diese Malabarischen heyden ein recht barbarisches volck und machten so gantz keine reflexion auf die ausübung der tugenden; so hab ich dieses kleine büchlein aus ihrer sprache im teutsche übersetzen wollen, um zu zeigen, wie

diese heyden in ihrem leben oftmahls die allermeisten Christen zu beschämen pflegen. Es wird aber dieses büchlein in den schulen von den kleinen kindedrn auswendig gelernet, welches wenn es geschehen, so haben sie nachmals noch weit höhere lebensreguln zu lernen, bisz sie endlich tüchtig sind in dem reguln der weisheit und der vielfältigen disciplinen unterrichtet zu warden. Ihre poeten geben vor, dasz diese büchlein nebst annoch viel andern, die ich auch in meiner bibliotheca habe, von der göttin der weisheit sol gemachet seyn, die sie Auweiyar nennen. Solches, sagen sie, sey geschehen vor 750 jahren, da diese göttin sic hunter den menschen wegen eines gewiszen verbrechens halben hat aufhalten müszen. Ob man aber schon solch fabelwerck nicht zu glauben hat, so musz man doch gestehen, dasz die reguln in diesem büchlein nicht eben wider die natürlich billigkeit straiten. Daher ich mich auch nicht befürchten darff, dasz diejenigen warden einigen schaden leiden in ihrem Christentum, die selbige lessen möchten, sondern vielmehr zum tugendwandel dadurch aufgemuntert warden, aufdasz dermahleins an jenem gerichtstage die heyden sie nicht beschämen möchten. Hiermit ergeb ich den geneigter leser götliche gnade und verbleibe seyn zu gebet und liebe verbundener AUTOR ZIEGENBALG.

37. *Der Königl. Dänischen Missionarien aus Ost-Indien eingesandter ausführlichen Berichten, Von dem Werck ihrs Ams unter den Heyden, angerichteten Schulen und Gemeinen, ereigneten Hindernissen und schweren Umstanden; Beschaffenheit des Malabarischen Heydenthums, gepflogenen brieflicher Correspondentz und mundlchen Unterredungen mit selbigen heyden* [...], 1710–72 Teil 1–9 [Continuationen 1–108] Waiserihaus, Halle (hereafter HB i.e., Hallesche Berichte), continuation 6, pp. 286-7; Arno Lehmann, *Es begann in Tranquebar: Die Geschichte der ersten evangelischen Kirche in Indien*, Berlin, 1956, pp. 57-8.

38. AFSt, M 2, B:11. The translation of the text runs: The Malabar Doctor which gives a brief account of the heathen principles of medicine; of the manner in which they cure the sick and the medicines they use: Collected and translated for the information of doctors in Europe from the medical books of the Malabarians by J[ohann] E[rnst] G[rundler]. Porayar, 1712.

39. HB, Continuation 7, p. 392; Johann Ernst Grundler und Bartholomaus Ziegenbalg, *Die Malabrische Korrespondenz: Tamilische Briefe an deutsche Missionare Eine Auswahl* (with an introduction and explanations by Kurt Liebau), Thorbecke, Sigmaringen, 1998, see the fifth letter, p. 114.

40. AFSt, MS M 2, B:11.

41. AFSt, MS Catalogue S.120-132; S.133-149.

42. Saraswathi Mahal Library, Thanjavur, Tamil Medical Manuscripts, no. 14; S. Venkata Rajan, ed., *Agathiyar Irrandayiram*, in II parts, Thanjavur, 1980.

43. BL, Oriental and India Office Collection (hereafter OIOC), MSS EUR.C1. The Latin Kural manuscript contains (1) Tamil text (2) A transliteration (3) A Latin translation (4) A word by word explanation (5) Exclusively a further note.
44. V. M. Gnanapragasam, ed., *Veeramamunivar Aruliya Lathin Thirukural Mozhi Peyarppu*, Palayamkottai, 1977; V. M. Gnanapragasam, *Veeramamunivar Thirukural: Lathin Urai*, Karumathur, 1977; V. M. Gnanapragasam, *Thirukural: Veeramanuinvar Lathin Mozhi Peyarppu*, Madurai, 2004.
45. SU. Innasi and S. Soundara Pandiyan, *Thirukural Veeramamunivar Urai*, Madras, 1985, p. 17.
46. K. Meenakshisundaram, *The Contribution of European Scholars to Tamil*, Madras, 1974, pp. 93-4.
47. G.U. Pope, *The Sacred Kural of Tiruvalluva Nayanar*, Oxford, 1886.
48. V. M. Gnanapragasam, 'Some Observations on Beschi's Latin Translation of Thirukural', *Proceedings of the International Conference - Seminar of Tamil Studies*, Madras, 1971, pp. 1531-5.
49. AFSt, M 2, K11:15.
50. Charles C. Prinsept, *Records of Services of the Honourable East India Company's Civil Servants in the Madras Presidency from 1741 to 1858, Compiled and Edited from the Records in the Possession of the Secretary of State for India*, London, 1885.
51. Nathaniel Edward Kindersley, *Specimens of Hindoo literature: Consisting of Translations, from the Tamoul Language, of Some Hindoo Works of Morality and Imagination, with Explanatory Notes: To which are Prefixed Introductory Remarks on the Mythology, Literature, & C. of the Hindoos*, Printed by W. Bulmer and Sold by F. Wingrave, London, 1794, see, Extracts from the Teeroo-vaulaver-kuddul or The Ocean of Wisdom, pp.51-82.
52. HB, vol. I, continuation 14, p. 419.
53. HB, vol. I, continuation 44, p. 489.
54. HB, vol. II, continuation, 7, pp. 885-9.
55. Georg Christian Knapp, et. al., Neuere Geschichte der evangelischen Missions-Anstalten zu Bekehrung der Heiden in Ostindien aus den eigenhändigen Aufsätzen und Briefen der Missionarien erausgegeben (hereafter NHB), Teil 1–8, (Stück 1–95) Waisenhaus, Halle, 1770-8/ 1795-1848, NHB, 42, p. v; NHB 66, St., 527.
56. BL, 14172.c.5, *Arappaal, Kural*, ed. F.W Ellis, Madras, 1816.
57. BL, 14170.e.42, Willem Germann, *Der Kural des Tiruvalluver, Ein Gnomisches Gedicht uner die drei Strebeziele des menschen Ubersetzung und Eklarung von Karl Graul*, 1865.

58. See, *Neues Hannoversches Magazin*, 1, 1791, pp. 1073-1120, 1137-48; AFSt, M 2 B 7:5; NHB 39, St., 263-5; See also, 'Das Sittenbuch Aattiswadi', *Deutsches Magazin* (1) 1791, pp. 161-65.
59. NHB, 39C, St., vi.
60. Albertine Gaur, 'Bartholomäus Ziegenbalg's Verzeichnis der Malabarischen Bucher', *Journal of the Royal Asiatic Society of Great Britain and Ireland*, no. 3-4, October, 1967, pp. 63-95, See pp. 85-6.
61. AFSt, M 2 B 7:6; NHB, 39, St., 267-9.
62. C.S. John, 'Beschreibung und Inhalt eines kleinen heidnischen sittenbuchleins in Tamulischen versen', *Brauschweigisches Magazin*, 3, 1790, pp. 681-702; 'Das Sittenbuch Pottiamalei', *Berlinische Monatsschrift*, 19:1, 1792, pp. 195-200.
63. See, 'Etwas aus Einigen Malabarischen Sittenbuchern, von Welchen Aweiar die Verfaaerin ist', Anhb, IV, 1796, pp. 263-9; BL, 14172.a.40, *Aweiar's Kalwi Orhuckam, Oder Sittenspruche aus Tamulischen palamblatten ubersetzt mit, Bemerkungen uber Indische Gelehrsamkeit, von. J.CC. Rudiger*, Halle, 1791.
64. BL, 14170.e.42, *Ubersetzung und Erklarung Ramanuja Kavirayar Athma Bhodaga Paritchai*, Bibliotheca Tamulica, 1854.
65. BL, 14170.k,72, *Fahrten und Abenteuer Gimpels und Compagnie Ein tamulischen Reise-und Scherzmarchen, Nacherzahlt von Dr. Johannn Georg Theodor Grasse*, mit 6 color irten Bildern, Dresden, 1856.
66. BL, 14172.a.39, *Indische Sinnpflanzen und Blumen, zur Kennezeichnung Indischen Vornehmlich tamulischen, Geistes*, Erlangen, 1865, pp. 37-147. See also, Karl Graul, 'Notizen, Correspondenzen und Vermischtes. Die tamulische Bibliothek der evan. luth. Missionsanstalt zu Leipzig', in *Zeitschrift der Deutschen Morgenländischen Gesellschaft*, H.VII, Leipzig, 1853, pp. 558-568.
67. *Et brev hvilket af de Kongelige Danske Missionarieri det Malabariske sprog er de Malabariske hedninger paa kystem Coromandel bleven tilsendt forst idet tydske sprog af Missionarierne oversat, og, nu fordansket af Rasmus Hansen Attrup*, Tranquebar: Trykt I det Kongel- Danske Missions-Bogtrykherie, 1719.
68. AFSt, M1 C10:44-45; HB, vol. III, continuation 33, p. 931.
69. National Archives of India, Southern Zonal Office, Pondicherry (hereafter NAIP), MSS Acte Tabelliones, Bundle no.1, document no. 1.
70. Ibid., document no.2.
71. Ibid., document no. 10.
72. Ibid., document no. 6, 12, 7, 15, 18, 19, 30, 31, 32, 40, 4 and 34.

73. Ibid., document no. 14, 28 and 29.
74. Ibid., document no. 8, 16, 37 and 41.
75. Jean Bernouilli, ed., *Description Historique et Geographique de l'Inde*, Berlin, 1789, pp. 64-5; Henry Hosten, 'Le Bhagawata- D'après Un Texte Sen Tamoul: Nouvelle Traduction de Maridas Poulle de Pondichéry, 1793-1795', *Revue Historique de L'Inde Française*, vol. XXXVIII, 1921, pp. xxxvii-xxxviii, see, p. xl.
76. Jean Bernouilli, Description historique, op. cit, pp. 65-6.
77. Court de Gerbelin, Compiled., *Le Monde*, Paris, 1773, p. 70; 1777, p.74.
78. Jean Bernouilli, Description Historique, op. cit, p. 64; BL, 279.d.21, Foucher d' Obsonville, ed., *Bagavadam ou Doctrine Divine, Ourage Indien Canonique, sur l'Etre Supreme Tradu., Sanskrit en français par Mariadass Poulle*, Paris, 1788, p. viii.
79. Maridas Poulle, *Memoire Sur L'Astronome en Vigueur Sur la Cote du Coromandel Envoye A.M. de Monneron en 1787 par Maridas Poulle, Interprete du Roi a Pondichery*, L'Impreimerie Royale, Paris, MDCCXC.
80. The nakshatarams include: (1) Ashvini, (2) Bharani, (3) Krittika, (4) Rohini, (5) Mriga, (6) Ardra, (7) Punarvasu, (8) Pushya, (9) Ashlesha, (10) Magha, (11) Purva phalguni, (12) Uttara phalguni, (13) Hasta, (14) Chitrai, (15) Swati, (16) Vishakha, (17) Anuradha, (18) Jyestha, (19) Mula, (20) Purvashadha, (21) Uttarashadha, (22) Shravana, (23) Dhanistha, (24) Shatataraka, (25) Purva-bhadrapada, (26) Uttara-bhadrapada, and (27) Revati.
81. The years include: (1) Jaya, (2) Manmatha, (3) Durmukha, (4) Hemalambi, (5) Vilambi, (6) Vikari, (7) Sharvari, (8) Plava, (9) Shubhakrit, (10) Shobhana, (11) Krodhi, (12) Vishwavasu, (13) Parabhava, (14) Plavanga, (15) Kilaka, (16) Saumya, (17) Sadharana, (18) Virodhakrit, (19) Paridhavi, (20) Pramadi, (21) Ananda, (22) Rakshasa, (23) Nala, (24) Pingala, (25) Kalayukta, (26) Siddharti, (27) Raudra, (28) Durmati, (29) Dundhubi, (30) Rudhirodgari, (31) Rakstashi, (32) Krodanaa, (33) Kshaya, (34) Prabhava, (35) Vibhava, (36) Shukla, (37) Pramoda, (38) Prajapati, (39) Angira, (40) Shrimukha, (41) Bhava, (42) Yuva, (43) Dhatri, (44) Ishwara, (45) Bahudhanya, (46) Pramathi, (47) Vikrama, (48) Vrisha, (49) Chitrabhanu, (50) Subhanu, (51) Tarana, (52) Parthiva, (53) Vyaya, (54) Sarvajit, (55) Sarvadhari, (56) Virodhi, (57) Vikriti, (58) Khara, (59) Nandana, and (60) Vijaya.
82. Maridas Poulle, Mémoire Sur L'Astronome, pp.65-144.
83. Ibid., pp. 145, 202. The signature of Mariadass Pillai was also finally reported as 'signed' in the book printed.
84. Ibid., p. 268.
85. BL, 14170.k.67, Jean Antoine Dubois, *Le Pantcha-Tantra, ou les cinq ruses*

fables du brahme Vichnou-sarma, Aventures de Paramarta et autres sur les originaux Indies Paris, 1826.

86. BL. 14170.k.68, Jean Antoine Dubois, *Le Pantch-Tantra*, 1872.

87. BL, 12315.h.3, *Aventures du Gourou Paramarta, conte drolatique indien*, Paris, 1897.

88. BL, 14172.h.5, *Leçons faciles de Français et de Tamoul Suivant la method de T. Robertson, Par Arpoudam fils de Saveriakuty Odear, Piranchu Thamizh Bhashiyin Yezhithaana Paadnagal*, Pondicherry, 1850.

89. 'Kural de Tiruvaluver, Fragments Traduits du Tamoul E. Ariel', *Journal Asiatique*, Quatrieme Serie tome XII, pp. 423-433, Paris, 1848, vol. XIX, pp. 381-435, Paris 1852.

90. BL, 14172.b.47, *Tiruvalluvar Maximes Traduites* par P.G. Dumast Paris, 1854; BL.14085.d.4, Guerrier de Dumast (Auguste Propser François) *Fleurs de L'Inde*, Paris, 1857.

91. BL, 14170.g.14, François Eugene Sice, *Legislation Hindoue*, Pondicherry, 1857.

92. BL, 14170.k.73, Philippe van der Haeghen, *Maximes populaires de L'Inde Meridionale*, Paris, 1858.

93. BL, 14170.1.34, Louis Jacollist, *La Devedassi, Bayadere* en quatre parties, Paris, 1868.

94. G. Deveze, 'Saakunthala Vilasam, de la version tamoule', *Revue de Linguistique et de Philology Compare,* tome, XIX, XX, Paris, 1886-1887.

95. Julien Vinson, 'Poeme epique Sindamani' Ecole special de langues orientales vivantes mélanges orientaux, 1883, pp. 547-577.

96. Niklas Thode Jensen, 'The Medical Skills of the Malabar Doctors in Tranquebar, India, as Recorded by Surgeon TLF Folly, 1798', *Medical History*, vol. 49, (4) October 2005, pp. 489-515.

97. KB, Kobenhavn, MSS no. Add 761a; T.L. Folly, *Bemerkungen der von Dr. Roxburgh entdeckten Fieber-Rindse Swietenia febrifuga*, 1792, fls.1-18;

98. KB, MSS no. Add 761e; T.L. Folly, *Nogle Anmaerkninger I Anledning af Doctor Kleins forsog omden veneriske syges helbredelse I ostindien*, Tranquebar, 1798.

99. Kirurgisk Akademi, Kobenhavn, MSS no. Add 333a; S. Jeyaseela Stephen, 'The Circulation of Medical Knowledge through Tamil Manuscripts in Early Modern Paris, Halle, Copenhagen and London', eds., Anna Winterbottom and Facil Tesfaye, *Histories of Medicine and Healing in the Indian Ocean World: The Medieval and Early Modern Period*, New York, 2016, vol. I, pp. 125-150.

100. Natural History Museum, Department of Botany Library, London, MSS Rox, see the letter of Christoph Samuel John written from Tranquebar dated 25 July 1793 to William Roxburgh; See also the letter of Christoph Samuel John and the Moravian Brothers written from Tranquebar to Andrew Ross in August 1793.
101. Tamil Nadu State Archives (hereafter TNSA), Chennai, *Surgeon General's Records* (hereafter SGR), vol.12, fl. 53.
102. Benjamine Heyne, *Tracts: Historical and Statistical on India with Journals of Several Tour through Various Parts of the Peninsula also an Account of Sumatra in a Series of Letters*, London, 1814, p.126.
103. Ibid. It must be stated that Heyne admitted the fact that he was going through a Telugu translation of a Tamil Kalpasthanam manuscript.
104. Ibid., pp. 127-44.
105. Ibid., pp. 149-67.
106. A. Muttusami Pillai "A Brief Sketch of the Life and Writings of Father C. J. Beschi or Viramamuni Translated from Original Tamil with a Portrait" *The Madras Journal of Literature and Science*, Vol. XI, January-June 1840, pp. 250-300, see p. 251.
107. *Tiruschabeiyin Charitra Posthagam,* Tranquebar, 1799.
108. BL, London, no. 14170.c.23, *Vethiyar Ozhukkam* (Instructions to catechists, in twenty chapters with an appendix of eight chapters preceded by a biography of Beschi in English and Tamil), Madras, 1844. This work is abridged and adopted to the use of the Protestant missions. See also, KB, NY KGl.Saml.589C, 'Mission yengira kirigaiinudaya nadathaiyaarai kanbikkira chuvadi'; Albertine Gaur, Bartholomäus Ziegenbalg's Verzeichnis der Malabarischen Bucher, pp. 92-4; A. Muttusami Pillai, A Brief Sketch, p. 258.
109. *Ibid.*, p.291.
110. *Ibid.*, p.267.
111. J. Ferd Fenger, p. 258.
112. J. Rhenius, *Memoir of Rev. CT.E.* Rhenius, London, 1841, p.220.
113. Stephen Neill, *A History of Christian Mission,* Revised by Owen Chadwick. Second Edition, Penguin Books, London, 1986, p. 468.
114. Ibid., p. 561.
115. BL, 14172.f.6, *A Tamil Expositor, Containing a brief account of its idiom by way of question and answer, composed and translated into English by Teroovercaudo Soobroya Modelliar*, Madras, 1811; BL, 14172.f.7, Second edition, Madras, 1817.

116. BL,14170.k.70, Benjamin Guy Babington, *The Adventures of the Goorooparamartan: A Tale in the Tamil Language, Accompanied by a Translation & Vocabulary together with an Analysis of the First Story*, London, MDCCCXXII.
117. BL, 14172.b.1, Hudleston Stokes, *Neethineri Vizhlakkam: Ttranslated into English with Notes*, Madras, 1830.
118. BL, 14003.d.5, *The Vedala Cadai, Translated by B.G. Babington*, 1831.
119. BL, 14170.k.35, J. Walker, *Neethimozhi Thirattu: Selections in Tamil and English*, 1841.
120. BL, 14172.f.10, *Grammatica Tamuliensis: An English Translation of the Nunool by W. Joyes and S. Samuel Pillay, Revised and Corrected by the Rev. T. Brotherton*, VI Parts, Madras, 1848-50.
121. BL, 14170.i.8, *Sothi saathiram, The Oriental Astronomer, Translated into English by Henry R. Hoisington*, Jaffna, 1848.
122. Henry R. Hoisington, 'Sivagnaana Bodham: Instruction in the Knowledge of God: A Metaphysical and Theological Treatise Translated from the Tamil with an Introduction and Notes', *Journal of the American Oriental Society*, vol. IV, Boston, 1854, pp. 31-102.
123. Henry R. Hoisington, 'Thaththuva Kattalai, Law of the Tattuvam, A Synopsis of the Mystical Philosophy of the Hindus Translated from the Tamil with Notes', *Journal of the American Oriental Society*, vol. IV, Boston, 1854, pp. 1-30.
124. Henry R. Hoisington, 'Sivaprakasam: Light of Sivan. A Metaphysical and Theological Treatise Translated from Tamil with Notes', *Journal of the American Oriental Society*, vol. IV, Boston, 1854, pp. 125-244.
125. BL, 14170.g.11. Thomas Lumisden Strange, *Manual of Hindoo Law*, Madras, 1857.
126. BL, 14170.e.36 (1), *Naanaseevavaatha Kattalai, or The Elements of the Controversy Respecting the Plurality of Souls, by Seshadrisiva Desikar, Translated from the Tamil by Thomas Foulkes*, Madras, 1860.
127. BL, 14170.e.36 (2), *Eclectic Vedantism: A Philosophical Poem in Frequent Use Amongst Hindu Women Translated from the Tamil by the Rev. Thomas Foulkes*, Madras, 1860.
128. BL, 14170.e.36 (4), *Sasivarna Potham or the Doctrine of Sasivarna A Vedantic Poem Translated by the Rev. Thomas Foulkes*, Madras, 1862.
129. BL, 14170.e.36 (6), *A Catechism of the Shaiva Religion, Translated by the Rev. Thomas Foulkes,* Madras, 1863.
130. BL, 14170.e.36 (5), *Elements of the Saiva Philosophy Translated by the Rev. Thomas Foulkes,* Madras, 1863.

131. BL, 14170.1.33, *Arichandra, the Martyr of Truth, a Tamil Drama translated into English by Mutu Coomara Swamy Mudeliar*, London, 1863.

6

The Conception, Production and Circulation of the Bible Translation from Latin to Tamil by the Catholic Missionaries, 1554-1857

The Bible contained two parts i.e., the Old Testament and the New Testament and its translation in the Christian Church had played a critical role in the transmission of the Gospel message. The church followed faithfully the command of Jesus Christ given to his Apostles 'Go to all nations to teach the Gospel'. The scripture played a pivotal role from the early history of the church in its missionary activity and evangelization. The four Gospels of the New Testament had been translated into only a few languages of the world by AD. 600. These were Latin and Gothic in the West, and Syriac, Coptic, Armenian, Georgian, Ethiopic, and Sogdian in the East.

The Old Testament in Hebrew had 39 books. The Septuagint translation of the Old Testament (had 46 books including the 15 books called Apocrypha/deuteron-canonical) into Greek laid the groundwork for Bible translation to the vernacular and it was the most important and influential translation of scripture.[1] It came about because the Jewish people were dispersed, and as a result they no longer spoke or read Hebrew. Koine Greek was the language in use at the time and so the legend has it that seventy-two Jewish scholars met at the court Ptolemy for a period of seventy-two days. It allowed Jews outside of Palestine to read the Jewish scriptures in a language in which they were familiar.

The New Testament in Greek had 27 books. This New Testament was remarkable being written in Koine Greek because it was the dialect understood by commoners in the Holy Roman Empire. This along with people evangelizing led to Christianity spreading far and wide by the second century. There was a need for a translation in the Syriac when Christianity began to spread east from Antioch. Syriac became the preferred language for Christians in eastern Syria, Persia, Mesopotamia, and later India, China, and Mongolia.[2]

The four Gospels in Greek were separate books and in the second century the Syrian theologian Tatian had combined the Gospels into one harmonious volume. If the Septuagint was the first influential translation of scripture ever produced, then it must be said that the Latin translation was the second. St. Jerome translated the Bible in Latin in the fourth century. As per the order of the Pope Damascene in AD 402 the Bible got translated was called Vulgate. There were many Latin translations around, but the most popular became known as the 'Vulgate', which means 'the language of the people' and it appeared in AD 405. Its influence was so immense that it was named the official translation of the Roman Catholic Church at the Council of Trent held in 1545-7, 1555 and 1562-3. Pope Sixtus V wrote in the Papal Bull *Aeternus Ille* that the Vulgate was to be received as 'true, lawful, authentic and unquestioned'.[3]

In Europe the people in the Catholic chapels and churches heard portions of the New Testament and the Old Testament read out to the congregation as lessons. The Portuguese missionaries in India too therefore did the same and they brought the Latin Bible and used.[4] The Council of Trent had declined to approve the vernacular translation of the Bible. The Old Testament with 46 books including Deuteron-canonical and the New Testament with 27 books of the Latin Vulgate was the only approved text for the doctrine, preaching and worship by the Catholic Church. There was restriction for translation of the Bible through the orders issued by various Popes like Pope Paul IV (in 1559), Pope Pius IV (in 1564) and Pope Benedict XIV. Thus the Catholic Church had widely prohibited the translation of Bible written in other languages. As a result, the Bishops of Goa and Cochin in India had declined to approve the vernacular translation of the complete Bible. Permission from the Holy inquisition and superiors had to be sought for publication of works composed in Tamil. Missionaries were satisfied in the beginning to keep their knowledge of Christian doctrine and literature within the local Tamil community in palm-leaf manuscripts. Further they felt that there was no necessity of publishing all the Tamil works composed through printing in paper and bound books which were intended for worship and use.

The Early Translation of the Biblical Passages from Latin to Tamil in Portugal and in Tamil Country, 1554-1586

The earliest portion of the Bible translation in Tamil is the Lord's Prayer from the Gospel of St. Mathew (Chapter VI, verses 9-13) found in a book printed titled Cartilha in Lisbon in 1554.[5] However, the script is not Tamil but transliteration in Roman characters. When the Catholic Christian liturgical prose in Tamil developed, the Jesuit missionaries commenced to write the contents of the Holy Bible. They felt this work very important in order to reach out to the Tamil converts with the message of the Holy Gospel. Hence missionaries prepared the translations of the Tamil Bible and circulated in palm-leaf manuscripts as per the Tamil tradition then in vogue. Anrique Anriquez, the Portuguese missionary was the first to start translating some selected portions of the New Testament into Tamil. We find translation of the Gospel of St. Mathew chapter V notably the passages related to the Sermon on the Mount by Jesus which had been found printed towards the end of the book of Thambiran Vanakkam in 1578.[6] It is the earliest Bible translated portion. The text of the book was examined by Dom Matheus de Medina the Bishop of Cochin and by the lords of inquisitors and they approved it for printing and so granted permission. Anriquez thus placed the holy book for the first time in the hands of the common and ordinary people and he wrote in such a style that was understandable to all. Anriquez called Bible in Tamil as *viviliyam* and we find mention of it in his another Tamil book printed on the lives of saints in 1586.[7]

Missionaries had aspired that the new Tamil converts should learn portions of the Bible by-heart and recite it from memory. Anriquez stated in his prologue of the book printed that he translated from Latin the passages of the four Gospels and also from the Acts of the Apostles. He said that he had to limit to himself and choose such printed matter which would be the best and suited to the needs of his new converts. The book of Anriquez had details on several parts of the New Testament such as the birth of Christ, visit of the three kings, purification, incarnation, crucifixion, death, resurrection of Jesus, his ascension, the descent of the Holy Spirit and the final judgement.[8] The missionaries ordered the use of this book and the catechists read out to the public during the divine service on Sundays.

Many words used had been found to be simple transliterations from Portuguese into Tamil in this book such as cruz (Kurusu-Cross), apostolo (apostalar-Apostle) Spiritu Santu (ispiritu santu-Holy Spirit) Iesu (yesu-Jesus) Christao (krisithu-Christian) Propheto (propethu-prophet) Pedro (Pethuru-Peter) Paulo (Pavulu-Paul) Simão (Simavu-Simon) Miguel (Mikkelu-Michael) and Purifição (puripikkasam-Purification).

Jesuits of the Madurai Mission and Translation of Passages of the Bible from Latin to Tamil, 1625-1760

Bible translation in Tamil that began with Anriquez had been subsequently continued by other missionaries. Roberto Nobili, the Jesuit in Madurai began to translate portions of the Bible in Tamil and composed Nithiya Jeevan Sallaapam (Dialogue on Eternal Life) and the prose developed with mixing Sanskrit words besides Portuguese and Latin terms. He prepared the sallaapam (literally dialogue/conversation) in 1625 based on the biblical passages from the Old Testament.[9] Thus he created and developed the basic Tamil Christian vocabulary for communication and the newly coined words were adopted both for worship and explaining the Catholic theology.

Subsequently Manuel Martins (1597-1656) another Jesuit of the Madurai mission composed various works such as Paththu Sallaapam (ten dialogues), Upadesa Sallaapam (catechetical discourse), Siluvaiyin Visesha Sallaapam (special dialogue on the Holy Cross) and Sathya Lakshana Sallaapam (dialogue on truth). Antão Proença (1625-1666) the Jesuit of the same period mentioned that Fr Martins had a good command of Tamil and so he composed the above said works.[10] These manuscripts are preserved in the State Central Library in Goa.[11] Manuel Martins wrote several writings in dialogue form and the sallaapams were based on the New Testament in the same style sheet and format of the question and answer model and it was specially prepared for the use of children. An example of this may be cited from the Gospel of St. Mathew chapter V, verses 23-24 which had been arranged thus:

> **Question**: What has Our Lord taught us we must do when one offers his gift at the altar and there remembers that his brother has something against him?
>
> **Answer**: Our Lord said, leave your gift there before the altar and go. First be reconciled to your brother and then come and offer your gift.

It is gleaned from the above that the content of the Bible is thus retained as an answer while each segment of the verse is re-moulded in the form of question. It is made easy thus by the kids to know what the Bible contained while Bible is being translated. Jesuits in due course of time came to incorporate the large translated parts of the Bible into their big catechisms, story books and devotional literature.

In addition to such things, we also find separate translation of the large portions of the Bible mainly for the use of the elders. In this type, question-answer format again we find interestingly matter related to the Bible. The first question of the sallaapam runs thus: Viviliyam enral yenna? (What is called Bible). Thus the word viviliyam was used to refer to the Catholic Holy Bible in Tamil even during the seventeenth century.

Further, the literal Tamil translation of the Gospel was prepared by the missionaries and it was meant for the readings on Sundays in the church. This translation of the Bible was based on the Latin Vulgate only. Scribes were appointed and employed exclusively for preparing the works on palm-leaf for wider circulation. These popular manuscripts were of the year 1666.[12] Manuscripts titled *Katholikkarin puthiyayerpattu sallaapam* (Catholic New Testament Sallaapam), *Pazahya yerpatin sallaapam* (Old Testament Sallaapam) and *Rajakkalin sallaapam* (Book of Kings sallaapam) prepared in 1666 and 1667 are now available at the Bibliothèque Nationale, Paris.[13] A glance at this Jesuit Tamil Bible translation shows that the words from Greek and Hebrew such as Amen, Allelulia, Pasca, Hosaana which were untranslatable in Tamil came to be retained as such. In addition, we find place names and the units of measurements such as dinarium and thaalanthu too were transliterated in Tamil. The only difference that the Jesuits had come to adopt and follow in translation was that they had very copiously used the words of Sanskrit origin in spoken Tamil. They did this in the course of translation because these terms such as jeevan, visvasam, ratchippu, rappojanam, maamisam, pithaa, puthiran, kaariyam, visesham, appam, jalam, saththuru, abishegam, aaradhani and jepam were widely used.

Jesuits began to make the Bible so Tamilized for we find the change of proper names in the Bible translation. We find replacements such as Pedro (Royappar-Peter), João (Arulappar-John), Paulo (Chinnapar-Paul) and Andrea (Bilavendirar-Andrew). Roman Catholic translations of the Bible thus moved away very slowly from limiting to biblical citations in liturgical, devotional and catechetical materials. Missionaries on a large scale began to undertake the complete translations of the New Testament and Old Testament, but the material was not allowed to be freely circulated to the Tamil public.

With the wide use of paper and ink, the Catholic missionaries on the Tamil Coast began to write the Bible translations in paper that was imported from Europe. As they were unfamiliar with the method of writing on palm-leaf, they did so. The translations from the Holy Bible was thought fit to be disseminated and the Jesuits came to recast the translated texts in a form of sermons as preached by them. These texts were given for spiritual reading under the relevant Biblical chapter headings for the express purpose of developing knowledge. The Jesuits thought this would help the elite and educated converts to understand the Bible very much.

Eventually, the New Testament on the whole which got translated was put for use in the Church. In one manuscript we find mention of the Holy Bible finished copying and the writing completed in paper on 22 May 1702 (on 8 vaikasi, *atchishsta viviliya posthagam yezhuthi mudinthathu*). The work was executed by a Tamil scribe namely Gnaanapragasan who was well trained in the art.[14] The manuscript begins at page two with invocation *Yesu Mari* (Jesus and Mary) and ends at fl. 210v. It has been written on both sides but pagination is done only on one side. The Jesuits in Pondicherry had sent this manuscript to France for posterity. Since road communications had well developed to Europe, this particular Bible manuscript was sent from Pondicherry to Paris via Constantinople.[15]

A further significant development of the portion of the Bible translation into Tamil poetry (verse) had emerged and this work was well executed by Constanzo Giuseppe Beschi the Jesuit. He had remarkably carried out this task and we find a total of 152 references cited in his Christian Tamil epic of Thembaavani in 1726.[16] It included details from the Gospels of St. Mathew, Mark, Luke and John, Letter of St. Paul to the Corinthians and the book of Revelation from the New Testament. Beschi had introduced mainly the Bible stories and events mentioned in the book of Genesis, Exodus, Numbers, Joshua, Judges, Samuel I, Samuel II, Kings I, Proverbs, Isaiah, Ezekiel, Daniel, Jonah, Macabi and Tobias from the Old Testament.[17]

The Gospels translated by the Catholic missionaries in Tamil were keenly noticed by the Protestant missionaries of Tranquebar. According to them six palm-leaf manuscripts had been then very popular which they could have access.[18]

1. Pazhaya yerpaatin vetha pusthakangkal: Korvaipaduthi uththamamaay visthaarikka pattathu (The books of the Old Testament: Arranged in an orderly manner)
2. Mattheu suvisesham: Thekkidathi-Bhaashai (The Gospel of St. Mathew: Translated in the southern language)
3. Lucas suvisesham (The Gospel of St. Luke)
4. Iovanne-suvisesham (The Gospel of St. John)
5. Aposthalarkaludaya nadapaddikaigal (The Acts of the Apostles)
6. Thirunaalkazhliley vasikkappadugira suviseshangalum nirubangalum. (The Gospels and epistles for reading on the feast days).

Bible translations of Tamil locally prepared in palm-leaf manuscripts were regularly sent in the ships that sailed from Pondicherry to France in 1739 and 1750.[19] Since Catholics had no Tamil printing press to print the Bible, the biblical passages translated and the writings known as sallaapams were sent to France for preserving in the repositories. While some of the manuscripts were on the New Testament and the others included Old and the New Testament.[20]

An examination of the Gospel of St. John in Tamil (*Yovaan yezhuthivaitha suvisesha aagaamam*) prepared in 1760 shows that there was a short introduction to each chapter. The titles were well assigned to the principal divisions. The chapter and verse numberings are also given in the translation. It is important to note that this Gospel had been translated by a French missionary, for we notice French words and phrases written under the most common Tamil verbs besides important theological terms. The translation is an improved version and made particularly in literary (High) Tamil and much better than the one that had been found in palm-leaf in colloquial (Low) Tamil.[21] This manuscript was sent from Pondicherry to France.

Jácome Gonçalves in Sri Lanka and his Chronicle of the History of the Old Testament in Tamil, 1725

Jácome Gonçalves the Catholic missionary of the religious order of the Oratorians of Goa wrote the chronicle of the history of the Bible. He translated several passages of the Old Testament from Latin into Tamil in 1725. It was titled 'Deva Arul Vetha Puranam'. The manuscript begins with the term 'sarvesaraya nama' (Praise be the name of the Lord). It is mentioned in folio 1 and 1v that that this Old Testament of the Bible Tamil translation was originally written in AD 1725 in two volumes (vol. I, 282 folios; vol. II, 175 folios). It has been also added that this Deva Arul Vetha Puranam was composed in Singala language by the same Jácome Gonçalves. This copy of the Tamil Bible was made in AD 1734 based on the original composed by him (the sanayasi of the order of the Holy Cross and the superior of the society in Langai (Sri Lanka) who was called in Tamil Sangopanganatha swami).[22]

Though the Tamil title Deva Arul Vetha Puranam was assigned, Jácome Gonçalves referred to this Old Testament in Tamil also as Purandima Kaandam (A Paraphrase of the Old Testament). It was also called by him as Purva Vetham. He mentioned that this book contained whatever happened from the creation of the world to the times of Christ. He said that the Old Testament was written in Hebrew and one or two sections were written in Aramaic language which was related to Hebrew. The period of the composition of these works were assigned between sixth-seventh centuries BC to 150 BC. It has been said that the text of Old Testament was written in prose and poetry. Gonçalves said that it contained prophecy, instructions, law, history and morals. Largely the subject matter had been slavery life, joint tribal society, pastoral life and settled agricultural life of one of the Semitic groups who became slaves under Egyptians, and later had a state for Palestine region and David and Solomon became the kings as political powers.

Jácome Gonçalves stated that there were seven yugams.[23] He explained them in the preface such as –

(a) anaathi yugam, Age of Adam, 3 chapters
(b) aathi yugam, Age of Noah nine chapters
(c) irandaam yugam, Age of Abraham, three chapters
(d) munraam yugam, Age of Moses three chapters
(e) nangaam yugam Age of Solomon, six chapters
(f) Aiynthaam yugam, Age of Holy Prophets, chapter 1, chapter 2, 2.1, 2.2, chapter 3, 3.1, 3.2, chapter 4, 4.1. 4.2, and
(g) Arraam yugam, Age of Christ, chapter 6, 6.1, 6.2, 6.3, 6.4.

He narrated the events of the Old Testament of the Bible under the Tamil title Deva Vetha Puraanathina Vivegam.

Jácome Gonçalves and his Chronicle of the History of the New Testament in Tamil, 1725

Jácome Gonçalves also wrote on 'The Chronicle of the History of the Bible' of the New Testament in Tamil and called it Pachima Kaandam.[24] He records in the preface the happenings of this yugam with the birth of Jesus Christ, his teachings, miracles, passion, death and resurrection and the following arrangements are given in the New Testament.

Chapter one	– 1, 2, 3
Chapter two	– 1, 2, 3, 4, 5, 6, 7, 8
Chapter three	– 1, 2, 3
Chapter four	– 1, 2, 3, 4, 5, 6, 7
Chapter five	– 1, 2, 3, 4
Chapter six	– 1, 2, 3
Chapter seven	– 1, 2, 3
Chapter eight	– 1, 2, 3, 4, 5, 6
Chapter nine	– 1, 2, 3
Chapter ten	– 1, 2, 3, 4, 5, 6
Chapter eleven	– 1, 2, 3, 4, 5
Chapter twelve	– 1, 2
Chapter thirteen	– 1, 2, 3, 4, 5, 6
Chapter fourteen	–1, 2, 3, 4
Iruthi athigaaram (Final chapter)	– 1, 2, 3

It is gleaned from the manuscript that the New Testament finally ends with the word 'Amen'. Jácome Gonçalves understood well that a large number of people though were very eager to read the Bible they could not get the facility and heard regularly only in the Church when read out by the Tamil catechist. Hence he planned to prepare some sort of a guide or booklet like the daily bread, for those who wished to know the contents of the Bible. As there was no history available of the Bible, its origin, its composition, its authors when and where the various books were written, what evidences were there and about their authenticity Gonçalves had decided and prepared the work in Tamil.

The Dictionary of Biblical Words in Tamil by Jácome Gonçalves, 1731

Jácome Gonçalves felt the need for compilation of the biblical terms used by him in the translation of the New Testament and Old Testament in Tamil titled Deva Arul Vetha Puranam. He finished the dictionary work in 1731 and it is titled in Tamil Suvisehsa vaakiya suluba agaraathi. There is a title page in Portuguese mentioning it as, '*Diccionario breve de Palavars selectas e difficeis da chronica e Evangelho*, (A glossary of the rare and difficult words for the better understanding of the Gospel). The manuscript is preserved at the Biblioteca da Ajuda and also at the Arquivo Historico Ultramarino, Lisboã, Portugal.[25]

The Suvisesha Suluba Agaraathi was prepared to help those who wished to read Purandima kaandam (Old Testament) and Pachima kaandam (New Testament) when they encounter the difficult Tamil words (latchana sollu). The meanings are given in the dictionary so as to help the reader easily. The words are arranged in the dictionary beginning with the alphabet A with the word 'Agosaamaa' and ends with the alphabet ve with the word 'Vaibhoga sugiya'.

Suvisesha Viruththi Urai: A Book of Gospel Reading for Sundays and Feast days Translated from Latin to Tamil by Jácome Gonçalves, 1732

Jácome Gonçalves was struck in his mind with the idea that the Holy Scripture, a book of large size, if placed with the Tamil Christian reader, would render great difficulty. Hence he planned to compose smaller texts in the exceedingly rich and edifying contents of the Bible. He felt that it would give great comfort to the readers to move spiritually fast and firm. This conviction had earlier gained ground among the Catholic missionaries in Tamil country too. Hence the most important work of the Bible passages translation though completed in full for the use of the native Christians, extracts from the New Testament, were given in expanded and commentary form and these were made popular. Therefore he composed the work called Suvisesha Viruththi Urai.

Jácome Gonçalves had also prepared the gospel readings from St. Mathew, Mark, Luke and John to be read during the Sundays of the year and feast days of the year particularly as special spiritual readings and

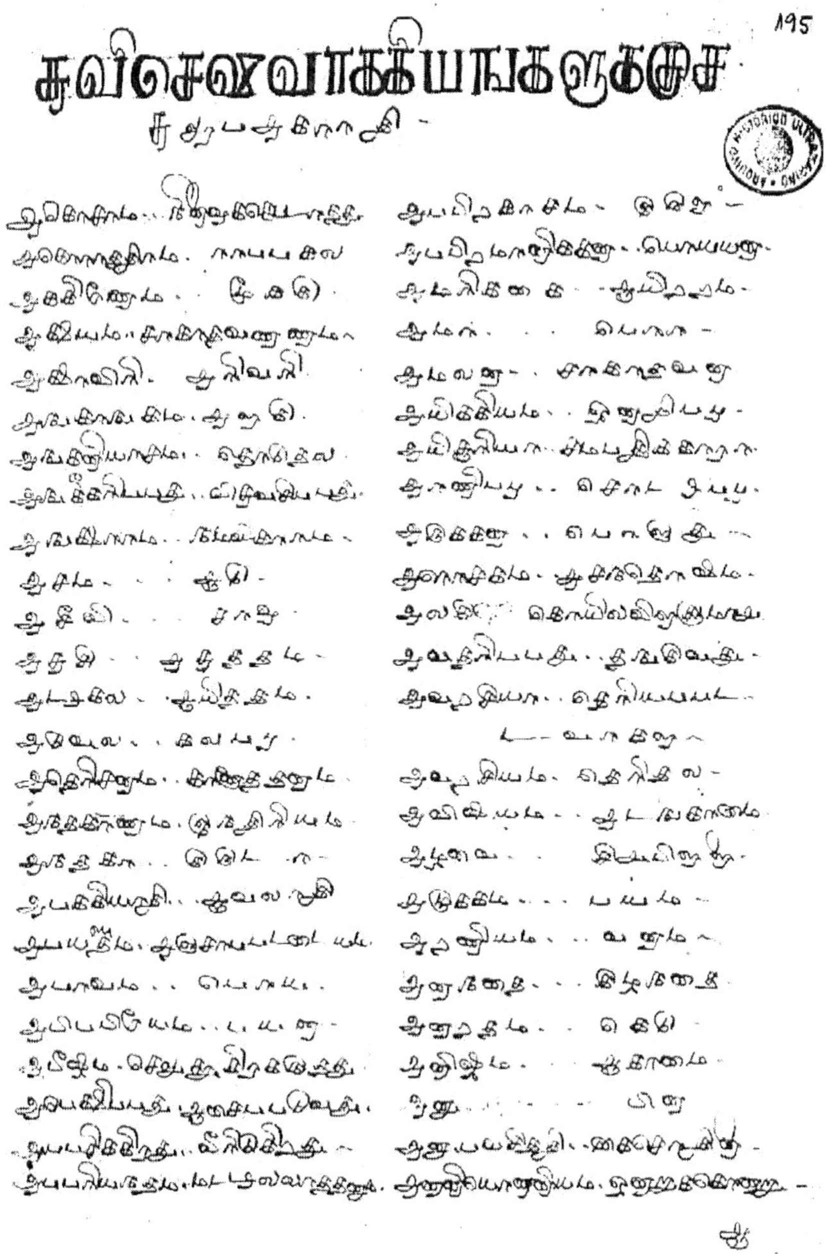

6.1: Suvisesha Vaakiya Suluba Agaraathi of Jacome Goncalves (Courtesy: Arquivo Historico Ultramarino, Lisboã, Portugal)

these had been very meaningfully provided. The Suvisesha Viruththi Urai (Gospel text expanded) was completed and the Tamil year Bhaadvaiya is mentioned in the manuscript. It corresponds to the Christian year 1732.

It may be said that words of new compounds such as Suvisesham (su-god and visesham-new) rendering the Greek meaning had been used to refer the Gospel. These are used as substituting terms with inappropriate synonyms for the sake of change from the Hindus and usage. However there were no arguments on them but terms came to be widely coined newly and introduced in Bible translation.

The manuscript of the Gospel readings begins with a sentence '*Suvisesha viruthi urai vasikiravargalukku vivekam*', (Those who read the Holy Scripture would become wise).[26] The Gospel readings begin with *agama kaalathin muthal Gnaanyiru* (The first Sunday of Advent) – St. Mathew Chapter I.

There is a preface wherein it is mentioned that reading of the Gospel for all the four seasons of the Church calendar had been included in this book for the year 1732. The Christian calendar is given and we find it in the preface.[27] Jácome Gonçalves mentioned in the preface that in the Gospel glossary, he had explained separately the difficult words of the Bible and it is appended to this work. The Gospel readings in Suvisesha Viruththi Urai begin for the season of Advent corresponding to the month of Margazhi in Tamil (December).

1 First Sunday Advent	- Mathew chapter I
2 Second Sunday Advent	- John chapter I
3 Third Sunday Advent	- Luke chapter III
4 First Sunday after Christmas	- Luke chapter II
5 Second Sunday after Christmas	- John chapter II
6 Third Sunday after Christmas	- Mathew chapter VIII
7 Fourth Sunday after Christmas	- Mathew chapter VIII
8 Fifth Sunday after Christmas	- Mathew chapter XIII
9 Sixth Sunday after Christmas	- Mathew chapter XIII
10 Seventh Sunday after Christmas	- Mathew chapter XX
11 Eighth Sunday after Christmas	- Luke chapter VIII
12 Ninth Sunday after Christmas	- Mathew chapter VI

13 Lent first Sunday	- Mathew chapter IV
14 Lent second Sunday	- Mathew chapter XIV
15 Lent third Sunday	- Luke chapter XI
16 Lent fourth Sunday	- John chapter VI
17 Lent fifth Sunday	- John chapter VIII
18 Lent sixth Sunday	- Mathew chapter XXI
19 Holy Week	- John chapter XIII
20 First Sunday after Easter	- John chapter XX
21 Second Sunday after Easter	- John chapter II
22 Third Sunday after Easter	- John chapter XI
23 Fourth Sunday after Easter	- John chapter XII
24 Fifth Sunday after Easter	- John chapter XI
25 First Sunday after Pentecost	- John chapter XV
26 Second Sunday after Pentecost	- Luke chapter XVII
27 Third Sunday after Pentecost	- Luke chapter XV
28 Fourth Sunday after Pentecost	- Luke chapter V
29 Fifth Sunday after Pentecost	- Mathew chapter V
30 Sixth Sunday after Pentecost	- Mathew chapter VIII
31 Seventh Sunday after Pentecost	- Mathew chapter VII
32 Eighth Sunday after Pentecost	- Luke chapter XI
33 Ninth Sunday after Pentecost	- Luke chapter XIX
34 Tenth Sunday after Pentecost	- Luke chapter XVIII
35 Eleventh Sunday after Pentecost	- Mark chapter XVII
36 Twelfth Sunday after Pentecost	- Luke chapter X
37 Thirteenth Sunday after Pentecost	- Luke chapter XVII
38 Fourteenth Sunday after Pentecost	- Mathew chapter VI
39 Fifteenth Sunday after Pentecost	- Luke chapter VII
40 Sixteenth Sunday after Pentecost	- Luke chapter XIV
41 Seventeenth Sunday after Pentecost	- Mathew chapter XXII
42 Eighteenth Sunday after Pentecost	- Mathew chapter IX
43 Nineteenth Sunday after Pentecost	- Mathew chapter XXII
44 Twentieth Sunday after Pentecost	- John chapter IV

45 Twenty first Sunday after Pentecost - Mathew chapter VIII
46 Twenty second Sunday after Pentecost - Mathew chapter XXII
47 Twenty third Sunday after Pentecost - Mathew chapter IX
48 Twenty fourth Sunday after Pentecost - Mathew chapter XXIV
49 Twenty fifth Sunday after Pentecost - Mathew chapter IV
50 Twenty sixth Sunday after Pentecost - Mathew chapter VII
51 Twenty seventh Sunday after Pentecost - John chapter XX
52 Twenty eighth Sunday after Pentecost - Mathew chapter XXIII

Thus readings of the Gospel included for 52 Sundays of a year and the readings had been well arranged accordingly. It may be mentioned that the Protestants in Tranquebar had also followed a similar liturgical calendar that began with the readings of the first Sunday of the advent season till next 25 Sundays and then we find the readings for the Sundays ending with the reading for the 27th Sunday after Holy Trinity thus making the gospel readings in total with 52 Sundays.

Further, the dates of the Catholic feasts were also given commencing from the Tamil month of Thai (January) -2 days, Masi 3 days, Panguni 2, Vaigasi 2, Aani 3, Aadi 2, Aavani 3, Puratassi 4, Aypasi 1, Karthigai 3 and Margazhi 7. The Gospel readings for the feasts are given separately such as Christmas day, Circumcision of Jesus Christ, Epiphany, The holy family in Jerusalem, the feast of the Holy Ghost, Holy Trinity, All Souls day (Motcha vaanavaraudyada utsavathiley vassikira suvisesha viruththi urai (scripture reading for the All Souls day), and the feast of the St. Andrew.[28] Then we find the Tamil calendar of the years containing sixty commencing from the year Pirabhava (1747) to the year Kishaya (1806).[29]

The fragrance of translations of the Bible from Latin to Tamil by the Catholic missionaries on the Tamil Coast and Sri Lanka have been known to us and the Tamil prose style had been in a different form than the one what existed prior to that time. The scent of the scriptures with several newly coined words for translation in Tamil therefore though interesting it had directed the development of pre-modern Tamil to modern Tamil. A serious question raised and a new challenge posed at that time was that whether the spoken Tamil should be adopted for translation or the literary Tamil style should be followed. However, there was no comprise and also no final solution could be reached in this regard since it was an ongoing process.

The New Testament Translation by Louis Marie Mousset and Arul in Pondicherry, 1844-56

Bible translation and printing in Tamil continued at a rapid speed by the Protestant missionaries in Tranquebar during the seventeenth and eighteenth centuries. This greatly worried the MEP missionaries who reached Pondicherry for apostolic work at the beginning of the nineteenth century. They were at once surprised to find that Tamil Catholics were reading the Bible printed by the Protestant missionaries since it was supplied free of cost. The first synod that held in Pondicherry between 18 January 1844 and 13 February 1844 discussed the matter as to which books should be used by the Catholic converts and which books must be assigned priority for printing in the first place. Incidentally it was also noted that would it not be good to translate some parts of the Holy Scripture in order to print them and which parts and in what style.[30] It was finally decided at the meeting, that the Gnaanopadesa kaandam of Roberto Nobili, the abridged edition of the Old Testament titled Purandima Kaandam and the New Testament titled the Patchima Kaandam composed by Jácome Gonçalves should be the three books to be propagated in Tamil country for the use of the Catholic Christians. The New Testament was felt to be newly translated into Tamil with notes. The members present in the synod unanimously opined that the New Testament should be prepared with a new translation. It should be one that should be highly edifying which the Christians would draw great inspiration and it was necessary to prevent them from going in search of the Word of God published by the Protestants in Tamil. They felt that the Bible translations of the Lutherans were always dangerous for the faith and unfortunately they were faulty, too difficult to comprehend and with a lot of differences from various printed ones from Tranquebar, Madras and Colombo. Hence the new Catholic translation of the New Testament proposed by the MEP missionaries in Pondicherry would certainly help and make the Catholic readers written for the defense of religion against heresy and become more popular and interesting. Since the complete translation work demanded a lot of work it had been declared that a priest who had good command over Tamil should be exclusively appointed and another second priest a Tamil should also be associated with the work of translation of the Holy Gospel.[31]

Fr Louis Marie Mousset (1808-1888) who knew Tamil very well was asked by Clement Bonnand (1796-1861) the Bishop of Pondicherry in 1845 to engage himself in the work.[32] Further, Fr Arul a Tamil priest ordained was also later appointed to assist and both were jointly entrusted with the work of translation.[33] They took all efforts and completed the translation of the four Gospels and the Acts of the Apostles. Fr Louis Savinien Dupuis who was the manager of the Catholic printing press was asked to oversee the work as he also had command over Tamil language. The New Testament finally saw the light of printing in Pondicherry in 1857.[34]

Louis Savinien Dupuis and Printing the First Catholic Tamil Bible at the Printing Press in Pondicherry, 1857

L.S. Dupuis in his letter dated 10 November 1856 to Jean Tesson the procurator of the missions for India in Paris mentioned that the translation of the four Gospels and the Acts of the Apostles had been completed and 3000 copies of the book would be printed. He said that this printing would soon begin and so he requested the required quantity of paper to be sent from France.[35] Dupuis in his letter of 22 December 1856 said to Tesson that he had earlier asked for the supply of 200 reams of paper which he placed an order vide his earlier letter. He stated not to forget to supply additional 200 more reams of paper which he needed at present. He categorically stated that this quantity of the supply of paper was immediately needed because the first Catholic Tamil Bible (New Testament) was going to be printed in 1857. Dupuis had also in this connection had asked for 100 glued papers. He said thanks to God, that the printing press in Pondicherry was flourishing.[36]

On arrival of the paper L.S. Dupuis began the work and the New Testament printed had the Tamil title page and it runs thus: '*Sesu kristhu Naatharudaya Parisuththa suvisesham: Ithu Anniya desaththu Pothagar sabaiyilulla Apostholikku Gurukkallil silaraal Mozhipeyarkapattu puthuvaiyil yezhuntharuliirukkum Mahaa Ganam Poruthiya Aandavrragiya Clemensu Bonnand Drusipare yennum Naamatheyamkonduirukkira mettraaniyaar anumathiyil Romapuriinnitru vantha uththaarathinpadiye 1857 am varusham Puthuvaiyir senmaraakini maatha koilaiserntha achchukudathir pathippikapattathu*'.

சேசுகிறீஸ்துநாதருடைய

பரிசுத்த

சுவிசேஷம்.

இஃது

அந்நியதேசத்துப்போதகர்சபையிலுள்ள
அப்போஸ்தொலிக்குக் குருக்களிற்
சிலரால்
மொழிபெயர்க்கப்பட்டுப்
புதுவையிலெழுந்தருளியிருக்கும்
மகாகனம் பொருந்திய ஆண்டவராகிய
கிளேமென்சு பொனாந்
துரிசிப்பாரென்னும
நாமதேயங்கொண்டிருக்கிற
மேற்றிராணியாரவர்களநுமதியின்
உரோமாபுரியினின்றுவந்த உத்தாரத்தின்
படியே

௲அ௱௫௰எ-௵
புதுவையிற் சன்மவிராக்கினிமாதாகோயிலைச்சேர்ந்த
அச்சுக்கூடத்திற் பதிப்பிக்கப்பட்டது.

6.2: The title page of the First Catholic New Testament printed in Pondicherry in 1857 (Courtesy: Bibliothèque Asiatique Missions Etrangères de Paris)

புதுவையி லெழுந்தருளியிருக்கும் மகாகனம்
பொருந்திய ஆண்டவராகிய இளெமேன் கபொனு
ந் துரிசிப்பாரொன்னும் மேற்றிராணியாரவர்க
ள் தமது விசாரணைக்குட்பட்டிருக்கிற சகலகிறீஸ
துவர்களுக்கும் ஆசீர்வாதங்கொடுத் தறிவிக்கிற
தாவது:

விசுவாசப்பிரமாணிக்கமுள்ள அப்போஸ்தொ
லிக்குக்குருக்களிற் சிலரால் நாலுசுவிசேஷங்களு
ம் அப்போஸ்தலர்களுடைய நடபடிகளுந் தமிழ்
ப்பாஷையிற் சுமுத்திரையாய் மொழிபெயர்க்கப்
பட்டதென்று நிச்சயித்துக்கொண்டு இவற்றின்
மொழிபெயர்ப்பையேற்றுக்கொண்டோம். இதனை
த்தக்கப்பத்தி விசுவாசத்தோடே வாசிப்பவர்கள் உ
லகவிரட்சகராகிய சேசுகிறீஸ்துநாதருடைய திவ்
வியபோதனைகளையுஞ் சுகிர்தமாதிரிகைகளையுங்கற்
றுக்கொண்டநுசரிப்பதினால் மிகுந்த ஞானப
லனை யடைவார்களென்று நம்பி யிதனை நமதச்சு
க்கூடத்திற்பதிப்பித்து வெளிப்படுத்தவுத்தரவுத
ந்தோம்.

புதுவையில் ௲அ௱௫௰௭ம் ௵ மேமீ -உ௫உ

† CL. EV. DE DRUSIPARE

V. A.

6.3: The message of the Bishop of Pondicherry in the First Catholic New Testament printed in Pondicherry (Courtesy: Bibliothèque Asiatique Missions Etrangères de Paris)

There is a foreword to the New Testament by Bishop Clement Bonnand dated 25 May 1857.[37] It states that the bishop thereby had extended his blessings to all the faithful in his jurisdiction and informed that the four Gospels and the Acts of the Apostles had been very well translated by some MEP priests into Tamil and he affirmed that it had been accepted. The Bishop believed that those who follow Jesus Christ and lead lives of good example and follow the teachings of Lord Jesus Christ would benefit much spiritual benefit through reading it with devotion and faith. Hence the book had been permitted to be printed at the printing press and the Bishop accorded permission for the same.

In the New Testament we find also an introduction of 13 pages by those who translated the Bible into Tamil.[38] The introduction mentions what is bible and says the meaning of it as 'Good News'. Hence the Tamil term 'suvisesham' is used in the book has been stated.[39] Then the translators mentioned that the Catholic Church had preserved the four Gospels which contain four parts but the subject matter had been one and the same being contained in a single treatise.

The biography of St. Mathew is next given and it stated the biblical scholars had mentioned that St. Mathew wrote the Gospel in Hebrew and it was translated into Greek during his life-time. Originals of the Gospel and the copies were also believed to exist till that date. The biography of St. Mark is next provided. It had been stated that some scholars opined that St. Mark wrote the Gospel in Latin while others ascribed that he wrote in Greek. The biography of St. Luke had been followed and it stated that St. Luke wrote the Gospel in Greek and scholars ascribed that he wrote in AD 15. It further added that St. Luke was a painter and he had painted a picture of the Blessed Virgin Mary the mother of Jesus. The biography of St John had been given and it stated that he wrote the Gospel in Greek. Then the details of the Acts of the Apostles had been given and it stated that the translations were available in Latin, Hebrew and Greek. The translation of the Bible into Latin was called 'Vulgata' which was believed to be good and accepted by the Catholic Church. Bible translations into other languages were accepted by the Bishops of the respective countries and nations.

இத்திருச்சுவிசேஷங்களைத்

தமிழில் மொழிபெயர்த்தவர்களால்

முகவுரை.

சுவிசேஷமென்பது சுபசெய்தி அல்லது நல்லசமாச்சாரமென்றர்த்தமாம். மனிதனாயவதரித்த சுதனாகியசர்வேசுரன் தாம்வாய்மலர்ந்து மனுமக்களுக்குப் பிரசங்கித்த அருள்வேதத்துக்குக்கட்டளையிட்டருளிய சிறந்தபெயரிதுவே. ஆதலாலித்திவ்வியநாதர் பிறந்தஆச்சரியத்துக்குரிய வகையுஞ்செய்துகாட்டிய வுத்தமபுண்ணியமாதிரிகைகளும் பண்ணின அதிசயத்துக்குரிய வற்புதங்களும் போதித்தவேதகற்பனை யுபதேசங்களும் மனிதருண்டாய விரக்ஷணியத்துக்கடைந்த கடின நிர்ப்பந்தமரணமு மறுபடியுயிர்த்தெழுந்தருளிய நிகரற்றவல்லபமகிமையு மனுக்குலமீடேறுவதற்கு விசுவசித்தநுசரிக்க வேண்டியசத்தியசுகிர்த ஒழுக்கமு மிவைமுதலியவிசேஷங்களும் அருள்வேதப்பொருளா யடங்கியவேதாகமங்களுக்கும் இத்திருப்பெயரேயுண்டாயிற்று.

இஸ்பிரீத்துச்சாந்துவினாற் படிப்பித்து நடத்தப்படுகிற திருச்சபையானது அப்போஸ்தலர்களின்கையால் நான்குசுவிசேஷங்களைப் பற்றிக்கொண்டு பாரம்பரியமாயவைகளை யிந்நாள்வரைக்குங் காப்பாற்றிக்கொண்டுவருகின்றது. அவைகள் ஒரேசுவிசேஷப்பொருளடங்கிய நாலுபிரிவுகள் போலேயாம். பரமகர்த்தாவுக்குச் சித்தமானால் அவைகளிலடங்கிய வர்த்தமானமெல்லாம் ஒரு

6.4: The foreword by the Translators of the First Catholic New Testament printed in Pondicherry (Courtesy: Bibliothèque Asiatique Missions Etrangères de Paris)

அர்ச். — மத்தேயுவென்பவர்

எழுதியருளிய

சேசுகிறீஸ்துநாதருடைய

பரிசுத்த

சுவிசேஷம்.

முதல் — அதிகாரம்.

மனுஷாவதாரத்திற் சேசுகிறீஸ்துநாதருக்குண்டான வமிசவரிசையும் அவருற்பவித்துப் பிறப்பதைக்குறித்துச் சம்மனசானவர் சூசையப்பருக்கறிவித்த விசேஷமுமாவன.

க. அபிரகாமின் * குமாரனாகிய தாவீதன்குமாரனான சேசுகிறீஸ்துநாதருடைய சன்மிப்பாகமமாவது.

* க. வேதாகமங்களில்வழங்கிய முறையின்படியே யிவ்வசனத்திற் குமாரனென்பது சந்ததியானென்றர்த்தமாம்.

A க

6.5: The first page from the Gospel of St. Mathew in the First Catholic New Testament printed in Pondicherry (Courtesy: Bibliothèque Asiatique Missions Etrangères de Paris)

The introduction explained the importance of translation too.[40] It stated that biblical languages were different from the rest of the other languages of countries and there existed vast differences between languages. The language difference in style and diction was also well known. The translators stated that the words in translation do not find always matching or equivalent words. The meanings of the text have to be kept in mind in the course of translation. The translators had mentioned that they have noticed the translations of the New Testament from Greek into Tamil by the Protestants and in the opinion of the Catholic missionaries it was found to be erroneous. They also stated that they had used the available Catholic commentaries of the New Testament. The translators have said that they have adopted the bracket symbols for the purpose of readability of the matter and they have used one or two words within the brackets to make sense of the Tamil text.[41] The translators had also said that the remarks and views of the Protestants in Tamil Country had been challenged and seriously called into question through the earlier publications such as *Vetha Vizhlakkam* of Beschi vide chapter 16 and *Vethapuratallai Neekum Sanjivi* of Louis Savinien Dupuis vide part 6, chapter 8. It had been also mentioned that though the verses of the Bible had been serially translated while publishing for the purpose of convenience to the readers in Tamil, three or four verses had been clubbed and put together in this New Testament then printed. It has been mentioned that the translation of the New Testament followed here was the common Tamil style and not in High Tamil of the literary style.

The verses of the New Testament texts were given in Tamil numerals only. Symbols like CROSS had been given for providing notes which would enable the reader to understand well. A summary had been given at the beginning of each chapter in about five or six lines. A comparison of the verses found in the Gospel of St. Mathew with other evangelists had been provided at various places.[42] There are some nice pictures printed in the book such as baptism of Jesus Christ given by John the Baptist (vide p. 13), the last supper (p. 149), Death of Jesus on the cross (p. 167) and carrying the cross by Jesus to Mount Calvary (p. 429). The complete text of the four Gospels ends at page 568 of the book. Then we find the Acts of the Apostles that begin at page 569 and it ends at page 725.

Finally, there is a reading list of the Gospels for all the Sundays and feast days for the whole year vide pages from 726 to 729. The last page at

நடபடிகள். ௭௨௯

௨௯. அவரிவைகளையுஞ்சொன்னபின்பு யூதர்
தங்களுக்குள்ளே மிகுந்த தர்க்கஞ் செய்துகொ
ண்டு அவரைவிட்டுப்போனார்கள்.

௩௰. மேலும் அவர்தமது கொடைக்கூலிவீட்
டில் இரண்டுவருஷமுழுமையும்வசித்தார். தம்மி
டத்திற்பிரவேசித்தயாவரையுமேற்றுக்கொண்டு

௩௧. சம்பூரண தைரியத்தோடே தடையின்றி
ச்சர்வேசுரனுடைய விராச்சியத்தையும்பிரசங்கி
த்துச்சேசுகிறீஸ்துநாதசுவாமிக்கடுத்தவைகளையு
ம் போதித்துக்கொண்டிருந்தார்.

முற்றிற்று.

6.6: The last of the Catholic New Testament printed in Pondicherry (Courtesy: Bibliothèque Asiatique Missions Etrangères de Paris)

730 contains the errata of 9 places only. Thus the book has been printed with reasonable care and attention. The credit goes to L.S. Dupuis for printing and overseeing the publication of the New Testament.

Scholars have so far quoted the Concordance of the Four Gospels prepared by J.B. Trincal, (1815-1891) the Jesuit in Madurai whose work got published from Madras in 1879 and from Pondicherry in 1887.[43] His version of the New Testament prepared with the assistance of brother Michael and got printed from the Catholic press in Pondicherry in 1890 is also made known.[44] Further, the translation of the Old Testament from Latin to Tamil by Hugues Madelain Bottero (1837-1913) published in 1904, 1912 and 1917 is also known.[45] However, there is a curious gap in which the Tamil Christian literary world and the Bible scholars have failed to note and underline the important contribution of Fr Mousset, Fr Arul and Fr Dupuis who were involved in translating and printing the first Catholic New Testament in Tamil from Pondicherry in 1857. A printed pastoral letter/ circular of Clement Bonnand the Bishop of Pondicherry dated 17 December 1844 having 16 pages issued to all the priests and the faithful of the diocese contains quotations from the texts of the Old Testament like Jeremiah I,7; Isaiah I, VIII.1; Ezekiel III, 17-19; Proverb. XXVII,23, and the New Testament of the Bible from Mathew XXVIII, 20; Luke X,16; John XX, 21 and the Acts of the Apostles XX, 28. Hence it is proved that Bible text in Tamil was available in Pondicherry earlier much before printing in 1857 and the same has been used for quoting copiously in 1844.[46] It may be said that the Vulgate version of 1598 was the official Latin Bible of the Catholic Church. Pope Pius XII had decreed through his encyclical 'Divino Afflante Spiritu' dated 30 September 1943 by permitting the translation of the Bible from the original texts. As a result in 1965, 1966 and 1967, the Catholic version of the Gospel of Mathew, Mark, John and Luke translated from Greek into Tamil appeared in print. Thus the scripture translated into Tamil language and history has been an invaluable tool with eternal significance.

NOTES

1. Larry Stone, *The Story of the Bible*, Nashville, 2010, p. 43.
2. Edward L. Smither, *Mission in the Early Church: Themes and Reflections*, Eugene, 2014, p. 93.
3. Francis E. Gigot, *General Introduction to the Study of the Holy Scriptures*, New York, 1900, p. 337.

4. *Sacra Biblia, acri studio, ac diligentia emendata, rerum, atque verborum permultis et perquamdignis indicibus aucta,* Venetiis, apud Iolitos, 1588, 2 volumes, pp. 1-696.
5. Fernando de Almeida, ed., *Cartilha em Tamul e Português: Impresa em 1554*, Ministerio da Edução Nacional, Direção-Geral do Superior do Ensino Superior e da Belas-Artes, Lisboã, 1970, pp. 8-9.
6. Anrique Anriquez, *Thambiran Vanakkam*, Kollam, 1578, ed., S. Rajamanickam, *Vanakkam*, Tuticorin, 1963.
7. Anrique Anriquez, *Flos Sanctorum*, 1586, ed., S. Rajamanickam, *Adiyaar Varalaaru*, Tuticorin, 1967.
8. Biblioteca Apostolica Vaticana (hereafter BAV), Città del Vaticano, VAT Baago 3; Det Kongelige Bibliotek (hereafter KB), Kobenhavn, MSS Orientalske Afdeling 1531.
9. Saraswathi Mahal Library, Thanjavur, MSS Tamil, no. 536, fls.1-88, Nithiya Jeevana Sallapam, 1625; S. Rajamanickam, ed., *Nithiya Jeevana Sallapam*, Tuticorin, 1964.
10. Archivum Romanum Societatis Iesu (hereafter ARSI), MSS Goa, vol. 53, fls.239-58.
11. State Central Library (hereafter SCL), Goa, MS 26, *Sermões para todos os dias do anno*, 3 vols (Sermons for all days in a year in Tamil); MS 27, *Sermões para todos os sabbados e segundas feiras do anno* (Sermons for Sundays and feast days in Tamil).
12. Bibliothèque Nationale, Paris (hereafter BNP), Rue Richelieu, MSS Indien, no. 452, *Dialogues sur Josue, les Juges, Ruth, le premier et le segond des roys*. This manuscript has 268 palm-leaves. The year mentioned is 1666. It deals with Old Testament, and found way to France in 1739.
13. BNP, MSS Indien no. 452 and 454. The manuscripts entitled *Katholikkarin Puthiyayerpattu Sallapam*, (The Catholics New Testament Sallapam) *Ubaagama Sallapam, Onnu Rendu*, (The Uba Aagamam, Part one and two) *Rajakkalin Sallapam*, (The Book of Kings Sallapam) and *Pazahya Yerpatin Sallapam* (The Old Testament Sallapam). The years mentioned are 1666-7.
14. BNP, MSS Indien, no. 453, *Dialogue sur les 3 e et 4 e des roys, paralipomenes, esdras, tobias, esther, judith, job et les machabees*, fls.1-312. The manuscript contains the book of Kings I and II, Chronicles I and II, Ezra, Tobias, Esther, Judith, Job and Mccabe of Old Testament. It was received in Paris in 1750. BNP, MSS Indien, no. 450, fls.1-210.
15. BNP, MSS Indien, no. 457.
16. Paa. Valan Arasu, *Thembaavani Thiran*, Chidambaram, 2012, pp. 249-252.

17. Ibid., pp 164-167.
18. KB, Kobenhavn, NY KGl.Saml.589C; Albertine Gaur, 'Bartholomäus Ziegenbalg's Verzeichnis der Malabarischen Bucher', *Journal of the Royal Asiatic Society of Great Britain and Ireland*, no. 3-4, October, 1967, pp. 63-95, see pp.91-2.
19. BNP, MSS Indien, no. 450, fls.1-210. It contains translation of the Gospels in Tamil. It was sent from Pondicherry to the library of the King of France in 1738.
20. BNP, MSS Indien, no. 456, fls.1-49, *Matheyu Enbavar Yezhuthiviaitha Suviseshagam*. This manuscript is the Gospel of St. Mathew in Tamil and it reached Paris in 1739. BNP, MSS Indien, no. 454, *Dialogues sur le nouveau testament les evangels du dimanche et des principaes fetes de l anne 1750*, fls.1-313, The year 1667 is mentioned. BNP, MSS Indien, no. 451, *Dialogues sur le levitique les numbers et le deutronome*, fls.1-324. This manuscript contains the book of Leviticus, the book of Numbers and Deuteronomy of the Old Testament. The year 1667 is mentioned in the manuscript and it found way to France in 1743.
21. BNP, MSS Indien, no. 450, fls.1-210.
22. Biblioteca da Ajuda (hereafter BA), Lisboã, MSS Codice, 44-XII-38, fls.1-90, see, fl. 1-1v, The Old Testament: In Portuguese it is written 'The Chronicle of the History of the Bible'. British Library (hereafter BL), London, no. 141170bbb. 44.1, A. Jose Anna Durai, ed., *Purandima Kaandam: Pazhaya Yerpaatin Sarithiram* (A Paraphrase of the Old Testament) second edition, Madras, 1913. The book has viii+349 pages.
23. BA, Codice 44-XII-38, fls.2-4.
24. Ibid, Codice, 44-XII-38, The New Testament, fls.92-189; BL, no. 14170bbb.44.2, Jacome Goncalves @ Sangopanga Natha Swami, ed., A. Jose Anna Durai, *Pachima Kaandam: Puthiya Yerpattin Sarithiram*, (A Paraphrase of the New Testament), second edition, Madras, 1914. The book contains v+250 pages.
25. BA, 44-XII-38, fls.279-82. This manuscript copy was made in 1734. Arquivo Historico Ultramarino (hereafter AHU), MSS Livro Reservado 375, *Suvisesha Vaakiya Suluba Agaraathi* (with the Portuguese title *Diccionario breve de Palavars selectas e difficeis da chronica e Evangelho*) fls.195-9. This manuscript copy was made in 1832.
26. AHU, MS Livro Reservado (hereafter LR), no. 375, fls.1-180v. The Suvisesha Viruthi Urai manuscript copy belonged to Fr. Zeferino Godinho who was born in Panjim in Goa 1776 and joined the order of the Augustinians on 12 March 1794. He made his vows of profession on 16 March 1795 and later became the procurator of the college of Populo de Goa in August 1802. He

did missionary work in Daman and died there in 1831. There is another copy of Suvisesha Viruththi Urai in the Ajuda Palace Library. See, BA, Codice 44-XII-38, fls.190-234. BL, London, no. 14170 c.31, Suvisesha Viruthi Urai, (Explicação dos Evangelhos Dominicaes e Festivaes of Jacome Goncalves, being the Texts from the Gospels for the Christian Year with Goncalves' Expositions), Yaazhpaanam, 1891 (year mentioned in Tamil characters). The book contains vii+301+iii+ii pages.

27. BA Codice, 44-XII-38, fls.191-191v.
28. Ibid., Codice 44-XII-38, fls.129-257v.
29. Ibid., Codice 44-XII-38, fls.235-57. The list of feast days from 1st day of the Thai month to 31st of Margazhi month and the list of moveable days of feasts (such as the ascension of our Lord, Assumption of the blessed virgin Mary, the holy spirit , Corpus Christ) are mentioned from 1st of Panguni month 1757 to 30th of Masi month 1758. AHU, LR/375, fls.111v-48v.
30. Thomas Anchukandam, *The First Synod of Pondicherry (1844): A Study Based on Archival Sources*, Bangalore, 1994, p. 48.
31. Archives de la société des missions étrangères de Paris (hereafter AMEP), MSS *Correspondance Pondichéry-Paris, Lettres*, vol. 1000, pp. 660-1; Thomas Anchukandam, The First Synod, p. 78.
32. Louis-Marie Mousset was born at Sanzay on 7 February 1808. He was ordained a priest on 28 May 1831 and he served in the diocese of Poitiers. He entered the MEP seminary on 7 February 1834 and sailed form France on 22 April 1835 and arrived Pondicherry on 31 August 1835. He was appointed the parish priest of Sarugani in 1836 and was at Kamanyakkanpatti in 1837 and at Dindigul in 1839. He wrote a letter to Jean Tesson in Paris on 16 September 1835 from Pondicherry and mentioned he learnt Sanskrit grammar during his voyage. Later he wrote another letter to Tesson on 29 November 1836 from Sarugani and mentioned that he learnt Tamil and begun to speak. He was with Fr Charles Evariste Mehay in 1836-41) and in 184243 he visited Coimbatore and Mysore. He took part in the first synod of 1844 and also in the second synod of 1849. He was appointed professor in 4e (=8th standard) at the Petit Seminaire in Pondicherry. In his letter to Tesson on 10 October 1851 he mentioned he was engaged on teaching geometry, translation working and preparing dictionaries. In his letter dated 25 November 1860 he said that he was teaching arithmetic. In his letter of 19 August 1845 he said that he was teaching Latin and French languages in the seminary. In his letter to Tesson on 10 February 1844 he mentioned he had composed a Latin-Tamil dictionary of 112 pages with 1200 words. Bishop Bonnand gave a high opinion of Mousset in his letter to Langlois dated 18 February 1841. In his letter to Tesson dated 10 February 1846 Mousset mentioned the plan of

L.S. Dupuis to compose a grand book contrary to Hindu puranams and vethams. In the letter of Mousset to Tesson dated 3 September 1860 Mousset mentioned that he was composing the French-Tamil dictionary. He died on 8 February 1888 at Pondicherry. Mousset's works include Pusai udhavi mandiram (manner of serving the Holy Mass) Latin grammar in Tamil of 1845, grammaire-franciase en tamoule of 1846, elements de geographie en francais et en tamoul and L'arithmetic tamoul in 1853.

33. Fr Arul was born in 1830 and he was ordained a priest in 1856 and he died in 1870.
34. Bibliothèque Asiatique des missions étrangères de Paris, (hereafter BAMEP) no. TA 46, See also, Madurai Province Jesuit Archives (hereafter MPJA), Shenbaganur, no. 221/265.
35. AMEP, MSS *Correspondance Pondichéry-Paris, Lettres*, vol. 1002, see the letter of L.S. Dupuis to Jean Tesson the procurator of the missions for India in Paris dated 10 November 1856.
36. AMEP, MSS *Correspondance Pondichéry-Paris, Lettres*, vol. 1001, see the letter of L.S. Dupuis to Jean Tesson dated 22 December 1856.
37. BAMEP, no. TA 46, p. 4. .
38. Ibid., pp. 5-17.
39. Ibid., see the introduction vide para 1.
40. Ibid., see the introduction, p. 14.
41. Ibid., p. 15.
42. Ibid., pp.186, 188.
43. J. B Trincal, *Yesu Kristhunaatharudaya Parisuththa Suvisesha Poruththam*, Indian Press, Madras, 1879; MPJA, J. B Trincal, *Yesu Kristhunaatharudaya Parisuththa Suvisesha Poruththam*, Catholic Mission Press, Pondicherry, 1887.
44. MPJA, J.B. Trincal, *Yesu Kristhunaatharudaya Parisuththa Puthiya Yerpaadu*, Catholic Mission Press, Pondicherry, 1890.
45. BAMEP, call no. 7/212, Hugues Madelain Bottero, *Sathya Vetha Aagamam*, vol. I, 1904, vol. II, 1910; BAMEP, *The Holy Bible: Old Testament, Sathyavetha Aagamam, Pazhaya Yerpaadu*, Second edition, Catholic Mission Press, Pondicherry, 1912; BAMEP, *The Holy Bible: Old Testament, Sathyavetha Puththagam, Pazhaya Yerpaadu, Rendaam Kaandam*, Catholic Mission Press, Pondicherry, 1917; BAMEP, *New Testament, Sesukristhunaatharudaya Parisuththa Suviseshamum, Aposthalargaludaya Nadapadigalum, Nirupangalum, Archsishta Arulapparudaya Kaatchiyaagamamum*, Second edition, Catholic Mission Press, Pondicherry, 1928 .

46. S. Jeyaseela Stephen, *Louis Savinien Dupuis, 1806-1874: A Biography of the MEP Missionary in Pondicherry*, 2017, p. 130. The document had been gifted by the author to the Archives of the Franciscan Sisters of the Immaculate Heart of Mary, Pondicherry.

7

The Bible Translation and Transmission from Hebrew, Greek, German, Portuguese and English into Tamil by the Protestant Missionaries, 1708-1850

Translation of the Bible into several languages of Europe took place around the Fourteenth century and particularly in German and four Low German and fourteen High German publications appeared in print before Martin Luther began translating the Bible in German. The first printed Bible in any modern European language came from the press of Johann Mentelin of Strasburg in 1466. In the translations and revisions, starting with the New Testament in 1522 Luther wanted to capture the spirit of the text and make it suitable for a German audience. He aspired to make Moses so German that no one would suspect that he was a Jew.[1] Luther's translation of the Bible was first published in 1534. Later Bible translation came to be revised and it had been reported that the Bible in German was so good and precious that it was better than all other former versions said Martin Luther in preparing the 1541 edition of the Holy Scripture.[2] In England from the time of the Reformation, the English Bible was closely associated with the monarchy, and it was used to invoke the nationalist feelings.[3] In 1604 King James took steps for translation of the Old Testament into English. Later it had impact for the translation of psalms, King Solomon's Song of Songs, the book of Isaiah prophet, book of Job and other books into various other European languages. The authorized version of the New Testament in English (King James) came to appear only in 1611.

Bible printed in Europe came to be widely circulated by the Jesuits in Goa. It may be mentioned that Akbar the Mughal emperor was delighted to receive in 1580 a copy of the Holy Bible written in four languages and bound handsomely in seven volumes, in Hebrew, Chaldean, Latin and Greek from the first Jesuit missionaries who came to his court. This was the polyglot Bible edited by Montanus and printed between 1569 and 1572. Akbar's interest in the Old and New Testament was stimulated by the Jesuits and he organized a special translation office and charged Abul Fazal his court historian for making the translations and the Gospels were the first to be ordered. The order for the translation of the Gospels into Persian, in the words of Badauini, the court chronicler may also been corroborated in this connection. Monserrat the Jesuit in the court of Akbar reported that the emperor in the presence of his great nobles and religious leaders most devoutly not only kissed the Bible but placed it on his head. The emperor was so keen and he had asked in which volume the Gospel was to be found. When he was shown the right volume he displayed even more marked reverence for it. He then requested the missionaries to come with their Bibles into his own private room, where he opened the volume once more with great reverence and joy. He closed the Bible again very carefully and deposited them in a beautiful book case, worthy of such sacred volumes, which stood in the same private room. He spent a great deal of his spare time and was anxious to have the Arabic and Persian translations of the Holy Books of Judaism and Christianity in his collection. The emperor wrote a letter to King Philip II of Spain in 1582, and stated that it has been brought to his kind notice the Pentateuch, the Gospel and Psalms, and should these books have been translated into Arabic and Persian, which are profitable to all, whether translated or not, be procurable in Europe could be send to him.[4]

Bartholomäus Ziegenbalg the Protestant missionary boarded the ship Princessa Sophia Hedwiga which left Copenhagen on 30 November 1705 and arrived at Tranquebar on the Tamil coast on 9 July 1706. He admitted that he began to use the Tamil translation of the Bible that was formerly carried out by the Jesuits. He stated that he read again and again the New Testament translated in parts by the Catholic missionaries and collected lot of terms required and the phrases needed by him for his work and he noted them carefully. In the letter of 12 June 1707 Ziegenbalg for the first time referred to a Tamil book containing the gospels translated by Catholic missionaries.[5] In his next letter of 24 June 1707 to pastor Lysius in Berlin he again referred to the same Tamil book containing the gospels translated by Catholic missionaries.[6] In his yet another letter of 22 September 1707 he added that he had received the gospels and some books in Tamil composed by the Catholic missionaries from a local gentleman.[7] In his opinion these works although full of errors none the less contributed very much to the study of Christian Tamil language. He further said that he could get accustomed to a proper Christian style and the best book among them was a gospel book composed by the Jesuits. He said that at first he worked with this Bible translation and he extracted a lot of words and phrases and then began to memorize them and later he used in his daily exercises.

After three years Ziegenbalg mentioned in his letter of 22 December 1710 about five books of the Catholic missionaries which he had made special use of–

(a) questions of Christian teaching—which after purification and correction by him is quite pleasant to read

(b) catechism (authored by Roberto Nobili)—which needed quite a strong acid and he had to cut out six chapters completely as being incurable

(c) 26 sermons (authored by Roberto Nobili)—which have a very pleasant language style

(d) Christian wreath of pearls (authored by Manuel Martins and titled as Gnaana Muthumaalai—the book which was the best of all and dealt with mystics and

(e) short prayers on the sufferings of Jesus Christ (authored by Manuel Martins and titled Siluvaiyin visesha sallaapam) containing also several prayers to Blessed Virgin Mary, to the guardian angel and other angels and to various saints in which Ziegenbalg was not at all interested and so that which he had omitted.[8]

Ziegenbalg came to know about the translated Tamil Bible with the Roman Catholic missionaries at Nagapattinam. Hence he requested them on 21 March 1711 to send it to him in exchange for a copy of the New Testament to be published by him from the Tranquebar printing press. The Bible under the possession of the Jesuits contained the Old Testament given in the form of question and answers.[9] Ziegenbalg also mentioned about the book in Tamil on the Bible translated by the Jesuits and said that it contained selected passages and incidents from the Bible vide his letter 10 October 1711 sent to Europe.[10] He said again in his letter of 5 December 1711 written from Mylapore to Anton Wilhelm Boehme that 'When in Madras he visited the house of the Capuchins and found there a Tamil book containing the stories of the Old Testament in question and answer format.[11] Ziegenbalg said that he had tried to improve it in manner and style and purified it from the eleven chapters and added here and there something, so that it could be used with great profit in the Protestant congregation because each book of the Old Testament had been presented quite well according to contents by question and answer. In the historical books he said that it had been done so well that no stories had been omitted by the Jesuits. Ziegenbalg in his letter dated 9 December 1711 to Joachim Lange, the Rector and pastor in Berlin referred to the Bible translation in Tamil by the Catholic missionaries in Santhome of Mylapore when he visited and he said that it had been written on paper and that it contained interestingly stories of Old Testament as well as from the New Testament.[12]

Ziegenbalg later mentioned that he obtained a palm-leaf manuscript containing the Sunday Gospels prepared by the Jesuits on the Tamil Coast. These were gospel passages assigned to be read on each Sunday which had been so well translated into Tamil and that no Tamil Christian was able to get hold of it and the Jesuits alone used it. He reported that a Jesuit who was in Thanjavur area handed over his collection of books to be preserved in the town of Tranquaber and such matter was unknown for long. It so happened in a wonderful manner that Ziegenbalg came to know of this Tamil Bible translations and manuscripts of Catholic literature. He sought ways and means to this library and finally had access and surprisingly found a copy of the gospel passages excellently translated in Tamil. According to Ziegenbalg the Gospels were pretty accurately translated and they were based on the original Greek. After bringing the text, he made a copy of it for his use and returned it. He then began to correct a few things here and there and did what best he could do. Mistakes were found and these occurred not due to the fault of the Jesuit translators but because of the copyists.[13]

Ziegenbalg and his Tamil Translation of the New Testament, 1710-1713

Ziegenbalg who had set his mind to learn Tamil, in the course of time while learning the language desired to use the New Testament in Portuguese translated by João Ferreira Annes d'Almeida a former Catholic priest who became a Protestant in Batavia (Jakarta). He was the first biblical translator into Portuguese, and the New Testament was published in 1681 in Batavia where Almeida lived most of his life. Thus the first Bible translated and printed in Portuguese went from Asia to Portugal and to the rest of the Portuguese speaking countries. Mudaliappa the teacher of Ziegenbalg who knew Portuguese well had agreed to teach with the help of Portuguese Bible.[14] Ziegenbalg later reported on 15 January 1709 that he had continued learning Tamil through catechist Malayappan. At that time he improved his language skill and wrote down things with his steel pen which portion of the Bible was to be translated from the Portuguese Bible into Tamil.[15] Thus it is neatly evident that Ziegenbalg had not actually commenced at all translating the Bible in Tamil till 1709 but the work was on his mind and way.

It must be said that Ziegenbalg had access for the first time to the Tamil New Testament on 12 June 1707. This work was earlier executed by the Jesuits in Tamil country and it had enormously helped him to have the first idea for Bible translation. He and Johann Ernst Grundler (1677-1720) the two protestant missionaries thereafter had a plan and in principle had decided to undertake the laborious work of translation.[16] Ziegenbalg went through the Tamil Bible of the Jesuits time and again and he made his own additions, deletions, corrections, and improvements and gave the translation a shape with a different tone than what was found to be Catholic. Ziegenbalg had referred to these changes which he had executed and it is evident through his letters and reports sent from Tranquebar to Copenhagen and Halle. Thus the New Testament translation cum revision in Tamil was carried out by Ziegenbalg and Johann Ernst Grundler had helped him at times and within three years the work was nearing completion between 1710 and 1713. Ziegenbalg contributed whatever best he could do to his ability and efforts. The view that Ziegenbalg was the first to translate the Bible into Tamil as opined by David Prabhakar is therefore called into question.[17]

It may be mentioned that there were translations of the Bible in Tamil made earlier and available by the Catholic missionaries but were not freely circulated which Ziegenbalg thought necessary to print and circulate. The Jesuits had though laid the foundation and groundwork but could not raise the structures owing to restrictions and regulations imposed by the Catholic Church in printing Tamil Bible. The Jesuits could not also raise the super-structure to see the light of printing the Holy Gospel in Tamil owing to prohibition of the Catholic Church. Ziegenbalg realized this fact and he started working on the translation into Tamil with the New Testament on 17 October 1708. Ziegenbalg's translation of the New Testament into the Tamil was interrupted on 19 November 1708 by his imprisonment. He took up the work again as soon as he was liberated, and continued the translation. The first draft was ready by 21 March 1711.

In a letter written in 1708 Ziegenbalg clearly said that he intended to be quite alone in his translation, merely employing a Tamil writer to put down what he would say and dictate. He added that he required no help from others, and even if he wished for it, he could not get. Neither amongst the Christians nor the Tamils in Tranquebar he could find one person who could translate a sentence without mistake. He mentioned that it is true that the interpreters knew several European languages, but they had been only able to help him in the meaning of words. He stated that the grammatical rules had to be found out only by him through a diligent study of Tamil books.[18] It may be pointed out that Ziegenbalg considered that his greatest literary achievement was to translate the New Testament from Greek into the spoken form of the Tamil language. To gain a deeper understanding of the Greek text, he consulted Latin, German, Danish, Portuguese and Dutch translations. This was a major task that he undertook, and over the period of years he took the assistance of Grundler. Therefore he added his name and the name of Grundler that appeared at the title page when the Tamil Bible was printed.

Printing the New Testament in Tamil in Two Parts by Ziegenbalg and Johann Ernst Grundler in 1714 and 1715

The missionaries of Tranquebar were granted permission for printing by King Friedrich IV (1671-1730) from Copenhagen vide letter sent in February 1714. It stated that there was no hindrance to the advantage which the missionaries expected from the Tamil and Portuguese printing press, and the king herewith sent them the most gracious privilege by allowing them to print without supervision from the censor, feeling confident that the missionaries would use it with such circumspection, that no one will have any reason to complain of them.[19] Ziegenbalg thereafter had undertaken the task of printing the Bible in Tamil and got printed it from Tranquebar Press in 1714.

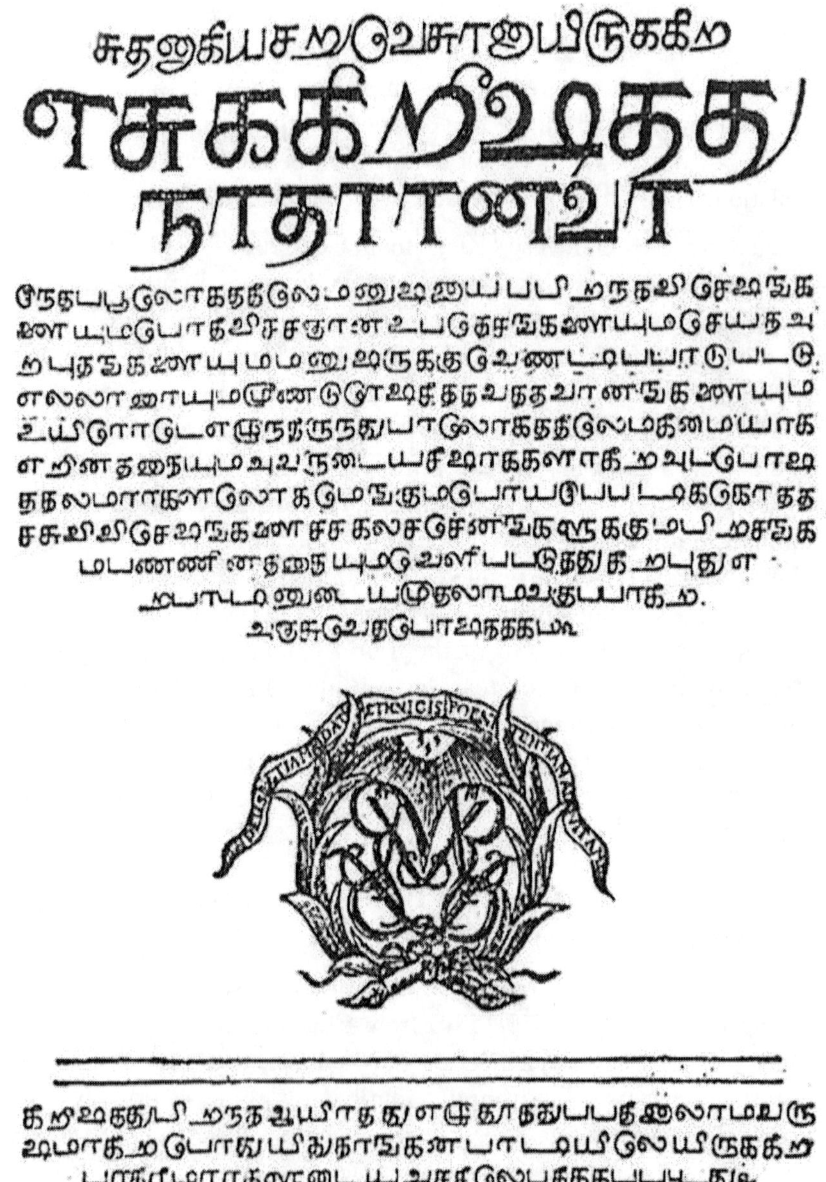

7.1: The first page of the first translation of the New Testament into Tamil (Anju Vetha Posthagam) by Bartholomaeu Ziegenbalg and Johann Ernst Grundler, printed in Tranquebar in 1714 (Courtesy: The American Bible Society Library, New York)

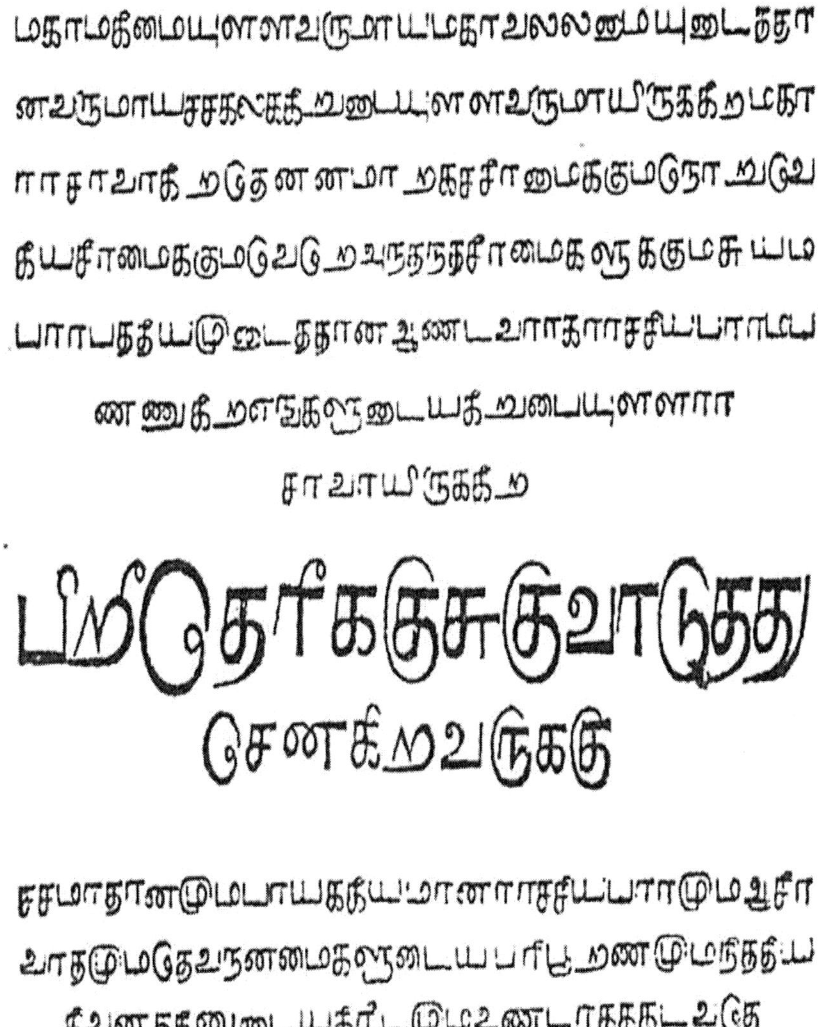

7.2: The Tamil page of dedication made to King Frederick IV of Denmark in the first translation of the New Testament into Tamil by Bartholomaeu Ziegenbalg and Johann Ernst Grundler, printed in Tranquebar in 1714 (Courtesy: The American Bible Society Library, New York)

The protestant missionaries wrote and said that it was the first part of the vetha containing the five books. The New Testament in Tamil was titled 'Suthanaagiya Sarvesuranaanirukkira yesykristhu naatharaanavar intha bhulogathiley manushanaai pirantha viseshangalaiyum bhoduvicha upadesangaliyum seytha arputhangalaiyum manusharukku vendi paadupattu yellaraiyum moondu raetchithuvithavanagalaiyum uyirodey ezhunthiruinthu paralogathiley magimaiyaga yerinathaiyum avarudaya seeshargalaagiya aposthalarmaargal logam yengum poey ippadikothavichu viseshangalai sagala senangallukkum pirasangam panninathaiyum vezhipaduthugira puthu yerpaadinudaya muthalaam vaguppagiya Anju vetha posthagam. Kristu piratha Ayirathu yezhunuthu pathinaalam varushamagirapothu Tharanganpadiyiley irukkira paathrimaargaludaya achiley pathipikka pattathu'.[20]

There is a page in Tamil dedicated to King Friedrich IV of Denmark in the New Testament. It is written 'Mahaa magimaiyullvarumai mahaa vallamaiudaithaanavarmai sagala kirubhai ullavarumaai irukkira maharaasavaagira thenn marga seemaikum Noruwayiga seemaikkum Vereyvundha seemaikum suyam paarpathiyam udaithana aandavaraaga racchiyapaaram pannugira yengaludaya kirubaiyulla Raasavay irukkira Preederickku kuvaduthu sengairavarukku samaathanamum pakkiyamaana rachiya paaramum aasirvaadhamum deva nanmaigaludaya parripuranamum nithiya seevanathinyudaya kiridamum undaga kadavathenru adiyengal vendikolgirom'.

There is also a page of dedication in German. It runs: '*Dem allerduchlauchtigsten, grosmaechtigsten und Allergnaedigsten souverainem ers-koenig und herren, Herrn Friderico Quatro Koenig zu Dannemaarck und Norwegen, der Wender und Gothen, Herzog zu schleswig, Holstein, stormarn und der Ditmaesche, grafen zu Oldenburg und Delmenhorst & Unserm Allegnaedigten erb-Koening und herrn, Wuncher win friede eine Seelige Regieruag, Seegen und die Fulle gottlicher Guter, wie auch die crone des ewigen Lebens*'.

There is a preface by Bartholomäus Ziegenbalg and Johann Ernst Grundler in German written from Tranquebar dated 25 September 1714 printed in the Tamil Bible. The New Testament contained Gospel of St. Mathew, Mark, Luke and John and the Acts of the Apostles only. Hence this is called in Tamil Angu vetha posthgam (five sacred books). It is also known as part one of the New Testament. The print copy of the New Testament was 500 at that time.

Part two of the New Testament was printed in 1715 at the Tranquebar press. It contained Letters of St. Paul to the Romans till the book of Revelation.[21] It had ii+176 pages in total. There is no Latin title page in the part two of the New Testament as found in the part one of the New Testament. It may be mentioned that the New Testament two volumes printed had no dots over consonants. Further, there is no difference made between the kuril and the nedil (the short and the long) letters. There is a letter of Ambrose the catechist in Tranquebar who wrote in Tamil to professor Francke in Germany wherein he profusely thanked him having sent the Bible to Tamil country and this letter is preserved at the Francke Foundation archives in Halle.

We are sure the translations were undertaken by the missionaries on paper and then composed or recast into palm-leaf by the Tamil scribes, for we find palm-leaf manuscripts sent to Europe. These are even now preserved in the Francke Foundation in Halle. The term 'Hebrew jaathi' is used in the translation in the Bible and we find mention *Archiyasishta Pauluosengiravar yebireya saathiyaarukku yezhuthi anupinna nirupam.*[22]

Reprint of the New Testament Translation of Ziegenbalg in 1722

Benjamin Schultze (1689-1760) thought it necessary to reprint the printed 1714-15 New Testament in Tamil. Schultze had not revised but he prepared it for publication. In this reprint edition of 1722 Schultze had mentioned in his Latin preface that this work was not his own work of translation or revision but in fact it was that of Ziegenbalg. Thus the New Testament had 27 books (4 gospels, acts, 14 epistles of Paul, 1 of Jacob, 2 of Peter, 3 of John, 1 of Juda (in total 21 epistles) and revelation chapter of St. John. Hence the two parts of the New Testament were printed in Tranquebar press in one volume and it appeared in 1722.[23] Michael Irudayam and Robinson Levi had mentioned that a revised version of the New Testament was done by Benjamin Schultze in 1722 and this view is incorrect.[24] Further it may be mentioned that the second edition of the New Testament in the title page is dated 1722 but according to records the printing was completed only in April 1724.[25]

Translation of the Old Testament by Ziegenbalg in 1711 and Printing Part I in 1723

Ziegenbalg came to know about the Tamil Old Testament with the Roman Catholic missionaries at Nagapattinam and Santhome of Mylapore. He stated that he had access to it for the first time in December 1711.[26] He used the Old Testament text of the Jesuits and made additions, deletions and carried on the work for publication. According to missionary records of Tranquebar we find that the work of printing the Old Testament was decided on 6 December 1718 to be done at the Danish mission press in Tranquebar.[27] Ziegenbalg could complete the work from the book of Genesis to Judges of the Old Testament and it was ready before his death on 23 February 1719. We find that the decision to print first five books of the Old Testament translation of the Bible had been made only in June 1720 and so the book in print appeared only in 1723, keeping to the tradition of the times beginning with the first five books (Torah) that were attributed to St. Moses who is considered the first prophet in the Old Testament till the book of judges. 400 copies were the print order. The Tamil title is 'Sarvathukkum vallavarumaay anaadhiyaai irukkiravarmaay yengum niranjavarumaay irukkira parraapara vasthuvaanavar poorva kaalathiley paramandalathil irunthu thiruvilampathina sathyama vetha posthagathin muthalaam vagauppu: Ithiley atchsishta mosesengiravar sarvesuranyadaya thiruvaayile ninru ketta gnayangalayum kartharaanavar aathiiley paralogathayum bhoologathayum yeppadi undaakinar yengirathayum avar sagala senangalukkile oru kosthirathaarai thammudaya sonthamaana senangkallaga therinthu kondaar engirathayum vezhipaduthugira mosesuvin anju posthagangalaiyum, yousuvaa vengiravarudaya gnaana posthagamum, neethikaaragaludaya vaththamanangalay kaanpikkira posthagamum, adangi irukkudhu'. Kristu pirandhu ayriath yezhuthnuthi irupathu moonam varushamgira poedhu, ithu tharanganpaadiiley irukkira paathrimargaludaya achiley pathipikka pattudhu.[28]

The Tamil Old Testament had a title page printed in Latin '*Biblia Tamulica seu Deus Omnipotentis simus semetipsum ex sua aeternitate clarius manifestatures de coelo est locutus Veteris Testamenti Pars Prima, Moses libri quinque, Josu e liber unus atque liber unus Judicum Studio & opera Bartholomaei Ziegenbalgii Missionarii ad Indos Orientales in Linguam Tamulicum versi continentur, Trangambariae, in littore*

Coromandelino, Typis & sumptibus Missionis Danicae, MDCCXXIII'.[29] It may be mentioned that this book printed had no dots over consonants. Further, there is no difference made between the kuril and the nedil (the short and the long) letters.

Translating the Book of Psalms by Benjamin Schultze and its Printing in 1724

Benjamin Schultze the missionary desired to translate the psalms into Tamil, without following the order of the Biblical books. As he preached in Tamil for the first time in April 1720 he realized soon the fact that of all the books of the Old Testament, the book of psalms are best adapted for public and private devotion. He made such progress that he successfully completed the translation of the psalms and it got printed at the Tranquebar press in 1724.[30] This book came out separately first and later the psalms were included after two years in the second part of the Old Testament which got printed in Tranquebar in 1726.

Translating the Old Testament from Hebrew into Tamil by Benjamin Schultze in 1723 and Printing Part II of the Old Testament in 1726

Benjamin Schultze started to do the translation of the Old Testament from Ruth to Song of Songs, though Ziegenbalg also did some work but left it incomplete. In 1723 Schultze began the continuation of Ziegenbalg's translation of the Bible, which had only reached as far as the book of Ruth. This little book was the first part of the Bible which he translated, and he carried out the work. Schultze took the Hebrew Bible and read a verse through; when he was certain that he understood it thoroughly, he repeated it to Peter Malayappan his writer in Tamil, when he and other natives thought that it was well expressed, Schultze dictated the verse for writing down, then Peter Malayappan the writer read it aloud to see whether anything had been left out, or whether perhaps some error had been made in writing it. There was also a learned brahmin present, whom Schultze had taken into his service in order to ask his advice.[31] Schultze who had thus did the work completed it and the book printing was finished on 5 August 1726.[32] 400 copies were the print order. This was called part two of the Old Testament with Book of Ruth, Prophets Samuel, Elijah and Elisha followed by wisdom books which again were written by David and

7.3: The first page from the first translation of the New Testament part two of the Acts of the Apostles into Tamil by Bartholomaeu Ziegenbalg and Johann Ernst Grundler, printed in Tranquebar in 1714 (Courtesy: Universiteits Bibliotheek, Leiden)

முதலாம அதிகாரம

7.4: The page in Tamil of the first translation of the New Testament Part Two, from the letters of St. Paul to the Romans, by Bartholomaeu Ziegenbalg and Johann Ernst Grundler, printed in Tranquebar in 1715 in small letters newly made (Courtesy: Universiteits Bibliotheek, Leiden)

7.4: The page in Tamil of the first translation of the New Testament Part Two, from the letters of St. Paul to the Romans, by Bartholomaeu Ziegenbalg and Johann Ernst Grundler, printed in Tranquebar in 1715 in small letters newly made (Courtesy: Universiteits Bibliotheek, Leiden)

Solomon, since earlier Ziegenbalg's translation had appeared (which contained from the book of Genesis to Judges).

The Old Testament had a title page printed in Latin '*Biblia Damulica seu quod Deus Sapientissimus in sua divina obconomia cum populo Israelitico & egit & locutus est Veteris Testamenti Pars Secunda, in qua libellus Ruth, Samuelis liber prior et posterior, Regum liber prior et posterior, Chronicorum liber prior et posterior, liber Esrae, liber Nehemiae, liber Esther, liber Jobi, liber Psalmorum Davidis, liber Proverbiorum, liber Ecclestiae, et liber Cantici Canticorum, Studio & opera Bartholomaei Ziegenbalgii & Benjamini Schultzii, Missionarorium ad Indos Orientales in Linguam Damulicum versi continentur, Tranquebariae, in littore Coromandelino, Typis & sumptibus Missionis Danicae, MDCCXXVI*'.

On the opposite page of the Old Testament printed in 1726 the Tamil title is rendered: 'Azhavillaatha gnaanamullavarumaay azhavillaatha kirubaiullavarumaay azhavillatha deivigiamullavray irukkira parraapara vasthuvaanavar pazhaya yerpaatinyudaya kaalathiley thiruvilampaththina vetha posthagathin rendaam vagauppu: ithiley archiyasishta ruth engiravazhludaya posthagamum, archiyasishta samuyel yengiravarudaya muthalaam posthagamum, rendam posthagamum Maarassakaludaya muthalam posthagamum, rendam posthagamum, paralipomvenru sollapatta muthalaam posthagamum, rendam posthagamum, echcheruvengiravarudaya posthagamum, neyemiyavengiravarudaya posthagamum, yesther engiravazhludaya posthagamum, yobu engiravarudaya posthagamum, Daavidengriavar ezhuthi vaitha gnaana sangeethangalengira posthagamum, Saalamon engiravar pesina vaakiyamgaludaya posthagamum, ekkeilsesiyesh engira naamathai kondirukkira posthagamum, unnathamaana paatinudaya posthagamum adangai irukkudhu. Kristu pirandhu 1726 varushamagira poedhu, ithu tharanganpaadiiley irukkira paathrimargaludaya achiley pathipikka pattudhu'.[33]

In the translation of the Old Testament there are several expressions which are colloquial. We find the name of God is rendered by *Paraaparavasthu*. We also find the vulgarisms, instead of *thiruvullam pathina* we have *tiruvilam pathina,* and for *vetha pusthakathin irandaam paakam,* we have *vetha posthakkin rendaam vakuppu*. In the list of books the title *arasiyasishta* is given to Ruth and Samuel but withheld from Esther, David and Solomon and this is the term that the Roman Catholics used for the term saint.

Michael Irudayam and Robinson Levi had mentioned that Benjamin Schultz had translated part two of the Old Testament and their opinion is incorrect.[34] In the title page of the book we find mention the names of both Ziegenbalg and Schultze being printed. Both of them were involved in part two of the translation of the Old Testament.

Printing the Old Testament of Part III in 1727

Schultze continued to do the translation of the rest of the books which Ziegenbalg began and left incomplete in the Old Testament. This included the books both from the major and minor prophets from Isaiah to Malachi. He completed the work and it got printed from the Tranquebar Press in 1727.[35] It was called part three of the Old Testament. According to missionary records printing work was completed on 3 October 1727.[36] 400 copies were the print order.

The Old Testament had a title page printed in Latin '*Biblia Damulica seu quod Deus Omniscius de gratia in Jesu Christo tempore Novi Testamenti revelanda per sanctos suos propheats est vaticinatus Veteris Testamenti Pars Tertia, in qua prophetae majores: Esaias, Jeremias, ejusdemque Lamentatiines, Ezechiel, Daniel,; prophetae minores Hosseas, Joel, Amos, Jona, Micha, Nahum, Habacuc, Zephanja, Haggi, Zacharias et Malachias, Studio & opera Bartholomaei Ziegenbalgii & Benjamini Schultzii, Missionarorium ad Indos Orientales in Linguam Damulicum versi continentur, Tranquebariae, in littore Coromandelino, Typis & sumptibus Missionis Danicae, MDCCXXVII*'.

There is also a title page in Tamil 'Anju kanda seeraay irukkiravarumaay, yellathayum arinthu irukkiravarumaay, azhavillaatha parisuthamullavarumaay irukkira parraapara vasthuvaanavar pazhaya yerpaadu irukkirapothu puthu yerpattinudaya magimaiyai vezhipaduthapora yesu kristhuvin periley thiruvilampaththina vetha posthagathin moonam vaguppu: Ithiley archiyasishta theergatharisigalaagira yesaypiya-vengairavar kanda therisanthaninudya posthagamum, yeremiyavengiravar pannina pirasangathinudaya posthagamum, avar paadina pulambalinyudaya posthagamum, ysekkiyelengiravarakku kaanpikka patta therisanathinudaya posthagamum, Daaaniyelengiravar therisanamaaga kanda varthamaananga-ludaya posthagamum, oseyaasum, yoyellum, Aamossum, obaadiyaavum, yonaasum, mikkavum, naahummum, abakukkum, sepaaniyavum, aakkayum, sakarayaasum, malayosum engiravargal theerkatharisanamaaga solli, yezhuthi vaitha posthagangalum adangi irukkudhu: Kristu pirandhu 1727 varushamaagira poedhu, ithu tharanganpaadiiley irukkira paathrimargaludaya achiley pathipikka pattadhu'.[37]

Michael Irudayam and Robinson Levi had again mentioned that Benjamin Schultz had translated part three of the Old Testament and their opinion is incorrect.[38] In the title page of the book we find mention of the names of Ziegenbalg and Schultze. Both were involved in translating part three of the Old Testament.

Translating and Printing the Book of Apocrypha in Tamil by Ziegenbalg and Benjamin Schultze in 1728

It should be noted that the Christian priests had rejected some parts of the Bible for being against the teachings of Jesus Christ in AD 369. These rejected books were called Apocrypha. Schultze carried out the translation of these books of Apocrypha which was earlier began by Ziegenbalg and left incomplete before his death on 23 February 1719. Schultze completed the translation of Apocrypha i.e., from Tobit to Prayer of Manasseh. If a verse or text were difficult in the original, Schultze had a Polyglot Bible and other good aids at hand. So he continued translating one Biblical book after another and successfully completed the whole.[39] The book of Apocrypha was published from the press in Tranquebar and the printing was finished on 26 September 1728.[40]

There is a title page printed in Tamil and it runs: 'Pazhaya yerpaattin kaalathinudaya theerkatharisagalikku pirakaalam undaayiruntha yutha samayathayaaraagiya punniya athumaakkal dharma nadakkaigalin perilleyum, akkaalam thuvakki Yesunaathar bhulogathiley manushanaga vanthu pirantha mattukkum thirusabaiiley nadantha kaaranangalin perilleyum yeuzthi vaitha apocripha yengira naamamulla gnaana posthangalaagiya gnaathinudaya posthagamum seeraakengirvarudaya posthagamum, yesderengiravar ezhuthina posthagamum, thobiasengiravarudaya posthagamum, yudithengirvazhludaya posthagamum, Estherengiravazhludaya posthagathodey sernthirukkirathum, Baaruchengiravarudaya posthagamum, eremiya yezhuthina nirupamum, Soolaiiley iruntha moonupergal Isha thothirathinudaya vaarthaigalum, Susaanengiravazhlukku sambuvicha sethiyum, bellengira vikkirathinudayavum, dhiraakonvengira

புணணியாததமாககள

ஞானபபொ

ஸததகஙகளாகிற

7.6: Tamil title page of the book of Apocrypha (Gnaana Posthagangal) translated by Benjamin Schultze into Tamil printed in Tranquebar in 1728 (Courtesy: Det Kongelige Bibliotek, Kobenhavn) malaipaambinudayavum varththamaanamum, makkabey engiravargaludaya muthalaam posthagamum, rendaam posthagamum, moonaam posthagamum, manassess engiravarudaya sepamum adangi irukkudhu: Kristu pirandhu 1728 varushamaagira poedhu, ithu tharanganpaadiiley irukkira paathrimargaludaya achiley pathipikka pattadhu'.

There is also a title page printed in Latin and it records: '*Libri Apocryphi seu libri aquibusdam piis viris ecclesiae antiquae judaicae post prophetas veterid tesatamenti scripti, continents partim supplementum historiae ecclesiasticae veteris testamenti, scilicet liber sapentie, ecclesiasticus sive Sirach, liber Esdre, liber Tobiae, liber Judith, adjectiones ad librum Esther, liber Baruch, epistola Jereiae, adjectiones ad Danielem seu trium virorum hymnologia, historia Sosanne, item Belis & Draconis, Maccabaeorum liber primus, secundas & tertius denique oratio Manassis; Studio & opera Bartholomaei Ziegenbalgii & Benjamini Schultzii, Missionarorium ad Indos Orientales in Linguam Damulicum versi, Trangambariae, Typis & Impressis Missionis Danicae, MDCCXXVIII*'. Thus the Protestant missionaries of Tranquebar had been successful in getting the Old Testament printed in Tamil for the first time. They had thus upheld the missiological meaning of Martin Luther's 62nd thesis that the true treasure of the church is the Gospel of God's glory and grace. Hence all 69 books of the Bible were made available in print in Tamil.

Ziegenbalg well understood and he said that there was almost so great a difference betwixt the vulgar and poetical Tamil, as there was betwixt Latin and High-Dutch. For notwithstanding the way of reading to be the same, no common Tamil could understand the writings of the poets without an interpreter. And this was the reason that there were so very few that are able to give a competent account of the principles of Hindu worship; the religious books written in so dark and abstruse a language, as no mean person was able to dive into.[41] Ziegenbalg therefore adopted a free style to translate the Bible in a different way to reach the Tamil protestant converts. The terms and words and the word formation in Bible translation by Ziegenbalg had been largely of Tamil spoken and ordinary usage. He used the word sarvesvaran for god, gnaanasnaanam (bath of knowledge) for baptism.[42]

Reprinting the Book of Psalms in Tamil, 1747

A second edition of psalms appeared in print in 1747. This book has 266 pages and is titled in Tamil 'Raasavum Thirgatharisiyumaayiruntha

Archisista Dhavidengiravar yezhuthi vaitha Gnaana sangeethangaludaya Posthagam: Ithilaye Dhavid enbavarum veru sila archisitavargalum paadina 150 sangeethangal adangiirukkuthu: Randaam pathithal, Kristu pirantha 1747 ile ithu Tharanganpaadiile achadikapattathu'.[43] The psalms are classified into ten categories and mentioned under a section titled in Tamil 'Achisishta Dhavid enbavarum veru sila archisitavargalum yezhuthi vaitha sangithangaliley adangi irukkira piradhaana kaariyangal vaguthu yezhuthapatta vivaramaavathu'.

1. Sarithira sangeethangal
2. Theergatharisana sangeethangal
3. Upadesa sangeethangal
4. Puththi solgira sangeethangal
5. Aarudhal sangeethangal
6. Jepa sangeethangal
7. Muraipadugira sangeethangal
8. Ilai thothira sangeethangal
9. Thuthiya sangeethangal sernthirukkum
10. Anathana varsaigalukkum vezhaigalukkum aduththa sangeethangal

Then the printed text begins from psalm 1 at page 10 to goes up to psalm 150 and the book ends at page 266. The last lines are, 'Alleluia, Gnaana sangeethangal mudinthathu, Muttrum' found in the end of the book. We do not find pulli (dot) used over the consonants in printing. But it is interesting to note that the long and short letter differences are found well in scripts and the words such as vey, veey, and sey/ seeye.

The Reading Habit of the Tamils and the Printing Impact

Some interesting episodes that created an impact through the printed Bible on the Tamils could be reported. A Catholic named Rayanayakkan was of pariah caste from Chinnanyan Palayam and he was a *servaikaaran* (subordinate officer) in the army of Serfoji, the ruler of Thanjavur. He obtained the New Testament of the Bible printed in 1714 and read it. It is said that by the age of 22 he and his younger brother Chinnappan had learned to read Tamil. They began reading palm-leaf books on the lives of saints, miracles of the Virgin Mary and Christ. The story of passion of Christ had caused such an emotion that they meditated on what sin was really and they began to fear god's judgment. Rayanayakkan wanted to know the history of Christ back to Moses, but the Catholic catechists whom he approached did not give him the books they had. This evidence shows that the Catholic missionaries never freely distributed the copy of the Bible translated to the people.[44]

Rayanayakkan said that he obtained Ziegenbalg's printed translation of the New Testament from a Catholic named Sathya Nathan. At first he thought that it was a Catholic publication because the title page with information that it had been printed in Tranquebar was similar to Catholic idea. Rayanayakkan began to read parts of the Bible in the beginning and he was moved by it greatly. He mentioned also that when he had obtained the book his longing desire to know was satisfied. He later used to read it all day and also then from the evening till midnight with the help of an oil lamp. When he had read the Bible thoroughly, he felt that the Lord our God had given him great light in understanding. The texts of the Bible that struck him most often he continuously read again and again. It was just like oil poured on the lamp upon his faith and it caused to burn very brightly. Thereafter he changed his faith and became a Protestant.[45]

Scathing Attacks and Criticism of the Catholic Missionaries on the Tamil Bible Translation of the Tranquebar Missionaries, 1728-1741

Since Martin Luther's Bible translation in German was based on common spoken language, the Protestant missionaries of Tranquebar also did the same in Tamil. After publication of the Tamil Bible, some remarks were made from several quarters regarding the style and form of the language used in the Holy Scripture. Bible translation was found to be faulty by the Catholic missionaries. Hence Protestant missionaries were blamed and it invited the ridicule of Constanzo Giuseppe Beschi (1680-1747) the Italian Jesuit. He expressed in his work *Vetha Vizhlakkam*, (The explanation of revelation) in 1728. Chapter 18 of this *Vetha Vizhlakkam* titled '*Deva Vaakkiya Vizhlakkam*' is very significant in this regard.[46] Beschi spoke here of the policy of the Catholic Church towards Bible translation in vernacular languages. He mentioned that the divine word or Word of God deals with all the truths to be accepted by Christians and also talks of the ways of observance and following to lead a good life. Hence if there is an error or mistake happens in the translation of the divine word so also there will be mistake in faith and also in life. Hence it was followed that without the permission of the superiors it should not be translated in native languages. Even so if translated, the people should not give their own interpretations and explanations and this was the order of the Catholic Church then in vogue.

Beschi also mentioned the charges commonly levelled against the Catholics by the Protestant missionaries. He provided the answers too. It has been said that the Catholic missionaries supplied and explained only some portions of the Bible to the people and the Catholic priests reserved the rest for themselves and this was considered a kind of cheating. In his view, Beschi replied that he gave milk to drink, not solid food, because the new converts were not yet strong enough then. The mother without giving the solid food that she took, and gave only the milk as food which the child needed, but poured her love and made it sweet. Thus Catholic missionaries also gave the spiritual food that the new Christian converts could digest. Beschi also asked that the child who did not know to read the four alphabets and if the baby is supplied with in his hand the grammar books of Nannul, Kaarigai and Alangaram would it help any way.

Beschi clearly exposed the poor standard and the language used by the Protestant missionaries in their Tamil Bible translations. He said that the Tamil translations found in the Holy Scripture by the Protestants would be mocked by people. He gave several examples from the printed Bible especially of Mathew 4:18; Mathew 18:17; Luke 6:14, Romans, 9:22; 1 Corinthians 7:3; 1 Peter 2:2 and 1Timothy 3:6.

Beschi pointed out the errors in ideas found mention in the Bible translations made by the Protestants. He gave examples from the printed Bible of Peter II, 1:10; Hebrews, 13:4 and 1 Corinthians, 9:5. He mentioned that translating the Bible into incorrect and inelegant Tamil was to burying a bright jewel in the mire, to mixing poison in the sea of Ambrosia and throwing charcoal on a lovely painting.

Beschi remarked the practices followed which were up till then. He stated that Tamil words of the south, allowing a few Sanskrit words in written Tamil usage had been the best adopted. He asked, can those books printed by the Tranquebar missionaries be fairly called the Word of God? He said that the Protestant missionaries do not at all write correctly the name of their country in Tamil. They have handed down to us pretending that they have translated the holy scriptures in Tamil. Whilst ignorant of that language, they have to the bitter paining of our ears, written them in barbarous words. By this means, the truth of God's word has been darkened, and by depriving it of its excellence.[47] Beschi could not accept the Bible translation of Ziegenbalg in spoken Tamil and he said 'when a person read the first sentence the reader's eye would burn, the tongue will become dry and the ears would blast. Then he would make a great laugh'.

Gauston Laurent Coeurdoux (1691-1779) the French Jesuit who lived at Karaikal mentioned in his letter dated 26 September 1741 that the Lutherans had translated the Bible into Tamil but its language, style and structure were not good and so it does not bring honour to the Holy Scripture. The defective translation carried out by the Lutherans had been mainly owing to their ignorance of the Tamil language.[48]

Prosper Giuliani another Jesuit in his annual letter also wrote that the Lutherans have printed and published the sacred scriptures in rather coarse Tamil and have disfigured them by their commentaries. Full of errors against the true faith, they have published a good many other books, more or less heretical. He said that the types used in printing were excellent, well cut, numerous and varied. The books were at least of seven to eight kinds and various sizes. Already a few Christians of the lower strata of Tamil society and some pariahs enticed by the love of rupees had fell away at their instigation. The number of apostates had been daily increasing. Giuliani said that the Jesuits wished to oppose the printed works of the Protestants from book to book, but there was no Catholic printing press and so Jesuits could not oppose that easily.[49]

Planning and Revising the Tamil Translations of the Gospel by the Missionaries of Tranquebar, 1737-39: Bible Translation from German to Tamil, 1740

It has been understood well and accepted by the Protestant missionaries of Tranquebar themselves that the ideas presented in the printed Bible in the spoken Tamil was erroneous.[50] The Protestant missionaries seven in number had agreed in principle and they had signed it in a correspondence as early as dated 5 December 1737. It had been also described that the method to be followed by them in revising the Gospel of St. Mathew since

அர்ச்சியசிஷ்ட அப்பொஸ்த்த

இவெஞ்ஞெலிஸ்த்தனாகிய

மத்தேவுசு

எழுதிவைத்த

எங்களுடையகர்த்தனுமிரட்சகருமாகிய

யேசுக்கிறிஸ்த்துவுடைய

சுத்தமான சுவிசேஷம்.

ஆதியிலெ எழுதப்பட்டகிரீக்ஸ்ப்பாஷையிலெயுன்னின்றுந்

தமிழ்ப்பாஷையிலெகொண்டுவரப்பட்டுத்

திருசபைக்கட்டளைப்படிக்குந்

திட்டவட்டமாகப்பரிசோதிக்கப்பட்டது

கொழும்பிலெ உத்தமகொம்பஞ்ஞியவின் அச்சுக்கூடத்திலெ
பதிக்கப்பட்டது [illegible] ஆண்டு.

7.7: The frontispiece of Gospel according to St. Matthew printed in Tamil by the Dutch East India Company in Colombo in 1741 (Courtesy: Bibliothek der Franckesche Stiftungen, Halle) numerous charges had been levelled against the printed Bible. They have stated that they had by now compared also two other Roman Catholic translations while one of them contained the ordinary Sunday gospels, and it was the book which had been used by the first missionaries (Ziegenbalg, Grundler and Schultze) who translated the printed Bible.[51] The other book was a complete one and it had been received from Pulicat through the catechist together with the gospel of St. John.[52] In sum, it may be said that Ziegenbalg's translation of the Tamil Bible involved mainly two other significant stages of work such as revision and reconstruction of the Bible prepared and used by the Catholic missionaries then.

Since Ziegenbalg's Tamil translation of the Bible was criticized, Christian Friedrich Pressier (1697-1738), Christoph Theodosius Walther (1699-1744) and Andre Worm (1704-1735) the missionaries in Tranquebar seriously undertook the steps to revise it. They completed the work and brought out the Gospel according to St. Matthew which was printed at the Tranquebar Press on 25 March 1739.[53] The Tamil title is Yesu Kristhu Swamiyin Seesanaagiya aposthalarum suviseshaganumaayiruntha archayasishta Mathei enbavar ezhuthivaitha suviseshath aagamam. The Latin title of the book is *Evangelium Matthaei de Domini Nostri Jesv Christi, qui est Filius Dei, nativitate humana, doctrina miraculis adserta, conversatione inculpate, morte expiatrice, gloriosa resurrectione et, instiuta in terries ecclesia, in coelos adscencu. Editio Tertia, prioribus ad genium linguae Tamulicae textumque originalem curatius exacta, succinstisque summaries atque parallelismo historico et exegetico adornata, Trangambariae, Missionis danicae, MDCCXXXIX*. The book has 110 pages. Paraaparan the Sanskrit word was used by Christoph Theodosius Walther and this Gospel was also put to a severe test and Johann Ernst Geister (1701-1746) and Benjamin Schultze (1689-1760) the missionaries in Cuddalore who raised serious objections. It had led to a linguistic dispute and they declared the revised edition was a miserable failure. Schultze declared that Ziegenbalg's translation was distinct and clear, and it has been understood by the *sudras* and the *pariahs*, besides by high castes and other low castes, and that many impartial brahmins had admired it too, praised it for its distinctness, and added that they would not take upon themselves to do it equally well. He therefore advised that the old translation of Ziegenbalg should be retained, and that no one should trouble themselves about the sneers of the Roman Catholic missionaries. The third edition of the New Testament in 1739 thus has an interesting history. A palm-leaf manuscript of 1740 preserved at the Archiv der Franckesche Stiftungen, Halle contains interestingly Bible verses simultaneously written in Tamil and German in each single leaf.[54] It goes to prove that Bible translation was also carried out through the palm-leaf writing system and not on paper from German to Tamil.

The radical revision with a view to issuing a new edition was subjected to very rigorous criticism and described as quite unintelligible to the natives. As a result the next edition that appeared in 1758 was of Ziegenbalg's original version.[55] There were two volumes and the first volume in Tamil has the title: Ualga retchakaraana yesu swamiyin muthinar manusharaagiya Mathei, Marku, Lukka, Yovan enpavargal avar peril yezhuthi vaitha naalu suviseshamath aagamangal. It has 430 pages. Volume one alone has a Latin title which runs: *Domini Nostri Jesu Christi, qui est servator mundi, novi foederis libri: S. Matthaei, Marci, Lucae et Joannis Evangeliaa, Apostolorum Jesu Acta, eorundem ad diversas ecclesiaes scriptas, et sancto Joanni revealtio, edition tertia Trangambariae, typis sumtibusque missionis danicae, anno 1758.* The volume two has the title in Tamil: Ulaga retchakraana yesu kristhu saami undupannina puthu udanpadikaiyin aagamangalaagiya Mathei, Marku, Lukka, Yovan enpavargal avar peril yezhuthi vaitha naalu suviseshamath aagamangal, printed in 1758. It has 471 pages.[56]

Bible Translation from Portuguese to Tamil by the Dutch

João Ferreira Annes d'Almeida's New Testament was printed in 1681 in Jakarta after reviewing and approval by the Dutch Reformed Church authorities. His first printed New Testaments and Old Testament editions of the eighteenth century became popular. The Dutch Reformed Church felt the importance of Bible teaching to the converts. Hence the missionaries made attempts to translate it from Portuguese to Tamil for use in Sri Lanka and wished to use in the churches on the Tamil coast. Francisco de Fonseca a native from Jaffna translated the Gospel of St. Mathew from Portuguese to Tamil. Philippus Baldaeus the missionary in his chapter 46 of the Ceylon portion had made it very clear which portions of translations intended for his churches had been left to his assistant, Francisco de Fonseca who revised it from Portuguese to Tamil.[57] Baldaeus also mentioned the translation of

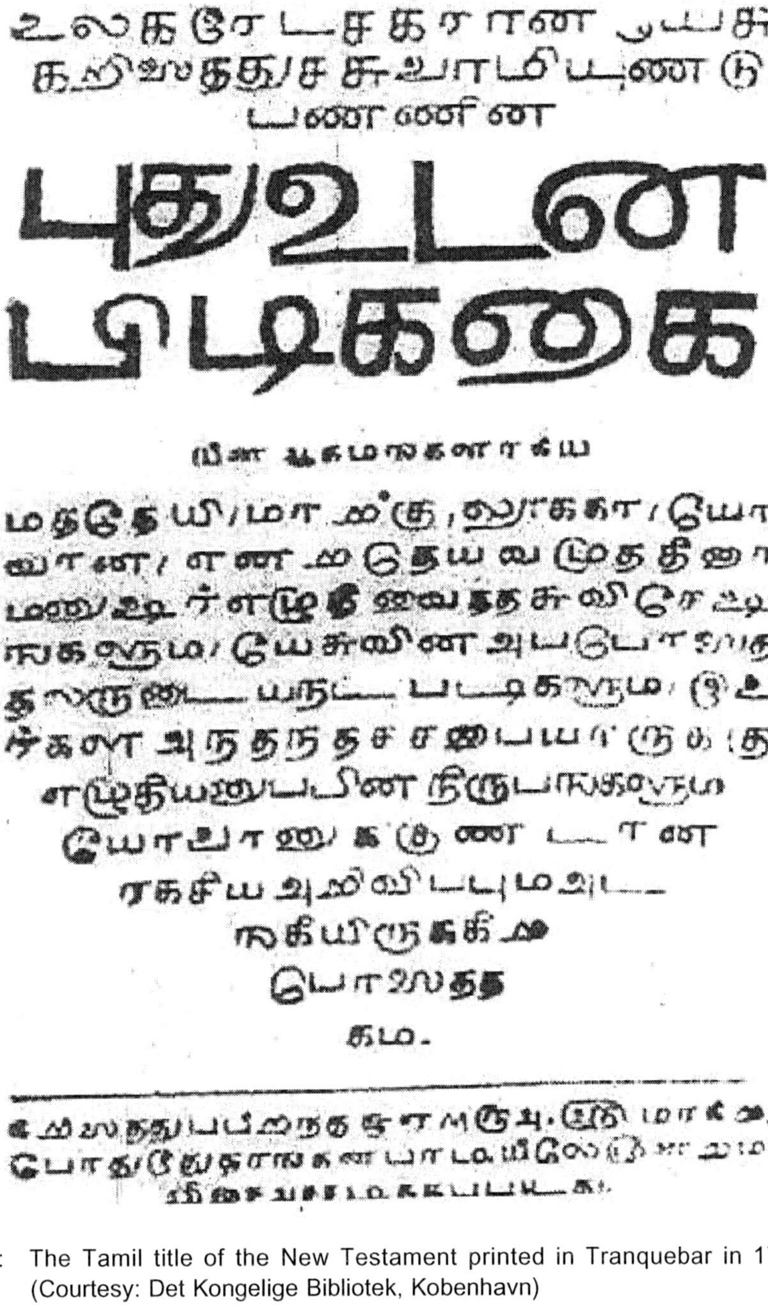

புதுஉடன்படிக்கை

7.8: The Tamil title of the New Testament printed in Tranquebar in 1758 (Courtesy: Det Kongelige Bibliotek, Kobenhavn)

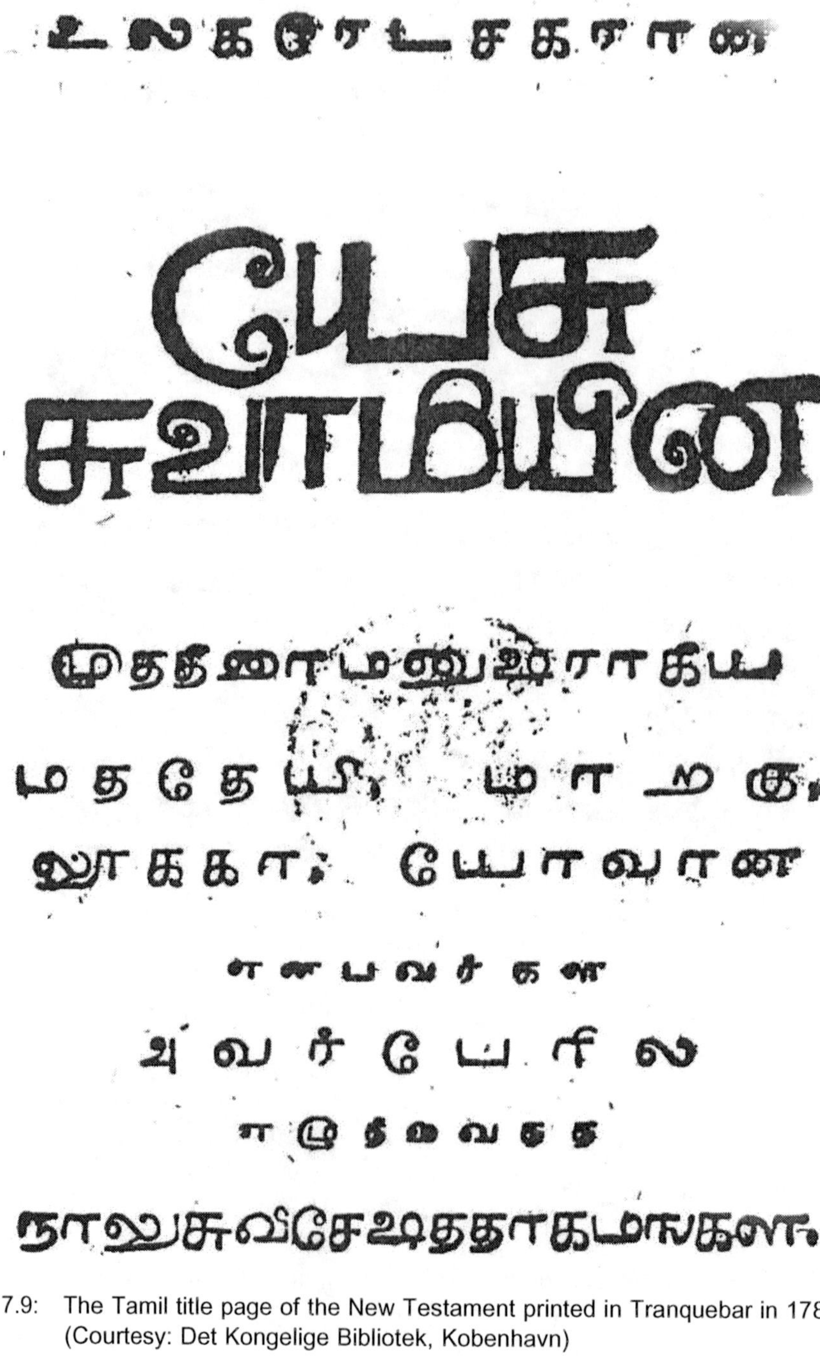
உலகரெட்சகரான

யேசு
சுவாமியின

மத்தேயு, மாற்கு,
லூக்கா, யோவான்
என்பவர்கள்
அவர் பேரில
எழுதிவைத்த
நாலுசுவிசேஷத்தாகமங்கள்.

7.9: The Tamil title page of the New Testament printed in Tranquebar in 1788 (Courtesy: Det Kongelige Bibliotek, Kobenhavn) the Psalms at various stages of work in progress. His language assistant, Francisco de Fonseca, was heavily loaded with the single responsibility of preparing the school texts books too. Baldaeus referred to a Bible printed in Rotterdam in Tamil as early as in 1671.[58]

Adrianus de Meij the Dutch *predikant* who came to Sri Lanka in 1678 was in Jaffna. He desired to do the Bible translations and in 1697 he translated the Acts of the Apostles in Tamil. He finished the translation of the New Testament into Tamil in 1692. It was available in manuscript form and the same was used by Simon Kar in Colombo in 1697.[59] Thus we notice that apparently Baldaeus's translation of the Bible was also used in Sri Lanka in manuscript form.

Bible Translation from Greek into Tamil by Adolphus Cramer in Colombo, 1732-48

A printing press was introduced by the Dutch in Sri Lanka in 1736. Translation of the Bible began to undergo several revisions at various hands. Adolphus Cramer translated parts of New Testament and he began the work in 1732 under the patronage of Gustavus Whilhem Baron Imhoff the Dutch Governor of Sri Lanka. Ziegenbalg's New Testament printed in Tranquebar was used by them. Cramer paid attention and used the pattern adopted in Greek original Bible. In a request made by Imhoff for the assistance of running the printing press, the son of Peter Michaelsen, the Danish type-founder in Tranquebar was sent to Colombo in 1737. He prepared the first Colombo type Tamil founts and these were used for the printing of the Lord's Prayer in Tamil on 28 April 1739.

In 1741, the Gospel according to St Mathew translation which was completed by Adolphus Cramer was printed in Colombo. The work is based partly on the Tranquebar New Testament. There was a Dutch title page printed and it runs: *Het Heylige Evangelium Onzes Heeren en Zaligmakers Jesu Christi na de Beschryvinge van den Heilingen Apostel en Evangelist Mattheus, uyt de Oorspronkelyke Grieske, in de Mallabaarse Tale overgebragt en behoorlyk na Kerken ordre gerediveert.* Then we find the Printers' mark, Gedrukt tot Colombo. Then we find in the book a rule, Compagnies Druckeryre, Anno 1741. There was also Tamil title page printed. Both the Dutch title and the Tamil title page had been printed with the help of woodcut made. The Bible has a preface and the Tamil text follows. It must be said that page four of the gospel is blank. The book has 120 pages in total.[60] The New Testament was printed in 1741 in Colombo under the auspices of Dutch Governor. It was in the Tamil language different from that of the earlier printed version by the missionaries in Tranquebar in 1714. Regarding the format we find the verses number of the gospel had been printed in the beginning of the verse in the Dutch version. The earlier Tranquebar printed Gospel of St. Mathew had the verse number at the end of the sentence. The Tamil word *senipithaar* (meaning born) had been used in Tamil in the Dutch version. The Tranquebar Gospel had the Tamil word *piranthaar* (meaning born). Hence it may be said that the Gospel of St. Mathew printed in Colombo had used sanskritized Tamil words. Thus the second Tranquebar edition was reprinted at Colombo in 1741-3, after having undergone some alterations adapting it to the Tamil spoken in Sri Lanka. This edition was designed for the Tamil Christians in the island, and was published under the auspices of L. B. von Imhoff, the Dutch governor.

Beschi introduced changes in Tamil scripts. He spoke of it in his Tamil grammar work Kodunthamizh (1728), Thonnul Vizhlakkam in his grammar in one Suththiram (1731) and in the preface of Chaturagaraathi (1732). He wrote that to the short letter (e) he added a slanting stroke and wrote the long form as (e/long) and similarly to the short 'O' Beschi added a loop at the bottom to make it the long letter 'O'. In vowel consonants the sound 'ye' is represented by a kompu. Beschi wrote that he added a loop at the top to this kompu to make it represent the long sound.[61] These changes made by Beschi came to be permanent features of the Tamils script as early as in 1741 and we find it in the Bible edition of 1741 by the Dutch in Sri Lanka. We find the use of a dash above the letter to indicate that the vowel sound is long. The short vowel sound has no special distinguishing marks. This must be said only a flourish and not used to denote any changes in sound.[62] It is interesting to find that the Bible in Tamil printed in Sri Lanka had Beschi's reformed Tamil letters or scripts. This copy of the Bible is preserved in the Colombo Museum.

Predikant J. Philip Wetzelius (1692-1751) and Adolphus Cramer translated the Gospel St. Mark, St. Luke and St. John in 1741 and we find a copy dated 1742. It is preserved at the British International Bible Society in London.[63] The edition of 1741 is of the original Dutch translation for we find the sacred name Jehovah is rendered 'Iyoavavakiya saruvesparan'.

The four Gospels and the Acts of the Apostles translated by Adolphus Cramer and group in Tamil was printed by the Dutch in 1748. The title page in Dutch runs: '*Het Heylige Evangelium onzes Heeren ende Zaligmakers Jesu Christi, na de Beschryvinge, van de Mannen Gods, en de H: Evangelisten, Mattheus, Marcus, Lucas, ende Johannes. Waar by nog komt het Tweede Boek, door Lucas, beschreeven, ende genaamt, de Handelingen de Apostelen, uit het Oorspronkelyke Grieks, in de Tamulsche Tale*'. It is followed by the Printer's mark, Gedrukt tot Colombo, a rule in's Compagnies Druckerye, Anno 1748. The Dutch title was followed by the Tamil title with vignette, and we find Voor-reden (Tamil preface), then begins the Tamil text. It has 212 pages in total. The text is completely set in two columns. It may be mentioned that this edition of 1748 had also used Beschi's reformed letters. We find here the dash is used occasionally, but generally it dispensed with the dash. From the context the reader has to decide whether the vowel sound is short or long.[64]

Bible Translation from Koine Greek into Tamil by Philippus de Melho in Colombo and Jaffna, 1759

The translations made by the missionaries of Tranquebar did not satisfy the Protestants of Sri Lanka either. Hence new steps were made and translation work was commenced by Philippus de Melho (1723-1790) who was the son of a wealthy Protestant *vellala* serving on the personal staff of the Dutch Governor in Colombo. He had learnt languages such as Hebrew, Greek, Latin, Dutch, Portuguese and Tamil and studied theology in Colombo. But he turned down an offer of further study in Leiden in favour of an appointment and began ministering to Sri Lankans. Six years later he was the first Sri Lankan to receive the ordination in the Church of Holland.[65]

Philippus de Melho translated 13 Psalms in Tamil and also other Bible songs and he completed the work in 1755. Hence the work in Tamil was printed in Jaffna in 1755. As customary in the Colombo printed books, the 1755 Psalter has both a Dutch and a Tamil title page (Iraasa Thirkatharisyaahiya Thaavidthinudaya sila sangeethangal). The title page in Dutch runs: *Eenige Psalmen des Koninglyken Prophete Davids en andere Lofzangen. Uyt den Nederduytschen in Tamulschen Digte overgeset door Philippus De Mello Bedienaer des H. Evangeliums in de Gemeente Jesu*

Christi, Te Jaffanapatnam: En uitgegeven naar gewoone Kerkorder, Anno 1755. It has 112 pages in total.[66] The date in old-fashioned Tamil numbers: 1,000 plus 700 plus 50 plus 5, really being letters with numerical values. Opposite the Tamil title page (verso of the Dutch) are two musical scales to illustrate the system. No textual explanation is included simply the ascending and descending scales with tonal names. Included are metrical Psalms numbers 1, 22, 23, 47, 51, 68, 69, 90, 100, 103, 110, 117, 118, 121, and 122. The six metrical 'Lofzangen' are known in Dutch as by a serious error (6) the words Simeon and Solomon have been confused. The Song of Simeon was printed at Colombo and the Song of Solomon was not. There is a note with mention of this first edition of David's psalms set to music by Philippus de Melho.[67] The Psalms he translated were in poetry as in the original and also he translated them as it could be sung in European music.[68] It would be interesting to know what portion of the 1755 Tamil poetry in this Psalter might be attributed to Clement Marat, through Philippus Baldaeus, and then through the revision by *predikant* Philippus de Melho. The 1755 Psalter in Tamil language and characters is the earliest vernacular book of music to be produced by a printing press anywhere in Asia.

Philippus de Melho was not pleased with the Tranquebar version of the Tamil Bible. He became the first Sri Lankan translator of the Tamil New Testament. He began revising it in 1746 so that it would follow more closely the original Koine Greek and worked at it for 13 years. In the mean time, he moved from Colombo to lead the Protestant Christians in Jaffna and, while there his New Testament translation appeared in print in 1759.[69] The New Testament in Tamil printed by the Dutch had a title page in Dutch. It runs as follows: *Het Nieuwe Testament, ofte Alle De Boeken Des Nieuwen Verbonds Van Onsen Heer Jesus Christus, Door Last van de Hooge Overheid Deeses Eilands Uit de oirspronglyke Grieksche Taal In de Tamulsche Spraak overgezet, En Naar Kerken-order behoorlyk overzien. It is followed by Vignette, Gedrukt te Colombo, in Dutch Company, gewoone Drukkery door Pieter Bruwaart. Anno MDCCLIX.*

After the Dutch title Dutch quotation from Openbaar, Voor-reden, Colombo, 24 December 1759 is mentioned and also signed by Sigisb Abraham Bronsveld and J. J. Fybrands. The Tamil title Puthiya Yerpaadu is found with vignette, Openbaar. Then we find the Tamil preface, Tamil text, and finally index in Dutch and Tamil index. The book has 256 pages.

The preface of the Bible is dated 24 December 1759 and the translators are Philippus de Melho and Simon de Zilva. It reports on the mission work by Philippus Baldaeus, Philippus de Vriest, Joan Anthony, Jan Philips, Philip Emanuels and Simon de Sylva.[70] It may be mentioned here that the translation was largely the work of J.P. Wetzelius assisted by Philippus de Melho and Simon de Sylva. Philippus de Melho had used Greek original Bible and Adrianus de Meij's translation for this work.

De Melho's translation of the Tamil Bible was publicly and solemnly read in the Jaffna Fort Church to a large body of learned Tamils and to other auditors. The assembly had agreed that it was intelligible to the common people and that its language was matchless, elegant and heart cheering.[71] It is the first Dutch translation of the entire New Testament in Tamil to be printed in Sri Lanka in 1759.

The Dutch in Sri Lanka printed the Psalms in 1776. This is a re-edition in Dutch of the 1773 Ledien edition. The title in Dutch printed runs: *Het Boek der Psalmen, Nevens de Gezangen, By de Hervormde Kerk van Nederland In Gebruik; Door Last van de Hoog Mogende Heeren Staaten Generaal der Vereenigde Nederlanden, Uit drie Berijmingen, in den Jaare 1773, gekooren, Met de noodige daar in gemaakte veranderingen tweede Oplage*. Then we find the double rule, followed by Te Colombo, By Johan Fredrik Cristoph Dornheim 1776, Drukker van de O.I. Maatschappy.

The approval by the authorities in Sri Lanka is stated on the verso reads as follows: *Dat deeze Kolombosche Druk naauwkeurig overeenstemt met de Eerste volledige openbaare Uitgaave te leiden gedrukt by C. van Hoogeveen Junior 1773, getuigt, als daar toe door de Regeering van Ceilon geautorizeerd*. Then follows the signature of M.J. Ondaatje VDM, followed by En rector van't Seminarium Te Colombo.[72] It may be said that the eldest grandson of Rector Ondaatje had compiled the 'Tabular list of original works and translations published by the late Dutch Government of Ceylon at their printing press at Colombo' and he had listed this 1773 Dutch Psalter found in 12 mm. Presently the Sri Lanka National Archives has this book in what was apparently an entire box of manuscript Dutch miscellaneous records has been segregated. Johan Fredrik Christoph Dornheim was the printer for the Dutch East India Company and he used the Dutch term Maatschappy rather than the more usual form Compagnie.

Translating the Old Testament from Hebrew to Tamil by the Dutch in 1790

The Dutch had mainly paid attention to translation and printing of the New Testament. It is found that after a long period they realized the need for the Old Testament translation in Tamil since the Tranquebar version of the Old Testament completed and published in 1723, 1726, 1727 and 1728 was for good reasons, considered to be imperfect and not good for public use. It was therefore in contemplation to prepare a new version in Sri Lanka and Tamil coast for the service of the Tamil Protestant congregation. With this view Rev. Ondaatje executed in 1774 a translation of the book of Genesis and presented it to the Governor Falk, who directed its revision according to the prescribed rule, previous to publication. But as it was deemed preferable to revise the Tranquebar version itself, directions to that effect were conveyed to him. But these were countermanded as soon as it was known in Sri Lanka that Johann Philip Fabricius the missionary in Madras had already begun that work and that the Pentateuch and the books of Joshua and Judges had been published. On the receipt of this order, Ondaatje represented to the Dutch Governor that he had read the revised version with great care and attention, and had also found it to be faulty stating at the same time his opinion, that it would be preferable to translate the Old Testament anew. He moreover added that he had received some portions of the Old Testament rendered by De Melho, which appears superior to the first (Ziegenbalg version) as well as the second (Fabricius) version. To this communication, the Governor replied that both he and De Melho had permission to commence a new version. De Melho accordingly in 1779 and 1780 submitted to the Governor the versions of the books of Genesis and Exodus made from the original Hebrew with the aid of the Septuagint, the Latin versions of Tremellius and Junius and the Netherlands State Bible.[73] It was however reported to De Melho that the Dutch Government in Sri Lanka would prefer a revision of the recently corrected Fabricius version; and they accordingly wished him such a revision, exhibiting in a separate paper of errors found thereto with the required corrections. Pursuant to this order, De Melho prepared and transmitted to Governor Falk a revised version of the Pentateuch, accompanied by a report on the subject and an annotation of the errors in the Fabricius version. The translation of the Old Testament was carried out by Philippus de Melho before his death on 10 August 1790.[74]

It has been mentioned by Johann Gottfried Klein (1766-1821) the missionary of Tranquebar who visited Jaffna that he heard De Melho's discourse on Tamil philology, in the presence of the Dutch commander. Klein candidly said that he thought he understood Tamil language very well, but after hearing De Melho's talk he confessed that he was yet a common learner, and wished his circumstances permitted him to remain some time longer to learn from De Melho something more of Tamil language. He also requested De Melho to give his fellow European missionaries and himself some instructions in the Tamil language by means of correspondence, to correct their writings and to point out the errors committed by them in the translation of the Scriptures.[75] Thus we find there was an open mindedness in improving the language of the Bible translation.

The Dutch administration assigned Philippus de Melho to review the Tamil translation of the New Testament by Ziegenbalg and his German successors at Tranquebar. De Melho in this respect had attacked it severely and found fault with its poor spelling, use of foreign words, erroneous translations, frequent interpretations, and lack of style appropriate to the subject. The views of De Melho were communicated and the Tranquebar missionaries in reply submitted several reasons for the differences between the two versions. First of all there was a difference in dialect. The missionaries considered the language spoken in Sri Lanka to be a perversion of the original Tamil, spoken on the Coromandel Coast which, the Tamils said had its origin from Madurai. Yet this was not the only difference. They also noted the differences in style. The prerogative of the Halle missionaries was not elegance but comprehension, and there were differences which could only be explained by the source-texts of their translations, the Lutheran Bible on the one hand and the Dutch Reformed Bible on the other.[76] As they had to work together in Tranquebar with Dutch Reformed and Anglican ministers they found a way to cope up with these differences.

When the Tranquebar missionaries replied that De Melho's own translation of the same texts was too high for common understanding, his rejoinder was that the words they found difficult were actually pure Tamil words, unintelligible to none but to such as to understand no other than the lame Tamil.[77] De Melho had raised a continuing issue in Tamil letters:

What is the standard of good Tamil prose? When an author addresses a general audience rather than the traditional elite, what style of Tamil should he use—the literary dialect of regional elites such as the *vellalars* of Jaffna or the dialects of the non-literate population or something created especially for the purpose? Though it was a century after the Tamil Hindus took up the issue, but Bible translation again was the starting point. Thus there were two groups of people found in the Bible translations. One was that those who accepted Christian Tamil and others who refused to accept the Christian Tamil style. This paved the way for the pure Tamil movement. The European translation of the Bible style was something new and different to Tamil prose language.

The inventories of the Dutch ships mention their number of Psalters such as 32 Psalters with locks, and 133 Psalters leather bound on a called ship Trincomalle. It is dated 20 February 1789 and preserved in the Sri Lanka National Archives.[78] As the Dutch Reformed Church was a psalm-singing communion, metrical versions of the Psalms, collected in Psalters, became part and parcel of the liturgical equipment of the congregation.

Translating the Bible from Greek into Tamil by Johann Philipp Fabricius and Printing in Madras and Tranquebar, 1772-96

Johann Philipp Fabricius arrived at Tranquebar in 1740 but two years later he entered into the service of the English East India Company as a missionary and moved over to Madras in 1743, where he began to read Ziegenbalg's translation of the Bible. He started revising the New Testament of Ziegenbalg and Schultze translation in 1752 through the critical guidance of a highly reputed Hindu Tamil scholar named Muthu. Noting the difficulty, he too set out to retranslate scripture from the original languages. Fabricius was going on with his revised New Testament for thirty years after having come to Madras and finally his New Testament with four Gospels and the Acts of the Apostles was published by the press at Vepery in Madras in 1772. It is to be noted that 1000 copies were printed. The Tamil title is Nammuda kartharum iratchakarumaahiya yesu kristhuvinaal undaana kirupayin udanpadikaiyaagiya puthu yerpaadu'. This book printing happened thirteen years after De Melho's version of New Testament that appeared.[79]

Fabricius in his Bible had listed the feasts of the birthday of Christ (Christmas), the circumcision of Christ or New Year day, the manifestation

7.10: A page from the Tamil New Testament of Fabricius printed in Madras in 1772 (Courtesy: Archives of the United Theological College, Bengaluru)

of Christ or epiphany, Good Friday, Easter day, Ascension day, Whit Sunday and Trinity Sunday in an appendix to the Tamil New Testament printed in 1772. Vethanayaga Sastri had also stated this information in the humble address Saathi Thirattu (Explaining caste) which he wrote.[80]

The four gospels of the New Testament in Tamil appeared in print from the Danish mission press at Tranquebar in 1788. It has 367 pages with a Latin title and a Tamil title. We find two pages are numbered as 304. This is the fourth edition of the New Testament in Tamil titled *Ulaga Ratchakaraana Yesu Swamiyin Muthinar Manusharaagiya Mathei, Marku, Lukaa, Yovaan Yenpavargal Avar Peril Yezhuthivaiththa Naalu Suviseshathaagamangal.*[81]

Fabricius also carried out the translation of the Old Testament in Tamil based on Hebrew Bible. He undertook the revision of Benjamin Schultze's version of the Old Testament preparatory to a second edition; but the work, as revised by him, has every claim to be considered new and independent. Fabricius sent the translation sheets for examination and correction to the missionaries at Cuddalore. It was passed on from there to the Danish missionaries and from them it was passed on to Daniel Pillai, the Tamil translator to the Danish government. The notes and corrections thus obtained were carefully collated by Fabricius, and the whole translation was again subjected by him to a searching revision. He worked at it for over twenty years. Daniel Zeglin the missionary (died in 1780) checked the translations. Daniel Pillai, the interpreter of the Danish East India Company helped Fabricius extensively. Excessive and slavish adherence to the word-for-word translation of the original was the change that has been well brought out which we find in his work. This Bible translation work when completed was printed at the mission press at Tranquebar under the special care of Johann Peter Rottler (1749-1836) who knew Tamil very well. It was printed in four volumes. The first volume from the Book of Genesis to Judges appeared from the press in Tranquebar in 1777.[82] The Tamil title is Manusasaathi ratchikapaduvatharkkaka sarvalogathaya paraaparanaana karthar aruliseytha sathya vetham: Muthalaam pangu. The Latin title is *Librorum sacrorum veteris testamenti pars prima. Contens libros mosis, josuae et judicum-edition secunda correctioner*. This Bible had to be printed in four volumes, because the letters/scripts were of large size and very big in printing and the textual pages were less in comparison.

In continuation of the New Testament printed in 1772, the New Testament of the Bible in Tamil by Fabricius contained from the book of Romans to Revelation appeared in print from the press at Tranquebar in 1778.[83]

The second volume of the Old Testament in Tamil by Fabricius from Book of Ruth to Job was published in 1782 from the press at Tranquebar.[84] The Tamil title is Manusasaathi ratechikka padavarkathakka sarvalogathaya paraaparanaana Karthar aruliseytha sathya vetham: Irandaam pangu. The Latin title is *Librorum Sacrorum Veteris testamenti pars secunda: continens Libros Ruth, II. Samuelis, II. Regum, II. Chronicorum, Esrae, Nehemiae, Esther et Jobi, Editio secunda Correctioner*. There are two pages numbered 320 in this printed book.

The third volume of the Old Testament in Tamil by Fabricius from the Book of Psalms to Song of Songs was printed at Tranquebar press in 1791.[85] The Tamil title is Manushasaathi retchikapattuvarathakka sarvalokathaya paraaparanaana karthar aruliseytha sathya vetham: Moonram Pangu. The Latin title is *Librorum Sacrorum Veteris, pars tertia, Continens Libros psalmorum, Proverbiorum, Ecclesiastae et Cantici Canticorum, Editio secunda Correctioner*. The book has 130 pages.

The fourth volume of the Old Testament in Tamil by Fabricius from the book of Isaiah to Malachi was printed from the Tranquebar press in 1796.[86] It has 287 pages and the Tamil title is 'Manushasaathi retchikapattuvarathakka sarvalokathaya paraaparanaana karthar aruliseytha sathya vetham: Naalaam pangu'. Fabricius who desired that Bible should be in readable form sought opinion of many others and made suitable changes. As a result the Old Testament in four parts came to be printed with 808 pages. He had omitted the books of Apocrypha from translation into Tamil.

Fabricius used the term *paraaparan* in his Old Testament printed in 1777 and he also later used the term kartharaagiya paraaparan (God who is Lord). The term *paran* in Tamil referred to Siva in Hinduism with the female power of the Hindu goddess Paravathi. Therefore in Jaffna it was opined that Fabricius translation, however was a mixture of all words current on the Tamil coast and was extremely uncouth, barbarous and ridiculous, owing to the grammatical errors and the vulgarism with which it abounded.[87]

Philippus De Melho in a report to Falk the Dutch Governor of Sri Lanka submitted a passage demonstratively showing the character of Fabricius version. It was stated that the language and style had not been arranged in accordance with the solemnity of such a divine revelation as the Holy Scripture. The spelling of a great many words is very defective. Foreign words have been introduced by Fabricius, which in Tamil style appear ungraceful and deform the language and disfigure it. Abundant errors had also crept into it consisting of unnecessary additions of words which were not in the sacred text and inadmissible omissions of those were in it, bad and incorrect renderings and incompatible interpretations, instead of translations and that in so many places as De Melho had noted down. The same as was to be seen in the accompanying statement of errors in the five books of Moses (Pentateuch) alone. De Melho's critique on Fabricius version was sent to the Protestant missionaries in Tranquebar along with a copy of his own translation. The missionaries in Tranquebar agreed that De Melho's translation used excellent and choice language, but they doubted that the common people would understand it.[88]

Scholars have agreed that his translation rendering is more faithful to the original tongues than either the English or the German, but his language was sometime obscure. Later translators in the nineteenth century like Karl Theophilus Ewald Rhenius (1790-1838) and Henry Bower (1813-1889) did not change from the style of Fabricius.

It may be pointed out that the Tamil gospels of Tranquebar New Testament of 1714 and 1715, Old Testament of 1723, 1726, 1727, part one two and three, besides printed New Testament of Colombo in 1748, New Testament of Madras printed in 1772 were by different missionaries at different times and places. Every translation of the Bible into Tamil reflects the socio-historic situation obtained at the time of translation. Each translation given the sincerity of the translators and need of the churches is one more attempt to get nearer the original text of the Bible as such is a faithful translation of the period. The denominational differences of the churches had continued and there was no cooperation at all between the churches in making an attempt for a common and good translation. The Catholic Church never allowed the Bible to be printed in any vernaculars but the Protestants were trying to get nearer to the Word of God and to the people which was the important strategy of the times. It may be mentioned that the scriptures translated at times were published even in the periodicals.

Not entire Bible stories but translations of Christian prayers which appeared at the end of a missionary diary. "Say among the heathen that the Lord Reigneth (psalm 96:10) was translated as Karthar ratshiabaram pannugirar ennu pura saathiyaaril sollungol.[89] This translation was reprinted also in Latin and Tamil scripts.

There were differences only in the use of words but not in the sense they conveyed. This was the opinion of native poets like Vethanayagam Sastri in Thanjavur who mentioned it in 1825 in his pamphlet, titled '*Puthu Thiruthuthalin Kookural*' (Noise of the New Corrections).[90] Vethanayagam Sastri also said that Fabricius' New Testament and Old Testament translations had created a language that 'could be plainly understood by the learned and unlearned, a most agreeable Tamil, rejoicing and edifying the mind like the joys of the garden of Eden and the gladness of the city of god.[91] Nevertheless, years later in 1829, the same Vethanayagam Sastri wrote in a bad taste condemning that the Bible translations and he said that they had spoiled our books. Sastri also affirmed in his humble address in 1829 that despite knowing these translations to be against their conscience and erroneous the Protestant missionaries had still continuously put them in print time and again publishing them incessantly.[92] Thus judgments about the Bible Tamil translations greatly varied. However, it has been the opinion of Sabapthi Kulendiran that Christian Tamil was created or founded by Fabricius.[93] His view needs seriously to be reconsidered in the light of our earlier discussion presented.

Printing the Tamil New Testament at Serampore in 1813

The Danish mission press at Serampore near Calcutta brought out the New Testament in Tamil in 1813.[94] The same press published the psalms translated by Christian David in 1818. Johann Peter Rottler (1749-1836), the protestant missionary in Madras had translated the psalms into Tamil and the book was also printed at Madras in 1819. An original is preserved at the American Bible Society Library.

Translating the New Testament from Greek into Tamil by Karl Theophilus Ewald Rhenius and Printing in Madras in 1827, 1833, and Printing in Jaffna in 1843 and in Madras in 1844

Karl Theophilus Ewald Rhenius the missionary translated the four Gospels and the Acts of the Apostles. The book was printed by the British

7.11: A page from the Tamil New Testament of Rhenius printed in Madras in 1827 (Courtesy: The American Bible Society Library, New York)

and Foreign Bible Society at Church Missionary Society (CMS) press at Madras in 1827.[95] As there was a lot of discussion among the missionaries regarding the various translations of the Bible, Rhenius composed a book on the principles of translation and it was printed at Nagercoil in 1827.[96] His version of the New Testament again got printed in Madras in 1833 by British and Foreign Bible Society. After ten years (in 1843) Rhenius translation of the New Testament was printed by the British and Foreign Bible Society in Jaffna.[97] In the next year (1844) the Old Testament translated by J.P. Fabricius and the New Testament translated by Rhenius was printed together and the full Bible appeared in print at the American Mission Press in Madras.[98] It may be mentioned that Rhenius translation was chaste in idiom though his renderings were often periphrastic and departed from the usual translations.

Translating the Bible from English to Tamil by Peter Percival and Arumuga Naavalar and Printing in Jaffna in 1850

Peter Percival who started his Methodist mission in Jaffna in 1826 desired translation of the Bible and took the assistance of Arumuga Naavalar. The full Bible translated was printed in Jaffna in 1850.[99] The translation work was started in 1840 and it included in its board the Anglican missionaries like Samuel Hutchings, H.R. Hoisington and Winslow. It was insisted that the authorized version of 1611 in English should be used for translation and it should strictly adhere to word for word. They were even told to use the extremity of maintaining the order of words, the idioms and punctuations. The Bible translated and printed was rejected by the British and Foreign Bible Society at Madras and it said that the new version did not follow the original text and the Tamil style in India was different from that of the Tamil of Jaffna. They further added that there were too many Sanskrit words used in translation and the grammar used in Jaffna in Sri Lanka and in Tamil country in India had been different.

A Dictionary of Biblical Tamil Words by Benjamin Schultze in 1728 and by Philippus De Melho in 1790

While translating the Bible in Tamil, the missionaries had prepared a dictionary of biblical words coined and used. Benjamin Schultze prepared the Tamil-Telugu biblical vocabulary of the New Testament in 1728. This he prepared with a view to serve the natives to understand the words used in the printed Bible of New Testament in 1722. This dictionary copy which he had sent to Europe is now preserved at the archives of the Francke foundation in Halle.[100] Schultze had also prepared similarly another Tamil-Telugu biblical vocabulary of the Old Testament which he completed in 1728. It was done to serve the needs of the natives in order to understand the words used in the printed Old Testament of the Bible part one in 1723, part two in 1726, part three in 1727 and the books of Apocrypha in 1728. The dictionary which he had sent to Europe is also now preserved at the archives of the Francke foundation in Halle.[101]

Over a period of time, Tamil catechists began to assist and do the translations of the Bible in Tamil and we find Philippus de Melho the native in Sri Lanka was employed and patronized by the Dutch East India Company. It was noticed then that some missionaries had introduced an improved system of orthography, with regard to the derivations of the words and had also been adopted by various other missionaries, including those of the various churches. Thus Tamil tongue in Bible translation came to have to its own peculiar idioms and the existing forms of its words changed invariably. Thus Catholic and Protestant missionaries had abundant opportunities to construct new words and formulate new terms for many things unknown to the Tamil Christians. To obviate all difficulty on this score, and to render the work generally useful, Philippus de Melho had prepared an alphabetical glossary of the words in question to be appended to his Bible translated version. It was published by the Dutch Company in 1790.[102]

It may be mentioned that religious idiom of Christian Tamil revealed some sort of parity with Hindu sacred usage. It denoted the significance of choice of particular terms and appropriateness of the sacred was only implied. A remarkable turn of event that happened was that there arose a necessity by the missionaries to compile a biblical and theological dictionary in Tamil so as to give proper meanings to terms used in the Gospel. The early efforts made in 1728 and 1790 had impact in the later period and we find Henry Bower who also did the same type of work and he compiled a biblical and theological dictionary in Tamil in 1841 which was called *Vetha Agaraathi*.

The translation committee of the Bible in Madras asked Rhenius to translate the scriptures into Tamil. In June 1823, Rhenius discussed with them. The translation committee wanted to adopt the English version as the standard one and resolved that the translation should be made according to the English version. In 1827 he published a pamphlet of sixty pages entitled, "An Essay on the Principles of Translating; the Holy Scriptures with Critical Remarks on Various Passages, Particularly in Reference to the Tamil Language.[103] He dealt with four main principles on translation. 1) The translation ought to be made from the original languages and not merely from another version. 2) The translation ought not to be literal; but the idiom both of the originals and of the language into which they are translated should be carefully attended to. 3) In countries where there is so great a difference between the language of the learned and of the unlearned as among the Hindus, the translation of the Bible ought to be made neither according to the style of the one nor according to that of the other; but the middle path should be kept between the two. 4) Passages which have been obscurely or incorrectly rendered in former translations should not be so rendered in new versions if their sense can be more clearly made out upon just evidence. Rhenius chose a style that was in-between that of the educated and the uneducated. He brought the language of the Bible more in the tune with the culture of the Tamils. The British members of the Revision Committee could not approve of it. The British notion was that all languages under the empire should be levelled down to English. On 21 August 1834, Rhenius published the review of Harper's Church and also an Address to all Christians on Union.

To conclude it may be mentioned that the churchly framework of philosophy and patristic theology was dominant in medieval Europe and so Martin Luther and his followers of Protestantism had freed the Bible and there was no ban for Bible translation and use by the Protestants. Hence printing the Bible also they did and this is the truth and fact in history. Ziegenbalg after two years of his stay in Tranquebar began to translate the Bible and finished the New Testament after living there for five years. In my opinion it is not a dangerous experiment but we know that he had been largely using the Roman Catholic translations then available to him. Though Ziegenbalg had completed it in 1711 the Bible awaited printing till 1715. Fabricius another translator of the New Testament did the work but published it after thirty years. Ziegenbalg's version began to be revised but the version of Fabricius after publication had remained unrevised for the next 130 years. This speaks of the quality of translation.

It has been now known that six editions of the New Testament in Tamil viz., four at Tranquebar, one at Colombo and one at Madras had appeared during the eighteenth century. The first edition was by Ziegenbalg in 1715, the same was reprinted in 1724, for the third time reprinted in 1739 and the fourth time in 1788. A translation of the New Testament at Colombo by the Dutch was printed in 1759 and the translation differed considerably from Tranquebar. The edition of the New Testament printed at Madras in 1772 was a revision of the Tranquebar New Testament and not a new translation.

After the death of Ziegenbalg and Grundler, the Old Testament translation work which was undertaken by them was continued by Benjamin Schultz. Rayanayakkan the catechist had been doing the work of translation of the Bible from 1727 and assisted Benjamin Schultze whose name had been mentioned in the missionary sources. In 1723 the Old Testament was printed and the first part appeared. Later in 1726 the second part and in 1727 the third part had been printed. The Old Testament was carefully revised by the Danish missionaries after 50 years and a new edition was printed in 1777. Later it was revised by Fabricius and Breithapt and it was reprinted at Tranquebar in 1786. Five books of Moses were translated by Philippus de Melho and it was printed at the press at Colombo in 1790. It was elegant and was also in High-Tamil. However it has been reported in missionary records that it was not understood by the common people. A complete edition of the Old Testament has never been printed at any place except Tranquebar. However, consecutive retranslation of the Tamil Bible had been undertaken. Many of the translations done had appeared in print at the various printing centres in India and Sri Lanka. There was a chain of link with the activities of Tamil translators of the Bible and the printers who operated from the interconnected networks that facilitated the production, distribution and reception of the translated and printed Bible besides making the cycle of print an open system, and not a closed one. We also find the royal favour at the court of King Friedrich of Denmark granting permission for printing the translation of the Bible in Tamil at Tranquebar. A page of dedication made to the king by Ziegenbalg proves transnational networks had played an important part in the circulation of translated and printed Bible in Tamil.

NOTES

1. Roland Bainton, *Here I Stand: A Life of Martin Luther*, London, 2002, p. 327.
2. Helmut T. Lehmann, ed., Theodore G. Tappert, trs., 'Table Talk no. 5324', in *Luther's Works,* vol. 54, Philadelphia, 1983, p. 408.
3. R. S. Sugirtharajah, *Postcolonial Criticism and Biblical Interpretation*, Oxford, 2002, p. 135.
4. Anthony Monserrat, *Mongolicae Legationes Commentarius*, 1582, F. Hosten, ed., trs., J. S. Hoyland, Oxford, 1922, p. 182; Payne, *Akbar and the Jesuits*, London, 1926, pp. 9, 221, 242; Edward Maclgan, *The Jesuits and the Great Moghul*, London, 1932; 'Jews and Judaism at the Court of the Moghul Emperors in Medieval India', *Proceedings of the American Academy for Jewish Research*, New York, 1949, pp. 137-77.
5. Arno Lehmann, ed., *Alte Briefe aus Indien: Unveröffentlichte Briefe von Bartholomäus Ziegenbalg 1706–1719*, Berlin, 1957, see the letter of Ziegenbalg dated 12 June 1707.
6. Ibid., see the letter of Ziegenbalg dated 24 June 1707.
7. Ibid., p. 59, see the letter of Ziegenbalg dated 22 September 1707.
8. Ibid., see the letter of Ziegenbalg dated 22 December 1710.
9. Henry I. Victor, 'Tamil Translation of the Bible by the Danish-Halle Mission during the Eighteenth Century', *Indian Church History Review*, vol. XVI, no, I, June, 1982, pp.72-85, see p. 75; Daniel Jeyaraj, 'Early Tamil Bible Translation in Tranquebar', *Dharma Deepika*, vol.1, no.1, June 1997, pp. 67-77; Sa. E. Arulsamy, *Viviliyam Vazhlarantha Varalaaru*, Coimbatore, 2000.
10. Arno Lehmann, Alte Briefe aus Indien, see the letter of Ziegenbalg dated 10 October 1711.
11. Ibid., p. 197, see the letter of Ziegenbalg to Anton Wilhelm Boehme written from Santhome of Myalpore dated 5 December 1711.
12. Ibid., see the letter of Ziegenbalg dated 9 December 1711 to Professor Joachim Lange.
13. Wilhelm Germann: *Ziegenbalg und Plütschau: Die Gründungsjahre der Trankebarschen Mission*, 2 vols., Erlangen, 1868, pp. 188-9.
14. Bartholomäus Ziegenbalg, *Propagation of the Gospel in the East: Being a Collection of Letters from the Protestant Missionaries, and other worthy Persons in the East-Indies, & c. Relating to the Mission; the Means of Promoting it; and the Success it hath pleased GOD to give to the Endeavours used hitherto, for Propagating True Christianity among the Heathen in those Parts, but chiefly on the coast of Coromandel. With a map of the East-Indies,*

Part III, Published by the direction of the Society for Promoting Christian Knowledge, London, Printed and Sold by J. Downing, in Bartholomew-Close near West-Smithfield, 1718, vol. III, pp. 41-50; Dennis D. Hudson, *Protestant Origins in India: Tamil Evangelical Christians, 1706-1835*, Surrey, 2000, p.12; Johann Ferdinand Fenger, *History of the Tranquebar Mission: Worked out from Original Papers*, trs., Emil Francke, Tranquebar, 1863, pp. 82-3.

15. Bartholomäus Ziegenbalg, Propagation of the Gospel in the East, vol. III, pp. 146-7.

16. Arno Lehmann, Alte Briefe aus Indien, see the letter of Ziegenbalg dated 12 June 1707; Ulla Sandgren, *The Tamil New Testament and Bartholomäus Ziegenbalg: A Short Study of Some Tamil Translations of the New Testament*, Uppasla, 1990; A. Daniel, *Vedagama Thamizh Mozhipeyarpil Lutheran Sabaiyaarin Pangu*, Madras, 1989.

17. David Prabhakar, *Krithava Thamizh Nadaiiyal Nokku*, Chennai, 2002, p. 10.

18. *Der Königl. Dänischen Missionarien aus Ost-Indien eingesandter ausführlichen Berichten, Von dem Werck ihrs Ams unter den Heyden, angerichteten Schulen und Gemeinen, ereigneten Hindernissen und schweren Umstanden; Beschaffenheit des Malabarischen Heydenthums, gepflogenen brieflicher Correspondentz und mundlchen Unterredungen mit selbigen heyden*, (hereafter HB), Teil 1–9, (Continuationen 1–108) Waiserihaus, Halle, 1710–1772, vol. 1, p.19; The text runs thus: *In der Translation selbsten aber gedenke ich ganz allein zu seyn, ohne daß ich nur einen malabarischen Schreiber bey mir habe, den ich alles in Griffel dictiren könne: Sintemal ich hierinnen keine Hülfe von anderen nötig habe, auch solche nicht bekommen könnte, wenn ich sie gleich verlangte. Denn es ist allhier weder unter den Christen noch Malabaren einer, so da verstünde nur periodum rechtmäßig ohne vitiis translatieren.* See also, Johann Ferdinand Fenger, History of the Tranquebar Mission, pp.84-5.

19. Daniel Jeyaraj, Early Tamil Bible Translation in Tranquebar, pp. 67-77; Johann Ferdinand Fenger, History of the Tranquebar Mission, p. 90.

20. The American Bible Society Library (hereafter ABSL), New York City, Accession no. 25060, Call no. 1481513, The Library of King George III, London, no.2.a.4; The New Testament has v+494 pages. There is a book containing the Gospels and the Acts of the Apostles printed in Tranquebar in 1714 at the Universitat Leipzig. The Tamil imprint found mentions the year 1715. There is another book printed available at the Bibliothek der Franckesche Stiftungen, Halle, 12D 7, pp. 1-494.

21. British Library, London (hereafter BL), Or.70.b.21; Universiteits Bibliotheek, Leiden (hereafter UBL), 877 C 2-3; ABSL, Accession no. 12226; New York Public Library (hereafter NYPL), OLB 1728.

22. Bibliothek der Franckesche Stiftungen (hereafter BFSt), Halle, 12D 7, see the letter of St. Paul to the Hebrews, pp. 107-23.
23. BL, no. 1410.g.1; *Novum Jesu Christi Testamentum, ex Originali Textu in Linguam Damulicum Versum Opera & Studio Bartholomaei Ziegenbalgi & Joh. Ernesti Grundleri, Editio Secunda*, Tranquebariae, 1722. There is a book available at the Universitat Leipzig and contains xv+1048 pages.
24. S. Michael Irudayam and Y. Robinson Levi, eds., *History of the Tamil Bible Translation*, Madurai, 2002, p. 66.
25. Det Kongelige Bibliotek, Kobenhavn (hereafter KB), 1-188; KB HJ, 46a-b; BL, London, Or.71.C.18; Rosenkilde Volmer, Printing in Tranquebar, 1712-1845, *The Library Series 5*, vol. 4, 1949, pp. 179-95, see p.186.
26. Arno Lehmann, Alte Briefe aus Indien, p. 206, see the letter of Ziegenbalg to Professor Joachim Lange written from Santhome of Mylapore dated 9 December 1711.
27. *Notices of Madras and Cuddalore in the Last Century from the Journals and Letters of the Earlier Missionaries of the Society for the Propagation of Christian Knowledge*, London, 1858, p.28.
28. ABSL, Accession number no. 15291; New York Public Library, OLB 1723-I vol; Archives of the United Theological College (hereafter AUTC), Bengaluru, Call no. A9/19; BL, London, Or.70.b.21; KB, 1-41, KB, HJ,7.
29. Ibid.
30. Biblioteca Nacional de Lisboã (hereafter BNL), Portugal, Reservados, A.6246; KB, 1-111; BL, London, no. 3090ccc.6; *Daavidengiravar Yezhuthivaitha Gnaana Sangeethangaludaya Posthagam*: *Liber Psalmorum Davidis Regis et Prophetae, ex Originali Textu in Lingua Damulicam Versus Opera & Studio Benjamin Schultze*, Tranquebariae, 1724. The book has iv+255 pages.
31. Johann Ferdinand Fenger, History of the Tranquebar Mission, pp. 131-33.
32. New York Public Library, OLB 1723; AUTC, call no. A9/21; BL, London, no. 3066.g.6.
33. KB, 1-41; KB, HJ 9; AUTC, call no. A9/21. This Old Testament has the pages continued from part I of the Bible published in 1724.
34. S. Michael Irudayam and Y. Robinson Levi, History of the Tamil Bible Translation, p. 66.
35. NYPL, OLB 1723; AUTC, Call no. Z/66.
36. Notices of Madras and Cuddalore, p. 28.
37. KB, 1-169; AUTC, Call no. Z/66.
38. S. Michael Irudayam and Y. Robinson Levi, History of the Tamil Bible Translation, p. 66.

39. Johann Ferdinand Fenger, History of the Tranquebar Mission, pp. 132-3.
40. KB, HJ, 10; KB, HJ 1-163; NYPL, OLB 1728, II vol., AUTC, Call no. Z/66.
41. Bartholomäus Ziegenbalg, Propagation of the Gospel in the East, vol. III, pp. 2-11; Dennis D. Hudson, *Protestant Origins in India: Tamil Evangelical Christians, 1706-1835*, Surrey, 2000, p. 145.
42. Archiv der Franckesche Stiftungen (hereafter AFSt), Halle, M 2 C10:59; Bror Tiliander, *Christian and Hindu Terminology: Study in their Mutual Relations with Special Reference to Tamil Area*, Uppsala, 1974, p. 127.
43. KB, 1-111; KB, HJ 490; BNL, MSS Cota Res.248v.
44. Dennis D. Hudson, Protestant Origins in India, p. 42; Rajaiah D. Paul, *Triumphs of His Grace: Lives of Eight Indian Christian Laymen of the Early Days of Protestant Christianity in India, Every One of Whom was a Triumph of His Grace*, Madras, 1967, pp. 17-27.
45. Rajaiah D. Paul, Triumphs of, p. 26.
46. C. J. Beschi, *Vetha Vizhlakkam*, Senmarakkini Maatha Achchukoodam, Pondicherry 1842, see chapter XVIII; see also, second edition, Pondicherry, 1855; third edition, Pondicherry, 1868.
47. Ibid., chapter XVI.
48. Madurai Province Jesuit Archives (hereafter MPJA), Shenbaganur, *Documents Bertrand,* vol. III, document, no. 362.
49. Leon Besse, *Father Beschi: His Times and his Writings*, Trichnopoly, 1918, pp. 84-5.
50. AFSt, M2 E 46:16 (2).
51. HB, continuation 6, p. 33.
52. HB, continuation 24, p. 1025.
53. KB, 1-209; BL, London, no. G. 20059.
54. AFSt, MS: P/TAM 97.
55. KB, 1-189, KB, HJ, 7a-b; HJ, 490; Rosenkilde Volmer, Printing in Tranquebar, p. 186.
56. KB, 1-189.
57. Philippus Baldaeus died in March 1671 and his travel account appeared in 1672 in Dutch, with an almost-simultaneous German translation. The English translation was from the German. Philippus Baldaeus, Philippus Baldaeus, *Nauwkeurige beschryvinge van Malabar en Choromandel, derhalver aangrenzende ryken, en het machtige eyland Ceylon. Nevens een omstandige en grondigh doorzochte ontdekking en wederlegginge van de afgoderye der Oost-Indische heydenen*, 3 vols, Amsterdam, Janssonius van Waasberge en

van Someren, 1672; Philippus Baldaeus, *Bahrhaftige Ausfuhr- liche Beschreibung,* Amsterdam, 1672; Philippus Baldaeus, *A True and Exact Description of the Celebrated East-India Coasts of Malabar and Coromandel as also of the island of Ceylon*, translated from the High Dutch London: Printed for Awnsham & John Churchill, 1703.

58. Ibid., see chapter. 46.
59. Simon Kar, Colombo, One folder Circa 1697, Oosterse Handschriften, Legatum Warnerianum, Or.4997. Sabapathi Kulendiran is incorrect with regard to the year 1692. Sabapathy Kulendran, *Kristhava Thamizh Vethaagamathin Varalaru*, Bangalore, 1967, p. 69; Esther Nancy Beulah is incorrect saying that Adrianus de Meij's translation of New Testament was not printed. Esther Nancy Beulah *Thamizhlil Vivilya Mozhipeyarppugal: Or Oppaivu*, Madurai, 2002, p. 33.
60. Hendrik Koaemer Institut (hereafter HKI), Oegstgeest, K-154; HKI, G-9-14; BL, London, 14170.cc.15.
61. S. Jeyaseela Stephen, *From Anrique Anriquez to Louis Savinien Dupuis: The Tamil Grammar and Dictionary Quest*, Pondicherry, 2017, pp. 83-86, 103, 106-7, 110, 202-03.
62. C. Balasingham, 'Some Unusual Characters Used in Tamil Printing in Ceylon during Dutch Times', *Proceedings of the International Conference-Seminar of Tamil Studies*, Madras, 1971, vol., II, pp. 528-30, see p. 529.
63. British International Bible Society, London, J. Philip Wetzelius and Adolphus Cramer, trs., *The Gospel St. Mark, St. Luke and St. John, 1742*. Sabapathy Kulendran, Kristhava Thamizh Vethaagamathin Varalaru, p. 29; J. S. M. Hooper, *Bible Translations in India, Pakistan and Ceylon*, Oxford, 1963.
64. Koninklijke Bibliotheek, Den Haag (hereafter KBDH), 662 B 23; HKI, K-155.
65. Simon Casie Chitty, *The Tamil Plutarch: Containing a Summary Account of the Lives of the Poets and Poetesses of South India and Ceylon from the Earliest to the Present Times with Select Specimens of their Compositions*, Jaffna, 1859, pp 69-76.
66. HKI, K-10; KBDH, 4 F 20; KBDH, 488 H 3.
67. Universiteits Bibliotheek, Amsterdam (hereafter UBA), 492 E27; 877 G 12; Universiteits Bibliotheek, Leiden (hereafter UBL), 1144 F 23.
68. Sabapathy Kulendran, Kristhava Thamizh Vethaagamathin Varalaru, p. 78.
69. Philippus de Melho and Simon de Zilva, *Het Nieuwe Testament: Ofte alle de Boeken des Nieuwen Verbonds van Onsen Heer Jesus Christus*, Colombo, Pieter Bruwaart, 1759; Bibliothèque Asiatique Missions Etrangères de Paris (hereafter BAMEP), Call no.27/21; Simon Casie Chitty, The Tamil Plutarch, pp. 69-76.

70. HKI, K-155; KBDH, 662 B 21; 622 B 22; UBA, 220 B11; BL, or.71.d.8.
71. Simon Casie Chitty, The Tamil Plutarch, p. 75.
72. M. P. J. Ondaatje, 'A Tabular List of Original Works and Translations Published by the Late Dutch Government of Ceylon at their Printing Press at Colombo', *Journal of the Royal Asiatic Society of Great Britain and Ireland*, new series, 1, 1865, pp. 141-4.
73. The Old Testament contains in Hebrew 39 books (from Genesis to Leviticus, five books; Joshua to Esther, twelve books; Job to Song of Songs, five books; Isaiah to Daniel, five books and Hosea to Malachi, twelve books). The Old Testament in Septuagint (Greek) contains 46 books.
74. British and Foreign Bible Society's Library (hereafter BFBSL), Cambridge University, Cambridge, *Het eerste deel des Ouden testaments van de Heilige Schrivtuur, vervattende de vye Boeken Mosis genaamd Genesis, Exodus, Leviticus, Numeri, en Deuteronomium gedrukt te Colombo, in's Komp: Boekdrukkery, by Johan Frederik Christoph Dornheim, anno 1790.*
75. Simon Casie Chitty, The Tamil Plutarch, p. 86.
76. Georg Christian Knapp, et. al., Neuere Geschichte der evangelischen Missions-Anstalten zu Bekehrung der Heiden in Ostindien aus den eigenhändigen Aufsätzen und Briefen der Missionarien erausgegeben (hereafter NHB), Teil 1–8, (Stück 1–95) Waisenhaus, Halle, 1770-8/ 1795-1848, NHB, 3, pp. 744-45. Miron Winslow marked about 3000 words in his dictionary as 'provincial' and explained the terms and meaning that most of them were peculiar to Jaffna. Miron Winslow, *A Comprehensive Tamil & English Dictionary of High and Low Tamil*, P.R. Hunt, Madras, 1862.
77. Simon Casie Chitty, 'Ceylon Celebrities: Philip de Melho, 1723-1790)', *Ceylon Literary Register*, Third Series, vol. II, no. 2, 1932, pp. 49-56.
78. Sri Lanka National Archives (hereafter SNLA), Colombo, *Dutch Miscellaneous Records*, no. 1/ 3446.
79. BL, London, or.72.b.11, *The New Testament of Our Lord & Saviour Jesus Christ, Translated into Malabar (Tamul)*, Vepery near Madras, 1772; AUTC, Call no. A11/14; HNB, III, p. 341; V, p. 635; VII, p. 925, IX, pp.1189, 1191; XI, p. 1474.
80. Dennis D. Hudson, Protestant Origins in India, p. 149
81. KB, 1-189. The Latin title is DOMINI NOSTRI JESU CHRISTI Qui est, SERVATOR MUNDI NOVI FOEDERIS libri pars prima S.MATTHEI, MARCI, LUCAE, et JOHANNIS EVANGELIA Editio Quarta, TRANGAMBARIAE, Typis Sumtibusque Missionis Danicae, Anno MDCCLXXXVIII.

82. KB, 1-41; AUTC, Call no. A9/19, *Librorum Sacrorum Veteris... Pars Prima, Continens Libros Mosis, Josuae et Judicum, Editio Secunda Correctioner*, 1777.
83. AUTC, Call no. A12/8.
84. KB 1-41; BL, or.71.d.6(2); AUTC, Call no. A9/21.
85. BL, or.71.d.6 (3); KB, 1-41; AUTC, Call no. A10/7.
86. KB, 1-41; BL, or.71.d.6 (4); AUTC, Call no. A10/8.
87. Simon Casie Chitty, The Tamil Plutarch, p. 75.
88. Ibid., pp. 75-6.
89. HB, vol. 1, continuation 7, p. 574.
90. AUTC, MSS VPC-VNS 27, Vedanayagam Sastri, Puthu Thiruthuthalin Kookural (Noise of the New Corrections).
91. AUTC, MSS VPC-VNS, 36, Vedanayagam Sastri, Puthu Thiruthuthalin Sothanai (The Ordeal of the New Corrections).
92. BL, Or.11.742, Vedanayagam Sastri, *Saathi Thirattu* (Explaining Caste), 1829.
93. Sabapathy Kulendran, Kristhava Thamizh Vethaagamathin Varalaru, p. 88.
94. New York Public Library, OLB/1813, The English title of the Bible runs: The Malabar New Testament of Our Lord and Savior Jesus Christ.
95. ABSL, Accession no. 1748. The Tamil title of the Bible runs: Ulaga Ratchagaraana Yesu Kristhuvin Udanpadikaiyaagiya Puthuverpaadu.
96. C. T. E. Rhenius, *An Essay on the Principles of Translating the Holy Scriptures with Critical Remaks on Various Passges, Particularly in Reference to the Tamil Language*, Printed at the Mission Press, Nagercoil, 1827. See, V. Richard, 'The Politics, Problem and the Beauties of Translating the Holy Bible', in C.T. Indra and R. Rajagopalan, *Culture, Language & Modernity: English-Tamil in Colonial India, 1750-1900*, Abingdon, 2018, pp. 48-65.
97. New York Public Library, OLB 1843; AUTC, call no. N532.
98. ABSL, Accession no. 6012; New York Public Library, OLB 1844. The English title of the Bible runs: Holy Bible in Tamil: The Old Testament translated from the original by the Rev. J.P. Fabricius, the New Testament by the Rev. C.T.E. Rhenius and revised by the committee of the Madras Auxiliary Bible Society, with contents of the chapters and chronology, from the English and occasional references.
99. AUTC, call no. H/77; ABSL, accession no. 6019.
100. AFSt, MS J.66, pp. 299-388, Benjamin Schultze, *Vocabularium Telugo-Tamulo Biblicum Novi Testamenti*.

101. AFSt, MS J.66, pp. 1-288, Benjamin Schultze, *Vocabularium Telugo-Tamulo Biblicum Veteris Testamenti.*

102. Simon Casie Chitty, *The Tamil Plutarch: Containing a Summary Account of the Lives of the Poets and Poetesses of South India and Ceylon from the Earliest to the Present Times with Select Specimens of their Compositions*, Jaffna, 1859, p. 88.

103. Rhenius, *An Essay on the Principles of Translating; the Holy Scriptures with Critical Remarks on Various Passages, Particularly in Reference to the Tamil Language*, Madras, 1827.

8

The Development of Tamil Prose, its Style and the Impact of Print in the Age of Translation, 1554-1857

Religions in the world had contributed towards the growth of language and literature so also the languages and literatures had caused the spread and development of religions. European missionaries had translated the Holy Bible in Tamil and it led to successful apostolic work. The development of Tamil prose through Bible has not caught the attention it deserves. Hence this chapter aims to trace the development of Christian Tamil prose through Bible translations carried out during the mid-sixteenth to the mid-nineteenth centuries.

At the outset it must be said that Bible translation in Tamil had been done at times by one individual and other times by a group of two or three persons. History of translation has shown that missionaries who learnt Tamil language both the Catholics and the Protestants in India and Sri Lanka used different language on the same passages of the text. With regard to the textual issue it is obvious that there was no uniform reading since we find numerous and far-reaching differences between quotations of the same passages. It is also true that some books were apparently translated a number of times, and no single translator worked on all the books of the Bible. It must be said that Bible was common to all, irrespective of the various denominations of the Church. While there has been no previous study of a holistic approach some scholars have touched upon the elements of translation of our subject from various angles.[1] Their initial attention has come mainly inspired by the study of church history. They have failed to note the concept of translation from classical languages of Hebrew, Greek and Latin besides Europeans tongues like Portuguese and English into Tamil.

A manuscript in paper preserved at Det Kongelige Bibliotek, Kobenhavn has been a study of Christoph Theodosius Walther (1699-1741) at Tranquebar who translated the Bible from Hebrew into Tamil. He had interestingly noticed the Hebrew-Tamil Synonymy and had prepared a vivid and valuable account of links between these two classical languages.[2] This shows that classical status to Tamil language had been realized as early as in 1740, though the Government of India officially declared Tamil as a classical language of India only in 2004. One can also understand the linkages of other classical languages like Greek and Latin through translation of the Bible noticed by the missionaries and so they assigned importance to Tamil.

The Translation of the Lord's Prayer into Tamil from the Gospel of St. Mathew, 1554-1739

The earliest portion of the Bible translation in Tamil is the Lord's Prayer from the Gospel of St. Mathew (Chapter VI, verses 9-13) found in a book printed under the title Cartilha in Lisbon in 1554.[3] However, the script is not Tamil but transliteration in Roman characters. The translated text runs as follows:

Pithaa yengalade nee agaasathil irukkiraay
Un thirunaaman punniyam agavenum
Un rajjiyam varavenum
Yengalukku un manathu aggave agaasathilum avvanam bumiilium
Yengaloda Aappam nazhlthorum kudukirapadi yengalukku inru thaa
Poruthukol yengalukku yengalledey pizhaigalai
Appadi naangal porukkum appale yengaloda pizhaiyaari
Yengali kondu varaathey karumathil
Mattrum Ratshishi kozl yengali yellaa pollangilillum
Amen Appadi Aaga

After many years we find again the Lord's Prayer further translated into Tamil by Anrique Anriquez the missionary on the Tamil coast. His translation is found printed in Tamil script for the first time in a book titled Thambiran Vanakkam from the printing press at Quilon in 1578.[4] It is an improvement in Tamil diction, language and usage of the words found in some form of proper grammatical order. The earlier printed translation in Portugal was in a crude form when we compare the version of Anriquez. The text of Anriquez runs thus:

Vaannangalil irukkira yengal pithaave
Unnudaya Naaman yellarukkung suththamaaga
Unnudaya virachiyam vara
Un manathin padi vaanathil vaanavargal seyyumaapoley
Bhumiyilum yellarung seyya
Anranruulla yengal appam yengalukku inro thaa
Engal pizhai kadankaararukku naangal porukkumaa poley
Neeyum yengal paava kadangalai poru
Yengalai doshathukku yethuvaaha ottathey
Yengalukku pollangu varaamal vilakku
Amen

Instead of the usage 'ummudaya' in a more respectable form we find the expression 'unnudaya' followed by Anriquez. The usage of the term 'thaa' (meaning give) and also the term 'vara' (meaning come) had been given in the form of command instead of making it in the statement form.

Gaspar da Aguilar (1588-1648) the Jesuit who worked in Tamil country had translated the Lord's Prayer in 1644. It was used by Philippus Baldaeus the Dutch missionary.[5] The text translated was though found to be same as that of Anriquez but very few changes had been incorporated by him. The text of Aguilar runs thus:

Vaanangalil irukkira yengal pithave
Unnudaya naamam ellaathukkum suththamaaga
Unnudaya raacchiyam vara
Un manathinpadi vaanavargzhal vaanathil seyyumaapoley
Bhumiyilum yellaarukkum seyya
Antrantrulla yengal appam yengalukku inru thaa
Yengal pizhai kadankarrarukku naangal porukkumaa poley
Neeyum yengal paavak kadangalai poru
Yengalai thosthangalukku yethuvaaga ottaathey
Yengalukku pollaangu varaamal vilagu
Amen Sesuia

After making some changes in the translation of the Catholic missionaries, the Dutch East India Company had printed the Lord's Prayer. The printing was carried out in Amsterdam in 1672.[6] The printed text runs thus:

Vaanangalil irukkira engal pithave
Unnudaya naamam ellaathukkunj suthamaaga
Unnudaya irracchiyam vara
Un manathinpadi vaanvargzhal vaanathil seyumapoley bhumiyilum ellaarum seyya
Antrantrulla engal appam yengalukk unavaa thaa
Yengal pizhai kadankarrarukku naangal porukkumaa poley yengal paava kadangalai poru
Yengalai thosthangalukku yethuvaaga ottaathe vilaguvathu
Yengalukku pollaangu varaamal, ennum unnudayya rachchiamum vallamum mokkilum seyya yeppothum undaavathaga
Amen

It is important for we find at end an insertion after the expression '*Yengalukku pollaangu varaamal*' found in the translation the Catholic missionaries. The new translation is added with an expression 'ennum unnudayya rachchiamum vallamum mokkilum seyya yeppothum undaavathaga.''

Bartholomäus Ziegenbalg and Johann Ernst Grundler the Protestant missionaries in Tranquebar had translated and printed the New Testament in Tamil at Tranquebar in 1714.[7] The Lord's Prayer translated is totally different from all the previous versions. The printed text runs as follows:

Paramandalangaliley irukkira yengal pithaavey
Ummudaya naamam archikkapaduvathaaga
Ummudaya rachchiyam vara
Ummudaya siththam paramandalaththiley seyyapadumaapolay
Bhumiyileyum seyyapaduvathaaga
Annannullzha yengal appam yengalukku innu thaarum
Yengal kadankaararukku naangal porukkumaapoley
Neerum yengal kadangalai yengalukku porum
Yengalai sothanaiyiley pravesippiyaatheyum
Aannaalo Thinmaiyiley ninru yengalai retchithuku kollum
Atheynenral rattchiyamum, belamum, magimaiyum umakku ennenaikum undaairuukudhu
Amen.

Time and again, the Lord's Prayer had been printed in Tranquebar on various occasions (30 June 1735 and 7 July 1735).[8] We find no change in translation and the same version of Ziegenbalg appeared in print and also in reprints. The text runs as follows:

Paramandalangaliley irukkira yengal pithaavey
Ummudaya naamam archikkapaduvathaaga
Ummudaya rachchiyam vara
Ummudaya siththam paramandalaithey seyyapadumaapolay
Bhumiyileyng seyyapaduvathaaga
Anrantulla yengal appam yengalukku innu thaarum
Yengal kadankaararukku naangal porukkumaapoley
Neerum yengal kadangalai yengalukku porum
Aanaalo sothanaiyiley pravesippiyaatheyum
Thinmaiyiley ninru retchithuku kollum
Atheynenral rattchiyamum, belanum, magimaiyum umakku ennenaikum undaanathu.
Amen.

The Dutch in Sri Lanka again began to translate and they printed the Lord's Prayer in Colombo on 28 April 1739.[9] The language and the translation had been completely different from that of the earlier ones. The text runs thus:

Vaanangaliley irukkira yengal pithaavey
Ummudaya naamam archikkapaduvathaaga
Ummudaya rachchiyam vara
Ummudaya siththam vaanathir seyyapadumaapolay
Bhumiyileyng seyyapaduvathaaga
Anrantulla yengal appam yengalukku inru thaarum
Yengal kadankaararukku naangal porukkumaapoley
Neerum yengal kadangalai yengalukku porum
Yengalai sothanaiyiley pravesippiyaatheyum
Thinmaiyiley ninru retchithuku kollum
Atheynenral rattchiyamum, vallabamum mokishamum yeppothaikkum
Ummakkey ullathathu thaan, Amen

les libertins, ornant des belles couleurs de l'éloquence leurs doctrines immorales et erronées, séduisent leurs imprudents lecteurs, et leur insinuent leur poison funeste, caché dans un miel délicieux. C'est pourquoi avant de lire un livre que vous ne connaissez pas, informez-vous auprès de personnes pieuses et instruites, s'il est bon ou mauvais, et suivez les sages avis qu'ils vous donneront.

Les bons livres sont un mets délicieux et salutaire à l'âme; ils ornent l'esprit, développent l'intelligence, et forment le cœur au bien. C'est par la lecture des bons livres que vous pourrez devenir en même temps vertueux et savants. La science sans la vertu ne vous rendra jamais heureux; mais la science et la vertu réunies, seront pour vous une source intarissable de joie pure et sincère.

8.1: Piranch Ilakkana Noorsurukkam page 167 showing translation from French into Tamil in 1845 (Courtesy: Bibliothèque Asiatique des missions étrangères de Paris)

௱௫௰. ௯ர். வகுப்பு.

Si என்னுங்கூட்டிடைச்சொல்லோடே நிகழிடைபிறந்தகாலமாவதுஇறப்பிடையிறந்தகாலமாவதுவந்தால்வியங்கோள்விதத்தைக்கேட்கும். உம். நீயென்னைப்பற்றி யிதைச்செய்துகொண்டிருந்தால் அல்லது முன்னமேசெய்திருந்தால், id si faceres vel si fecisses causâ meâ.

Si என்னுங்கூட்டிடைச்சொல்லோடே வருகிறவினைச்சொல் லுக்குப்பின் வேறேவினைச்சொல் எதிர்காலத்திலாவது இறப்பிடையெதிர்காலத்திலாவதுவந்தால் முதனின்வினைச்சொல்லு மதற்கொத்தகாலத்தில்வருவதே நலம். உம். நீவந்தா லெனக்கு மிகவுஞ்சந்தோஷமானகாரியஞ்செய்வாய், si veneris, pergratum mihi feceris; நீயிந்தப்புஸ்தகத்தை வாசித்தால் அகமகிழ்வேன், quem librum si leges, lætabor.

Ut படிக்கு என்னு மர்த்தங்கொண்டிருக்கிறபோதெல்லாம் வியங்கோள்விதத்தைக்கேட்கும். உம். நான்பகலி லிளைப்பாறும் படிக்கு, luce ut quiescam.

Ut போல அல்லதுமாத்திரத்திலே என்னும்அர்த்தங்கொண்டிருந்தாற் காட்டல்விதத்தைக்கேட்கும். உம். மனிதர்சொல்லுகிறதுபோலே, ut aiunt; நான்பட்டணத்தினின்று புறப்பட்டமாத்திரத்தில், ut ab urbe discessi.

௩ம். வகுப்பு.

இலத்தீன்பாஷைக்குந் தமிழ்ப்பாஷைக்கும்வித்தியாசமானவசனங்களைமொழிபெயர்க்கும் வகை.

விவரம். பெயர் - உரி - வினைமுதலியசொற்கள்மட்டிலும் அதுகளின்பால் வேற்றுமைக்கிரமம்விகுதிக்கிரமமுதலியவைகளின் மட்டிலு மிலத்தீன்பாஷைக்குந் தமிழ்ப்பாஷைக்குமுள்ள வித்தியாசங்களிந்தப்புஸ்தகத்தின் முதல்வகுப்பிலே பொதுவாய்விளங்குகிறதுமன்றி அகராதியி லந்தந்தச்சொல்லோடேகுறிக்கவும்படும். ஆதலால் அகராதியிலொருபெயர்ச்சொல்லைத்தேடும்போது அதின்பாலேது வேற்றுமைக்கிரமமேதெனவும ஒருபெயருரிச்சொல்லைத் தேடும்போது அது எந்தவேற்றுமைக்கிரமத்தைச்சேர்ந்ததென்றும் ஒருவினைச்சொல்லைத்தேடும்போது அதுசெய்வினையோ தன்வினையோ செய்பாடுவினையோவென்றும அது கேட்கிறவேற்றுமையேதென்றும் பிரதானமாய்க்கவனித்தாராயவேண்டும்.

8.2: The page explaining translation from Latin into Tamil in Lathinilakkana Noorsurukkam in 1845 (Courtesy: Madurai Province Jesuit Archives, Shenbaganur)

The Sermon on the Mount of Jesus and its Translation into Tamil from the Gospel of St. Mathew, 1578-1857

Another important passage of the Bible from the New Testament that attracted the attention of the missionaries was the Sermon on the Mount by Jesus from the Gospel of St. Mathew (Chapter V, verses 3-12). Anrique Anriquez was the first to translate this portion from the Bible and he printed it in the book Thambiran vanakkam (which had 16 pages) at Quilon in 1578.[10] There is no dot over the consonants in the printed Tamil text and this was the practice followed at that time in the palm-leaf writing system of the Tamils. The text runs thus:

Nammudaya naayan Yesu Kristhu
Oru murai thiruvullam pattriya pothu
Mokkisha pergaliley yettu vagai ariviththaar athil muthalaavathu

Manathiley midyaraai irukkiravargal mokkisha pergalaaly irukkiraargal
Athenenraal avargal vaanagalil ratchiyaththukku utpattavargal

Rendaavathu, amainthu nadakkiravargal mokkisha pergalaaay iruukkiraargal
Athenenraal avargal bhumiyai aandiruppaargal

Munraavathu, azhugiravargal mokkisha pergalaay irukkiraargal
Athenenraal avargal santhosha pattiruppaargal

Naalavathu, niyayam nadakka venumyenru pasiththavannam undaayirukkiravargal
mokkisha pergalaay irukkiraargal
Athenenraal avargal pasiththavannam thirnthu sampoornamaay iruppaargal

Anjaavathu, irakkamullavargal mokkisha pergalaay irukkiraargal
Athenenraal avargal irakkam peruvaargal

Aaraavathu, mana suththamaay iruukiravargal mokkisha pergalaay irukiraargal
Athenenraal avargal thambirannay kaanpaargal

Yezhaavathu, uravukku thendikkiravargal mokkisha pergalaay irukkiraargal
Athenenral avargal thambiranudaya makkalenru pesappaduvaargal

Yettaavathu, niyayaththukku vendi paadupadugiravargal mokkishapergalaay irukkiraargal
Athenenrall avargal vaanagalil ratchiyaththukku udaiyavargal.

Ithu thavira namakkaaha vendi manushar ungalai thittum pozhluthum, nerungacheyyum pozhluthum, pollangkellam ungalai kondu poyyaaga sollum pozhluthu mokkisha pergalaay irukkirreergal. Ullam kazlikoornthu santhoshamaay iruungal.

Athenenraal vaanagalil ungal peru miguthiyum undaai irukkirathu. Ivai yellam nammudaya naayan Sesu Kristhu thiruvullam pattrinathu.

Amen Isesu

It is clear that the job of translation posed difficulty to Anrique Anriquez. He chose and used the equivalent/matching words in the language of the source (Latin) and the proposed textual part in the target language (Tamil). Anriquez hailed from a Jewish family. His parents became Catholic and he joined the Society of Jesus and entered into priesthood. Hence he must have had an excellent knowledge of the Hebrew Bible. He used the term 'viviliya' very rightly and coined it to refer the Tamil Bible. It is evident that Anriquez had kept his Jewish culture and Portuguese identity since the Bible was born on that soil though Christians in Europe accepted the Bible.

Bartholomäus Ziegenbalg and Johann Ernst Grundler had translated and printed the New Testament in Tamil at Tranquebar in 1714.[11] Ziegenbalg's translation of the Sermon on the Mount runs as follows:

Dharithira manuthullavargal bhakkiyavaangal
Atheynenral vaanaratchiyathukudayavargal

Rendaavathu, methamaay irukkiravargal bhakkiyavaangal
Atheynenral bhumikaandavargalaay iruppaargal

Munraavathu, azhuthukondirukkiravargal bhakkiyavaangal
Atheynenraal aarudhaladaivaargal

Naalaavathu, needhiyudaya-pasiyum thaagamumaay irukkiravargal bhakkiyavaangal
Atheynenraal thiruthi adaivaargal

Anjavaavathu, kirubhaiyaay irukkiravargal bhakkiyavaangal
Atheynenraal kirubhaiyadaivaargal

Aaraavathu, manasil suththammay irukkiravargal bhakkiyavaangal
Atheynenral saruvesuranai kaanbhaargal

Yezhaavathu, samaathanaththai thedurgiravrgal bhakkiyavaangal
Atheynenral sarvesuranudaya pillaigalyena azhaikkapaduvaargal

Yettavathu, Neethikkaaga thunpappadugiravargal bhakkiyavaangal
Atheynenral vaanaratchiyathukkukudaiyavargal.

A comparison of the texts of Anriquez and Ziegenbalg shows that different words were used in translation. The word dharithiram is used by Ziegenbalg for spiritual poverty. The term moksham of Anriquez has been replaced by translation as vaanaraatchiyam referring to heaven. The expression methamaay irukkiravargal is referred to by Anriquez in his translation to the word gentle. The expression azhuthukondu iruuppavargal is referred to those who mourn. The expression needhiyudaya pasiyum thaagamumaayirukkiravargal is referred to those who are hungry and thirsty for righteousness. Finally the term samaathanaththai thedurgiravargal is referred to the word peace-makers. Thus the prose translation of the same passage between 1578 and 1714 had undergone drastic change for the style of the language was on progress. The term irakkam (mercy) used by Anriquez has been substituted by Zigenbalg with kirubhai. So also the term thambiran (God) used by Anriquez has been substituted by Ziegenbalg with sarvesuran. Johann Philipp Fabricius, the missionary in Madras had translated the Sermon on the Mount of Jesus from Greek into Tamil. The textual translation of Fabricius runs as follows:[12]

Manaddharithirar bhakkiyavaangal
Athenenraal vaanarachchiyam avargaludayathaay irukkirathu

Thuyarapppadugiravargal bhakkiyavaangal
Athenenraal avargal thettrappaduvaargal

Methanaullavargal bhakkiyavaangal
Athenenraal avargal bhumiyai suthanthariththu kollvaargal

Neethiyinperiley pasi thaagam ullavargal bhakkiyavaangal
Athenenraal avargal thirupthi adaivaargal

Irakkam ullavargal bhakkiyavaangal
Athenenraal avargal irakkam peruvaargal

Irudhayathil suththamaanavargal bhakkiyavaangal
Athenenraal paraaparani dharisippaargal

Samaathaanathai nadathugiravargal bhakkiyavaangal
Athenenraal avargal paraaparanudaya pathirenapaduvaargal

Neethin nimiththamaga thunpapadugiravargal bhakkiyavaangal
Athenenraal vaana rachchiyam avargaludayadhaay irukkiradhu

Yen nimithamaaga dhushanithu thunpapaduththi theethu mozhi yellam ungal peril poyyaay sonnargalaanaal bhakkiyavangalaay irukkireergal

Santhosthapattu kazhikurungal. Yenenraal ungal palan paramandalanggalil thirallay irukkum. Yenyenil ungalukku muniruntha dheerkatharisigalai ippadiye thunpap paduthinnaargal.

Louis Marie Mousset and Fr Arul had translated the Lord's Prayer from Latin. This is the first Catholic Tamil Bible translated and printed in 1857 at Pondicherry by Fr Louis Savinien Dupuis.[13] The textual translation of the Sermon on the Mount runs thus:

Manadharithirar bhakkiyavaangal
Yenanil motchrachiyam avargaludayathu

Saantha gunaththor bhakkiyavaangal
Yenanil bhumai sudanthariththu kolluvaargal

Azhuvor bhakkiyavaangal
Yenanil aarudhal adaivaargal

Neethiyin mer pasi thaagam ullavargal bhakkiyavaangal
Yenanil thirithi yadaivaargal

Irakkam ullavargal bhakkiyavaangal
Yenanil irakkam adaivaargal

Thooya virdhayamulloor bhakkiyavaangal
Yenanil avargaley sarvesuranai dharisippaargal

Samaathaana gunaththor bhakkiyavaangal
Yenanrir sarvesuranudaya pillaigalyenapaduvaargal

Neethin nimiththam upathiriya padugiravargal bhakkiyavaangal
Yenanil motcha rachchiyam avargaludayadhe

Yennai pattri manidhar ungali sabiththu thunpappaduththi
Ungalperil sagala thinmaiyum abaandamaay sollumpoethu
Neengal bhakkiyavaangal

Adinaaley parlogathil ungal sambhaavanai yeraalamaay irukkiramaiyaar
Santhosthithu akkaliungal
Yenanil ungalukku muniruntha dheerkatharisigali appadiye ubhathiriya paduththinaargal.

In the above translation, Mousset and Arul replaced the term vaanarachchiyam of Ziegenbalg and it has been substituted by motcharachchiyam. The expression methamaay iirukkiravargal has been substituted by saantha gunaththor. Ziegenbalg's usage of the term kirubahi is changed into irakkam by Mousset and Arul. However, the term sarvesuran (for God) is retained by the Protestants and Catholics. The usage azuthukonduirukkiravargal is substituted by azhuvor and here we find the present tense has been changed to the future tense. It shows not only the progress of translation but also growth and development of Tamil prose.

The Translation of the Genealogy of Jesus Christ from the Gospel of St. Mathew Printed by Ziegenbalg in Tranquebar and its Comparison with the Dutch Printed Version of Colombo, 1715-1741

The textual portions of the New Testament translation of Bartholomaeu Ziegenbalg and Johann Ernst Grundler printed in Tranquebar in 1714 (Mathew Chapter I, verses, 1-3: A Book of genealogy of Jesus Christ son of David, son of Abraham. Abraham was the father of Issac, Issac of Jacob, Jacob of Judah and his brothers) runs as follows:[14]

Dhavidudayvum abiramudayavu kumaranaagiya yesu kristhuvinudaya posthagammaavathu
Abiramengiravrukku yeesaaku yengiravar piranthaar
Yeesaaku engiravrukku yakkobengiravar piranthaar
Yakkobengiravrukku yudasengiravarum avarudaya sagotharargalum piranthaargal

The same text which had been translated and printed by the Dutch runs as follows:[15]

Aavarum udaya kumaranaagiya davidinudaya kumaaran Yesus kristhusvinudaya angishaththin posthagam
Aavarum issakkuvai senipiththaar
Yeesaaku yakkobuvai senipiththaar
Yakkobu yudasuvaiyum avarudaya sagotharargaliyum senipiththaar.

On examination of the two texts, we find translations done differently with use of words. The terms senipiththaar and piranthaar had been used to convey the same meaning. The proper name of persons like Abraham had also been referred to differently as abiram and aavarum. It may be said that the usages at Tranquebar in India and at Colombo in Sri Lanka were different and puzzling to note.

Psalms Translated and Printed by Benjamin Schultze in Tranquebar and its Comparison with the Version of Johann Philipp Fabricius in Madras, 1724-1772

Benjamin Schultze translated the Psalms and the book was printed at Tranquebar in 1724. It witnessed the second edition from the same printing press in 1747. His translation (of psalm 23, verse 1-3: The Lord is my shepherd; I shall not lack. He makes me to lie down in green pastures. He leads me beside restful water) runs as follows.[16]

Aandavar yennudaya idaiyanaay irukkirar engira padiyinaalaye
Yennaku kuraichal varapporathillai
Avarennay pillugallukkulla sthalanagkaliley meychchu kondu yennai thaaganthirkirra kulirintha thanneer andaiiley kootti konu poey vittaar

Fabricius the missionary in Madras had also translated the same text and it appeared in print in 1772. The text of runs thus:[17]

Karthar Yen meyparray irukkirar
Naan Thzhchi adaiyeen
Avar yennai pullulla sthalngalil meythu yennai amarntha thaneergal andaikku kondu poey vidugirar

Little wonder in both the translation has been that the earlier version has been retained while the terms are made to change.

An Assessment on the Translation of the New Testament by Ziegebalg in Tranquebar (1715), Fabricius in Madras (1772), and Mousset in Pondicherry (1875)

The translation of the New Testament by Johann Philipp Fabricius was from Greek into Tamil and he did not deviate from the source text. He could do the work because he had command over the language. Fabricius used the term paraaparan (transcendent and immanent) referring to God. Ziegenbalg had already used the term Paraaparavasthu in his translation. The translation of Ziegenbalg in 1714 and Fabricius of 1774 could be compared through the Gospel of St. Luke (Chapter 16, verse 19: There was a rich man dressed in purple and fine linen, who enjoyed luxurious living every day). The text of Ziegenblag in Tamil runs thus:

> *Aysuriyam udaiththaanay irukkira yaathory manushan undaay irunthaan. Avan sagalaathukalaiyum vilaiyerappeththa pidavaigaliyum tharischchu kondu anuthunamum santhoshapattu piruthaapichchu kondirunthaan.*[18]

Fabricius had also translated and his text in Tamil runs thus:

> *Aisuvariyamulla oru mansuhan irunthaan. Avan raththaambaramum vilaiyerappettra pudavium thariththu kondu anuthinamum sampiramaay vaazhthirunthaan.*[19]

An investigation into the two above texts shows that Fabricius in his translation desired to present the idea very clearly and he did not wish to mix up, though he was prepared to give up the style of Tamil language in a limited way while translating. His translation appeared in print from the press at Vepery in Madras in 1772 and again at Tranquebar in 1891. Fabricius wrote 'vithaigal vizhunthathu' and 'paravaigal patchiththathu' in the translation and these are grammatically incorrect in Tamil. Fabricius therefore was at loss to distinguish between the usage of singular and plural for neuter gender particularly while using the subject and predicate. In the translation of the Gospel St. Luke (chapter XV, verse 20: I have sinned against heaven and before you) he wrote again the expression incorrect in Tamil as vaanathkku virodhamaagavum umakku virodhamaagavum'. Thus several statements and expressions are found incorrect in the translation.

Ziegenbalg translated the text of the Acts of the Apostles (Chapter XXV, verses, 1-3: Three days after he had arrived in the province Festus went up from Caesarea to Jerusalem. The chief priests and the most prominent Jews appeared before him against Paul and begged it as a favour to them that Paul be sent to Jerusalem-they planning to form an ambush and to murder him on the road) and the text runs thus:

> *Besethus yengiravan antha seermayiley piravesithu moonu naalaikku pirpaadu sesaariyae yengira pattanthiley irunthu yuthargaludaya moopaana pergalum pavulusukku virodhamaaga*

> *avarandaiiley sanirudhayama vanthu avari vendikondu ivan yerusalemukku vanthanuppa venumengira upagaarathai mannadikondu ivari vazhiyiley konru poda vengum enirukkirasarpanaigali panni kondirunthaargal.*[20]

The same passage translated in Tamil appeared differently in the Catholic printed text of 1875 and it runs as follows:

> *Appadi irukka Besthus yenbavan annaatukkkul vanthu moonru thinathukkupin cesaaraiyya nagarininru yerusalemukku ponnaan. Appothu piradhaana achariyargalum yuthargalil muthanmaiyaanavargalul Sinnappanmer piriyaathu seyya avanidarthir ponnaargal. Melum avanai mandradi vazhiyir kolai seyyap pathividai karuthi avar yersalemukku kootikondu varappadumpadikku kattalai idavenumenru avarkku virodhamaay upagaaramaay kettaargal.*[21]

An Analysis on the Translation of the New Testament by Karl Theophilus Ewald Rhenius (1827), and Louis Marie Mousset (1857)

The Bible translation of Fabricius printed in 1772 does not have the pulli (dot) over the consonants as it was the form of style then adopted in the palm-leaf writing system. The Gospel of Mathew translated (chapter VI, verses, 3-4: When you give charity, do not blow a trumpet ahead of you as the hypocrites do in the streets to gain glory from men. I assure you, have reward. But when you practice charity your left hand must not know what your right is doing, so that your charity will be in secret. And your Father who sees in secret will reward you) by Fabricius runs thus:

> *Aanapadiyaal nee dharmang seygirapoethu maayakkaarar thaangal manusharaaley pugazhlapaduvatharkku aalayangalilum veedhigalilum seygiraapoley un munpaaga thaarai voothu viyaathey. Meyyagavey ungalukku sollugireyn avargal thangal palani adaithu theerthathu.*
>
> *Neeyovenil dharmang seygirapoethu un dharmam antharangamaay irukkirathukkaaga un valathu kai seygirathai un idathu kai ariyaathirukkakadavathu. Appo antharangathil paarkira un pithaa thaamey vezhiarangamaay unakku palan azhippaar.*[22]

The text of the Catholic Bible printed in 1857 has pulli (dot) over the consonants. The text from the Gospel of St. Mathew translated (chapter VI, verses, 3-4) runs as follows:

> *Aagaiyaal Nee Dharmanj seygirapoethu kazhlla Gnaanigal manitharaar sangikkappaduvatharkku devaalayangkalilum veedhthigalilum seygirathu poela unakku munney yekkaazhlam moothuvikka vendaam. Avargal thangal sambhaavanaiyai adaithanaaittru yenru nichayamaa ungalukku sollugireyan.*
>
> *Neeyovenildharmanj seygaiyil un dharman maraivaay irukkathakkathaaga un valathu kai seyvathai un idathu kai ariyaathirukkakadavathu. Appothu maraiviley kaangira un pithaa unakku sambhaavani azhippaar.*[23]

The study of the two above texts shows variance in translation for the source languages used were different. While the Protestants used Greek and the Catholic missionaries used Latin.

Karl Theophilus Ewald Rhenius translated the Bible from Greek into Tamil and got printed in Madras in 1827, 1833, and again printed in Jaffna in 1843 and in Madras in 1844. It was during this period there had been a lot of discussion centered on the different styles of (literal and free) and methods (from source languages like Hebrew and Greek) adopted in translating in the receptor language of Tamil among the missionaries. Therefore Rhenius wrote on the principles of translating the Holy Scriptures. He outlined main principles such as translation should be from the original source language and no literal translation.[24] In Hebrew language the impact/effect of an event was said in the beginning of a sentence and the details of the same were mentioned later. Hence Rhenius translated the book of Genesis (chapter XIX, verse 3) in Tamil 'Lothu appangalai suttu virundhu azhiththaan' (while the English translation runs: Loth made them a feast and did bake the unleavaned bread). This was carefully done in translation by Rhenius to avoid the reader from confusion if the translation otherwise meant that Loth threw a dinner first and then went to bake the bread doing another job.[25] Rhenius said that a word was normally in all languages used to convey different meanings. Therefore the translator ought to be careful while translating by noting the circumstance under which it has been referred to in the source language. Further when equivalent words from the source language could not be found in the language of the targeted translation, the meaning of the term could be explained in words. According to Rhenius this was unavoidable in any translation. Those who found such explanation in his Bible translation therefore did not approve of. Rhenius was of the firm of opinion that there should be a new style in which Tamil

Bible should be translated and it should bridge the gulf that existed between the literates and the illiterates. He also pointed out not to follow the style of a single dominant group in Tamil society. This he learnt after finding the inequalities present in the then caste ridden Tamil society.

Though Greek had been the only source language of the same two translators (Fabricius and Rhenius) we find different expressions and the words used were also varied. Fabricius used the term velichcham (bright instead of light) while Rhenius used the right word ozhi (light). Fabricius mentioned the word inthalogam (this world) while Rhenius wrote ivvulagam. The term vaana rachchiyam (for heaven) of Fabricius was substituted by paraloga rachchiyam by Rhenius. The expression Samaariyyvin urukku vanthaar of Fabricius was drafted by Rhenius as samaariya urinal serthaar. Further the expression Vezhipaduthina vayanamaavathu of Fabricius (Gospel of St. John 21:1) had been found in translation of Rhenius as kaanpithapiragaaramaavathu. Similarly Uyirodirukkiravraaga prasannapaduthinar (Acts of the Apostles 1:3) had also been translated as Uiyroduirukkiravryenru kaanpithaar. The expression Visuvaasathai kaikondeyn by Fabricius (2 Timothy 4:7) had been translated as visuvaasathai kaathukoneyen. The translation of Fabricius expressed Nambugira kaariyangalin thida asthipaaram (Hebrews 11:1) while Rhenius wrote Nambappadugiravaigalin urudhi. Again Fabricius translation mentioned Satchigalin iththani periya megam (Hebrew 12:1) while Rhenius wrote Megampol iththani thiralaana satchigal. Thus the arrangement of the subject, predicate and object in the sentences greatly differed. The term used by Fabricius Sneham (1 Corinthians 13) was mentioned by Rhenius with the term anbu. The expression of Fabricius Osaitharum kinkini was translated (1 Corinthians 13) by Rhenius as osaiidugira kaithaalam. Thus words from Sanskrit were freely used by Fabricius in 1772 while Rhenius began to correct the version of Fabricius and he made translation independent and he abundantly used pure Tamil words in his Bible translation.

The text of Rhenius in 1827 (Gospel of St. Mark verse 1: Some days later he returned to Capernaum, and it was learned that he was at home. So many congregated that shortly there was no longer any room even at the door. He was preaching the word to them) runs thus:

> *Sila naalakai pirpaadu avar thirumba Capernaumukkuul piravesiththaar. Avar veetilirukkirarrenru kezhviyaay udaney anegar*

> *vaasalpadikku munnum idang kollaatha padiyaay koodi vanthaargal. Avargalukku vasanaththai sonnaar.*[26]

The same text is found in the Catholic printed Bible runs thus:

> *Sila thinaththukku pinbu avar Capernaummenumuril marupadiyum pravesiththaar. Avar Veetilirukkiraar enru kezhivipadavey vaasalil muthalaayidam patrraathirukumpadiyaay thiralzhlaana per koodinaargal. Avaro (Deva) vaakkiyamavargalukku solli kondu irunthaar.*[27]

Though both the translations were refined the terms used were different. This had happened within a span of thirty years between 1827 and 1857. It has been noted that in the structure of the sentence formation there has been a close link between Tamil and Latin. This was pointed out by missionaries.[28] Therefore translation of the Vulgate Bible from Latin into Tamil would not have presented a lot of difficulty unlike from Greek and Hebrew which had different language style and structure.

A reading of the Catholic Bible printed in Pondicherry in 1857 shows that several Sanskrit terms were freely used and we find terms like kirubai (grace), paralogam (heaven), bhulogam (earth), motcham (paradise), bumi (land), sarirum (human body), devasneham (love of God), sirushtithaar (created), maamisam (meat), machchangal (fish), sthree (woman), kumaaran (son), kumaarathi (daughter), pirathaana (main), purushan (husband), giraamangal (villages), pithaa (father), maathaa (mother), vasthiranagal (dress), sishar (disciple), asanasaalai (dining hall), sagotharan (brother), sagothari (sister), niththirai (sleep), varusham (year) and pravesikka (enter). Further several words of Sanskrit origin were Tamilized without using Sanskrit alphabets like Sha, Ja, Shi. We find siviyam (life), pirasaigal (citizens), sanangal (people) and sepam (prayer)

The Christian terminology mentioned is something interesting for we find words like sammanasu (angel), royappar (Peter), arulappar (John), yagappar (James), ispiriththu saanthu (Holy Spirit), ratchippar (saviour), manumahan (son of God), ratchchaniyam (salvation), sarvesuranyuda rajyyam (kingdom of God), sarvesvaran (lord of all/almighty), dirkadarisanam (prophecy) and daavidin puththiran (son of David). Personal names have been given as found in Latin such as yeraemiyas and isaiyaas.

The formation of words making expressions included kirayathuuku vangi (price purchased at), appam posippaan (one who eats bread,) paanam seythaargal (drank), kuttram pidithaargal (found fault with) and saaya ratchayyaana poethu (in the evening). We find also other words like thagappan (daddy) thaii (mummy) vasanithaar (told) thiruvulam pattrinarr (said) devallaayam (house of God) mesai (table) urgal (places) pattanangal (towns) nagaram (city) manaivi (house-wife) musthippu (preparation) aishwaryavaan (rich man) kothumbai (wheat) kaliyaanam (marriage) and servaikaaran (office on duty).

M. Varadarasan had opined that Anrique Anriquez though used Tamil it was only after Ziegenbalg a branch of language that had developed differently and exclusively for the Christians.[29] David Prabhakar is of the view that Christian Tamil did not take any proper shape till the middle of the nineteenth century.[30] These views are called into question for we find production of abundant literary works before Ziegenbalg that have come to new light. In fact these texts have set the trend for later development of prose throughout the eighteenth century.

Catholic and Protestant missionaries had very much contributed not only to the liturgical prose but the printed books became a new genre of Tamil Christian literature. G.U. Pope (1820-1908) a missionary scholar in his preface to his translation of Thiruvaasagam in 1900 had envisaged the creation of such a protestant Tamil literature as a triumphant literary fruition of the Christian Tamil produced by the combined efforts of several missionaries. He said that there existed then much of what was called Christian Tamil, a dialect created by the Danish missionaries of Tranquebar, enriched by a few generation of people in Thanjavur, German and other missionaries, modified, purified and refrigerated by the Swiss Rhenius and very composite Tirunelveli school; expanded and harmonized by English men. Amongst whom Henry Bower (1813-1889) was foremost in his day; and, finally waiting then for the touch of some-heaven-born genius among the Tamil community to make sweet and effective as any language on earth, living or dead.[31] This sentiment was though often quoted and repeated, on the contrary we find Catholic literature in Tamil by the missionaries had established a new school of language and style of Tamil prose different from the Protestants. The various translations in parts and full circulated prove the fact. A Catholic printed Bible which had been pending finally appeared in print only in 1857. On examination it is gleaned that most of the fine translation parts of the two Protestant missionaries like Fabricius and Rhenius had been incorporated by Catholic missionaries

Fr. Mousset and Fr. Arul. They also dropped those passages which were different from the Latin version of the Bible because the Protestants had translated from Hebrew and Greek.

It is interesting to find that most of the translated works of Protestant Christian literature in Tamil were printed and these had interested the Hindu audience. Perumal Nayak the ruler in December 1742 came to the school of the missionaries in Poraiyar one day and after a few days he borrowed some of the printed books for reading. Thus books had been issued or borrowed for reading.[32] Further the reading habits of books among the Tamils had developed very much after printing of the books in Tamil language. On 5 January 1746, Ramalinga Nayak of Tranquebar had his usual visit to the missionaries on Pongal day. He was asked by the missionaries at that time whether he was reading the books that they had given to him. He told them that he not only read seriously but had also successfully learnt a lot. He also gladly admitted to the missionaries that he had passed on the books to some of his friends living in the north of Udaiyar Palayam.[33] The Catholic translation had a colloquial style of Tamil language in the beginning but later translations were a mixture of senthamzih and kodunthamizh. In fine it may be concluded that all the Tamil translations of the European missionaries had only directed gradually towards an idiomatic style.

NOTES

1. J. S. M Hooper, *Bible Translation in India, Pakistan and Ceylon*, Oxford, 1963; Ulla Sandgren, *The Tamil New Testament and Bartholomäus Ziegenbalg*, Uppsala, 1991; Sarojini Packiamuthu, *Viviliya Mozhipeyarppu Varalaaru*, Madras, 1990; Sarojini Packiamuthu, *Vivilyamum Thamzhium*, Chidambaram, 2000; T. Nancy Beualh, *Thamzhili Vivilya Mozhiperpupgal Or Aayvu*, Madurai, 2002; Sabapathi Kulendiran, *Kristhava Thamizh Vethaagamaththin Varalaaru*, Bangalore, 1967; S. Michael Irudhayam and Y. Robinson, Levi, eds., *History of Tamil Bible Translation*, Madurai, 2008; Hephzibah Israel, *Religious Transactions in Colonial South India: Language, Translation and the Making of Protestant Identity,* London, 2011.
2. Det Kongelige Bibliotek, Kobenhavn (hereafter KB), MS Ny kgl.Saml.154.
3. Fernando de Almeida, ed., *Cartilha em Tamul e Português: Impresa em 1554*, Ministerio da Eduçāo Nacional, Direção-Geral do Superior do Ensino Superior e da Belas-Artes, Lisboã, 1970, pp. 8-9.
4. S. Rajamanickam, ed., *Vanakkam*, Tamil Ilakkiya Kazhagam, Tuticorin, 1963.

5. Staats-und Universitatsbibliotheek Hamburg Carl von Ossietzy, Cod. Orient 283, fl. 70, *Arte Tamul Sive Instituto Gramatica Linguae Malabaricae Sum Philippi Baldej. UDM in Regno Jaffnapatam, 1659, Philippi Baldeyusu.*
6. Philippus, Baldaeus, *A True and Exact Description of the Most Celebrated East India Coasts of Malabar and Coromandel as well as of the Isle of Ceylon with their Adjacent Kingdom and Provinces*, London,1703, rpt., New Delhi, 2000, vol. III, p. 665.
7. Archiv der Franckesche Stiftungen (hereafter AFSt), Halle, *Oru Kristhavan Mokshathai Adaikirathukku Vetha Piramaanathinpadiye Ariyavendiya Vizhlakkangkalaiyum Mandirangalaiyum Paduchchu Seyya Vendina Gnaayangaliyum Pothidichivikkira Gnaana Upadesam: Sumario das Doutrinas Christaas por uso dos catechumenos*, Tranquebar, No Anno de Christo de 1715.
8. AFSt, G 11: 59.
9. AFSt, B 6:54a.
10. Houghton Library, Harvard University Library, USA, *Thambiran Vanakkam*, 1578, p. 15.
11. The American Bible Society Library (hereafter ABSL), New York City, Accession no. 25060, Call no. 1481513, The Gospel of St. Mathew, Chapter V, verses 3-12.
12. British Library (hereafter BL), London, or.72.b.11, *The New Testament of Our Lord & Saviour Jesus Christ, Translated into Malabar,* Vepery near Madras, 1772, Gospel of St. Mathew, chapter V, verses, 3-12.
13. Bibliothèque Asiatique des missions étrangères de Paris (hereafter BAMEP), *Sesu Kristhu Naatharudaya Parisuththa Suvisesham*, no. TA 46; Madurai Province Jesuit Archives (hereafter MPJA), *Sesu Kristhu Naatharudaya Parisuththa Suvisesham*, no. 221/265.
14. ABSL, Accession no. 25060, Call no. 1481513, The Gospel of St. Mathew Chapter I, verses, 1-3.
15. BFSt: MISS C 150.
16. Biblioteca Nacional de Lisboã (hereafter BNL), Cota Res.248v.
17. BL, or.72.b.11, psalm 23, verses 1-3.
18. ABSL, Accession no. 25060, Call no. 1481513, The Gospel of St. Luke, Chapter XVI, verse 19.
19. BL, or.72.b.11, The Gospel of St. Luke, Chapter XVI, verse 19
20. BFSt, 12D 7, The Acts of the Apostles, Chapter XXV, verses, 1-3, p. 471.
21. BAMEP, *Sesu Kristhu Naatharudaya Parisuththa Suvisesham*, no. TA 46, The Acts of the Apostles, Chapter XXV, verses, 1-3, p. 705.

22. BL, or.72.b.11, p. 16.
23. BAMEP, *Sesu Kristhu Naatharudaya Parisuththa Suvisesham*, no. TA 46, p. 26.
24. C. T. E. Rhenius, *An Essay on the Principles of Translating the Holy Scriptures with Critical Remaks on Various Passges, Particularly in Reference to the Tamil Language*, Printed at the Mission Press, Nagercoil, 1827.
25. Sarojini Packiamuthu, *Viviliyamum Thamizhum*, Chidambaram, 2000, p. 133.
26. ABSL, Accession no. 1748, p. 72.
27. BAMEP, *Sesu Kristhu Naatharudaya Parisuththa Suvisesham*, no. TA 46, p. 178.
28. C.T.E. Rhenius, *Memoirs of the Rev. C.T.E. Rhenius by his Son*, James Nisbet & Co., London, MDCCCXLI, pp. 564-5.
29. M. Varadarasan, *Thamizh Ilakkiya Varalaru*, Madras, 1912.
30. David Prabhakar, *Krithava Thamizh Nadaiiyal Nokku*, Chennai, 2002.
31. G.U. Pope, *Tiruvaacagam or 'Sacred Utterances' of the Tamil Poet, Saint and Sage Maanikkavaacagar*, Oxford, 1900, see, preface, p. xx
32. *Der Königl. Dänischen Missionarien aus Ost-Indien eingesandter ausführlichen Berichten, Von dem Werck ihrs Ams unter den Heyden, angerichteten Schulen und Gemeinen, ereigneten Hindernissen und schweren Umstanden; Beschaffenheit des Malabarischen Heydenthums, gepflogenen brieflicher Correspondentz und mundlchen Unterredungen mit selbigen heyden*, Teil 1–9, (Continuationen 1–108) Waiserihaus, Halle, 1710–1772, vol. 5, continuation 56, pp. 1321-2.
33 Ibid., vol. 6, continuation 65, pp. 788-9.

9

Conclusion

The prose development in the history of Tamil literature since the medieval period was not much. The process was also slow while poetry continued to flourish. With the advent of the missionaries from Europe, Tamil prose came to be well developed through translation when simplicity and vividness the two essential features gradually came to be present. The first missionaries arrived had felt the need to produce authentic translation of prayers and catechism and the later missionaries felt the need to translate the Christian doctrine from various printed books of Europe. As Tamil prose had not developed when compared to Europe, the missionaries recognized the significance of translation from European languages besides Hebrew, Greek and Latin in which Bible was available. They did translations into Tamil using the two kinds of Tamil, namely literary Tamil (cultivated dialect) and colloquial Tamil (uncultivated dialect). Though Tamil language had grown and developed since the dawn of civilization it took uncountable forms in the early modern age. By bringing Christianity to the locals on the Tamil coast the missionaries found in the beginning that they lacked expertise and knowledge of the local language that acted as a barrier. Hence they learnt to speak and write well. To bridge gaps that existed in communication they gradually developed translation as a link and it had a humble beginning.

The art of translation into Tamil the target language came to develop but the missionaries could not produce authentic translation from the source language. They initially struggled and aimed to do translation with substitution of equivalent words. The ideas and not word became important to them. Adherence to the original was also not possible because of their limited skill in Tamil. Hence the translations produced did not reveal the true spirit of the original as we find in the case of the prayers like *Pater Noster* and *Ave Maria*. Hence texts have come to be retranslated several times. Early translation of prayers was simply colloquial and not produced in chaste or cultivated Tamil. The usage of the words had also been not orderly in the proper form.

Anrique Anriquez made the pioneering effort at translating and adapting Christian terms to Tamil. His translation of the book *Flos Sanctorum* that dealt with the subject matter of the lives of saints had been riddled with hybrid language wherein Portuguese and Tamil words were phonetically adapted. He inserted them in large numbers with less Tamil syntax. The word '*thambiran*' he used for addressing the God was used by the Saivities in Tamil country. Roberto Nobili began to rewrite or retranslate the Christian Tamil catechism by eliminating Portuguese and Latin words which Anriquez had done earlier. This new effort was seriously objected to by Fr. Pero Francisco the Jesuit Provincial of the Malabar who opined that it was a deviation from the old version. Nobili expounded the Christian doctrine in Tamil and he coined several words to communicate the message to his Tamil audience. He used the word *kovil* for a place of worship, *arul* and *prasadam* for grace, *guru* for priest or teacher, *vetham* for the Bible, and *poosai* for Holy Mass. These words were not used earlier by Anriquez because he felt that these terms were associated with Hinduism. Pero Francisco said that this new emerging practice may be a novelty but plainly he stated that the proper names and those terms relate to the Catholic Church were not found common with the Hindus, and so he was of the opinion that they should be safely retained and preserved in Latin or Portuguese words. He said that it would be better to retain than to invent or coining new/other words in Tamil. Pero Francisco also suggested that some words like baptism, confirmation and eucharist denoted the holy sacraments and so sacredness should be attached to only in Latin and Portuguese usage and they were simply untranslatable into any other foreign language like Tamil. He said that equivalent Tamil names gnaanasnanam, uruthiyil pusthal and divya nanmai are unsuited to articulate the Catholic Christian ideas. Nobili made best of his efforts to translate and coin new terms for sacraments in Tamil carefully using etymology. However, Christian vocabulary for Tamil language was in the beginning stage. Hence it was extremely difficult for acceptance by some missionaries. To some extent there appeared some critical views and comments as gleaned from a manuscript (Goa vol. 51, fls.191-92) preserved at the Archivum Romanum Societatis Iesu in Rome. But there was no debate on this topic during the seventeenth century.

Catholic prose translations and writings in Tamil were the first great footsteps towards growth of literature and most of the missionaries devoted much time to study of Tamil language and came to produce several texts. The literary genres cultivated by Jesuits were decided by the daily spiritual needs of the new converts in Tamil country and evangelization concerns. Hence they wrote the books and sermons in Tamil. They used the printing press, which they brought to, as a tool in the world of texts. These missionaries wanted mass conversion and so they undertook in mass production of texts. Tamil Catholic religious literature had a dual purpose and we find firstly, to deepen the faith of the converts and secondly, to teach the natives how to read and write.

Missionaries have ventured into the literary scenario in Tamil country and they made great contributions in translation and caused changes in the field by altering the situation that prevailed then in the stage of Tamil prose. The appearance of Christian Tamil prose and a dramatic shift from verse to prose composition in the language was a momentous transformation in the literary form. Prose commentaries earlier developed into different types, from simple annotations to more complex dissections and criticism of poetic texts were different. They functioned mainly as critical commentaries on other commentaries. Tamil prose of the earlier period could not be considered as an appropriate genre for secular and sacred Tamil literature. The poetic verse in Tamil enjoyed traditionally a higher status while prose did not have any form and shape and came to enjoy a less equal literary status.

When the missionaries translated and brought out prose works in Tamil they wrote in palm-leaf. When they communicated their activities in the annual letters we find mention of the Christian themes that they had been covering. Hence we are able easily to know the Jesuit missionary writings in Tamil Christian translation and prose. Missionary translations appeared from Latin and Portuguese into Tamil Christian literature but so the religious Tamil development compared to Hindus took place in a different mode.

Catholic missionaries acquired mastery and skill in Tamil language and they composed new writings and these were widely circulated and made popular among the native Christians. The Jesuits prepared several copies of palm-leaf manuscripts and they also made numerous copies in paper. All these manuscripts in Tamil were shipped to Europe particularly to Lisbon, Rome and Paris. The religious dialogue and instruction for the Catholic converts had been completely different from the one that existed among the Hindus. Spoken Tamil in the beginning gained priority and later came to be converted into literary Tamil by the missionaries.

Jesuit missionaries have contributed enormously to the development of translation and Christian literature in prose. Tamil literary texts in palm-leaf manuscript production, distribution and acquisition in Europe developed and the intellectual impact had been far too deep and great in the early modern age. The study of language was of course oriented towards propagating the Word of God and the missionaries soon got down to the business of producing books. By 1713 the list of Tamil manuscripts, which have been composed by the missionaries themselves, or translated from other European languages, chiefly for the use of the Tamil Church and school was truly impressive.

1. The whole New Testament
2. A collection of the Gospels and Epistles used throughout the year done in a volume
3. Luther's short catechism, with an Exposition, and without it
4. A short history of the Old Testament, with the arguments of each chapter
5. A collection of some short rules or directions for a Christian life
6. Twenty-six sermons upon the article of the Christian faith
7. Eleven sermons upon some other subjects of Divinity
8. Fourteen sermons upon Mr Freylinghausen's short system of divinity
9. The history of the life of Christ
10. The order or method of salvation
11. An abridgement of the Old and the New Testament
12. A succinct narrative of the Christian, Jewish, Mohomedan and Hinduism
13. A compendium of divinity

14. A church history of the Old Testament, by way of questions and answers
15. A monitory letter, directed to the Hinduism by one of the missionaries
16. A collection of letters sent to some particular Tamil Hindus
17. A Tamil translation of some exhortatory letters, sent from Europe
18. A monitory letter written to the Tamil congregation by one of the missionaries in Madras
19. The Danish liturgy
20. A book of hymns set to European tunes
21. A book of hymns set to notes after the manner of the Indians
22. A book of devotions, or prayers
23. The articles of the Christian religion broke into short questions
24. A reading book containing some moral rules of life
25. A body of divinity (not yet finished)
26. Dr. Philipp Spener's exposition upon the catechism (not yet finished).

Apart from these texts the Protestant missionaries in Tranquebar sought out some few theological manuscripts, written by the Roman Catholic priests and after being carefully revised and purged of whatever might favour popery were included in their collection. These included:

(1) Some questions relating to the Christian doctrine
(2) A catechism
(3) Some orations upon theological subjects
(4) A collection of prayers, according to the order of the passion of Christ, and
(5) A string of pearls: Or an old mystical treatise upon the Christian virtues.

Christian terminology in Tamil prose had largely come to emerge and develop and we find several words used in the works of the Protestant missionaries. Their meanings are also sometimes to be understood not as the Hindus used because the missionaries have coined new terms or equivalent words. We find expressions such as aiyroppa seemai (country of Europe), denmarku mannar (King of Denmark), missiyon muthalaaligal (superiors of the mission), upadesimargal (catechists), thiruchabai (church), naatu thiruchabai (local church), paapumaar thiruchabhai (Roman Catholic church), naatupura kristhavargal (local Christians), sarvesuranyuda naamathinal (in the name of god), aathuma visarippu velai (conversion of souls), Kiristhava maargam (Christian religion) oru idayan (a priest, preacher/a shepherd), missionanan thevai (need of the mission), kristhuvinudya oozhiyakkaran (servant of Christ), sagala janangal (all people), aposthalar (apostle), muthirai manushar (prophets), adhigaaram (chapter), vasanam (verse), thiruvasanam (word of god), parisuththa aaviyaanavar (Holy Spirit), pethuru (Peter), pirasangam (preaching/ sermon), agnnaanathukku yethiraga (against heathenism), Kiristhuvin vetham (religion of Christianity), vinnappan seyvom (will be praying), usaavinathu (consulted), avanaukku tharipikkirathukku (to be given to him), karthar (God), kartharin bhayathil (fear of god), rajayam paravi belapadukiratharakkagavum (to spread and strengthen the kingdom), kristhuvin nimithamaay (for the sake of Christ), paaskaa thirunaal (Easter festival), paddrimaargalil (among the priests), gurupattam (priestly ordination), youtheya seemai (Judea country) yutha sabhai (Jews), thiruvulam pattinaar (said), sugithirulkkum (will be good), deva kiriyai (god's work), idettram (redemption), kettiyaai (firmly), ulliyangali seyyurathukku thiraani (strength to do service) and yesunaathar munnirha (Jesus First).

It may be said that translation played an important role in the transfer of Catholic religious knowledge in Tamil. In order to overcome the difficulties of translation and to facilitate communication, the Jesuits tried to introduce their knowledge by using the colloquial Tamil terms that were comprehensible by the common man. The method adopted by the Protestants had been in many ways different. We find the general translation process was that a German/Danish missionary orally translated the German texts and dictated it to a Tamil, who turned it into colloquial/literary Tamil terms and concepts. So, the translation work was in fact a cooperative work done by the Protestant missionary and Tamil literati. Between 1712 and 1799 the Protestants translated, wrote and also printed many Christian works in the forms of booklets, tracts, pamphlets and books including Tamil Bible.

Catholic missionaries had encountered certainly grammatical difficulties while making the Tamil translation of the Bible from Latin. Mention may be made of the two kinds of first person plural in Tamil, inclusive and exclusive (example such as *engal*, *namakku*) as Latin (including Greek) do not have this distinction in some contexts the missionaries were at puzzle to use inclusive or exclusive first person and what was meant exactly. The translation of words and phrases posed numerous problems. The proper names in the Bible posed a great difficulty for translation. But the trend earlier set by Anrique Anriquez was mainly followed. As there was nobody to speak authoritatively on the communication of the Bible message it was carried out in Tamil the way missionaries felt good. The best and the acceptability had been left to the people who had their mother-tongue Tamil. The message of the original Bible had to be also condensed and adapted itself to the new language Tamil mixing only with the written Tamil medium and not the spoken colloquial. Tamil Bible translation was silently going on in Tamil country as there was no ban for translation by the missionaries but its use and printing was not allowed by the Catholic Church. Thus before the advent of the Protestants, the Jesuits had created a language in Bible translation that could be plainly understood by the learned and the unlettered a most agreeable Tamil.

The Tranquebar missionaries found it difficult to use the Tamil word for God. There was an objection to use the word devan for God since it meant numerous Hindu Gods. They looked for alternative usages and found with the Tamil understanding of the unrevealed state of God as the supreme-being such as paraaparavasthu, sarveswara (the lord of all/almighty God), nithyaananda (the God of eternal bliss), aathiinaayaka (the first lord) and sarvalokadayaapara (the compassionate one of the entire world). They began to use the same Tamil epithets for God in their Christian writings, but understood them differently. Some of these epithets include kadavul (the one, who has gone through everything and resides inside/ the supreme that surpasses thought, word and reality), swami (the good one), karthar (the lord, the doer). These words meant for the missionaries the triune God as Father, Son and the Holy-Spirit, as revealed in the Bible. Likewise, the Tamil understanding of the vethas or scripture had specific meanings and implications but the missionaries also along with Tamils prided over possessing the sacred books instead of four vethas, they said the Bible had five vethas meaning the five books of the Bible when printed. Hence they called it as *anju vetha posthagam*.

It is evident that translation of Tamil Bible had no role to play with reference to the plan of the missionaries for cultural domination and for moral and religious improvement of Tamils. The missionaries did not engage themselves into rewriting or creatively translating sections of the Bible into Tamil. They did not believe that translated Bible would have the potential to effect conversion without human intervention. In Tamil country and Europe people believed that God understood all human languages. In the age of Portuguese expansion in the early modern world it was revealed that no one language can have singular monopoly both in terms of trade and religion. Missionaries took over the Gospel message of Jesus Christ to the converts and realized at that time that Gospel in every language should be incorporated to express better because the mother-tongue served the best medium of socialization. They thought that Gospel presented in Tamil the mother-tongue would produce better results and the success of the missionary works could be gauged and measured.

It must be mentioned that five different stages of Bible translations occurred in Tamil such as:

(a) telling the Bible by beating around the bush such as touching upon Bible but writing around the theme of Bible;

(b) avoiding the foreign words or terms derived from other languages;

(c) avoiding the colloquial usages in translation;

(d) avoiding spoken language;

(e) names written in pure Tamil and translation made in high standard Tamil.

Coining words, conveying ideas through proper expression, word translation assigning proper meaning are important in translation. The problem encountered by translators, and the solutions they gave, also need to be considered. Among Indian languages Bible was translated first into Tamil. If we look very closely we find both spoken Tamil and also commentators or the then prose literary writer's style being mixed and written. The translation gave respect to only to the Holy Trinity. All other respectable persons in Bible translation had been made disrespectful by using the words such as Avan and Ivan. Hence a question arose as to whether the Holy Scripture should be in spoken or written Tamil. As there was no standard format for Tamil prose it had created difficulty. The new form of Tamil prose was being created and the translations could not be done in a uniform style.

Tamil prose writing had not well developed in the strict sense of the word prose. The specific purpose and function of Tamil prose began with the missionaries to spread the Gospel. The style of prose writing of these missionaries was not generally spontaneous as they had different culture and purpose. Their prose works were situated within a framework to communicate the message to the different strata of Tamil society and merely for the purpose of conversion. There was sweetness indeed in their prose style and not like the modern Dravidian Tamil. However the missionaries fundamentally contributed the system of punctuation marks in Tamil prose in their Tamil religious texts, particularly in the translation of the Bible in Tamil. It may be mentioned that Bible translations were available to the missionaries in many languages like the Portuguese, Dutch, German, Latin, Greek and Hebrew. Had it been available in a single language, rendering translation of the Bible in Tamil would have been simple. Ziegenbalg used New Testament in Greek by Schmidt, Latin New Testament by Ariae Montani, German New Testament of Luther and Offenbach New Testament for Tamil Bible Translation. Philippus de Melho in Sri Lanka had used the original Hebrew with the aid of the Septuagint, the Latin versions of Tremellius and Junius and the Netherlands State Bible for Tamil Bible translations. It may be also said that owing to the different construction of the languages, what would come first in Greek or Hebrew would come last in Tamil, had thus caused confusion. There were grammatical difficulties because of two kinds of first person plural in Tamil inclusive and exclusive such as nammudaya and engaludaya. It may be said that in Greek, Latin and English we do not have this distinction.

Gradually evolved was the examination of the link between Bible translation and glossary making such as *suvisesha vaakiya suluba agaraathi* which was introduced to mean and understand the difficult words used in the manuscript Bible. However there also developed by the Protestants a work of dictionary writing and Bible translation after printing the Bible. Putting the local language and the relevant parts of local culture on par with the missionary language was viewed seriously, challenged, reviewed by people in the Scripture for Tamils. Over a period, the Catholic, Danish Lutheran, Dutch Reformed church, and the Anglican that began to translate the Bible from different locations such as Tranquebar, Colombo and Madras came up for the debate by the end of the eighteenth century.

The major issues and problems in translation of the Bible had haunted even during the later period of the nineteenth century. It was said that authors of some versions did not follow the original text. It was added that the Tamil style in India was different from the Tamil of Jaffna. The grammar used in Sri Lanka translation was different from the one prevalent in Tamil country. There were too many Sanskrit words used in translation. In Madras the British insisted on the following word for word translation of the authorized version of the Bible of 1611 and they went to the extreme of insisting to maintain the order of words, the idioms and even punctuations of the authorized version.

However it must be said that the work of translations has been thus viewed from different angles like that the ordinary service of a missionary either Catholic or Protestant, also of a learned biblical scholar or a instructor in a theological seminary or as a minister and pastor of a particular church congregation, and of a native Tamil scholar and author/translator of Christian writings for some years worked among the Tamils. Translation had stimulated to which Tamil either kodunthamizh or senthamizh for use and it opened up and demonstrated new possibilities for prose development.

It may be pointed out that the Gospel of St. Mathew in Hebrew characters had been found among the Christians of Malabar on the west coast. The presence of the Jewish merchants had been also noted by John of Monte Corvino sent by Pope Nicholas IV to China as early as in 1289 and he said that the Hebrew Bible was already used in South India. Anrique Anriquez the Jesuit on the Tamil coast in the sixteenth century knew Hebrew very well because he was of Jewish origin. Therefore he could have translated the Bible from Hebrew into Tamil but he could not, owing to restrictions placed by the Catholic Church which authorized the use of the Latin vulgate of the Bible.

Martin Luther's use of Hebrew version of the Bible for translation into German was popularly known in Europe. The Protestant missionaries hailing from Germany were also well trained in Hebrew and so missionaries like Ziegenbalg and Schultze used the Hebrew Bible for translation into Tamil. Some more Lutheran missionaries of Tranquebar like Christoph Theodosius Walther had remained strongly committed to Hebrew studies and Hebrew Bible text. As he knew Hebrew very well he desired to translate Bible into Tamil from Hebrew. He therefore in the beginning began to study the relation between these two languages. He also aimed to compile a dictionary of Hebrew-Tamil words. This dictionary he compiled successfully and it has been particularly important from the context of translating the Bible from Hebrew into Tamil. Further, Johann Philipp Fabricius the missionary also began to translate the Bible from Hebrew into Tamil between 1772 and 1796.

The circle of Protestant missionary Hebrew scholars being active in Tamil country in translating the Bible is interesting. They had though failed to relate the individual words of scripture (verba) to their subject matter (res), their role was that of a philologist without leaving the theological aspect for others to clarify. Translating the Bible into Tamil from Hebrew was felt very important by all of them. The study of theological and grammatical aspects of particular verses could not be separated as Fabricius had done. These missionaries read carefully first and then discussed with Tamils and argued against some of them in the course of translation from Hebrew into Tamil. The Protestant missionaries wished to be content with Hebrew text and tied to no other translation. They always desired both in grammar and sense the Bible in Tamil must be translated. It may be mentioned that Hebrew scholarship had a significant impact on the translation of the Bible into Tamil. Though the Dutch in the beginning began to use the Greek Bible for translation into Tamil, later they also switched over to Hebrew translation. They felt the Word of God from Hebrew into Tamil would be the best. Therefore they began the work in that direction. They found Greek, Latin and other Europeans languages did not have root words in them but had them in Semitic language families.

Translation was carried out more diligently on certain parts of the Old Testament like the circumcision found mention in the book of Genesis (17:1) and the missionaries felt that the matter should not be slighted. Further, prophetic passages found in the book of Daniel, Haggai and Isaiah had also been found difficult for translation. Missionaries noticed that Tamil grammar and lexicon were beautifully adequate dealing with figures of speech and proverbs. Hence they were wondering how best to do the translation of the Word of God into Tamil. In the New Testament translation the missionaries noticed the parallels of the gospel found particularly some like the resurrection of Jesus and his message to his disciples in Mathew (28:19) 'Go therefore and make disciples of all nations, baptizing them in the name of the father and of the son and of the holy spirit; and in the gospel of Mark (16:15) 'And he (Jesus Christ) said to them (his disciples) go into all the world and proclaim the good news to the whole creation; and in the gospel of John (20:21) 'Jesus said to them again, peace be with you. As the father has sent me, so I send you'. It has been noticed and identified such important passages, having a view to examine their close personal and professional connections. It is significant to record that Christian Hebrew scholarship that grew at a dramatic rate in Germany in this period was found useful and it had a deep impact in Tamil country. The Catholic opposing camp in Tamil country had fundamentally a different approach to Bible translation tied to Latin studies and not Hebrew. However they began to relate it concerning the use of spoken language of Tamil without laying emphasis on the Jewish biblical and linguistic scholarship.

Translation in the early modern period in Tamil country implied carry across or transfer from one language and the other under the Catholic missionaries. However, its problems were numerous in the course of time under the Protestants in the intellectual and cultural context of spoken and written language. The various processes involved in translation came explicit. Religion and development of words and inter-religious dialogue between Hinduism and Christianity brought the dialogue of translation to the forefront in Tamil country. Until the seventeenth century Catholic translations of the Bible and parts of the Bible were available and not the whole and they were usually in manuscript used by the catechists. This type had changed when the Protestant missionaries of Tranquebar when they decided to print and distribute widely as possible among all the classes and caste in Tamil country. The diffusion of the divine word brought the ideas of transferability or translatability whatever term we may use did not demand to the original but was understood as re-creation in change form and the notion of faithfulness to the original gained momentum in the history of translation. The translation of Bible into Tamil was useful to their mission and it must be said that for the missionaries it was an obligation and a strategy of soteriology. It is visible that all the translators of the Bible in Tamil had at least allowed their own pride as better or more effective translators having overconfidence. They have portrayed their translations without seeking corrections or revisions from others and scholars before printing the Bible. Hence criticisms appeared after making it available to the readers.

The New Testament and the Old Testament of the Bible in Tamil (in several parts and full) was printed and reprinted by the Protestant missionaries at Tranquebar nineteen times and in Jaffna and Colombo it was done seven times, and at Serampore near Calcutta twice and at Madras six times. Among all the books, Tamil Bible had the exclusive privilege of being printed and circulated with the maximum number of books to the tune of 31,500 copies in total between 1714 and 1850. However, the Catholic edition of Bible first got printed at Pondicherry only in 1857 and the print order was only 2000 copies. Hence the Protestants were the pioneers in printing Tamil Bible and placed the Holy Scripture in the hands of the Tamils. Thus the Christian literary production, intellectual life and literary history that were newly linked with missionary expansion helped to move away from the earlier multiple literary cultures in Tamil such as the royal court, temple and public.

Translation was not looked down on as second-class work in the early modern age. However discourse around Bible translation had tended to focus on how faithful a translation was to its original or whether the translator had somehow betrayed that original and debates had developed how to determine equivalence in translation. Europeans understood translation involved a dual process wherein at first the translator had to read and understand and thereafter the translator had to re-create in another language which involved certain amount of difficulty. There were no strict rules set forth for translation in the early stage. Since translation came to be said later a scientific exercise and also an art we find several translations appear for a single book like the Bible in Tamil. Translating from the original without any deviation was the general principle accepted and adhered to in the early modern age. Contacts with various other language speaking societies of Europe enabled for growth and transformation of translation in Tamil. Translation over a period of time was insisted that it should be like as found and said in the original and therefore translation was called an art. It was believed that if the translation was not done as composed by the original author it had no life and such a translation was considered both dry and dead. The word formation in the early modern age depended on the root language, qualifications of the translators, knowledge skill in two languages besides the acceptable approach and its style. The problems and difficulties besides complexities in translation of the Bible had mainly included peculiar and special characteristics of the language, culture and the cultural gaps, in addition to usage of respect and orthographical variations. The role of dictionary in translation was felt important and so a glossary of terms of biblical terms used in translation had appeared. The main three activities of translation in the early modern age included informative function, expressive function and the imperative function. The adaptability and versatility of the missionaries, the servants and officials of the East India trading companies made translation popular on the Tamil coast. All of them left their own mark on the translations in Tamil language and Tamil translations underwent a colourful growth as time passed on by coining new words and adding new dimension in the translation of documents, besides use in the civil, military and judicial administration of the government, a climb that one way up in British and French India of Tamil region. The connections between Europeans and the Tamil language had strengthened over the years. We notice multiple varieties of Tamil translations that were birthed over three centuries leading to overwhelming success of the language. Tamil underwent transformation in prose and it is gleaned that Tamil had adapted to the European languages and the European languages too have also adapted Tamil through translation. Further, Tamil had become a foreign language and popular in Europe and it was possible mainly through the translations.

Bibliography

PRIMARY SOURCES

I. MANUSCRIPTS

DENMARK

1. *Det Kongelige Bibliotek, Kobenhavn*

   Collectanea Europaeorum de Lingis et Litteris Indicis, MSS no. 31; 33, 34, 35

   MS NY. Kgl. Saml. 154, Christoph Theodosius Walther, Synonyma Ebraeo-Tamulica. Anno MDCCXL.

   MSS no. Add 761a; T.L. Folly, Bemerkungen der von Dr. Roxburgh entdeckten Fieber-Rindse Swietenia febrifuga, 1792, fls.1-18

   MSS no. Add 761e; T.L. Folly, Nogle Anmaerkninger I Anledning af Doctor Kleins forsog omden veneriske syges helbredelse I ostindien, Tranquebar, 1798

   Oriental Manuscripts: Codice no. LVIII: The gospel of St Mathew, Cod. 58.1; and 58.2; The gospel of St Mark, Cod Tamul 58.3; 58.4 and 58.5; The gospel of St Luke, Cod Tamul 58.6; The gospel of St John, Cod Tamul, 58.7; 58.9; 58.8; 58.13; 58.14; 58.15; 58.16; 58.17; 58.20; 58.21; 58.22; 58.23; 58.24; 58.25; 58.26; 58.27; 58.28; 58.29; 58.31; 58.50.

   Oriental Department, Cod Tamul 5, Ulaha Nidi oder Weltliche Gerechtigkeit

2. *Kirurgisk Akademi, Kobenhavn*

   MSS no. Add 333a

FRANCE

3. *Archives de la Societe des Missions Etrangères de Paris*

   MSS Correspondance Pondichéry-Paris, Lettres, vol. 1000, 1001, 1002.

4. *Bibliothèque Nationale, Paris, Rue Richelieu*

   MSS Indien

   no. 450. Translation of the Gospels in Tamil, 1738

   no. 451. Dialogues sur le levitique les numbers et le deutronome

   no. 452. Katholikkarin Puthiyayerpattu Sallapam, Ubaagama Sallapam: Onnu Rendu, Rajakkalin Sallapam and Pazahya Yerpattin Sallapam, AD 1666-7

   no. 453. Dialogue sur les 3 e et 4 e des roys, paralipomenes, esdras, tobias, esther, judith, job et les machabees, 1750

   no. 454. Dialogues sur le nouveau testament les evangels du dimanche et des principaes fetes de l anne 1750

   no. 456. Matheyu yenbavar yezhuthiviaitha suviseshagam, 1739

   no. 459, Roberto Nobili, Gnaanopadesam, Catechismus Romanus, fls.1-366

   no. 460, Roberto Nobili, Catechismus Romanus, Tertia Pars, fl. 1-362

   MSS Nouvelles acquisitions françaises

   no. 1168

GERMANY

5. *Archiv der Franckesche Stiftungen, Halle*

   MS J. 66, Benjamin Schultze, Vocabularium Telugo-Tamulo Biblicum Novi Testamenti

   MSS MI B59:22; M1 K5:16; M1 C10:44-45; M1 C29b:106

   MSS M2 B7:8; M2, B:11; M2, K11:15

   MSS S.120-132; S.133-149

   P: TAM 36; P: TAM 37C, 91r-151r; P: TAM 37G, fls.194-196r; P: TAM, 37 I, fls.196v-200v; P: TAM, 37 J, 200v-202r; P: TAM, 37 K, 202r-207r; P: TAM 62; P: TAM 69, fls.1-165; P: TAM 71 fls.1- 214; P: TAM 72 fls.1-175; P: TAM 73 fls.1-200; P: TAM 74; P: TAM 75; P: TAM 76; P: TAM 77; P: TAM 81, fls.1-242; P: TAM 85; P: TAM 88; P: TAM 97; P: TAM 99.

6. *Bibliothek der Franckesche Stiftungen, Halle*

   Kleinere Schriften, A12

7. *Staats*-und Universitatsbibliotheek Hamburg Carl von Ossietzy, Hamburg

   Cod. Orient 283, fl. 70, Arte Tamul Sive Instituto Gramatica Linguae Malabaricae Sum Philippi Baldej. UDM in Regno Jaffnapatam, 1659, Philippi Baldeyusu.

INDIA

8. *Archives of the Gurukul Lutheran Theological College and Research Institute, Chennai*

Microfilm accession no. 578, Roll no. 53, Johann Philipp Fabricius, *Hymn Book* (Tamil & English), Fourth edition, Vepery, Madras, 1825.

9. *Archives of the United Theological College, Bengaluru*

MSS VPC-VNS 27, Vedanayagam Sastri, Puthu Thiruthuthalin Kookural (Noise of the New Corrections).

MSS VPC-VNS 36, Vedanayagam Sastri, Puthu Thiruthuthalin Sothanai (The Ordeal of the New Corrections)

10. *Madurai Province Jesuit Archives, Shenbaganur*

Archive object 47, Shelve "Nobiliana", Typescripts, Roberto Nobili, *Catecismo em que se expliÇão todas as verdades catholicas necessarias pera a salvação com excelentíssima ordem.*

Documents Bertrand.

vol. III, document no. 362

11. *National Archives of India, Southern Zonal Office, Pondicherry*

MSS Acte Tabelliones, Bundle no.1, document no. 1, 2, 4, 6, 7, 8, 10, 12, 14, 15, 16, 18, 19, 28, 29, 30, 31, 32, 34, 37, 40, 41.

12. *Saraswathi Mahal Library, Thanjavur*

MSS Tamil, no. 536, Nithiya Jeevana Sallaapam

Tamil Medical Manuscripts, no. 14.

13. *State Central Library, Goa*

MS no. 6, Pe. Roberto Nobili, *Catecismo em que se explicaõ todas as verdades catholicas em tamul por ... & traduzido pelo Pe. Balthazar da Costa*, 1661.

MS no. 26. Sermões para todos os dias do anno, 3 vols. (Sermons for all days in a year in Tamil)

14. *Tamil Nadu State Archives, Chennai*

Surgeon General's Records, vol.12.

ITALY

15. *Archivum Romanum Societatis Iesu, Roma*

MSS Goa, vol. 51, 53.

16. *Biblioteca Apostolica Vaticana, Città del Vaticano*

VAT Baago 3.

PORTUGAL

17. *Arquivo Historico Ultramarino, Lisboã*

Livro Reservado, 375, fls.195-9. Suvisesha Vaakiya Suluba Agaraathi

18. Biblioteca da Adjuda, Lisboã
Codice 44-XII-38, fls.279-82.

SRI LANKA

19. *Sri Lanka National Archives, Colombo*
Dutch Miscellaneous Records, no. 1/ 3446.

UNITED KINGDOM

20. *British Library, London*
Oriental Manuscripts, no. 13864
Oriental and India Office Collection, MSS EUR.C1.

II. PRINTED DOCUMENTS, CONTEMPORARY CHRONICLES, TRACTS AND ACCOUNTS

IN DANISH

Et brev hvilket af de Kongelige Danske Missionarieri det Malabariske sprog er de Malabariske hedninger paa kystem Coromandel bleven tilsendt forst idet tydske sprog af Missionarierne oversat, og, nu fordansket af Rasmus Hansen Attrup, Tranquebar: Trykt I det Kongel- Danske Missions- Bogtrykherie, 1719.

IN DUTCH

Anthonisz-Pieters, S., *Memoir of Gustaaf Willem Baron van Imhoff to His Successor Willem Maurits Bruynink, 1740*, Colombo, 1911.

IN ENGLISH

Babington, Benjamin Guy., *The Adventures of the Gooroopáramartan: A Tale in the Tamil Language, Accompanied by a Translation & Vocabulary Together with an Analysis of the First Story*, London, MDCCCXXII.

– –, *The Vedala Cadai, Translated by B.G. Babington*, MDCCCXXXI.

Brotherton, T., *Grammatica Tamuliensis: An English Translation of the Nunool by W. Joyes and S. Samuel Pillay, Revised and Corrected by the Rev. T. Brotherton*, VI Parts, Madras, 1848-50.

Foulkes Thomas., *Eclectic Vedantism: A Philosophical Poem in Frequent Use Amongst Hindu Women Translated from the Tamil by the Rev. Thomas Foulkes*, Madras, 1860.

– –, *Naanaseevavaatha Kattalai, or The Elements of the Controversy Respecting the Plurality of Souls, by Seshadrisiva Desikar, Translated from the Tamil by Thomas Foulkes*, Madras, 1860.

– –, *Sasivarna Potham or the Doctrine of Sasivarna: A Vedantic Poem Translated by the Rev. Thomas Foulkes*, Madras, 1862.

– –, *A Catechism of the Shaiva Religion, Translated by the Rev. Thomas Foulkes*, Madras, 1863.

– –, *Elements of the Saiva Philosophy Translated by the Rev. Thomas Foulkes*, Madras, 1863.

Heyne Benjamine., *Tracts*: *Historical and Statistical on India with Journals of Several Tour through Various Parts of the Peninsula also an Account of Sumatra in a Series of Letters*, London, 1814.

Hoisington, Henry R., *Sothi Saathiram, The Oriental Astronomer, Translated into English by Henry R. Hoisington*, Jaffna, 1848.

– –, 'Thaththuva Kattalai, Law of the Tattuvam, A Synopsis of the Mystical Philosophy of the Hindus Translated from the Tamil with Notes', *Journal of the American Oriental Society,* vol. IV, Boston, 1854, pp. 1-30.

– –, 'Sivagnaana Bodham: Instruction in the Knowledge of God: A Metaphysical and Theological Treatise Translated from the Tamil with an Introduction and Notes', *Journal of the American Oriental Society,* vol. IV, Boston, 1854, pp. 31-102.

– –, 'Sivaprakasam: Light of Sivan. A Metaphysical and Theological Treatise Translated from Tamil with Notes', *Journal of the American Oriental Society,* vol. IV, Boston, 1854, pp. 125-244.

Kindersley, Nathaniel Edward., *Specimens of Hindoo literature: Consisting of Translations, from the Tamoul Language, of Some Hindoo Works of Morality and Imagination, with Explanatory Notes: To which are Prefixed Introductory Remarks on the Mythology, Literature, & C. of the Hindoos*, Printed by W. Bulmer and Sold by F. Wingrave, London, 1794.

Modelliar, Teroovercaudo Soobroya, *Tamil Expositor, Containing a brief account of its idiom by way of question and answer, composed and translated into English by Teroovercaudo Soobroya Modelliar*, Madras, 1811.

Mudeliar, Mutu Coomara Swamy, *Arichandra, the Martyr of Truth, a Tamil Drama translated into English by Mutu Coomara Swamy Mudeliar*, London, 1863.

Notices of Madras and Cuddalore in the Last Century from the Journals and Letters of the Earlier Missionaries of the Society for the Propagation of Christian Knowledge, London, 1858.

Prinsept, Charles C., *Records of Services of the Honourable East India Company's Civil Servants in the Madras Presidency from 1741 to 1858, Compiled and Edited from the Records in the Possession of the Secretary of State for India*, London, 1885.

Rhenius, Carl Theophilus Ewald., *An Essay on the Principles of Translating the Holy Scriptures with Critical Remaks on Various Passges, Particularly in eference to the Tamil Language*, Printed at the Mission Press, Nagercoil, 1827.

– –, *Memoirs of the Rev. C.T.E. Rhenius by his Son*, James Nisbet & co, London, MDCCCXLI.

Stokes, Hudleston., *Neethineri Vizhlakkam: Ttranslated into English with Notes*, Madras, 1830.

Strange, Thomas Lumisden., *Manual of Hindoo Law*, Madras, 1857.

Walker, J., *Neethimozhi Thirattu: Selections in Tamil and English*, 1841.

IN FRENCH

Ariel, E., 'Kural de Tiruvaluver, Fragments Traduits du Tamoul', *Journal Asiatique*, Quatrieme Serie tome XII, pp. 423-433, Paris, 1848, vol. XIX, Paris 1852, pp. 381-435.

Aventures du Gourou Paramarta, Conte Drolatique Indien, Paris, 1897.

Bernouilli, Jean., ed., *Description Historique et Geographique de l'Inde*, Berlin, 1789.

Dubois, Jean Antoine., *Le Pantcha-Tantra, ou les cinq ruses fables du brahme Vichnou-sarma, Aventures de Paramarta et autres sur les originaux Indies* Paris, 1826.

– –, *Le Pantch-Tantra*, Paris, 1872.

Dumast, Guerrier de., *Fleurs de L'Inde*, Paris, 1857.

Dumast, P.G., *Tiruvalluvar Maximes,* Paris, 1854.

Jacollist, Louis., *La Devedassi, Bayadere* en Quatre Parties, Paris, 1868.

Leçons faciles de Français et de Tamoul Suivant la method de T. Robertson, Par Arpoudam fils de Saveriakuty Odear, Piranchu Thamizh Bhashiyin Yezhithaana Paadangal, Pondicherry, 1850.

Obsonville, Foucher d'., ed., *Bagavadam ou Doctrine Divine, Ourage Indien Canonique, sur l'Etre Supreme Tradu., Sanskrit en français par Mariadass Poulle*, Paris, 1788.

Poulle, Maridas., *Memoire Sur L'Astronome en Vigueur Sur la Cote du Coromandel Envoye A.M. de Monneron en 1787 par Maridas Poulle, Interprete du Roi a Pondichery*, L'Impreimerie Royale, Paris, MDCCXC.

Sice, François Eugene., *Legislation Hindoue*, Pondicherry, 1857.

Van der Haeghen, Philippe., *Maximes Populaires de L'Inde Meridionale*, Paris, 1858.

IN GERMAN

Aweiar's Kalwi Orhuckam, Oder Sittenspruche aus Tamulischen palamblatten ubersetzt mit, Bemerkungen uber Indische Gelehrsamkeit, von. J.CC. Rudiger, Halle, 1791.

Der Königl. Dänischen Missionarien aus Ost-Indien eingesandter ausführlichen Berichten, Von dem Werck ihrs Ams unter den Heyden, angerichteten Schulen und Gemeinen, ereigneten Hindernissen und schweren Umstanden; Beschaffenheit des Malabarischen Heydenthums, gepflogenen brieflicher Correspondentz und mundlchen Unterredungen mit selbigen heyden, Teil 1–9, (Continuationen 1–108) Waiserihaus, Halle, 1710–1772.

Fahrten und Abenteuer Gimpels und Compagnie Ein tamulischen Reise- und Scherzmarchen, Nacherzahlt von Dr. Johannn Georg Theodor Grasse, Dresden, 1856.

Germann, Wilhelm., *Der Kural des Tiruvalluver, Ein Gnomisches Gedicht uner die drei Strebeziele des menschen Ubersetzung und Eklarung von Karl Graul*, 1865.

– –, ed., *Ziegenbalg und Plutschau: Die Grundungsjahre der Trankebarschen Mission: Ein Beitrag zur Geschite des Pietismus nach handscriftlichen Quellen und altesten Drucken*, 2 vols., Erlangen, 1868.

Graul, Karl., 'Notizen, Correspondenzen und Vermischtes. Die Tamulische Bibliothek der Evan. Luth. Missionsanstalt zu Leipzig', *Zeitschrift der Deutschen Morgenländischen Gesellschaft*, vol. VII, Leipzig, 1853, pp. 558-568.

Grundler, Johann Ernst und Bartholomaus Ziegenbalg, *Die Malabrische Korrespondenz: Tamilische Briefe an deutsche Missionare Eine Auswahl* (with an introduction and explanations by Kurt Liebau), Thorbecke, Sigmaringen, 1998.

Indische Sinnpflanzen und Blumen, zur Kennezeichnung Indischen Vornehmlich tamulischen, Geistes, Erlangen, 1865.

John, Christoph Samuel., 'Beschreibung und Inhalt eines kleinen heidnischen sitten-buchleins in Tamulischen versen', *Brauschweigisches Magazin*, 3, 1790, pp. 681-702.

– –, 'Das Sittenbuch Aattiswadi' *Deutsches Magazin* (1) 1791, pp. 161-65.

– –, 'Das Sittenbuch Pottiamalei', *Berlinische Monatsschrift*, 19:1, 1792, pp. 195-200.

Knapp, Georg Christian., et.al., *Neuere Geschichte der evangelischen Missions-Anstalten zu Bekehrung der Heiden in Ostindien aus den eigenhändigen Aufsätzen und Briefen der Missionarien erausgegeben*, Teil 1–8, (Stück 1–95) Waisenhaus, Halle, 1770-8/ 1795-1848.

Lehmann, Arno., ed., *Alte Briefe aus Indien: Unveröffentlichte Briefe von Bartholomäus Ziegenbalg 1706–1719*, Berlin, 1957.

Ubersetzung und Erklarung Ramanuja Kavirayar Athma Bhodaga Paritchai, Bibliotheca Tamulica, Leipzig, 1854.

Ziegenbalg, Bartholomäus., *Propagation of the Gospel in the East: Being a Collection of Letters from the Protestant Missionaries, and other worthy Persons in the East-Indies, & c. Relating to the Mission; the Means of Promoting it; and the Success it hath pleased GOD to give to the Endeavours used hitherto, for Propagating True Christianity among the Heathen in those Parts, but chiefly on the coast of Coromandel. With a map of the East-Indies,* Part III, Published by the direction of the Society for Promoting Christian Knowledge, London, Printed and Sold by J. Downing, in Bartholomew-Close near West-Smithfield, 1718.

IN ITALIAN

Confessionario Raccolto da Dottori Catolici, Per lo Revr. Maestro Girolamo Panormitano del Ordine de Predicatori, con Privilegio, in Napoli, Appresso Gio Mario Scotta, 1564.

Palmero, Girolamo da., *Confessionario Raccolta da i dottori Catolici Nuouamente ampliato di alcutli avisi & osservationi d'importanza Per F. Andrea Alchero de Materno*, Brescia, 1567.

Ribadeneyra, Pedro de., *Vita del p. Ignatio Loiola fondatore della Religione della Compagnia di Giesù*, In Venetia, appresso i Gioliti, 1586.

IN LATIN

Catechismus ex Decreto Concilii Tridentini ad Parochos, Roma, MDLXVI.

Catechismus ex decreto Concilii Tridentini ad parochos. Pii V pont. max. iussu editus, Venetiis : apud Fabium, August, Zoppinos, fratres, MDLXXXIII.

Codices Orientales Biblithecae Regiae Havniensis Jussu et Auspiciis, Regis Daniae Augustissims Christiani Octavi Enumerati et Descripti, Pars Prior Codices Indicos Continens Havnicae, Exofficina Fratrum Berlin, 1846.

Franco, Antonio., *Synopsis Annualium Societatis Jesu in Lusitania ab annis 1540 usque ad annum 1725*, Haeredum, Anno MDCCXXVI.

Maffei, Giovanni Pietro., *De vita et moribus Ignatii Loiolae, qui Societatem Iesu fundauit*, libri III, Venetiis, apud Iolitos, 1585.

Polaco, Juan de., *Breve directorium ad confessarii ac confitentis munus recte obeundum*, Roma, apud Antonium Bladum, 1554.

Sacra Biblia, acri studio, ac diligentia emendata, rerum, atque verborum permultis et perquamdignis indicibus aucta, Venetiis, apud Iolitos, 2 volumes, 1588.

Vita Christi domini saluatoris nostri a r.p. Ludolpho Saxone Cartusiano ante CCL annos ex sacris evangelijs, veterumque patrum sententijs contexta, atque ita disposita, nihil ut eorum, quae tum ad historiae, tum ad homiliarum totius anni rationem spectant, deesse quidquam possit. Opus ut vere pium, ac eruditum, ita singulis christianae pietatis alumnis plurimum & solatij, & utilitatis allaturum. A Io. Dadraeo, Parisiensis scholae doctore theologo, multis notationibus illustratum, postrema hac Venetaeditione innumeris mendis purgatum, pulcherrimisque figuris exornatum. Indices accessere necessarii, Venetiis: apud Guerraeos fratres, & Franciscum Zilettum, 1581.

Sacra Biblia, acri studio, ac diligentia emendata, rerum, atque verborum permultis et perquamdignis indicibus aucta, Venetiis, apud Iolitos, 1588.

IN PORTUGUESE

Castanheda, Fernão Lopes da., Manuel Lopes de Almeida, ed., *Historia do descobrimentos e conquista da India pelos portugueses*, 2 vols., Porto, 1979.

COMPENDIO SPIRITVAL DA VIDA CHRISTAA, tirade de muitos autores pello primeiro ARCEBISPO de Goa, ó per elle pregado no primeiro anno a seus fregueses, pera Gloria ó horra de IESV CHRISTO nosso SALVADOR, ó edificacam de suas. Na seguinte folha se decrara o conteudo neste Tratado. Impresso em Goa: por Ioão Quinquencio, ó Ioao de Endem, ó por madao do Senhor Arcebispo, 1561.

Cortesão Armando and Luis de Albuquerque, ed., *Obras Completas de Dom João de Castro*, 4 vols., Coimbra, 1968-1981.

Costa, Balthasar da., *Catecismo em que se Explição Todas as Verdades Catholicas Necessaraias para a Salvação com Excellentissima Ordem*, 1661.

Differenca da Christandade: Em que Claramente de Manifesta a Grande Desconformidade Traduzida da Castelhano em Portuguez Pelo P. Joãm Ferreira A. d'Almeida, Ministro Pregador do S. Evangelho na India Oriental: Conforme a Impressão de Batavia de 1668, Segunda Impressão, Trangambar, na Officina da Real Missão de Dinamarca, 1728.

Ho flos sanctorum em lingoajem portugues, Lisboã, Hermão de Campos e Roberto Rabello, 15 Março 1513.

Jorge, Marcos., *Doctrina Christam, Ordenando a maneira de dialogo, para ensiar os minios*, Lisboã, 1561.

Orta, Garcia da., *Coloquios dos simples, e drogas he cousas medicinais da India*, Lisboã, 1963.

Rosário, Diogo do., *Historia das vidas & feitos heroicos & obras insignes dos sanctos, que nesta segunda parte se contem: com muitos sermões & praticas spirituaes que servem a muitas festas do anno. Reuistas & cotejadas cõ os seus originaes autenticos: de mãdado do muy Illustre & Reuerendiss. senhor dõ frey Bartholomeu dos Martyres Arcebispo & senhor de Braga, Primas das Hespanhas, & c.*, Braga, António de Mariz, 1567.

Silva Rego, António da., ed., *Documentação para a historia das missões do Padroado Portugues do oriente*, 12 vols., Lisboã, 1947-1958.

Torres, Alvaro de., *Directório de confessores e penitentes*, Lisboã, João Blavio, 1556.

Vagad O. Cist, Gauberto de., *O Flos Sanctorum em Linguagem Português*, 1513.

VIDA DA SANTISSIMA VIRGEM MARIA MAY DE DEOS, Senhora Nossa, Composto pello Padre Antonio Fernandes da Companhia de Iesvs Portuguez natural de Lixboa, Em Goa co licenca dos Inquisidores & Ordinario, Impresso no Collegio de Sam Paulo da Companhia de Iesv, anno, de 1652.

Wicki, Jose, and J. Gomes., *Documenta Indica*, 19 vols., Roma, 1948-1988.

– –, *Tratado do P.e Gonçalo Fernandes Trancoso sobre o Hinduismo, Madure, 1616*, Lisboa, 1973.

IN SPANISH

Bataillon, Marcel., *Erasmo y España: Studios sobre la historia spiritual del siglo XVI*, 2nd edn, trans. Antonio a la Torre, Mexico, Fondo de Cultura Económica, 1966.

IN TAMIL

Aandavarudaya suthamaana Raaposanathukku sera virumbugiravargal ariya vendina Krisithavargaludaya vethaa padippinaiyin surukkamaana thogai: Kort Begryp Der Christelyke Religie, Voor Die zig willen begaven tot des Heeren heilig Avondmaal; ten dientse der kerken en Schoolen, In de Tamulsche Spraak overgezet, En, op Goed-keuring Van de Hooge Overheid deezes Eilands, In t' Licht gegeven, Door Sigisbertus Abrahamsz Bronsveld Bedienaar des H. Evangeliums in Christi gemeinte Te Colombo, Comps: gewoone Drukkery: Door Johann Bernhardt Arnhardt, MDCCLIV.

Aathichuvadi, Mission Press, Pondicherry, 1844.

Aganaanuru, eds., N.M. Venkatasamy Nattar and R. Venkatachalam Pillai, 3rd edn., South India Saiva Siddhanta Pathippu Kazhagam, Madras,1957.

Almeida, Fernando de., ed., *Cartilha em Tamul e Português: Impresa em 1554*, Ministerio da Edução Nacional, Direção-Geral do Superior do Ensino Superior e da Belas-Artes, Lisboã, 1970.

Anriquez Anrique, Krisiththiyaani Vanakkam, AD 1579, ed., S. Rajamanickam, *Vanakkam*, Thamizh Ilakkiya Kazhagam, Tuticorin, 1963.

– –, *Flos Sanctorum enra Adiyaar Varalaaru*, ed., S. Rajamanickam, Thuthukudi, Thamizh Ilakkiya Kazhlagam, 1967.

Arappaal, Kural, ed., F.W Ellis, Madras, 1816.

Archasishta Apostalanum Suviseshakanumaagiya Mathevusu enbavar Yezhuthi vaitha Yesuchristuudaya suthamaana suvisesham: Het Heylige Evangelium Onzes Heeren en Zaligmakers Jesu Christi na de Beschryvinge van den Heilingen Apostel en Evangelist Mattheus, uyt de Oorspronkelyke Grieske, in de Mallabaarse Tale overgebragt en behoorlyk na Kerken ordre geredíveert, Gedrukt tot Colombo. Compagnies Druckeryre, Anno MDCCXLI.

Archayasista Narkarunaikku Paathiram Ullavanaka: *Solidissima Instituto Sanctae Coenae: Inqua Ostenditu qua Praeparatione Ante: Qua Exteriorum Interiorum que Morum Observationae irca: et qua Novitiate Vitae post Usum Sanctae Coenae Digne Sacramentum Celebraturus se Probare Debeat in Gratiam Christianae Gentis Damulorum Exhibita a Missionaria Danica Benjamin Schultze*, Trangambariae, Typis ac Sumptibus Missionis Danicae, MDCCXXII.

Archiasishta Ignaasiyaar Sarithiram, Pondicherry, 1869.

Athma Bhodaga Paritchai, Madras, 1840.

Ayyar, U.V. Swaminatha., Pattinapaalai in *Pathupaatu*, Madras, 1974.

Beschi, Constanzo Giuseppe., *Vetha Vizhlakkam: Beschi yennum veeramaamunivar iyattriya nool: Romaapuriyinninru vantha uththarvinpadi puthuvai periya koilyaiserntha Achchukudathil pathipikkapattathu*, Pondicherry, 1842.

– –, *Paramaartha Guruvin Kathai*, Third edition, Mission Press, Pondicherry, 1904.

Borstius Jacobus, *Kristhavargaludaya Veda Padippinaiyin Surukkamaana Thogai*: Kort Begryp Der Christelyke Religie, Voor Die zig willen begaven tot des Heeren heilig Avondmaal; ten dientse der kerken en Schoolen, In de Tamulsche Spraak overgezet, En, op Goed-keuring Van de Hooge Overheid deezes Eilands, In t' Licht gegeven, Door Sigisbertus Abrahamsz Bronsveld Bedienaar des H. Evangeliums in Christi gemeinte Te Colombo, MDCCLIV.

– –, Sirupillai kathekisamu: *Vraagen en antwoorden voor de eerst beginnende kinderen ... in de Tamulsche sprakk overgezet ... door Sigisbertus Abrahamsz Bronsveld.. Gedrukt te Colombo in s' Comps: gewoonw drukkery door Johann Bernhardt Arnhardt, anno* MDCCLIV.

Bronsveld, Sigisbertus Abrahamsz., *Kathekisamu: Aththaavathu thiruthapatta sabaigalilum pallikudangalilum padipikkapadugira krisithamaana deva araathanaiyin upadesam*: Catechismus, Ofte Onderweyzing In de Christelicke Leere Die In de Hervormde Kerken en Schoolen geleerd word, Ten Dienst der Kerken en Schoolen In de Tamulsche Spraak Overgezet, En Op Goed-Keuring van De Hooge Overheid Deezes Eilands, In't licht gegeven,

Door. Sigisbertus Abrahamsz Bronsveld, Bedienaar des H. Evangeliums in Christi Gemeinte Te Columbo. Gedrukt in's Comps: gewoone Drukkery, Door Johann Bernhardt Arnhardt. Anno MDCCLIV.

Cramer, Adolphus., *Archasishta Apostalanum Suviseshakanumaagiya Maarku, Lukka and youvan enbabavargal Yezhuthi vaitha Yesuchristuudaya suthamaana suvisesham,* Colombo, MDCCXLII.

De Melho, Philippus, *Sathiyathin Jeyam*: Triumph der Waarheid Zynde Eene beknopte en kragtige wederlegging van der Voornaamste dwaalingen der Roomsche kerje, Med verdediginge van daar tegen gestelde Catholyke Waarheid, die in de gereformeerde kerke geleers word. Door Last van den Wel-Edelen groot-Agtbaaren here Julius Valenthyn Stein van Gollenesse, Eersten Raad En Directeur Generaal van Nederlnads Jndia Ten tyde van des zelvs Regeeringe op Ceilon gegeven, in de Tamulsche Taale Opgesteld, Ten dienste van de Christelyke Tamuklsche Gemeenten, Door. Philippus De Melho, Beroepen Praedikant te Jaffanapatnam, Gedrukt te Colombo, s' Compagnies gewoone drukkery door Johann Bernhardt Arnhardt, Anno MDCCLIII.

– –, *Thiruthapattta Thiruchabaigazhin Vazhipaatu Allatha Murai Noolhal*, Liturgie der Gereformeerde Kerken ofte de Formulieren by dezelve in den uiterlyken dienst gebruykelyk, Colombo, MDCCLX.

Devapadikku thakathaay irukkira sathiyathinaaya padippinnaiyinudya surukkamaana thogai: Kort Uittrekzel Van De Leere der Waarheid die na de Godsaaligheid is ten dienste der Schoolen Uit de hollandsche in de Tamulsche taale Overgezet Door Mattheus Jurgen Ondaatje, Proponent in de Hervormde gemeente, En Gerediveerd Door den mede Proponent Mattheus Jurgen Ondaatje. In de Tamulsche Gemeente, En door de Taalkundigen Philip Jansz: en Adrian Frans Farnando, Te Colombo; Joh: Christoph Dornheim, Anno MDCCLXXXIX.

Durai, A. Jose Anna., ed., *Purandima Kaandam: Pazhaya Yerpaatin Sarithiram*, Second edition, Madras, 1913.

– –, ed., *Pachima Kaandam: Puthiya Yerpattin Sarithiram*, Second edition, Madras, 1914.

Fabricius, Johann Philipp., *Nammuda kartharum iratchakarumaahiya yesu kristhuvinaal undaana kirupayin udanpadikaiyaagiya puthu yerpaadu*: Krsithu pirantha (1772 numeral in Tamil) varushaththil Chennapattanathil achadikaapattathu: The Malabar New Testament of Our Lord and Saviour Jesus Christ, Vepery near Madras, MDCCLXXII.

– –, *Manushasaathi ratchikaapattu varathakka sarvalogathaya Paraaparanaana Karthar aruli seytha Sathya vetham: Muthalam Pangu*: Librorum Sacrorum Veteris Testamenti Pars prima, continens Libros Mosis, Josuae et Judicum,

Editio secunda Correctioner, Trangambariae, Typis sumptibus Missionis Danicae, MDCCLXXVII.

– –, *Manusasaathi ratechikka padavrakathakka sarvalogathaya paraaparanana Karthar aruliseytha sathya vedam, Irandaam pangu*: Librorum Sacrorum Veteris testamenti pars secunda: continens Libros Ruth, II. Samuelis, II. regnum, II. Chronicorum, Esrae, Nehemiae, Esther et Jobi, Editio secunda Correctioner, Trangambariae, Typis sumptibus Missionis Danicae, MDCCLXXXII.

– –, *Ulaga Ratchagaraana Yesu Swamiyin Muthinar manusharaagiya Mathei, Marku, Luka, Yovaan yenbavargal peril yezhuthi vaitha naalu suviseshath thaagamangal*: Domini Nostri Jesu Christi qui est Servator Mundi Novi Foederis Libri Pars Prima S. Matthei, Marci, Lucae et Johannis Evangelia, Editio Quarta, Trangambariae, Typis Sumtibusque Missionis Danicae, Anno MDCCLXXXVIII.

– –, *Manusasaathi retchikapattuvarathakka sarvalokathaya paraaparanana kartar aruli seydha sathya vedam, Munraam pangu*: Librorum Sacrorum Veteris, pars tertia, Continens Libros psalmorum, Proverbiorum, Ecclesiastae et Cantici Canticorum, Editio secunda Correctioner, Trangambariae, Typis sumptibus Missionis Danicae, MDCCXCI.

– –, *Manusasaathi retchikapattuvarathakka sarvalokathaya paraaparanana kartar aruli seydha sathya vetham, Naalam pangu*: Librorum Sacrorum Veteris Testamenti, Pars Quarta, In qua Libri Prophetarum Majorum & Minorum continentur, editio secunda Correctioner, Trangambariae, Typis sumptibus Missionis Danicae, MDCCXCVI.

Gnaana Kannadi: Joannis Arndtii...de Vero Christianismo Liber Primus...Ex Germanico in Tamulicum Convertit Benjamin Schulzius, Halle, 1751.

Gnaana Mandira Selva Pungaavanam, 4 pts, Halle, 1749-1750.

Gnaana Paatugalin Posthagam: Hymnologia Sagrada: Isto he, Espirituaes Cantigas Para Excitação da Christaa Devoção, E para Edificação em Fe e Piedade, Com Real Licenca, Tranquebar, Em India Oriental na Costa de Coromandel, em a Estampa da Real Missão de Dennemark, no Anno MDCCXIX.

Gnaana Paatukkal Adangiirukkira Posthagam: Hymnologia Tamulica: Sive ex Germanico, Partiam Etiam Latino Sermone, nec non e Textu Sacro in Tamulicum Idioma Translatorum Ducentorum et Nonaginta Hymnorum Spiritualium Fasciculus: Quos in Gratiam Ecclesiae Tamulicae ...Successive Collegerunt Missionarii Danici, Editio Quarta, Trangambariae, MDCCXXXIII.

Gnnanapattugalin Posthagam, Munraam pathithal: *Kiristhu pirantha aayiraththi elunuthi naarpathi naalam varusham aagira pothu ithu tharanganpaadiyile irukkira paathirimaargaludaya acchile pathipikka pattathu*: Psalmodia evangelica, ou livro de cantigas espirituais, tirades de varios textos e muytos lugares da escritura sagrada, da theologia positica e moral, e de outros livros asceticos, para os Christaos se excitarem a hua santa devocao, e se edificaram na verdadeira fee hua pia convesacao: traduzidas pela mayor parted a lingoa Alemaa pelos padres missionaries de trangambar, Terceira impressao, Trangambar, na officina da real Missao de dinamarca anno MDCCXLIV.

Gnaana Paatukkal Adangi Irukkira Posthagam: Hymnologia Tamulica sive ex Germanic, partim etiam Latino sermon, nec non e textu scaro in tamulicam idioma transaltorum et nonaginta quinque hymnorum spiritualism fasciculus: quos in gratiam eccelasie tamulicas, Christu nomen dantis, succeive collegerunt missionary danici- edition quinta, Trangambariae, in littore Choromandelino: Typis sumptibus Missionis Danicae, anno MDCCLVI.

Gnaana Paatukkal Adangiirikira Posthagam: Hymnologia Tamulica: Sive Trecentorum et Octo Hymnorum Spiritualium Fasciculus, Quos in Usem Ecclesiae Christianiae inter Tamulos Successive Collegerunt Missionarii Danici; Editio Sexta, Auctor et Emendiatior, Trangambariae in Litore Choromandelino, Typis Missionis Danicae Anno MDCCLXXIX.

Gnaanapragasanathar, C., *Aathuma Nesam*, Mission Press, Pondicherry, 1860.

– –, *Kristhunaathar Anusaaram*, Mission Press, Pondicherry, 1863.

– –, *Sathiya Vetha Sarithira Surukkam*, Mission Press, Pondicherry, 1865.

Gnaanaupadesam: *Thathuvapothaga Swamigal Udayathu, Muthal Kaandam*, Ambalakaadu, 1677, *Catechismo Madurense: Escripta em Tamul pelo Padre Robert Nobili S.J. em 1674 e divido em duas partes, Impressoe em Ambalacatta no officina de Ignacio Archamanio em 1677.*

Gnaanaupadesam: Rendaam Kaandam, Catechismo Madurensa em lingoa Tamulica, por Pe. Roberto Nobili da Companhia de Jesus, e 2a parte, Ambalakaadu, 1677.

Gnaanaupadesam: Thathuvapothaga Swamigal Udayathu, Munram Kaandam, Ambalakkadu, 1678; *Catechismus P. Roberti Nobili, Tamulico idiomate scriptus ... Pars Tertia*, Ambalacatta: no officinal de Ignacio Archamonio, 1678.

Gnaanopadesam: Thathuvapothaga Swamigal Udayathu, Naankaam Kaandam, R.P. Roberti Nobili Romani Societate Iesv, *Catechism Romani Qvarta Pars, Ambalacatta, no officinal de Ignacio Arcchamonio*, 1678.

Gnaana upadesathinyuday kurippidam, Tranquebaria, MDCCXIX.

Gnaana upadesathinyuday kurippidam: Doctrina de ordine quo Homines Peccatores Salvari atque Felicis immortalitatis participes fieri debent, Editio tertia, Trangambariae Anno Christi, MDCCXXXIII.

Gnaana upadesathin kurippidam, Irandam pathithal: Ithu kiristhu pirantha aayiraththi yezhunoothi enpaththi munaam varushathil tharanganpaadiyil achchadikkapattathu, MDCCLXXXIII.

Gnaana upadesthainyudaya kurippidam, Irandaam pathithal: Kiristhu pirantha aayiraththi yezhunoothi yenpatthettaam varushamagira pothu ithu tharanganpaadiyile achchiley Pathipikkapattathu, MDCCLXXXVIII.

Goncalves, Jacome., *Suvisesha Viruththi Urai*, Yaazhpaanam, 1891.

Henrique Henriques, *Flos Sanctorum*: *Adiyar Varalaru*, ed., S. Rajamanickam, Tuticorin, 1967.

– –, *Thambiran Vanakkam, AD 1578*, ed., Thamizh Naadaan, *Thamizh Mozhhiyin Muthal Achchu Puththagam*, Salem, 1995.

– –, *Thambiran Vanakkam: Thamizh Mozhiyin Muthal Achchu Puthagam*, ed., Victoria, Mo. Nevis, Chennai, 2011.

Iguthu Thandavaraya Mudaliyaaraal Mozhipeyartha Panchathanthira Kathai, Madras, 1826.

Innasi SU., and S. Soundara Pandiyan, *Thirukural Veeramamunivar Urai*, Madras, 1985.

Iraasa Thirkatharisyahiya Thaavidthinudaya sila sangeethangalum veru pugazhlchi paatukalum adangiulla posthagam: Eenige Psalmen des Koninglyken Prophete Davids en andere Lofzangen. Uyt den Nederduytschen in Tamulschen Digte overgeset door Philippus De Mello Bedienaer des H. Evangeliums in de Gemeente Jesu Christi, Te Jaffanapatnam: En uitgegeven naar gewoone Kerkorder, Anno MDCCLV.

Kalithogai, ed., M. Kasi Visvanatha Chettiar, Third edition, Madras, 1947.

Karaiyerugiradhukku Surukkamaaha Ariya Vendina Gnaana Upadesathinudaya Kurippidam, Tranquebar, 1717.

Kathekisamu: Mallebaars Catechismus, en Gebede-boek Gedrukt tot Colombo ten dientse der Scholen Anno MDCCXXXIX.

Kristumarkattina Surukkamaana Vizhlakam: Doctrinae Christiane Rudimenta olim ab autore Beato A.H. Franckio theologo Halensi Germania edita: Nunc in lingual Tamulicam translata: Accessit brevis notitia de S. Scriptura religione, Trangambariae, Typis Missionis Danicae, MDCCXXXIV.

Kirisithamaana Upadesathin Surukkamana Vizhlakkam: Ithiley aynthu manditrangalum athugalin Viyavarthangalum anthantha vezhaikaliley sebika padathakka sepangalum adangi irukkuthu, Aram Visai, Ithu kiristhu pirantha aayiraththi elunuthi arupathi onaam varushathiley tharanganpaadiyile paddrimaargal achchukudathile achchadikkapattathu, MDCCLVI.

Kirisiththa Maarkathin Surukkamaana Vizhlakkam: Principia religionis Christiane, in usum scholarum Tamulensium missionis region Danicae, Edition secunda, Trankenbariae, sumptibus Missionis, MDCCXCVI.

Kristhavargaludaya Veda Padippinaiyin Surukkamaana Thogai, Colombo, 1754.

Manimegalai, ed., N.M. Venkatasamy Nattar, South India Saiva Siddhanta Pathippu Kazhagam, Tirunelveli, 1992.

Manushavathaaram pannina Devasuthanaagira Yesu Christu Swami Manusha Jathiyai Retchikka Paadupattu Marithanri Uyirthu Paralogathuku Yezhuntharliya Sarithiram, Iraanaddam Pathihthal: Historia passionis, mortis, resurrectionis et ascenscionis Jesu Christi Fili Dei et Mariae Virginis, Tamulice, ex quatour Evangelistis Conscripta,Editio secunda, Penitus Recognita Er Ad Textum graecum conformata), Trangambariae, Missionis Danicae, anno MDCCXL.

Martin Luther Enbavarin Gnaanopadesa Kuripidathai Vistharikkum Vina Vidaigal, Translated into Tamil by Bartholomäus Ziegenbalg, Revised by A. Blomstrand, third edition, Tranquebar, 1872.

Nobili, Roberto., *Punar Janma Atchepam*, S. Rajamanickam, ed., Tuticorin, 1963.

– –, *Archsishta Devamatha Sarithiram*, ed., S. Rajamanickam, Tuticorin, 1964.

– –, *Nithiya Jeevana Sallapam*, S. Rajamanickam, ed., Tuticorin, 1964.

– –, *Sesunathar Sarithiram*, S. Rajamanickam, ed., Tuticorin, 1964.

– –, *Gnaanopadesam*, vols. I-II, S. Rajamanickam, ed., 1966, vol. III, Tuticorin, 1968.

– –, *Robert de Nobili on Adaptation*, S. Rajamanickam, ed., Palayamkottai, 1971.

Ondaatje, Matthias Jurgen., *Tamitbhaashaiyir Sirupillai Kathekismu*, Colombo, 1788.

Oru Kiristhavnavedapramaanathina padiye ariya vendina mandirangalaiyum padichu seyyavedia gnayangaliyum podhichivikkira gnaana upadesam: A explicacao da doutrina christaa Segundo a ordem do catecismo do B. Luthero, em perguntas e repostas proposta, e com necessaries testemunhos da escritura Sagrada provada: traduziada em Lingoa portugueza pelos Minsitros da Palavra de Deus e Missionarios del rey de Dennemark, Tranquebar Em India Oriental na Costa de Coromandel, na Estampa dos dittos Missionarios, no. Anno de MDCCXIII.

Oru Kristhavana motchathai adairathukku vethapiramaanithina padiye ariya vendina vilakangaliyum mandirangaliuym padichu seyya vendia nayangaliyum pothichivikira gnaana upadesam, Tranquebariae, MDCCXV.

Oru Paradesi Intha Logathaivittu Marumaikku Nadantherinathu Sorpanamenru Uvamaiyiley Kaanpikkapattirukkuthu, Vepery, MDCCXCIII.

Paavikalaana manusar yenta ozhungunpadiey retchikapattu pakkiyam ullavargalmay motchavangalumay pogaveneum engira vetha padippiinai: Doctrina de ordine quo Homines Peccatores Salvari atque Felicis immortalitatis participes fieri debent, editio secunda, Trangambariae: Typis Missionis Danicae, Anno Christi, MDCCXXVIII.

Paramandalangali Thangal Pokkisham Undenirukkira Paraaparanudaya Pillaigalin Aabarana Petti, Translated into Tamil by Daniel Pillai, Vepery, 1800.

Pazhaya Yerpaddu: Het eerste deel des ouden testaments van de heilige Schrivutur, vervattende de vye Boeken Mosis genaamd genesis, exodus, Leviticus, Numeri, en Deuteronomiun, gedrukt te Colombo, in 's komp: Boekdrukkery, Johan Fredrik Christoph Dornheim, anno MDCCXC.

Pillai, Daniel, trs., *Paramandalangali Thangal Pokkisham Undenirukkira Paraaparanudaya Pillaigalin Aabarana Petti* , Vepery, 1800.

Pillai, Yagappa., ed., *Gnaanopadesam*, Second edition, St. Joseph's Printing Press, Madras, 1891.

Puranaanuru, ed., U.V. Swaminatha Ayyar, Madras, 1971.

Puthiya Yerpaadu: Het Nieuwe Testament, ofte Alle De Boeken Des Nieuwen Verbonds Van Onsen Heer Jesus Christus. Door Last van de Hooge Overheid Deeses Eilands Uit de oirspronglyke Grieksche Taal In de Tamulsche Spraak overgezet, En Naar Kerken-order behoorlyk overzien, Gedrukt te Colombo, gewoone Drukkery door Pieter Bruwaart. Anno MDCCLIX.

Puthithaay Thamizha Paduthapatta Gnaana Paatukkal, Ithu kiristhu pirantha aayiraththi elunuthi ampaathai rendaam varushathiley tharanganpaadiyile achchadikkapattathu: Hymnologia Tamulica, Tharanganpadi, MDCCLII.

Puthithaay Thamizha Paduthapatta Gnaana Paatukkal, Tharanganpadi, MDCCLVI.

Retchippin Ozhlukkam: A ordem da salvacao, ou doutrina Christaa Brevemente en perguntas e repostas declarada e provada com principaes testemunhos da escritura Sagrada, Juntamente com alhuas Oracoens e Castigas, Tranquebar, En India Oriental na costa de Coromandel, na Estampa dos missionaries del Rey de Dennemark, Anno MDCCXII.

Retchippin Ozhlungu: *Ithiley Paraaparavasthuvukkum manusha saathikkum mathiyasthanaakiya yesu kristhu thedivaitha paakiyam manusharuku paalikum vazhivagai yethenru solli irrukuthu, Irandaam pathithal*, Kiristhu pirantha aayiraththi elunuthi naarpathi yezhaam varushathiley ithu tharanganpaadiyile achchadikkapattathu, Trangambariae, Typis missionis Danicae, MDCCXLVII.

Retchiththalin Ozhlungu: *Paraaparamaakira sarvesuranukkum manusharukkum mathiyasthan ahiya yesu kristhu thedivaitha paakiyam manusharuku paalikum vazhivagai yethenru solli irrukuthu*: Ordo Salutis methodo Catechetica, pro diverso Catechumenorum captu trifaria froma exhibitus, & notis quibusdam in usum catechetarum instructus, Trangambariae, Typis missionis Danicae, MDCCXXX.

Sangeethangalum Veru Pugazhlchi Paatukalum Adangiulla Posthagam: Het Boek der Psalmen, Nevens de Gezangen, By de Hervormde Kerk van Nederland In Gebruik; Door Last van de Hoog Mogende Heeren Staaten Generaal der Vereenigde Nederlanden, Uit drie Berijmingen, in den Jaare 1773, gekooren, Met de noodige daar in gemaakte veranderingen tweede Oplage, Te Colombo, Johan Fredrik Cristoph Dornheim MDCCLXXVI.

Saruvesaparanuk Kuganthavarkalul Suthamaana Suviseshagarumaana Mathevus, Maarkku, Lukkaas, Yovannes Yezhuthina Posthagam: Het Heylige Evangelium onzes Heeren ende Zaligmakers Jesu Christi, na de Beschryvinge, van de Mannen Gods, en de H: Evangelisten, Mattheus, Marcus, Lucas, ende Johannes. Waar by nog komt het Tweede Boek, door Lucas, beschreeven, ende genaamt, de Handelingen de Apostelen, uit het Oorspronkelyke Grieks, in de Tamulsche Tale, Gedrukt tot Colombo, in's Compagnies Druckerye, Anno MDCCXLVIII.

Sathiya Vethabhodhaga Surukkam, Mission Press, Pondicherry, 1846.

Schultze, Benjamin, *Narkarunai Posthagam*, Kristhu pirantha 1721 varusham Tharangapaaddi achchile pathipikkapattathu : Solidissima Instituto Sanctae Coenae: inqua ostenditu qua praeparatione ante: Qua exteriorum interiorumque morum observationae circa: et qua novitiate vitae post usum sanctae coenae digne sacramentum celebraturus se probare debeat in gratiam christianae gentis Damulorum exhibita a missionaria Danica Benjamin Schultze, Trangambariae, Typis ac sumptibus Missionis Danicae, MDCCXXI.

– –, *Suthanaagiya Sarvesuranaanirukkira yesukristhu naatharaanavar inda bhulogathiley manushanaai pirantha viseshangalaiyum bhoduvicha upadesangaliyum seytha arputhangalaiyum manusharukku vendi paadupattu yellaraiyum moondu raetchithuvitha vaanagalaiyum uyirodey ezhunthiruinthu paralogathiley magaimaiyaga yerinathaiyum avarudaya seshargalagiya apostalarmaargal logam yengum poey ippadikothavichu viseshangalai sagala senangallukkum pirasangam panninathaiyum vezhipaduthugira puthu yerpaadinudaya muthalam vaguppagiya Anju veda posthagam*: Novum Jesu Christi Testamentum, ex originali textu in linguam damulicam versum opera & studia Bartholomaei Ziegenbalgi & Jo. Ern. Grundleri. – Daniae Regis Friederici IV. Ad Indos orientles missionariorum, Editio secunda correctior et accessione summariorum, cujusvis capitis auctior, Tranquebariae, Typis Damulicis missionis Danicae, MDCCXXII.

– –, *Archayasishta Narkarunaikku Paathiram Ullavanaka*: Solidissima Instituto

Sanctae Coenae: Inqua Ostenditu qua Praeparatione Ante: Qua Exteriorum Interiorum que Morum Observationae irca: et qua Novitiate Vitae post Usum Sanctae Coenae Digne Sacramentum Celebraturus se Probare Debeat in Gratiam Christianae Gentis Damulorum Exhibita a Missionaria Danica Benjamin Schultze, Trangambariae, Typis ac Sumptibus Missionis Danicae, MDCCXXII.

– –, *Meyyana Sarvesuranum meyyana Manushanum onnaairukkira yesu Christu Naatharaanavar inda Bhoologathiley salga manusargalay paavathinudaya adumaithanuthuleyum yenyennaikkum nirkira naragathinudaya akkiineyulum ninru meelkkathakathaga thammudaya sarirathileyum thammudya aathumathulayeum yethinai ninaivulagaiyum vethanaigaleyum kadaisiliey maranathilum nangu sollappadaatha porumaiyodu paddupattaryenru surukkamaaga vezhipaduthugira sarithira posthagam*: Historia passionis Jesu Christi Filii Dei et Mariae Virginis damulice ex quatour Evangelistis conscripta a Benjamin Schultze missionario Danico, Tranquebariae, in officina Missionis Danicae, anno MDCCXXIII.

– –, *Daavidengiravar Yezhuthivaitha Gnaana Sangeethangaludaya Posthagam*: Liber Psalmorum Davidis Regis et Prophetae, ex Originali Textu in Lingua Damulicam Versus Opera & Studio Benjamin Schultze ad Indos orientales Missionarii, Tranquebariae, MDCCXXIV.

– –, *Azhavillatha gnnanamullavarumaay azhavillatha kirubaiullavarumaay azhavillatha deivigiamullavray irukkira parraapara vasthuvaanavar pazhaya yerpaatinyudaya kaalathiley thiruvilampathina veda posthagathin rendaam vagauppu: ithiley archiyasishta ruth engiravzhludaya posthagamum, archiyasishta samuyel yengiravrudaya muthalaam posthagmum, rendam posthagamum Maarassakaludaya muthalam posthagamum, rendam posthagamum, paralipomvenru sollapatta muthalaam posthagamum, rendam posthagamum, echcheruvengiravarudaya posthagamum, neyemiyavengiravrudaya posthagamum, yesther engarivaludaya posthgamum, yobu engiravaruday posthagamum, Daavidengriavar ezhuthi vaitha gnnana sangeethngalengira posthagamum,Salamon engiravr pesina vaakiyamgaludaya posthagamum, ekkeilsesiyesh engira naamathai kondirukkira posthagamum, unnathamaana paatinuduaya posthagamum adangai irukkudhu.* Kristu pirandhu 1726 varushamagira poedhu, ithu thatanganpaadiiley irukkira paathrimargaludaya achiley pathipikka pattudhu: Biblia Damulica, seu quod Deus Sapientissimius in sua Divina oeconomia cumn Populo Israelitico et Egit t et Locutus est. Veteris Testanenti Pars Secunda, in qua Libellus Ruth, Samnzelis Liber Prior et Posterior, Liber Nehemiae, Liber Esther, Liber Jobi, Liber Psalmorum Davidis, Liber Proverbium, Liber Ecclesiastae, et Liber Cantici Canticorum, studio et opera Bartholomaei Ziegenbalgii et Benjamin

Schultzi Missionariorum in linguam Damulicam versi continentur, Tranquebariae, MDCCXXVI.

––, *Anju kanda seeraay irukkiravarumaay, yellathayum arinthu irukkiravarumaay, azhavillatha parisuthamullavarumaay irukkira parraapara vasthuvaanavar pazhaya yerpaadu irukkirapothu puthu yerpadinyadya magimaiayai vezhipaduthapora yesu kristhuvin periley thiruvilampathina veda posthagtahin moonam vagauppu: Ithialey archiyasishta theergatharisigalagira yesaypiyavengairavr kanda therisanthaninudya posthagamum, yeremiyavengiravar pannina pirasangathinyudaya posthgamum, avar paadina pulambalinyudaya posthgamaum, ysekkiyelengiravrakku kaanpikka patta therisanathinyadya posthagamum, Daaaniyelengiravar therisanamaaga kanda vathamaanagaludaya posthagamum, oseyaasum, yoyellum, Aamossum,obaadiyaavum, yonaasum, mikkavum, naahummum, abakukkum, sepaaniyavum, aakkayum, sakarayaasum, malayosum engiravargal theerkatharisanamaaga solli, ezhuthi vaitha posthagangalum adangi irukkudhu*; Kristu pirandhu 1727 varushamagira poedhu, ithu thatanganpaadiiley irukkira paathrimargaludaya achiley pathipikka pattadhu: Biblia Damulica, seu quod Deus Omnniscius de gratia in Jesu Christo tempore Novi Testamenti Revelanda per Sanctos suos Prophetas est Vaticinatus. Veteris Testamenti Pars Tertia, in qua Prophetae Majores, Esaias, Jeremias, ejusdemque Lamentationes, Ezechiel, Daniel; Prophetae Minores, Hoseas, Joel, Amos, Obadia, Jona, Micha, Nahum, Habacuc, Zephania, Haggai, Zacharias, et Malachias, studio et opera, Ziegenbalgii et Schultzi, Tranquebariae, MDCCXXVII.

––, *Gnaana Paatugalin Posthagam*: Hymnologia Damulica, Sive ex Germanico in Damulorum Idioma, Observatis usque et Melodiis et Rhythmis Odarum, Translatorum Centum et Sexaginta Hymnorum Spiritualium Fasciculus, in Gratiam Juventutis Damulicae Aeque ac Ecclesiae Hujus Gentis, Christo Nomen Dantis, Exhibita a Benjamin Schultze, Tranquebariae, MDCCXXIII.

– –, *Raasvum Thirgatharisiyumayiruntha Archisista Dhavidengiravar ezhuthi vaitha Gaana snageethangaludaya Posthgam*: *Ithilaye Dhavid enbavarum vaeri sila archisitavargalum paadina 150 sangethangal adangiirukuthu, Randaam pathithal*, Kristu pirantha 1747 ile ithu Tharanganpaadiile achadikapattathu: Liber Psalmorum Davidis, Regis et prophetae: ex originali textu in linguam Tamulicam versus, opera & studio Benjamin Schultze, ad Indos orientalesmissionarii, Editio secunda, Trangambariae: typis missionis danicae, anno MDCCXLVII.

––, *Gnaana Mandira Selva Pungaavanam*, 4 pts, Halle, MDCCXLIX- MDCCL.

––, *Siraakku engiravr yezhuthi vaitha Gnaanam-Irandam Visai*, Kristhu pirandha 1760 varushamaagirapothu, tharanganpaadiyile paadirimaargal achchukudathiley pathipikkapattathu, Trangambariae: typis missionis danicae, anno MDCCLX.

– – *Gnaana Kannadi*: Joannis Arndtii...de Vero Christianismo Liber Primus...Ex Germanico in Tamulicum Convertit Benjamin Schulzius, Halle, 1751.

– –, *Gnnaana Sangeethangaludaya posthagam: Ithiley Davidenpavarum veru sila archaysistavargalum paadina 350 sangethhangal adangi Irukkuthu, Muntram Pathithal*, kristhu pirantha 1785 varushathiley ithu tharangapadiyile missiyon achchukudathileypathika pattaththu. Trangambariae: typis missionis danicae, anno MDCCLXXXV.

Sesu kristhu Naatharudaya Parisuththa suvisesham: Ithu Anniya desaththu Pothagar sabaiyilulla Apostholikku Gurukkallil silaraal Mozhipeyarkapattu puthuvaiyil yezhuntharuliirukkum Mahaa Ganam Poruthiya Aandavrragiya Clemensu Bonnand Drusipare yennumNaamatheyamkonduirukkira mettraaniyaar anumathiyil Romapuriinnitru vantha uththaarathinpadiye 1857 am varusham Puthuvaiyir senmaraakini maatha koilaiserntha achchukudathir pathippikapattathu.

Silapthikaaram, ed., N.M. Venkatasamy Nattar, South India Saiva Siddhanta Pathippu Kazhagam, Tirunelveli, 1992.

Thamizh Bhaashayir Sirupillai Kathekisamu: Tamulsch Kinder-catechismus. Inhoudende het Gebed des heeren e XII, Geloovs Artykelen; de X. Geboden Gods; het Morgen en Avond Gebed; het Gebed voor en na den Eeten, de Instelling van den H. Doop, van 't H. Nagtmaal, en van de Kerkelyke Tugt; nevens den Christen Zegen: Als mede Korte Vraagen en Antwoorden Noopens De Grondstukken der waare Leere, En De Geschiedenissen des Ouden en Nieuwen Testaments; Gelyk ook de Register der H. Schrift. Ten dientse der Schoolen in een evervolg geschikt en uitgegeven Door Sigis: Abrah: Bronsveld, Bedienaar des H. Euangeliums en Rector in't Seminarium Te Colombo. De derde Druk, Gedrukt in 's Comp: gewoone Drukkey door Johann Fredrik Christoph Dornheim, MDCCLXVIII.

Thamizh Saathyaarukku Yezhuthuna Nirupam, Kiristhu pirantha aayiraththi elunuthi aimpaththi anjaam varusham aagira pothu ithu tharanganpaadi acchile pathipikka pattathu.

Tharanganbadiyile Irukkura Gurumargal Indha Desaththaaraay Irukkira Thamizhar Yellarukkum Yezhuthina Nirupam, Irandaam Pathithal, Kiristhu pirantha aayiraththi elunuthi irupathi rendaam varusham aagira pothu ithu tharanganpaadi acchile pathipikka pattathu.

Tharangambadiyile Irukkum Gurumaargal Thamizh Saathiyarrukku Yezhuthina Nirupam, Munraam Pathithal, Kiristhu pirantha aayiraththi elunuthi muppathi munraam varusham aagira pothu ithu tharanganpaadi acchile pathipikka pattathu.

Tharangambadiyile irukkura Gurumaargal Thamizh Saathiyaar Yellorukkum Yezhuthina Nirupam, Naalam Pathithal, Kiristhu pirantha aayiraththi elunuthi naarpathi naalam varusham aagira pothu ithu tharanganpaadiyile irukkira paathirimaargaludaya acchile pathipikka pattathu.

Tharangambadiyile Irukkura Gurumargal Thamizh Saathiyaar Yellorukkum Yezhuthina Nirupam, Ainthaam Visai, Ithu kiristhu pirantha aayiraththi elunuthi ampaathai rendaam varushathiley tharanganpaadiyile paddrimaargal achchukudathile achchadikkapattathu.

Tharanganbaadiiley navamayamaakkapatta Thiruchabaiyaagira Yerusalem engira kovilukku ulpatta kristhavargal paadugira naarpaththettu piratiniaigaludaiya posthagam, Tharangambadi, 1714.

Tharankanpaadi Thiruchabaiyil Valangum Gnaana Muramaigalin Vilakkam: Ithu kiristhu pirantha aayiraththi yezhunoothi yenpaththi onaam varushathiley tharanganpaadiyile paddrimaargal achchukudathile achchadikkapattathu: Rituale Trangambaricum, Trangambariae, Typis Missionis Danicae Anno MDCCLXXXI.

Thiruthapattta Thiruchabaigazhin Vazhipaatu Allatha Murai Noolhal: Liturgie der Gereformeerde kerken, ofte De Fornulieren by Dezelve in den uiterlyken dienst gebruykelyke: I in't doen van de gemeene gebeden; II. In de bedieninge der H.Sacramenten; III. Ind'inzegeninge des Houwelyks; en Iv.int' vertroosten der zicken. uit de hollandsche in de tamulsche taale overgezet ten dientse van de Christelyke Tamulsche gemeenten, door Philippus de Melho, Bedienaar des Godlyken words, in de Gemeente jesu Christi te Jaffanapatnam, En naar kerk order behoorlyk overzien, Gedrukt te Colombo, in's comps: gewoone drukkery, door Pieter Bruwaart, Anno MDCCLX.

Thiruvilaiyaadar Puranam, Chintadripettai, 1850.

Tholkaappiyam, South India Saiva Siddhanta Pathippu Kazhagam, Tirunelveli, 1982.

Ulaga Retchakaraaana Yesu Swamiyin Muttinar Manusharagiya Mathei, Maarku, Lukka, Yovan Yenpavargal Avar Peril Yezhuthi Vaitha Naalu Suviseshamath Aagamangal: Munraam Visai: Domini Nostri Jesu Christi, qui est servitor mundi, noui foederis libri: S. Matthaei, Marci, Lucae et Joannis Evangelia, Apostolorum Jesu Acta revelation, Editio tertia, Trangamabriae, typis sumtibusque missionis Danicae, anno MDCCLVII.

Ulaga Retchakraana Yesu Kristhu Sami Undupannina Puthu Udanpadikaiyin Agaamangal: (No Latin title for vol. II) Trangambariae, Typis sumtibusque missionis Danicae anno MDCCLVIII.

Ulagathin Retchakaraana Kristhu Pirantha Aayiraththi Thonnoothi Rendaam Varushaththukku Sellum Panjangam: Itha panjangam tharanganpayil irukkum misiyon achchukudathil pathipikkapattathu, MDCCXCI.

Veeramamunivar Thamzhililum Lathinilum Thanthapadi Aaranynthu Sutha Prathiyakkapatta Paramaarthaguruvin Kathai, Puducherii, E Typographio Missionariorum Apostolicorum Congregationis Missionum as Exteros, 1845.

Venkata Rajan, S., ed., *Agathiyar Irrandayiram*, in II parts, Thanjavur, 1980.

Vetha Vaakiyangal: Itukal Paraaparan Aruliseytha Vetha Agamangalil Yezhuthi Vaikka Pattathu: Dicta Biblica, ex codice sacro slectaa, secundum ordinem articulorum theologiae thetica collecta, in usum scholarum ecclesiae Tamulicae ad perdiscendum spatio LII. Hebdomadum, accomodata, et in duas partes repartita, Trangamabariae, Typis missionis danicae, anno Christi MDCCLXII.

Walther, Christoph Theodosius., *Yesu Kristhu Swamiyin Seensanagiya Aposthalanum Suviseganumaay Iruntha Archaysishta Mathei Yenbavar Yezhuthivaitha Suviseshath aagamam*: Evangelium Matthaei de Domini Nostri Jesv Christi, qui est Filius Dei, nativitate humana, doctrina miraculis adserta, conversatione inculpate, morte expiatrice, gloriosa resurrectione et, instiuta in terries ecclesia, in coelos adscencu, Editio Tertia, prioribus ad genium linguae Tamulicae textumque originalem curatius exacta, succinstisque summaries atque parallelismo historico et exegetico adornata, Trangambariae, Missionis Danicae, MDCCXXXIX.

Ziegenbalg, Bartholomäus., *Akkiyanam Yethanai Aruvarakkap Padatthakka Kaariyam Yendrum, Adhile Nikkikra Pergal Yeppadi Retshikkappattu Karai Yeralam Yendrum Vezhippaduthugira Veda Pramaanam*, Tranquebar, MDCCXIII.

– –, and Grundler, *Suthanaagiya sarvesuranaanirukkira yesukristhu naatharaanavar inda bhulogathiley manushanaai pirantha viseshangalaiyum bhoduvicha upadesangaliyum seytha arputhangalaiyum manusharukku vendi paadupattu yellaraiyum moondu raetchithuvitha vaanagalaiyum uyirodey ezhunthiruinthu paralogathiley magaimaiyaga yerinathaiyum avarudaya seshargalagiya apostalarmaargal logam yengum poey ippadikothavichu viseshangalai sagala senangallukkum pirasangam panninathaiyum vezhipaduthugira puthu yerpaadinudaya muthalam vaguppagiya Anju veda posthagam.* Kristu piratha aayirathu yezhunuthu pathinaalam varushamgairapothu tharanganpadiyiley irukkira paathrimaargaludaya achiley pathipikka pattathu: Novum Testamentum Domini Nostri Jesu Christi, ex Originali Texte in Linguam Damulicam o Versum, in Usum Gentis Malabaricae, opera et studio Bartholomrei Ziegenbalg et Joan. Ernesti Grundleri Serenissimi Danise Regis Friderici IV ad Indos Orientales Missionariorum, Tranquebariae, MDCCXIV.

– –, and Grundler, *Archasishta aposthalarmaargalaay irukkira pavulos engiravar romaa pattanathaarukku yezhuthi anuppina nirupamum, korinthiya engira pattanathaarukku yezhuthi annupina rendu nirupamum, kalaachiya engira thesatthaarukku yezhuthi annupina nirupamum, yebesiyaa engira pattanathaarukku yezhuthi annupinna nirupamum, philippa engira pattanathaarukku yezhuthi anuppina nirupamum, kolossey engira pattanatharukku yezhuthi anuppina nirpamum, thessaloniya engira pattanathaarukku yezhuthi anupinna rendu nirupamum, thimotheus engiravarukku yezhthuthi anuppina rendu nirupamum, filiomin engiravarukku yezuthi annupina nirupamum, yebireya saathiyarukku yezuthi anuppina nirupamaum, yakobus engiravarukku yezhuthi anuppina nirupamum, pedurus engiravarukku yezuthi anuppina rendu nirpamum, yoennans engiravarukku yezuthi anuppina moonu nirupamum, yudasengirvar yezhuthi anuppina nirupamum, yoyannansengiravrukku vantha arivippinudaya parama ragasiya posthagamamumagira puthu yerpaatinudaya rendaam vaguppagira irupathi rendu vetha posthagam,* Kristu piratha Ayirathu yezhunuthu pathinainthaam varushamgairapothu Tharanganpadiyiley irukkira paathrimaargaludaya achiley pathipikka pattathu.

Ziegenbalg, *Tharanganpadiyiley irukkira kurumargal Indu thesathaaray irukkira thamizhlar yellarukkum yezhuthina nirupam*, Tranquebariae, MDCCXVII.

– –, *Tharangambadiyile irukkura gurumargal indha desaththaaraay irukkira thamizhar yellarukkum ezhuthina nirupam*, Tranquebariae, MDCCXVIII.

– –, and Grundler, *Suthanaagiya Sarvesuranaanirukkira yesykristhu naatharaanavar inda bhulogathiley manushanaai pirantha viseshangalaiyum bhoduvicha upadesangaliyum seytha arputhangalaiyum manusharukku vendi paadupattu yellaraiyum moondu raetchithuvitha vaanagalaiyum uyirodey ezhunthiruinthu paralogathiley magaimaiyaga yerinathaiyum avarudaya seshargalagiya apostalarmaargal logam yengum poey ippadikothavichu viseshangalai sagala senangallukkum pirasangam panninathaiyum vezhipaduthugira puthu yerpaadinudaya muthalam vaguppagiya Anju veda posthagam. Kristu piratha Ayirathu yezhunuthu pathonpathaam varushamgairapothu Tharanganpadiyiley irukkira paathrimaargaludaya achiley pathipikka pattathu*: Novum Jesu Christi testamentum ex originali textu in usum gentis Malabaricae in linguam Damulicam.vulgo Malabarica dictam, versum opera & Studio Bartholoamei Ziegenbalg & Joh. Ernesti Grundler, serenissima Daniae Regis Frederici IV ad Indos Orientales missionariorum, Tranquebariae in littore Coromandelino Typis Damulicis Missionis Danicae, MDCCXIX.

– –, Grundler and Schultze., *Gnaana Paatugalin Posthagam*: Hymnologia

Damulica, sive ex germanico in Damulorum idioma, observatis usque et melodiis et rhytmis odarum, transaltorum centum et sexaginta Hymnorum Spiritualium fasciculus: in gratiam juventutis damulicae eque ac Ecclesiae hujus gentis, Christo nomen dantis, exhibita a Benjamin Schultze missionario ad Indos Orientales, edition tertia, Tranquebariae, in littore Coromandelino: Typis & sumptibus Missionis danicae, anno MDCCXXIII.

Ziegenbalg, *Sarvathukkum vallavarumaay anaadhiyaai irukkiravarmaay yengum niranjavarumaay irukkira parraapara vasthuvaanavar poorva kaalathiley paramadalithil irunthu thiruvilampathina sathyama vetha posthagathin muthalaam vagauppu: ithiley atchshista mosesengiravar sarvesuranyadaya thiruvaayile ninru ketta gnayangalayum kartharaanavar adiilay paralogathayum bhoologathayum yeppadi undaakinar yengirathayum avar sagala senangalukkiley oru kolaithirathai thammudaya sonthamaana senangkallaga therindu kondaar engirathayum vezhipaduthugira mosesuvin anju posthagangalaiyum, yousuvaa vengiravarudaya gnaana posthagamum, neethikaaragaludaya vaththamanangalay kaanpikkira posthagamum, adangi irukkudhu.* Kristu pirandhu ayriath yezhuthnuthi irupathu moonam varushamgira poedhu, ithu thatanganpaadiiley irukkira paathrimargaludaya achiley pathipikka pattudhu: Biblia Damlica, seu quod Deus est locutus Veteris Testamenti, pars prima, in qua Mosis libri quinque, Josuae liber unus atque liber unus Judicum, studio & opera Bartholomaei Ziegenbalgi, Missionarii, ad Indos orinetales in lingua Damulicam versi continentur, Tranquebariae, in littore Coromnadelino typis et sumtibus Missionis Danicae, MDCCXXIII.

– –, *Martin Luther Yenbavarin Gnanaopadesak Kuripidathai Vistharikkum Vina Vidaigal*, Tranquebariae, MDCCXV.

– –, and Grundler, *Vetha Saasthiram: Ithiley karaierugiradhukku ariya vendina gnaana upadesamagira Sarvesvaranukku adutha upadesathamum, manushanukkadutha upadesamum, Sathiya vedathiley adangi irukkira piradhana upadesangalyellaam thezhiva vezhipadutha pattirukkuthu*: Theologia Thetica, in qua omnia Dogamata as salutem cognoscendi necessaria perspicua methodo tractantur, ac Dictis classics probantur, ad propagationem Evengaelii Christi inter gentes Orientales in lingua Damulica scripta a missionis Danicis B.Z. et J.E.G, Tranquebariae, MDCCXVII.

Ziegenbalg and Schultze, *Pazhaya yerpattin kaalathinudya theerkatharisagalikku pirakaalam undaayiruntha yuthasamayathayaragiya punniyathumakkal dharma nadakkaigalin perilleyum, akkaalam thuvakki Yesunaathar bhulogathiley manushanaga vanthu pirantha mattukkum thirusabaiiley nadantha kaaranagalin perilleyum yeuzthi vaitha apocripha yengira naamamulla gnaana posthangalagiya gnaathinudaya posthagamum seeraakengirvarudaya posthagamum, yesderengiravar ezhuthina posthagamum, thobiasnegiravarduaya posthagamum, yudithengirvazhludaya posthagamum, Estherengiravazhludaya posthagathodey sernthuirukkirathum, Baaruchengiravarudaya posthagamum, eremiya ezuthina nirupamum, Soolaiiley iruntha moonupergal Isha thothirathinduaya vaarthaigalum, Susaanengiravazhlukku sambuvicha sethiyum, bellengira vikkirathinudayavum, dhiraakonvengira malaipaambinudayavum vaththammanamum, makkabeyengiravargaludaya muthalaam posthagamum, rendaam posthagamum, moonaam posthagamum, manassessengiravarudaya sepamum adangi irukkudhu*; .Kristu pirandhu 1728 varushamagira poedhu, ithu thatanganpaadiiley irukkira paathrimargaludaya achiley pathipikka pattadhu: Libri Apocryphi, seu Libri a quibusdam Piis Viris Ecclesice Antiquce Judaicaepost Prophetas Veteris Testamenti Scripti, continentes partim Varias Regulas Vitce Utiles,partim Supplementum Historic Ecclesiasticae Veteris Testamenti, scilicet Liber Sapientiae, Ecclesiasticus sive Sirach, Liber Esdrce, Liber Tobice, Liber Judith, A djectiones ad Librum Esther, Liberaruch, Epistola Jeremice, A djectiones ad Danielem seu Trium Virorum Hymnologia, Historia Sosannae, item Belis et Draconis, Maccabaeorum Liber Primus, Secundus, et Tertius, denique Oratio Manassis, studio et opera, Ziegenbalgii et Schultzii in linguam Damulicam versi, Trangambariae, Typis & Impressis Missionis Danicae, MDCCXXVIII.

III. TRAVELOGUES

Baldaeus, Philippus., *Nauwkeurige beschryvinge van Malabar en Choromandel, derhalver aangrenzende ryken, en het machtige eyland Ceylon. Nevens een omstandige en grondigh doorzochte ontdekking en wederlegginge van de afgoderye der Oost-Indische heydenen*, 3 vols, Amsterdam, 1672.

– –, *A True and Exact Description of the Most Celebrated East India Coasts of Malabar and Coromandel as well as of the Isle of Ceylon with their Adjacent Kingdom and Provinces*, III vols., London,1703, rpt., New Delhi, 2000.

IV. EPIGRAPHICAL SOURCES

South Indian Inscriptions, (Publications of the Archaeological Survey of India) vols., I to XXVI, New Delhi, 1890-1990.

Epigraphia Indica, vol. XXIII, Calcutta/Delhi, 1892.

V. SECONDARY WORKS

ARTICLES

Anonymous, 'Etwas aus Einigen Malabarischen Sittenbuchern, von Welchen Aweiar die Verfaaerin ist', Anhb, IV, 1796, pp. 263-9.

Balasingham, C., 'Some Unusual Characters Used in Tamil Printing in Ceylon during Dutch Times', *Proceedings of the International Conference-Seminar of Tamil Studies*, Madras, 1971, vol., II, pp. 528-30.

Barraccini, Rosa Marisa., 'An unknown bestseller: The Confessionario of Girolamo da Palemero' in Flavia Bruni & Andrew Pettegree, eds., *Lost Books: Reconstructing the Print World of Pre-industrial Europe*, Leiden, 2016, pp.291-309.

Chitty, Simon Casie., 'Ceylon Celebrities: Philip de Melho, 1723-1790)', *Ceylon Literary Register*, Third Series, vol. II, no. 2, 1932, pp. 49-56.

Gaur, Albertine., 'Bartholomäus Ziegenbalg's Verzeichnis der Malabarischen Bucher', *Journal of the Royal Asiatic Society of Great Britain and Ireland*, no. 3-4, October, 1967, pp. 63-95.

Gensichen, Hans-Werner., 'Abominable Heathenism': A Rediscovered Tract by Bartholomäus Ziegenbalg', *Indian Church History Review*, vol.1, no.1, 1967, pp. 29-40.

Gnanapragasam, V.M., 'Some Observations on Beschi's Latin Translation of Thirukural', *Proceedings of the International Conference - Seminar of Tamil Studies*, Madras, 1971, pp. 1531-5.

Grafe, H., 'Benjamin Schultze and the Beginnings of the First Indian Protestant Church in Madras', *Indian Church History Review*, vol. III, 1969, pp. 35-41.

Hosten, Henry., 'Le Bhagawata- D'après Un Texte Sen Tamoul: Nouvelle Traduction de Maridas Poulle de Pondichéry, 1793-1795', *Revue Historique de L'Inde Française*, vol. XXXVIII, 1921, pp. xxxvii-xxxviii.

Jensen, Niklas Thode., 'The Medical Skills of the Malabar Doctors in Tranquebar, India, as Recorded by Surgeon TLF Folly, 1798', *Medical History*, vol. 49, (4) October 2005, pp. 489-515.

Jeyaraj, Daniel., 'Early Tamil Bible Translation in Tranquebar', *Dharma Deepika*, vol.1, no.1, June 1997, pp.67-77.

Liebau, Heike., 'German Missionaries as Research Workers in India: Their Diaries as Historical Sources (Benjamin Schultze, 1689-1760, Exception or Norm?)', *Studies in History*, New series, vol. 11, no. 1, 1995, pp.101-18.

Prasad, G. J. V., 'Caste in and Recasting Language: Tamil in Translation' in

Decentering Translation Studies: India & Beyond, eds. Judy Wakabayschi and Rita Kothari, Amsterdam, 2009, pp. 17-28.

Richard, V., 'The Politics, Problem and the Beauties of Translating the Holy Bible', in C.T. Indra and R. Rajagopalan, *Culture, Language & Modernity: English-Tamil in Colonial India, 1750-1900*, Abingdon, 2018, pp. 48-65.

Schurhammer Georg., and G.W Cotrell, 'The First Printing in Indic Characters', *Harvard University Library Bulletin*, vol. VI, no.2, Spring 1952, pp. 147-160.

Shaw G. W., 'A Lost Work of Henrique Henriques: The Tamil Confessionary of 1580', *The Bodleian Library Record*, vol. 11, 1982, pp. 26-34.

Stephen, S. Jeyaseela., 'The Circulation of Medical Knowledge through Tamil Manuscripts in Early Modern Paris, Halle, Copenhagen and London', eds., Anna Winterbottom and Facil Tesfaye, *Histories of Medicine and Healing in the Indian Ocean World: The Medieval and Early Modern Period*, New York, 2016, vol. I, pp. 125-150.

Thaninayagam, Xavier., 'The First Printed Books in Tamil', *Tamil Culture*, vol. VII, no.3, July, 1958, pp. 288-308.

Victor, Henry, I., 'Tamil Translation of the Bible by the Danish-Halle Mission during the Eighteenth Century', *Indian Church History Review*, vol. XVI, no, l, June, 1982, pp. 72-85.

Volmer, Rosenkilde., Printing in Tranquebar, 1712-1845, *The Library Series 5*, vol. 4, 1949, pp. 179-95.

Zupanov, Ines G., 'I Am a Great Sinner: Jesuit Missionary Dialogues in Southern India, (Sixteenth Century)', *Journal of the Economic and Social History of the Orient*, vol. 55, 2012, pp. 415-446.

BOOKS

Anchukandam, Thomas., *The First Synod of Pondicherry (1844): A Study Based on Archival Sources*, Bangalore, 1994.

Anselmo, António Joaquim., *Bibliografia das obras impressas em Portugal no seculo XVI*, Lisboa, 1926.

Arulsamy, Sa. E., *Viviliyam Vazhlarantha Varalaaru*, Coimbatore, 2000.

Besse, Leon., *Father Beschi: His Times and his Writings*, Trichnopoly, 1918.

Beulah, Esther Nancy., *Thamizhlil Vivilya Mozhipeyarppugal: Or Oppaivu*, Madurai, 2002.

Blackburn, Stuart., *Print, Folklore and Nationalism in Colonial South India*, New Delhi, 2003.

Caland, Willem., ed., *Ziegenbalgs Malabarisches Heidenthum: Herausgegeben und mit Indices versehen von W(illem) Caland*, Amsterdam, 1926.

Caland, Willem., ed., *Bartholomäus Ziegenbalg's Kleinere Schriften*, Amsterdam, 1930.

Chakravarti, Ananya., *The Empire of Apostles: Religion, Accommodation and the Imagination in Modern Brazil and India*, New Delhi, 2018.

Chitty, Simon Casie., *The Tamil Plutarch: Containing a Summary Account of the Lives of the Poets and Poetesses of South India and Ceylon from the Earliest to the Present Times with Select Specimens of their Compositions*, Jaffna, 1859.

Costelloe, M. Joseph., trs., *The Letters and Instructions of Francis Xavier*, Anand, 1993.

Daniel, A., *Vedagama Thamizh Mozhipeyarpil Lutheran Sabaiyaarin Pangu*, Madras, 1989.

Dias, João Jose Alves., ed., *No Quinto Centenario da Vita Christi, Os Primeiros Impressores Alemaes em Portugal*, Lisboã, 1995.

Fenger, Johann Ferdinand, *History of the Tranquebar Mission: Worked out from Original Papers*, trs., Emil Francke, Tranquebar, 1863.

Ferroli, D., *The Jesuits in Mysore*, Calicut, 1955.

Filliozat, Jean., *Un Catechisme Tamoul du XVIe Siecle en Lettres Latines*, Pondicherry, 1967.

Gigot, Francis E., *General Introduction to the Study of the Holy Scriptures*, New York, 1900.

Gnanapragasam, V.M., ed., *Veeramamunivar Aruliya Lathin Thirukural Mozhi Peyarppu*, Palayamkottai, 1977.

– –, *Veeramamunivar Thirukural: Lathin Urai*, Karumathur, 1977.

– –, *Thirukural: Veeramanuinvar Lathin Mozhi Peyarppu*, Madurai, 2004.

Hooper, J. S. M., *Bible Translations in India, Pakistan and Ceylon*, Oxford, 1963.

Hudson, Dennis D., *Protestant Origins in India: Tamil Evangelical Christians, 1706-1835*, Surrey, 2000.

Indra C.T. and R. Rajagopalan, eds., *Culture, Language, Identity: English-Tamil in Colonial India, 1750-1900*, Abingdon, 2018.

Irudayam, S. Michael and Y. Robinson Levi, eds., *History of the Tamil Bible Translation*, Madurai, 2002.

Israel, Hephzibah., *Religious Transactions in Colonial South India: Language, Translation and the Making of Protestant Identity*, London, 2011.

Jeyaraj, Daniel., ed., *Olai Chuvadigalil Thodakakaala Thamizh Kristhava Iraineri Paadalgal, 1714: Mulamum Vizhakkamum*, Chennai, 2014.

Kailasapathy, K., *Thamizh Naaval Ilakkiyam*, Madras, 1968.

Khan, Tariq., ed., *History of Translation in India*, Mysuru, 2017.

Kulendiran, Sabapathi., *Kristhava Thamizh Vethaagamaththin Varalaaru*, Bangalore, 1967.

Leão Gaspar de and Eugenio Asensio, ed., *Desengano de Perdidos*, Coimbra, 1958.

Lehmann, Arno., *Es begann in Tranquebar: Die Geschichte der ersten evangelischen Kirche in Indien*, Berlin, 1956.

– –, *It Began at Tranquebar* (trs., M.J. Lutz), Madras, 1956.

Madhavan, Chitra., *History and Culture of Tamil Nadu as Gleaned from the Sanskrit Inscriptions, vol. I, Up to C. AD. 1310*, New Delhi, 2005.

Martins, Jose Vitorino de Pina., *Au Portugal dans lle Sillage d'Erasme*, Paris, 1977.

Matos, Luis de., ed. *Imagens do oriente no seculo XVI: Codice Casanatense*, Lisboã, 1889, rpt., Casa da Moeda, 1985.

Meenakshisundaram, K., *The Contribution of European Scholars to Tamil*, Madras, 1974.

Meenakshisundaram, T.P., *History of Tamil Literature*, Madras, 1965.

Meersman, Achilles., *The Franciscans in Tamilnad*, Fribourg, 1962.

M. P. J. Ondaatje, 'A Tabular List of Original Works and Translations Published by the Late Dutch Government of Ceylon at their Printing Press at Colombo', *Journal of the Royal Asiatic Society of Great Britain and Ireland*, new series, 1, 1865, pp. 141-4.

Naadaan, Thamizh., *Thamizh Mozhhiyin Muthal Achchu Puththagam*, Salem, 1995.

Packiamuthu, Sarojini., *Viviliya Mozhipeyarppu Varalaaru*, Madras, 1990.

– –, *Vivilyamum Thamzhium*, Chidambaram, 2000.

Pandiyan, N. Murugesa., *Mozhipeyarppiyal*, Chennai, 2016.

Pollock, Sheldon., *The Language of the Gods in the World of Men: Sanskrit, Culture and Power in Pre-modern India*, Berkeley, 2006.

Pope, G.U., *The Sacred Kural of Tiruvalluva Nayanar*, Oxford, 1886.

– –, *Tiruvaacagam or 'Sacred Utterances' of the Tamil Poet, Saint and Sage Maanikkavaacagar*, Oxford, 1900.

Prabhakar, David., *Krithava Thamizh Nadaiiyal Nokku*, Chennai, 2002.

Rajamanickam, S., *The First Oriental Scholar*, Palayamkottai, 1972.

Sandgren, Ulla., *The Tamil New Testament and Bartholomäus Ziegenbalg: A Short Study of Some Tamil Translations of the New Testament*, Uppasla, 1990.

Sauliere, A., *His Star in the East* (Revised and reedited by S. Rjamanickam), Anand, 1995.

Schurhammer Georg., and E. A. Voretzsch, *Ceylon zurr Zeit des Konigs Buvaneka Bahu und Franz Xaviers, 1539-1552,* 2 vols., Leipzig, 1928.

– –, *Epistolae S. Francisci Xaverii alia que eius Scripta*, Roma, 1944.

– –, *St. Francis Xavier: His Life, His Times,* 2 vols., Rome, 1977.

Shaw Graham., *The South Asia and Burma Retrospective Bibliography, Stage 1: 1556-1800*, London, 1987.

Silva Rego, António da., *Historia das Missões do Padroado Portugues do Oriente*, Lisboã, MCMXLIX.

Simoes, Maria Alzira Proença., *Catalogo dos impressos de tipografia do seculo XVI: A Coleção da Biblioteca Nacional*, Lisboã, 1990.

Sivasubramanian, Aa., *Sirukathaiku Vitthitavar*, Tuticorin, 1982.

Smither, Edward L., *Mission in the Early Church: Themes and Reflections*, Eugene, 2014.

Stephen, S. Jeyaseela., *Portuguese in the Tamil Coast: Historical Explorations in Commerce and Culture, 1507-1749*, Pondicherry, 1998.

– –, *Letters of the Portuguese Jesuits from Tamil Countryside, 1666-1688*, Pondicherry, 2001.

– –, *A Meeting of the Minds: European and Tamil Encounters in Modern Sciences, 1507-1857*, Delhi, 2016.

– –, *Missioner Tamil Written and Printed in Pondicherry: Literature and Louis Savinien Dupuis, 1841-73*, Pondicherry, 2017.

– –, *Louis Savinien Dupuis, 1806-1874: A Biography of the MEP Missionary in Pondicherry*, 2017.

– –, *From Anrique Anriquez to Louis Savinien Dupuis: The Tamil Grammar and Dictionary Quest*, Pondicherry, 2017.

Stone, Larry., *The Story of the Bible*, Nashville, 2010.

Sugirtharajah, R.S., *Postcolonial Criticism and Biblical Interpretation*, Oxford, 2002.

Tiliander, Bror., *Christian and Hindu Terminology: Study in their Mutual Relations with Special Reference to Tamil Area*, Uppsala, 1974.

Trautmann, Thomas R., *The Madras School of Orientalism, Producing Knowledge in Colonial South India*, New Delhi, 2009.

Varadarasan, M., *Thamizh Ilakkiya Varalaru*, Madras, 1912.

Index